CONVICTION OVERTURNED

JESUS, THE BIBLE, EVIDENCE, AND REASON,
A TRIAL ATTORNEY'S PERSPECTIVE

Willard Bakeman

Copyright © 2024 by Willard Bakeman

All rights reserved.

No part of this book may be used or reproduced in any manner
without written permission of the author,
except for brief quotations used in reviews and critiques.

Printed in the United States of America

To Carl Miller and Howard Loehne

TABLE OF CONTENTS

CHAPTER ONE—LAW AND THE SEARCH FOR TRUTH 1

CHAPTER TWO—THE RESURRECTION: PART ONE

SURROUNDING CIRCUMSTANCES 15

    Peculiar surrounding circumstances which serve to undermine the certainty of execution: The Reluctant Executioner: Level 1 15

    The Reluctant Executioner: Level 2 16

    Mysterious, Ambiguous Death 18

    Sixty Years Later — Patch the hole in the story by making a hole in Jesus 19

    Body in Possession of his Disciples 19

    A Non-burial Interment 20

    No Guard at the Tomb 21

    Likelihood of Belief by Disciples that Jesus was Alive 24

    More surrounding Circumstances — Evidence of Phenomenal Occurrences 28

CHAPTER THREE—THE RESURRECTION: PART TWO

THE APPEARANCES 34

    General Observation Number One: The Drift from Clarity to Darkness — The Journey to the "F" Zone 48

    General Observation Number Two: Progressive Embellishment 50

    Third Observation: The Flawed Argument from Martyrdom .. 53

    Fourth Observation: "People are the same everywhere" (Or, who were the Pentecostals before they were Pentecostals? Answer: The Pentecostals) 61

    When Does Rumor become *Legend*? 65

    A Criticism of the Christian Apologists' Critique of the Gospels 66

CHAPTER FOUR— THE NATIVITY 68

CHAPTER FIVE— FULFILLMENT OF PROPHECY IN THE LIFE OF JESUS 75

    Prophecy: The messiah would be born in Bethlehem 77
    Prophecy: Born of a Virgin 80
    Evidence from Surrounding Narrative 81
    Who is Immanuel? 83
    Evidence from Linguistic Background 85
    Prophecy: Messiah would come out of Egypt 89
    Prophecy: He would grow up in Nazareth 91
    Prophecy: The infants would be massacred in Bethlehem 92
    Prophecy: The messiah would be a descendant of King David ... 95
    Prophecy: The Bible Correctly Foretold the Exact Time of Jesus' Ministry and Crucifixion Hundreds of Years Before. 98
    The Christian Argument 99
    "Prophetic Years" v. Solar Years 102
    Observations: Starting Point and Bifurcation of Prophecy 105
    A Prophecy that Begs Self-Fulfillment: Jesus Proclaimed Self as the Son of Man Described in Daniel 113
    Prophecy: The messiah would have to come before Israel became a Roman province in 6 A.D. 115
    Christ would be crucified — Psalm 22 116
    Isaiah Chapter 53 117
    Jesus rides into Jerusalem on a donkey 121
    Sold for thirty pieces of silver — Zechariah 11:13 121

CHAPTER SIX—FAILED BIBLE PROPHECIES 124

    Biblical Editing 125
    Functionally Conditional Prophecies 125
    Vaticinium Ex Eventu — Prophecy After the Fact 127
    A Wild Ride on Daniel's Time Machine — through the past, present and future 129

Egypt Would Suffer Destruction and Captivity for Forty Years 140
The Ten Northern Tribes Would be Reunited in Israel 142
The Death of Jehoiakim 144
Jeconiah would be childless; Jehoiakim would have no heir to the throne 145
Destruction of Tyre by Babylon 146
Judah (i.e., the House of David) Would Always Provide a King of Israel until the Kingdom of God Arrived (Gen. 49:10) 146
Jesus Would Return to the World in Glory within a Generation 147
Conclusion.. 149

CHAPTER SEVEN—JESUS OF NAZARETH: SAVIOR AND SODOMIST..... 150

Jesus on Transsexualism 152
Who Wrote the "Gospel of John"?.. 156
An Evening at Dinner... 158
An Embarrassing Incident in a Garden 161
The Secret Gospel of Mark 165
Conclusion.. 169
The Gospel of Thomas 170
Postscript and Apology 173

CHAPTER EIGHT—PROGRESSIVE DEVELOPMENT OF DOCTRINE IN THE BIBLE: ORTHODOXY SPRINGING FROM DIVERSITY IN THE NEW TESTAMENT..175

New Testament Development of Doctrine............................ 177
Acceptable Heresy: That which "made it" into our New Testament 189

CHAPTER NINE—THE PROGRESSIVE DEVELOPMENT OF DOCTRINE: THE OLD TESTAMENT 196

Who made the ark?..202

Why does Ezra ignore the Day of Atonement
(Yom Kippur)? 204

Similar problems with the practice of the Passover...............206

Why do people in the Old Testament consistently violate
the solemn injunction to worship and sacrifice to God
only at the Temple in Jerusalem and that sacrifices can
only be offered by the priests? 207

Why was the Second Temple a copy of the tabernacle,
in its dimensions, features and furnishings, but the first
Temple — the Temple of Solomon — was not?.................210

When Solomon built his temple, what happened to the
furnishings that were in the tabernacle? What ever
happened to the gold cherubim that were built in
the desert?..212

Why do the prophets not refer to the Law of Moses?...........215

Why are there two laws of slavery? 219

If God directed that only the sons of Aaron be priests, why
are the priests of Shiloh descendants of Moses? And
why are the Aaronite priests, and even the high priest,
not mentioned in Deuteronomy? And why did David, a
"man after God's own mind", choose two high priests,
with only one a son of Aaron? 220

Why are there two versions of so many things? 223

Why does God condemn a monarchy for Israel if he has
specifically allowed it in Deuteronomy?...........................226

Why do Isaiah, Job, and the Psalmists, multiple times
refer to the Canaanite creation account, and never refer
to the Genesis creation account?..228

Chapter Ten—The Bible and the Origin of Religion..........234

The Origin of Religion 236

The World of Early Man and his Religions 240

Man was Originally an Atheist...245

Early Religion as the Religion of the Concrete — Light versus Darkness=Good versus Evil 247
The Next Phase — Solar Fertility Cults Translated into Ancient Religions 251
Christ and Chrishna 255
The Cross, the Crown, and the Eucharist 258
Genesis and Ancient Cosmogonies 263
Summary of Comparison of Bible with Pagan Mythology ... 268
Pre-Bible Hebrew Religion 269
The Urim and the Thummim 276

CHAPTER ELEVEN—THE EVIDENCE OF CHANGED LIVES 284
Holy Spirit Influenced Thoughts and Behavior 284
The Effectiveness of Prayer 292
The Bible as a Moral Standard 296
The Basis of Morality 300
America — "A Christian Nation" 302
The Problem of Self-Esteem 306

POSTSCRIPT AND CONCLUSION OF THE CASE 311

FOOTNOTES 317

BIBLIOGRAPHY 327

CHAPTER ONE

LAW AND THE SEARCH FOR TRUTH

Over a century and a half ago, American attorney Simon Greenleaf, an authority on the early law of American evidence, wrote a book called *An Examination of the Testimony of the Four Evangelists by the Rules of Evidence Administered in the Courts of Justice.* After examining the Gospel narratives in light of the rules of evidence, Greenleaf concluded that the narrative of the four Gospels establish a convincing foundation for the Christian faith and to prove "that Christ had risen from the dead, and that only though repentance from sin, and faith in him, could men hope for salvation." **[1]** As Greenleaf stated:

> "All that Christianity asks of men…is, that they would be consistent with themselves; that they would treat its evidences as they treat the evidence of other things; and that they would try and judge its actors and witnesses, as they deal with their fellow men, when testifying to human affairs and actions, in human tribunals. Let the witnesses be compared with themselves, with each other, and with surrounding facts and circumstances; and let their testimony be sifted, as if it were given in a court of justice, on the side of the adverse party, the witness being subjected to rigorous cross-examination."[2]

Rather than tarry on lengthy introductions, I instead wholly endorse and accept the above partial paragraph as the actual introduction and preface to this work. An introduction is meant to state the reason why an author is writing what he is writing and the above fully accomplishes this function. In point of fact, I give a hearty *amen* to the above and say

"Let the work begin!" In a spirit of cooperation I will gladly join Mr. Greenleaf in this noble endeavor.

Greenleaf's work has long been heralded by Christian apologists as the definitive evidentiary work in this field, claiming that it has never been refuted, and that the work establishes the Gospel accounts as the definitive evidentiary proof of the material facts they assert. That is because of Greenleaf's conclusion, which is summarized by the conclusion of the above quoted paragraph: "The result [of the above evidentiary analysis], it is confidently believed, will be an undoubting conviction of their integrity, ability and truth."

I believe that the idea is a very sound one and that such critical evidentiary analysis by common principles of jurisprudence may yield useful results to those willing to follow the natural course of where those principles will direct us. There are certainly other approaches to testing the truth of any historical hypothesis or doctrine. In the introduction to his apologetical anthology, *Evidence that Demand a Verdict,* author Josh MacDowell cites the primary proof of the divinity of Jesus to rest in "The impact of his life, though his miracles and teachings, upon history..." **[3]** followed, apparently in order of importance, by fulfilled prophecy in his life, and the resurrection. In other words, if we are to accept his first order of proof, we can test truth, by looking at how many people have believed something and the impact that such belief has had. This is an argument that certainly has in its favor the element of universal appeal, something we boring evidentialists lack, since the argument is also a popular one with Mohammedans, Buddhists, and Marxists alike. But the great drawback is that this approach certainly puts the cart before the horse, saying essentially that something is true because people believe it's true.

But Christianity is a doctrine, and a religion, that is claimed to be based upon historical fact, almost uniquely so among the great religions of the world (Not to ignore Judaism and Islam, the former stemming from the same Bible). Historical facts are routinely litigated in legal forums. Sometimes they are great cases of major import and sometimes, usually, they are small cases of benefit and interest solely to the involved parties. Therefore it is altogether fitting that we should undertake such an approach with something of monumental significance, which the supporters of Christianity claim involves the very nature of our reality and the destiny of the universe — the very nature and meaning of our existence. And so it is with this resolve and intent that we should examine the fundamental facts and reliability of the Bible, to determine if it truly informs us of historical facts vital for our eternal salvation, as its adherents claim. Why should we not submit the testimonies included in the Bible to the same type and degree of scrutiny as testimony in a court of law?

When I consider the gravity of the questions presented in the Bible, as matters of life and death for every human being, and the degree of commitment demanded by its adherents in the life of the individual, I cannot help but to be reminded of the standard of evidence commonly employed in criminal cases of **"Beyond a Reasonable Doubt"** to obtain a conviction. This remark requires some explanation. In the first place, the very term "conviction" indicates a mental belief, and more than a mere belief, a *certainty of belief.* Ironically, this is the same term we use in relation to a person's determined beliefs in life — we might say a person has a conviction in the principles of American democracy. And it is used in regard to religion — a person's "religious convictions" — those spiritual matters he holds true as guiding principles in life. Conviction is another past perfect form of the word convinced. To say a person has a conviction simply means that a person is *convinced of something.* We could also use the term *convicted,* but this is a term used solely by evangelists in our current age (John 16:8, *"And when he is come he will convict the world of sin..."* NASB), although it is grammatically correct and probably brings out the true depth of meaning when a person comes to believe and accept something that has life-changing consequences, especially in regard to his understanding of his own nature, character, and destiny. Such is the nature of the religious conversion process, and undoubtedly more than simply religious, but rather a conversion to any belief system. And as every evangelical preacher knows, the religious conversion process occurs when an individual is "convicted" in his or her heart of the fundamental precepts of the Gospel — that he is a sinner lost without Christ, that Christ died on the cross for his sins, and that he must turn to Christ. "Conviction" , the past perfect, simply means that a person is *convinced.* The person has a conviction. Christian evangelists use the expression of "giving your life to Christ."

Conviction Overturned

And most ironically, this is the term — conviction - we employ to say that judgment has been passed upon an accused because a jury of twelve persons has unanimously felt *convinced* of his guilt, and so he sustains a *conviction*. It is an appropriate term and also an appropriate comparison to one surrendering one's life to a belief system because he is *convicted* or convinced of the truth of that which is charged to him. In the most severe penal cases the accused "gives his life" for his crime, by death or life imprisonment.

I have been involved in multitudes of criminal cases, both as a prosecutor and defense attorney. A person's life, in one form or another, is on the line, because a criminal conviction is a mark on the character of a person, and often involves confinement in jail or prison. Sometimes a person's very life is at stake in a capital case, or at least where the accused will spend the rest of his life. So the standard to find the accused guilty is a high one. Just as Christianity asks that the individual believe the Gospel and commit his life to Christ and to follow him, so in the criminal system a life is committed to judgment, often to the point where the life is even taken. Perhaps now my point is understood. Should not the same standard apply for you to give up your own life, whether it be to a person or cause, as you would apply to commit the life of another?

Hence the value and superiority of this standard of "Beyond a Reasonable Doubt" when it comes to making the most important decisions of life. Should matters of life and death be made on any less a standard? Would you even get on an airplane to fly unless you are convinced that the plane was safe beyond a reasonable doubt? Or conversely, if you were told that there was a reasonable doubt whether the plane was safe, would you not choose another plane or delay your trip? Would you use a parachute when there was a reasonable doubt whether it would open? Then you would indeed require that the standard of "beyond a reasonable doubt" be employed for the most important decisions in your life.

Let us examine this standard as employed by the court system. California Criminal Jury Instructions 219 (CALCRIM) is the jury instruction given to jurors in all criminal cases in California, and it parallels all other states and the English common law from which it is derived:

> **A defendant in a criminal case is presumed to be innocent. This presumption requires that the People prove a defendant guilty beyond a reasonable doubt. Whenever I tell you the People must prove something, I mean they must prove it beyond a reasonable doubt [unless I specifically tell you otherwise]. Proof beyond a reasonable doubt is proof that leaves you with an abiding conviction that the charge is true. The evidence need not eliminate all possible doubt because everything in life is open to some possible or imaginary doubt. In deciding whether the People have proved their case beyond a reasonable doubt, you must impartially compare and consider all the evidence that was received throughout the entire trial. Unless the evidence proves the defendant[s] guilty beyond a reasonable doubt, (he/she/they) (is/are) entitled to an acquittal and you must find (him/ her/them) not guilty.**

This is the formulation used in California since 2006 but I personally strongly prefer the definition of reasonable doubt in the prior version, as it existed until 1995, which was age old and had another philosophical dimension to it. The former CALJIC instruction, at least in the form that was used until 1995, and which was given to jurors for centuries, stated that:

> **Reasonable doubt is defined as follows: It is not a mere possible doubt; because everything relating to human affairs is open to some possible or imaginary doubt. It is that state of the case which, after the entire comparison and consideration of all the evidence, leaves the minds of the jurors in that condition that they cannot say they feel an abiding conviction to a moral certainty of the truth of the charge.**

The standard of proof of beyond a reasonable doubt is that which leaves the mind "with an abiding conviction *to a moral certainty* of the truth of the charge." Courts felt that the term *moral certainty* was ambiguous and nebulous. I feel, on the contrary, that it establishes a degree of certainty, other than mathematical certainty, upon which the most important decision of life can be made. We can be certain of things which are not capable of mathematical certainly but which we are convinced are true, and we live accordingly. Indeed, *MORAL CERTAINTY* is exactly what this is all about. It is the certainty on which we stake all of life's bets. It is the certainty that will send a man to the grave at your behest, as a juror. It is the certainty with which you will make a decision, or contribute to a decision, to commit the troops of your own nation, and possibly even your own children, to war and possible death. It is the certainty of the principles on which you live your life. We should not expect a person to "give his life to Christ" on anything less than moral certainty, should we?

Now there are related jury instructions which embrace the application of the law of evidence. These are equally essential to a juror's decisions. The first is the law of direct and circumstantial evidence. The traditional instruction given to juries is as follows, being the text of CALJIC (California Jury Instruction) number 2.00:

> **Evidence consists of the testimony of witnesses, writings, material objects, or anything presented to the senses and offered to prove the existence or non-existence of a fact.**
>
> **Evidence is either direct or circumstantial.**
>
> **-Direct evidence is evidence that directly proves a fact. It is evidence which by itself, if found to be true, establishes that fact.**
>
> **-Circumstantial evidence is evidence that, if found to be true, proves a fact from which an inference of the existence of another fact may be drawn.**
>
> **-An inference is a deduction of fact that may logically and reasonably be drawn from**

another fact or group of facts established by the evidence. *[It is not necessary that facts be proved by direct evidence. They also may be proved by circumstantial evidence or by a combination of direct and circumstantial evidence. Both direct and circumstantial evidence are acceptable as a means of proof. Neither is entitled to any greater weight than the other.]*

The California Judicial Council further simplified this instruction in the new CALCRIM Instruction 223, as follows:

Facts may be proved by direct or circumstantial evidence or by a combination of both. Direct evidence can prove a fact by itself. For example, if a witness testifies he saw it raining outside before he came into the courthouse, that testimony is direct evidence that it was raining. Circumstantial evidence also may be called indirect evidence. Circumstantial evidence does not directly prove the fact to be decided, but is evidence of another fact or group of facts from which you may logically and reasonably conclude the truth of the fact in question. For example, if a witness testifies that he saw someone come inside wearing a raincoat covered with drops of water, that testimony is circumstantial evidence because it may support a conclusion that it was raining outside.

Both direct and circumstantial evidence are acceptable types of evidence to prove or disprove the elements of a charge, including intent and mental state and acts necessary to a conviction, and neither is necessarily more reliable than the other. Neither is entitled to any greater weight than the other. You must decide whether a fact in issue has been proved based on all the evidence.

Direct evidence would include eyewitness testimony. There is a unique approach to proof by circumstantial evidence. The analysis of circumstantial evidence, as opposed to direct evidence, has its own nuances. The traditional instruction given to juries is as follows, being the text of CALJIC (California Jury Instruction) number 2.01:

> **However, a finding of guilt as to any crime may not be based on circumstantial evidence unless the proved circumstances are not only (1) consistent with the theory that the defendant is guilty of the crime, but (2) cannot be reconciled with any other rational conclusion.**
>
> **Further, each fact which is essential to complete a set of circumstances necessary to establish the defendant's guilt must be proved beyond a reasonable doubt. In other words, before an inference essential to establish guilt may be found to have been proved beyond a reasonable doubt, each factor or circumstance on which the inference necessarily rests must be proved beyond a reasonable doubt.**
>
> **Also, if the circumstantial evidence [as to any particular count] permits two reasonable interpretations, one of which points to the defendant's guilt and the other to [his] [her] innocence, you must adopt that interpretation that points to the defendant's innocence, and reject that interpretation that points to [his] [her] guilt. If, on the other hand, one interpretation of this evidence appears to you to be reasonable and the other interpretation to be unreasonable, you must accept the reasonable interpretation and reject the unreasonable.**

The California Judicial Council attempted to further simplify this instruction in the new CALCRIM Instruction 224, as follows:

> **Before you may rely on circumstantial evidence to conclude that a fact necessary**

to find the defendant guilty has been proved, you must be convinced that the People have proved each fact essential to that conclusion beyond a reasonable doubt. Also, before you may rely on circumstantial evidence to find the defendant guilty, you must be convinced that the only reasonable conclusion supported by the circumstantial evidence is that the defendant is guilty. If you can draw two or more reasonable conclusions from the circumstantial evidence, and one of those reasonable conclusions points to innocence and another to guilt, you must accept the one that points to innocence. However, when considering circumstantial evidence, you must accept only reasonable conclusions and reject any that are unreasonable.

As can be readily seen, the Judicial Councils' revisions of the California jury instructions in no way change existing law of evidence. They are merely designed to simplify and make more understandable the instructions, although in my opinion the older formulation was equally clear. In my opinion the traditional wording of the 2.00 instruction on direct and circumstantial evidence, as well as the following instructions on the rules of circumstantial evidence, and for that matter on reasonable doubt, were brilliantly crafted, meticulously calculated, perfectly worded and stood the test of time. But that is another matter and the most salient fact is that fortunately the new instructions are merely re-wordings of exactly the same principles.

How would we craft this wording to the case before us? In this case, we would not be concerned with guilt or innocence, but with the truth of the claim asserted, in this case that Jesus was the son of God and that he rose from the dead. So we should disregard the references to "guilt or innocence" and instead perhaps substitute the phrase "the truth of the charge" or "truth of the claim." For surely the proponents of the Bible would be the first to admit that that they charge the Bible and its claims as true, and that they ask all of humanity to first and foremost *BELIEVE* the Bible's claim that Jesus is the son of God, that his death was a substitutionary sacrifice for the sins of the world, that he rose from the dead, and that believing on his name, believing in the account given in the Bible, is the only means to eternal salvation. No Christians would deny the above. They demand belief and so it is their burden to prove to the world why individuals should commit their lives, destinies and identities to the facts and doctrines enunciated in the Bible. It is only fair to place the burden on the Christians to prove *their case,* as they are so eager to do.

We will deal much with purported circumstantial evidence. If we accept circumstances to prove the truth of the Bible, the circumstances, or chain of circumstances, must themselves be proven true beyond a reasonable doubt, and then the inferences we draw must only be compatible with the claim asserted. If circumstantial facts are equally susceptible of two explanations, one pointing to the truth of the Gospel assertions, and the other having another, reasonable explanation, then we must adopt the other reasonable, interpretation. Remember, it is *our life* we are committing and the lives of others!

When it comes to direct evidence, in particular to witnesses, then we are dealing with an issue of credibility, and there are rules of credibility which apply. CALCRIM Instruction 226 is given to the jury:

> **You alone, must judge the credibility or believability of the witnesses. In deciding whether testimony is true and accurate, use your common sense and experience. You must judge the testimony of each witness by the same standards, setting aside any bias or prejudice you may have. You may believe all, part, or none of any witness's testimony. Consider the testimony of each witness and decide how much of it you believe. In evaluating a witness's testimony, you may consider anything that reasonably tends to prove or disprove the truth or accuracy of that testimony. Among the factors that you may consider are:**
>
> - **How well could the witness see, hear, or otherwise perceive the things about which the witness testified?**

- How well was the witness able to remember and describe what happened?

- What was the witness's behavior while testifying?

- Did the witness understand the questions and answer them directly?

- Was the witness's testimony influenced by a factor such as bias or prejudice, a personal relationship with someone involved in the case, or a personal interest in how the case is decided?

- What was the witness's attitude about the case or about testifying?

- Did the witness make a statement in the past that is consistent or inconsistent with his or her testimony?

- How reasonable is the testimony when you consider all the other evidence in the case?

- [Did other evidence prove or disprove any fact about which the witness testified?]

- [Did the witness admit to being untruthful?]

- [What is the witness's character for truthfulness?]

- [Has the witness been convicted of a felony?]

Of particular importance is the issue of whether a witness is found to be willfully lying. The old, traditional CALJIC 2.21.2 instruction provided:

> A Witness who is willfully false in one material aspect of his or her testimony is to

be distrusted in others. You may reject the whole testimony of a witness who willfully has testified falsely as to a material point, unless, from all the evidence, you believe the probability of truth favors his or her testimony in other particulars.

It has been reworded by the new CALCRIM instructions as follows:

If you decide that a witness deliberately lied about something important, you should consider not believing anything that witness says. Or, if you think the witness lied about some things, but told the truth about others, you may simply accept the part that you think is true and ignore the rest.

These then are the basic instructions given to juries to decide criminal cases. The instructions are merely a rewording of basic legal principles of how to evaluate evidence. And as such, they are merely a formulation of common sense principles that have been accepted for ages.

My own position in all of this is probably a very good one to prompt this undertaking. I am not naturally antagonistic to the claims of the Bible's proponents. Apart from my legal background, I am a long-time evangelist, preacher, chaplain and Baptist seminarian. I have preached the Gospel to countless jail and prison inmates and been instrumental in countless conversions. The Bible adherents have been my colleagues. I am aware of the arguments of the Bible adherents and hope to give all of their arguments a full and fair hearing, without exception.

A word as to methodology. True to the pleadings of the Bible adherents, in the portion of this work which deal with the Bible texts themselves, I will at the outset test the Bible only by the Bible, and to the extent possible, avoid analysis by works outside the Bible, except where necessary to refer to commonly accepted contemporaneous sources, such as the histories of Josephus. Naturally, we can never reject common sense, and common sense necessarily includes a degree of common historical fact. Just as we cannot ignore the law of gravity from common sense, so there is an element of what we call common sense that is only common sense because it is common historical fact. If I said a Prussian officer at Waterloo showed up on the battlefield in a tank, you would say it is contrary to common sense. Actually, driving a tank on to a battlefield, especially where there are no armored units, is a splendid idea. The problem is that tanks were first used in 1916 at the battle of Cambray in France, and even if we do not know this trivia, we do know that tanks are a 20th century phenomenon and so this is a historical anachronism. As such, this innate *historical sense* forms a part of our *common sense,* and cannot truly be separated from it. Later in the work, we delve into such matters as the dating of Bible texts, the development of doctrine, and the impact of the Bible on the lives of people, which necessarily will involve a review of external texts. Later, when dealing with such sundry issues as "evidence of changed lives", and scholarly research on the history of the Bible, I will necessarily look to sources outside of the Bible.

It is only fair that we begin our analysis with what Christians call the central claim of the Bible — the resurrection of Jesus. As the Apostle Paul said in I Corinthians 15:14, *"And if Christ is not risen, then our preaching is empty and your faith is also empty. Yes, and we are found false witnesses of God, because we have testified of God that he raised up Christ, whom he did not raise up — if in fact the dead do not rise. For if the dead do not rise, then Christ is not risen. And if Christ did not rise your faith is futile..."* Indeed, no evangelical Christian would disagree with the view that the truth of the resurrection account is essential to a belief in the doctrine of Christianity and that without the resurrection there is no Christianity.

One issue that has thus far been left mute, and indeed it has in the law also, is a term that the law does not define, but which some, but not all, would find fundamental. That is the question of what truth is? Some would say that this question - "what is truth?" - is philosophical and therefore out of the realm of legal definitions. Others would say that this issue is too abstract to be legally manageable. Others would say that the question is so fundamentally simple and obvious that any person of normal intelligence simply knows what truth is and doesn't need any definition. In any event, I will attempt an answer and gladly inform the world of Bible proponents that I heartily endorse the definition of knowledge that is generally accepted among Christian theologians:

Truth is that which is internally coherent and which corresponds to reality.

This is as good a definition as any. It probably leaves open the definition of reality, but if sane, we all seem to grasp what is real around us and what is not. So we can safely say that we are off to a start.

There is one other issue. It involves our mindset as we search for the truth. Over 2400 hundred years ago, Socrates opened his debates with his opponents, and his dialogues with his audience, by asking of them only one commitment — only one promise —before he would engage them. He asked them if they would commit to following the thread of whatever they could establish as the truth no matter where it led. If they could be convinced that something is true, would they follow that truth to wherever it led them? Virtually all reasonable people would accept this proposition. My own request is nothing less than this.

However, this seemingly harmless exercise in intellectual honesty calls to mind a very relevant story. The story is told by a close friend and colleague of evangelist Billy Graham from the very early days of Graham's ministry. The man was, like Graham, a sincere, ardent Christian and evangelist, but he increasingly became a skeptic. He would share his increasingly skeptical views with Graham, and at the outset would have open conversations. Then one day Billy Graham went for a walk in the country. He came to a large rock on his walk and he got down on his knees and prayed. And he made a commitment to God that no matter what he found, heard, or was told in his life, that he would never lose his faith in Jesus and the Bible. And guess what? He never did. He became the Billy Graham that we know today. I relate this story because there are many people who will do what Billy Graham did, or perhaps they have already done it. They will find their own metaphorical rock to kneel at. Their response to the observations and facts contained in this book will be to seek that rock of comfort and to pledge to close their eyes for the rest of their natural lives. But for those who do not, there may be a new adventure at hand - the adventure discovering what is true and what is not, and of possibly discovering from this the meaning of life and truth.

Chapter Two

THE RESURRECTION: PART ONE
SURROUNDING CIRCUMSTANCES

Peculiar surrounding circumstances which serve to undermine the certainty of execution.

The Reluctant Executioner: Level 1

The Bible account makes it clear that Pilate ordered the execution of Jesus. And yet the Bible makes it equally clear that Pilate believed that Jesus was innocent, and that the Jewish leadership wanted to kill Jesus "out of envy" or out of a perceived threat to either their own religious power base or their religious norms. So one of the paramount points of the Bible narrative is that Pilate, the person with the authority to execute Jesus, and who in fact ordered his execution and was ultimately in charge of carrying out the execution, did not *want* to kill him. The natural and unavoidable corollary is that he wanted to *spare* him. He clearly either wanted to kill him or he didn't. The Bible says Pilate spoke out on behalf of Jesus but that he feared the crowd and feared a riot would break out so he gave in to them. This is of great significance — the person who was the principal representative of the emperor, with plenary power to execute the laws, with the power to condemn or acquit, wanted to *save* Jesus. This begs the question — Did Pilate lack the power to get his way? Was he going to allow himself to be "bossed around" by the Jewish leaders?

The portrait of Pontius Pilate depicted by the historian Josephus is of a severe man, who had contempt for the Jews. He had a confrontation with the Jewish authorities because of the eagles depicted on Roman standards, violating the Jewish ban on images. He slaughtered a number of Jewish rebels. [1]Indeed, Christian debunkers often doubt as unlikely the entire Bible account that the Jewish leaders supposedly forced the hand of this supposedly ruthless despot. This author does not see the account of Pilate's hand being forced as an untrustworthy account on the surface. Being tough does not require one to be politically stupid or abrasive. In point of fact, it may just be that his confrontations with the Jews had awakened him to the need for compromise. Pilate's toughness may simply be an indication of the increasing political turmoil during the period of Pilate's term of office as proconsul, 26-36 A.D. The need for a bloody crackdown on dissidents was a sign of the increasingly politicized and violent times, not a product of a particularly oppressive governor, who may not have been more naturally oppressive than preceding governors.

But rather, Pilate's admitted opposition to the execution tends to undermine, and not support, the claim of his execution. If the claim to the veracity of the Christian faith hinges initially on the fact of the crucifixion, and God, in his infinite wisdom and providence, both creates events that result in Jesus' crucifixion, and later provides us with an accurate written account of the crucifixion which is "written that you may believe that Jesus is the Christ, the Son of God, and that believing you may have life in his name" (John 20:30), then we would wonder why we would not have a Roman governor hell-bent on crucifying Jesus, so we would know that a determined, ruthless Roman governor deliberately put Jesus to death.

The Reluctant Executioner: Level 2

But this is but the first level of consternation and of surrounding countervailing facts which undermine the certainty of this essential article of faith, an article of faith without which, mind you, the entire doctrinal and historical artifice collapses. On another factual level, it just so happens that the figure in charge of *actually* killing Jesus, the Roman centurion, happens to believe that Jesus is "the son of God!",or at least "a righteous man", and so presumably does not want to see him killed (Matthew 28:54; Mark 15:39; Luke 23:47). A word is in order about Centurions. A Centurion is usually depicted as a lowly rank in the Roman army, the equivalent of the foot soldier in modern times. Such is not the case. Originally a Centurion was in charge of 100 men, hence a "century" of men. The Roman Republic's political system was originally based on centuries of 100 persons, who would vote as centuries in electing consuls in the primitive Roman Republic. These centuries would double as units of a citizen's army in times of war. So the Centurion was an important person. The centuries remained a vital and fundamental unit in the Roman legions, such as the platoon or company in our day. Although the history and structure of Roman ranks is somewhat different than our own, the Centurion would be the equivalent of either a Marine Corps Gunnery Sergeant, or Army Master Sergeant, in other words a fairly high-ranking non-commissioned officer, or possibly a second lieutenant, the lowest ranking commissioned officer. He is *not* the buck private or private first class, as he is usually represented.

We do not know how many Roman soldiers were sent to crucify Jesus, and we could only speculate using common sense to calculate this. It is usually estimated that a Roman squad of eight was sent, and this is as good an estimate of any. That would seem to be a likely and sufficient number. The point is that there would have only been *one* Centurion present, and so he was *the only* Centurion, and as such he was *in charge of the crucifixion detail!*

So all of this is indeed a peculiar backdrop for a world-changing and world significant event, whose truth must be proven in order for Christian doctrine to be founded in truth and believed. The Roman governor who sentences him to death, a person accustomed to getting his way by all accounts, doesn't *want* see him killed, and actually goes to the extent of earnestly pleading for his life in public in front of a crowd, and searches for other alternatives, such as scourging, as a way out of execution, before sentencing him; and then the man *in charge* of actually directing the crucifixion and ensuring that he is crucified thinks Jesus is *the son of God* or *a righteous man*, and in either event definitely is not thrilled at the chore of killing this "righteous man."

So the Bible narrative is clear. The people who actually killed Jesus didn't want to kill him. We would think a narrative that wished to convince anyone of the historical fact of Jesus' death would go about the task from a different angle. But this is *not all!* There is yet at least a third level of difficulty to be overcome.

Mysterious, Ambiguous Death

We know from a variety of ancient observers, including Josephus, and from common sense, that crucifixion was a deliberately long, slow, painful process. Those who were crucified often lingered days before their death, even weeks. Jesus was a young man in his early thirties with no evidence given us of infirmity. Yet he dies, depending on which Gospel version is accepted, within six hours (in the Gospel of Mark) or three hours (Gospel of Luke, Gospel of Matthew, both of which have him on the cross at noon). The Gospel of John shows him condemned to death at about noon and dying at 3 p.m. In any event he dies surprisingly quickly, and this is not only a modern, critical observation, this is the undoubted conclusion drawn at the time! When it is reported that Jesus has died, Pilate "marvels" (Mark 15:44) that he has died so suddenly. Interestingly, how did Pilate find out Jesus was dead in the first place? Was it from a reliable source? He found out from *Jesus' disciples,* presumably Nicodemus and Joseph of Arimathea, members of the Jewish ruling Sanhedrin, who presumably were prominent enough to approach Pilate.

Christian apologists insist that Pilate, the tough, stern, severe governor would have *insisted* that his orders were followed out and would have verified that Jesus was dead, and that the Roman soldiers, had they not ascertained the death of Jesus, would have been crucified themselves in retaliation (something which is absolutely without foundation and the mere product of fertile minds). In fact, Mark tells us that Pilate sent to make sure that Jesus was dead. We do not know how he *verified* this. Presumably he simply sent to the Centurion (the same one who thought Jesus was the son of God) to find out if it true. We also are told that although the legs of the other two persons crucified were broken to hasten their death, the legs of Jesus were not broken because he was already dead. It is interesting to note that Christian apologists often cite this sudden death as itself *a miracle* — the only explanation for why Jesus supposedly died in three hours. Absent the a posteriori conclusion of a miracle — a method of escaping the straightforward application of reason and the normal laws of nature for evaluating occurrences — a more likely conclusion is that he had not died. In fact, Josephus tells us an account of a man who survived after a week of crucifixion, was cut down, and survived.

Sixty Years Later — Patch the hole in the story by making a hole in Jesus

Now this narrative leaves such a gaping hole in the middle of it, that doubt of Jesus' death would be inescapable. So, according to *Christian* estimates, some sixty years after the event, we have another narrative, the Gospel of John, which claims that a Roman soldier placed a spear through Jesus' side to make sure he was dead, and that water and blood spewed out from the wound. Time and vigilant minds have been known to "cure" many such gaping holes in stories, and to remedy implausibility in narratives. Unfortunately, the writers of the synoptic Gospels, supposedly written by illustrious disciples of Jesus at or near the time of the events, did not know about this event.

Body in Possession of his Disciples

We already have three surrounding factors that create uncertainty in the narrative. The governor who orders his execution and the man in charge of carrying it out, believed that Jesus was being unfairly victimized and were against killing him. He dies suddenly and mysteriously. His legs are not broken to ensure his death.   But this is not the end of the thread. Although it well could have been if the Roman authorities did the natural next thing — dispose of the body themselves. Instead, amazingly, they grant the request of the *disciples of the man they had just sentenced to death to <u>give the body to them!</u>* (The people, keep in mind, who are telling you that he is the Messiah of the Jews who could, would, and did come back from the dead). We could only imagine the consternation of the Jewish authorities at this turn of events. And nothing could further demonstrate the antagonism of Pilate toward the Jewish leaders that wanted Jesus executed, or his sympathy for Jesus' followers, than his decision to present them with the body. From the moment his body was taken off the cross, it remained in the custody of his own disciples, the very ones who later supposedly announced that Jesus had come back from the dead — but nobody saw him but them!

We have a doctrine in the law that relates to the law of negligence, because that is the area of the law where the issue arises, that is called *Res Ipsa Loquitur*, which means the thing speaks for itself. Where negligent injury occurs and the exact cause cannot be determined, but the instrumentality that caused it was always in the possession and control of a particular person, then that person is deemed to be responsible for causing the injury. Now this might seem like comparing oranges to apples, but the concept is the same here. We would be correct in presuming that whatever happened to the body, at least some disciples should be held responsible for it, because *they had the body*, and so this should be at least the first place we should look, certainly before we look to supernatural causes.

A Non-burial Interment

This is a narrative that already at four major levels creates confusion and doubt rather than certainty. But this is not all. There yet another level which can only create consternation in the reasonable mind. Is Jesus buried in a grave? Is earth put over him? No, amazingly to our minds, although befitting Jewish customs, his body is placed into an open sepulcher, a mere cave in the rocks, with a large rock placed at the door. It was the Jewish custom to allow the body to decompose, at which time the bones would be placed in a smaller stone box called an ossuary. And the sepulcher in which Jesus' body is placed just so happened to be, *you guessed it*, the sepulcher belonging to one of his disciples, Joseph of Arimathea. So Joseph just happened to have a sepulcher handy, very close to the scene of the crucifixion.

Now this is an area that Christian apologists just love. And indeed they have a field day. The proof of Christianity, they say, is that the body of Jesus was behind a large stone (we have no idea whatsoever how large — that is mere speculation). Frank Morrison, a journalist, wrote a famous book, Who Moved the Stone, arguing that mortals could not have moved the stone out of place [2]. This argument seems specious. A more logical observation would be that if human beings rolled the stone into place, then human beings could unroll it. We know that female disciples, who saw the body placed behind the stone, visited the sepulcher two days later, knowing the stone was there, and according to all the Gospel narratives, were in no way stymied by the presence of the stone at the entrance and saw no problem in the idea of finding someone to roll the stone back for them (Mark 16, Matthew 28, Luke 24). But Christian apologists seem to think this was an insurmountable task. Who rolled the stone? Likely answer: Whoever rolled it there in the first place. The whole idea of placing the stone in front was that *in every single case, without exception,* the stone would eventually be rolled back so the bones could be placed in an ossuary. Yet Christian apologists claim that rolling back the stone was an exceptionally, outlandishly unusual and strange thing that no human being could ever possibly do! This is nonsense. The whole idea was to be able to fairly easily move it away.

But the fact that the body, whether living or dead, was placed in a spot by his disciples easily accessible to anyone is not the end of the story. In fact there is another layer of baffling doubt stretched over this picture. The final level of doubt to be cast over this story is that *there was absolutely no guard at the tomb*! This statement will immediately be hailed as sloppy slander and falsehood by Christian apologists, but this is not the author's assertion — this is the flat assertion of the Bible itself. The Gospel of Matthew makes it very clear that the Jewish leaders asked for a guard to be placed *the next day!!* (Matt. 28:62-65).

No Guard at the Tomb

If the disciples believed, rightfully or wrongfully, that Jesus was still alive, or simply decided to remove the body, the most likely time to do so would have been the same night he was interred, *especially* if there was any doubt about his actual death. It would not have been on Saturday night. It would have been on Friday night (assuming that the Bible is correct that the women disciples did not return to the tomb the day *after* the crucifixion because it was the Sabbath, but they *did* return the *day after that* — Sunday, making the crucifixion take place on a Friday, despite strenuous and somewhat foolish efforts by some apologists to claim it was any day other than Friday, in light of the obvious and direct chronology stated above). One might argue that this means that the body had disappeared from the tomb by the time the guards arrived on Saturday. In the first place, this assumes the veracity of the story of the guards. This story is not attested by the other three Gospel writers, who had an equal interest in convincing the world of their Lord's veracity and marshalling every possible fact at their disposal in support, and they presumably also had equal access to the facts. In the second place, the tomb may have actually been discovered as open on Saturday. But because of the Jewish Sabbath's prohibition of walking more than a mile on the Sabbath the disciples did not come until Sunday, and hence *their discovery*, the recorded one, and truly the only important one, was on Sunday morning.

A more likely conclusion is that the story of the guards, which seems so crucial, and in fact is so strongly heralded by Christian apologists, is a later fabrication designed to patch up an otherwise gaping hole in the historical legitimacy of the resurrection — to escape the patent vulnerability of a resurrection that depends on Jesus' body entrusted to the disciples to be buried in the private sepulcher of one of his disciples, unguarded. Admittedly, the fact of a guard posted to the tomb would be a vital fact. So vital indeed, that it would hardly be missed by writers determined to prove the Lordship of their leader, including the authors of the Gospels of Luke, Mark, and John. But remarkably, such is not the case. Mark, Luke and John never heard this story, because if they did we can be assured that it would *be there!*

But the story of the guards is especially interesting in another light. The disciples did not steal the body, we are told, because they were ignorant of the fact that Jesus would be resurrected. And yet what did the Jewish leaders tell Pilate as the reason they wanted a guard? They said "Sir, we remember when he was still alive, how that deceiver said 'After three days I will rise.' Therefore command the tomb be made secure until the third day." (Matt. 28:63). Supposedly the disciples were simply unaware or unconvinced that Jesus would arise from the dead. When Marie Magdalen, or alternatively the several women, who visited the tomb on Sunday morning reported the tomb empty (or depending on the alternative versions to be discussed later, they reported that they had seen the risen Jesus) they are met with

The Resurrection: Part One

skepticism and doubt by the disciples. This is despite the fact that the Gospels clearly state that Jesus three times predicted that they would rise from the dead the third day. Indeed, the two disciples on the road to Emmaus were discouraged and dispirited over the death of their leader and seem to have not been aware of, or at least were doubtful of, any resurrection. This is used by Christian apologists to bolster their repudiation of any suggestion that any disciples were involved in the disappearance of the body. And yet here we see that the *enemies* of Jesus and his disciples, the Jewish leaders, were very aware of the predictions of Jesus' resurrection and took such pretensions, according to the account of Matthew, very seriously, fearing in advance that as a result of zealous disciples the body would end up disappeared — which is exactly what happened.

The story of the guards poses another interesting issue. If the women at the tomb arrived to find an empty grave, then wouldn't the soldiers have been the first to witness the resurrection? That would be the logical conclusion based on the renditions of Mark, Luke and John. But Matthew has a ready answer for that. The women and the soldiers were both present when the rock was rolled back by an earthquake and the appearance of an angel. And the frightened guards fell to the ground like dead men. We will address this more in the accounts of the empty tomb.

I am hinting in a gentle and subtle fashion at something very reasonable and natural. If I go to my Uncle Charlie's grave, and lo, and behold, it is empty, do I say, "Uncle Charlie must have gotten up and gone to the town bar for a drink!" Or do I say, "Who took the body?" This is not a supernatural bias, as Christian apologists say. It is certainly a tendency to look for answers that correspond to reality as I know it, and therefore which conform to natural laws. It is also a penchant to accept the maxim that "Extraordinary claims require extraordinary proof", which no reasonable person will disagree with (Tell me your wife drove you to work today, and I will as a gentlemen accept it with no further adieu. Tell me that a flying saucer kidnapped you this morning and took you to Jupiter, and I will be *leery* to believe you based on your own word alone — sorry!) But more on all of this later.

Likelihood of Belief by Disciples that Jesus was Alive

The suddenness of death after a short time on the cross and the fact that one of the disciples brought the news to Pilate suggest that the disciples' believed or reasonably hoped that Jesus was not dead. And his subsequent retrieval is the basis for an empty tomb — a more logical answer than the one of Uncle Charlie in the town bar. Clearly, leaving the shroud in the tomb is proof that those that retrieved the body believed or suspected that Jesus might still be alive — otherwise they would have removed the body still covered by the shroud (John 20:5). If Jesus had been alive, considering the lack of medical capacity to deal with infection at the time, Jesus would have soon died of his wounds, probably from infections.

Christian apologists make much of the supposed surrounding circumstances to show lack of intent on the part of *"the disciples"* to remove the body. They cite the dedication of the small band of later disciples as depicted in the Acts of the Apostles. *"They"* could not have removed the body, so the argument goes. They claim this is preposterous considering the dedication and loyalty of the early Christian cult members. In the first place, this argument relies upon an assumption of a monolithic group of disciples with one, single mind. I *also* fully agree that two hundred, three hundred, or a thousand, whatever the number, of disciples did not march over together on Friday night and removed the body. Only a few were needed. And the disciples did not have a monolithic, central mind such that whatever a few disciples did was immediately known by every, single disciple in Jerusalem, not to mention all Judea. In point of fact, considering the claims of resurrection, would those who took the body, being disciples themselves, have stood up and openly proclaimed that they had taken it, and that there was no resurrection? That all the claims of appearances were false? I hardly think so. Why would they?

Christian apologists make much of the term "hoax." They proclaim this could not have been a "hoax." In fact they like to put all alternatives theories into neat straw man packages. According to them, skeptics claim that either Jesus was alive and merely fainted, then *he* personally pushed the stone away and got away; *or "the* disciples"

The Resurrection: Part One

stole the body as a *hoax* in order to fool every one (and then supposedly were willing to die for their hoax). These are always presented as exclusive, alternative explanations, which they are not. If the disciples believed with good reason that Jesus was still alive, then the retrieval of the body was anything but a hoax. And the few that took the body, which if not dead would soon be dead, had no reason to proclaim this to the world. It is hardly helpful to the Christian apologists that almost all the future evangelization and proselytization was done overseas, and mostly under the leadership of a foreigner, the Apostle Paul, who was not from Jerusalem and had no first-hand knowledge of events, and who directed himself exclusively to an audience equally distant from the events he related. The people who were in the vicinity where these events happened, and should have been the most acquainted with them, were not a natural or accepting audience of these claims — but rather only people hundreds of miles away who were not acquainted with the facts.

And incidentally, as a closely related matter, we should pause to consider: What *did* actually happen to such figures as Nicodemus, Joseph of Arimathea, Mary Magadalen, and the other women who were in Jesus' group? Why do we *never* hear a word of them in the Acts of the Apostles or any later accounts? These people, so important to Jesus' ministry and, in the case of Joseph and Nicodemus, certainly highly esteemed both in the Christian and the larger Jewish community, being members of the Sanhedrin, just disappear off the historical radar screens. *These* are the key players and supposed witnesses who should be out proclaiming the resurrected Christ, not a person from Tarsus, in far away Cilicia, who was not even there, and had a flash of bright light and a loud voice (that no one else present saw or heard), which knocked him off his horse and revealed to him the truth of these events. And yet curiously we are expected to adhere to his vision (remarkably similar in many respects to our own American Apostle, Joseph Smith, and the Arab Mohammed, whom we are *not* supposed to adhere to). Is it any wonder, after all, that the Christ, the resurrected Savior, was never accepted in Jerusalem and Judea, the place where it supposedly all happened, but was accepted in remote regions many miles away? Of course the Christian apologists have a ready answer, the same answer as Apostle Paul — God "blinded their eyes" until in

Conviction Overturned

the "fullness of time" they could recognize their savior, which is a part of the end times. A much more down to earth and likely explanation, and a far simpler one, for their rejection is that *they were there* and so will not be bamboozled. It is amazing that the people who would be the best witnesses, those who were *there*, reject the Christian claim and in fact, according to the Gospel of Matthew, and apparently to the Jews over one hundred years later referred to by Justin Martyr in his *Dialogue with Trypho,* claim that *the body was stolen!* The likely reason for this is that *the body was stolen*!

So then, in light of the claims of abundant, incontrovertible *proof* of the resurrection made by Christian apologists, let us provide them with a reality check. Here is a summary of the typical claims made and the reasonable responses to each which we have observed:

Pilate was a ruthless, severe governor who would have insisted that his orders to execute Jesus be carried out.

According to the Bible, Pilate strongly opposed the crucifixion, disliked and distrusted those that wanted to kill Jesus, and only submitted to immense political pressure to keep the peace. Could not this powerful, severe ruler, used to getting his own way, have made an apparent political concession and still gotten his way and contrived that Jesus survived? With what determination did Pilate resist the suggestion, when a disciple came after only several hours and told him Jesus had expired and requested that the disciples be given the body?

The ruthlessly efficient Roman guards would have would have ensured his execution. They would have feared that if Jesus did not die they would be executed in his place.

Are we talking of the same people? With what alacrity would the Centurion in charge of the execution, who thought Jesus was "the son of God" and a "righteous man" have carried out his task? And we can easily estimate with what enthusiasm he would have gladly followed the order to cut the body down and deliver it to the disciples? Fear of reprisal because Jesus did not die? Fear of whom? The governor that opposed his execution in the first place and wanted him kept alive? Would not the order from Pilate to cut the body down have seemed a

The Resurrection: Part One

natural one to the Centurion, in light of Pilate's known opposition to the execution.

The Roman guards thrust a spear into Jesus' side to make sure he was dead.

This is a convenient story, devised at lead fifty years after the event (according to Christian reckoning). The Gospel of Mark, written closer in time, knows nothing of so probative and critical an event, and instead has the unusual situation of a disciple going to inform the already reluctant executioner Pilate that Jesus is already dead and asking that the body be taken down and given to them! Not surprisingly, Pilate does just that! Supposedly he sends to find out if it is so that Jesus is dead — to whom, if in fact he did this? To the Centurion who thought Jesus was the "son of God"?

Jesus was *buried* in a tomb with a huge rock placed at the door, that nobody, *but nobody* could have ever moved.

The tomb was an open sepulcher, with the body laid in the open on top of the ground. The rock at the door was designed to be moved in order to later put the remains in an ossuary. The women arrived at the tomb Sunday morning to put spices on the body, with full confidence that someone could open it for them.

Now the more obvious, and probative fact, is that amazingly the body is entrusted to his very disciples, <u>the ones who later proclaimed him resurrected!!</u> Wouldn't an all-knowing, all-powerful God, who providentially planned and moved events to give us a verifiable, world historical cosmic event, and who later providentially inspired trustworthy accounts of that event, have at least contrived events so that somebody other than his own disciples had care of Jesus' body? And that maybe his body was disposed of in some manner other than an open burial in a sepulcher that anyone could have entered? I guess God is just not the planner and story-teller that some of us are. Let's keep him away from Hollywood!

There was a guard on the tomb and a Roman seal, forbidding any one from entering the tomb.

*There was **no guard at all** on the first day, the most likely day for any one to enter to rescue the body (Read the Bible!), and it is in*

Conviction Overturned

fact unlikely there was ever a guard, since three other Gospel writers, all equally anxious to prove the case of resurrection are all quite pointedly ignorant of this crucial fact, which they would not naturally fail to inform us of if it were true.

More Surrounding Circumstances—
Evidence of Phenomenal Occurrences

But there is more proffered circumstantial evidence to be considered. In fact, there is more proffered evidence which is in point of fact is of the most convincing form — evidence that can only be described as phenomenal and which, if believed, is so powerful that it leaves no doubt in the mind of supernatural intervention. Yet ironically, Christian apologists are almost universally loath to refer to this evidence, and in fact would usually prefer that it be forgotten. We will soon understand why. But it is a part of the narrative and a part of the proffered evidence and there is a very pertinent reason why it *must* be considered, because the evidence relates not only to the truth of the Gospel writer's proposition as the resurrection, but to his own credibility as a witness.

This evidence is of three claimed events that occurred at the time of the crucifixion. It is claimed that there was an unnatural darkness for three hours, from twelve noon to three p.m., the time of Jesus' death; that there was a large earthquake which split rocks around Jerusalem and actually ripped in two the veil of the Holy of holies in the Temple; and that some corpses in graves came alive and walked out of their tombs. These are phenomenal events, which if they can be proven true, demonstrate an event of cosmic proportions beyond the confines of our own natural, physical laws. Such is obviously the import and design of this narrative and that is the calculated effect upon the mind of the hearer.

The Gospel of Mark states "Now when the sixth hour [of the day, twelve noon] had come, there was darkness over the whole land until the ninth hour"(16:33). In Luke we have additional information: "Now it was about the sixth hour, and there was darkness *over all the earth* until the ninth hour. Then *the sun was darkened,* and the veil of the Temple was torn in two" (Luke 23:44-45). In Matthew, we have even

The Resurrection: Part One

additional information, "Now from the sixth hour until the ninth hour there was darkness over all the land..."(27: 45). Then Jesus dies on the cross with the famous "My God, My God why have you forsaken me?", and then cries out with a loud voice and dies. "Then, behold, the veil of the temple was torn in two from top to bottom; and the earth quaked, and the rocks were split, and the graves were opened; and many bodies of the saints who had fallen asleep were raised; and coming out of the graves after his resurrection, they went into the city and appeared to many"(27:51-53). So much for progressive development of a narrative, which we will see elsewhere.

The author of Gospel of John is the only author who actually claims to be present at the crucifixion. He had followed the arrest entourage to the high priests house (John 18:15) and he is expressly present when the spear is thrust into Jesus' side by the guard (John 19:34-35). But this claimed eyewitness knows nothing of any of these supernatural, phenomenal events. The sun disappearing and it becoming nighttime at noon, not to mention an earthquake, or for that matter people walking out of their graves, are hard things to miss, or forget! When you are trying to prove a supernatural, cosmic salvation event beyond our natural, physical laws and experience, you do not forget such details as these.

But there is more to be observed about these statements. As to the "unnatural darkness" much has been said by critics to dispute the possibility of a solar eclipse at the time, declaring that the Passover is at the time of the full moon and an eclipse cannot occur at the full moon. These arguments may be fairly gratuitous since physical laws render an eclipse impossible. In the first place the earth is traveling though space at more than 66,000 mile per hour at the same time that it is spinning about 1,000 mile per hour, and the moon is racing around the earth. So an eclipse could not last more than six minutes. But more importantly, since the courses of the earth, moon, and sun follow exact courses we can mathematically determine the time and place of every eclipse that has ever occurred or will occur. There was no eclipse in that locale for any time anywhere near the period of Jesus' death. Now of course the Christian apologists will respond that if there is a God with infinite power, who stands above and controls physical laws, then he can suspend physical laws in one part of the world, and blot our the sun, causing the people there to experience unnatural darkness. Of course when you accept this *assumption* the conclusion is undeniable. But of course this requires an *a priori* assumption of the truth of the very thing you wish to prove, rendering this of no value to us. But, claims the apologist, it is of use to us because there is *corroboration*.

Christians claim that this event is chronicled by Phlegon, a chronicler from the reign of Hadrian during the 130's A.D., in chapter 16 of his book *The Olympiads*. Tertullian, in the third century, quotes Phlegon as supposedly saying that in the fourth year of the two hundred and second Olympiad (32-33 A.D.) there was "the greatest eclipse of the sun" and that "it became night in the sixth hour of the day so that stars even appeared in the heavens. There was a great earthquake in Bithynia [western Turkey today], and many things were overturned in Nicea [also western Turkey]." **[3]** We are given more facts in this account, such as it being actual nighttime and the stars being out, which seems like even more progressive embellishment, although the non-canonical *Gospel of Peter*, which had wide currency, indicates that the stars were out. He also tells us the epicenter was in Bithynia, in western Turkey, which would be the North Anatolian fault line, an historically very active one.

Now the *Olympiads* is a book which chronicles highly unusual, bizarre events. Chapter 16 no longer exists, but the other parts of the book chronicle such bizarre events as finding the bones of a forty foot man in Sicily, and other such far-fetched events. None of the events are ever documented or ascribed to worthy sources. So Phlegon's *Olympiads* is sort of an ancient world *Guinness Book of World Records* but even more fantastic and without any proof to back up the claims made. But more importantly, what are the sources for Phlegon's claim for unnatural darkness at midday in first century Israel, assuming that is what he said? Where did he get his material? Did he receive it from the Christians? Did he obtain it from an early Gospel account? If so, then it is a circular argument. Phlegon would obviously put in anything that sounded exotic, strange, or astounding; and the Christian gospels were already in circulation.

Christians also claim that the darkness is referred to by an historian named Thallus in "his third book." The reference, by a church father, Julius Africanus, writing in the third century, is that "Thallus in the

The Resurrection: Part One

third book of his histories, explains away the darkness as an eclipse — unreasonable it seems to me." The sole reference quoted is that Thallus attempts to ascribe some darkness, presumably that alleged to have occurred at the crucifixion, to an eclipse, which is argued as impossible. But the first problem is that the writings of Thallus do not exist and we do not know with any certainty when they were written (although Christians proclaim, with scant reason, that it was 52 A.D). It is apparent from the excerpt from Julius Africanus that Thallus does not believe that anything supernatural took place. Even more probable is that Thallus is refuting claims, presumably by Christians, that something supernatural took place, meaning that Thallus was probably one of the many critics and skeptics that Christians have periodically been forced to refute through the ages, most of whose works are conveniently lost . It is more than presumptuous of us to assume, without further facts, that Thallus even claimed or conceded that there had been an unnatural darkness at the time of Jesus' crucifixion. It is much more likely that Christians had made that claim, and that Thallus was refuting the claim, insisting that even if there *had been* any such darkness that it was an eclipse. This was a poor refutation, admittedly, by our modern standards and knowledge. A more likely one could be that it simply became a dark day because of excessive cloudiness, but through multiple retellings and exaggerations (God bless the "Pentecostal" mind) it wound up being "the sun was darkened", i.e., it became nighttime. But even more importantly, since we do not have the writings of Thallus, we do not know what it was that Thallus was attempting to refute, or in other words, we do not know what Thallus' sources were. Was Thallus referring to an account given him by early Christians, or to an early Gospel account? Did he obtain it from the Gospel of Mark? If so, then the reference is of no use to us.

As to the earthquake, there is an even greater problem. Much as with solar eclipses, we have a perfect seismographic history of the world from time immemorial. We know when and where every single earthquake occurred in history and how powerful it was. There *simply was no earthquake* in the area of Israel, either the North Anatolian fault line or any other, any where near the time period we are talking about. As with the earthquake at the empty tomb in Matthew chapter

28 (Matthew loves earthquakes) it is a fairly crucial question as to credibility. For instance, if right now it is October 10, 2011 at 4:34 P.M., there is either an earthquake right now powerful enough to split rocks, or there isn't. There is no *maybe* involved. There either is or there isn't. And a person is either lying or telling the truth. The above assertion is, quite frankly, a *lie*.

As to dead people coming out of their graves, none of the Gospel authors other than the author of Matthew are apparently aware of this absolutely astounding information. And yet they are all just as eager as the author of Matthew to prove that Jesus is the Son of God and that he rose from the dead. Their silence on this point is astounding, since such supernatural phenomena is a herald of supernatural world cosmic events unfolding around them.

Now how do the above narratives affect our interpretation of the Gospel narratives? Do we merely say, "Well, this purported evidence does not really prove the resurrection very much, so let's just ignore it and move on?" Further reflection is merited. Because we must ask ourselves how these accounts reflect on the credibility of the authors, remembering the legal maxim included in standard jury instructions, that:

> "If you believe that a witness has been willfully false in part of his testimony, you should reject all of that witness' testimony…"

But, you may respond, you yourself admit that these authors were not eyewitnesses, they were merely reciting what others had told them. But are they not claimed, according to the Christian dating methods, to be first century persons living for the most part in Israel? (Luke being there at least two years, twenty five years later on Paul's expedition). Then they must have known that these accounts were false at the time they wrote them. Plainly put, a person who tells you it's night when it's day, or there was an earthquake when there was not, or that a bunch of corpses came to life when they did not, cannot be relied upon to tell you that someone who was dead came back to life and cannot be relied upon to base your life, ideals, hopes, property, wealth, and aspirations on the absolute certainty of such a belief. Even absent the above jury instruction, only a fool would do so. It is no wonder that pop Christian apologist and anthologist, Josh McDowell wrote a comprehensive book, *The New Evidence that Demands a Verdict,* and never once refers to the above Gospel texts. That is because while these narratives were obviously written to impress and convince ancient audiences, they prove the incredibility and unreliability of the Gospel authors and therefore the untrustworthiness of the Gospels themselves. And as such they are a source not of support, but of embarrassment, to the Christian apologists.

Chapter Three

THE RESURRECTION: PART TWO
THE APPEARANCES

Thus far we have observed some of the surrounding circumstances such as they may be probative of the issue of the resurrection of Jesus. The next order of evidence are the alleged "eyewitnesses" of the resurrection. These are the witnesses that historical Christianity has relied upon who claim to have seen, or who are claimed to have seen, the resurrected Jesus in the flesh. Let us examine carefully each incident.

We find first of all, surprisingly, that we do not have a single first hand account of an individual who narrates an account of his having met the resurrected Christ. There are only hearsay accounts of third persons who claim to be writing what others have supposedly seen in the past. Some will argue with me that the Gospel of John is written by one of Jesus' closest disciples who was presumably present for all of the events described, but such is not the case. In the first place, there is some considerable contention, as we shall later see, over who wrote the "Gospel of John" but more importantly for our purposes here, the Gospel of John itself states "This is the disciple who testifies of these things and *we* know that his testimony is true" (John 21:24, referring to Jesus' disciple that Jesus loved described in the incident at the Sea of Galilee in that chapter). This is an account written by persons who claim to have heard it from an original source that was present at the events narrated. So at the outset, let us remember one of the factors in the evaluation of a witness:

> "In evaluating a witness's testimony, you may consider anything that reasonably tends to prove or disprove the

The Resurrection: Part One

truth or accuracy of that testimony. Among the factors that you may consider are: How well could the witness see, hear, or otherwise perceive the things about which the witness testified?"

In this case, the witnesses who narrate the matter to us did not see, hear or perceive anything. So there are no "eyewitnesses" to the resurrection in the Gospel accounts. It is rather unsettling, since we are told an all-powerful God, who loves us and wants to save our souls, providentially moved events to provide us a world cosmic salvation event unparalleled in eternity, and also provided us an inspired written account for the purpose of our information and belief, that we would not see any eyewitness account in the most important and foundational of all documents — the Gospels — anyone who would say "I sat at my table on Sunday morning and suddenly there was Jesus, the Jesus I knew, standing beside me, and I touched him and spoke to him , and he spoke to me"... or "I attended a gathering along with hundreds of others, and there speaking to us was none other than Jesus himself.." But alas, we and the Christian apologists must take the Gospels as we find them.

If we look to the Epistles we purportedly find eyewitness references. One purported exception is from the Apostle Paul, who claims he saw the resurrected Jesus on the road to Damascus, but this is never one of the sightings claimed by Christian apologists. This happened an unknown period of time afterwards, at least three years later, and perhaps considerably more. It was long after the claimed ascension of Jesus to heaven which was supposed to be forty days after the resurrection, and the form that appeared was a highly supernatural, flaming form that did not resemble the earthly Jesus, or even a human form, in any way. In fact this was described as merely a great light and a voice proclaiming itself Jesus.

Likewise we have the First Epistle of John and the Epistle of Second Peter (II Peter 2:16-18). As we will see later, the authenticity of the latter is greatly doubted. It is almost certainly from the second century, it was not included in many early collections of purported apostolic writings, and it is without question written by a different person from the First Epistle of Peter, long regarded by the church as genuine. [1] As we will see in a later chapter, pseudepigraphic and pseudonymous writings were very commonplace in the first few centuries of our era, as they were in the centuries before Christ, particularly in Second Temple Israel. Especially among the Christians the pious fraud, far from being an anomaly, was actually seen as constructive of the faith. They were difficult to detect and gradually gained widespread adherence because of the apparent soundness of the doctrines they expressed, their use to the church, and the superior quality of the writing. [2]

So we must look to the other claimed appearances beginning on the Sunday morning after the resurrection — Easter Sunday. By all accounts it was between one and several women who arrived at the empty tomb. And that is all we can say as a nucleus of fact common to all accounts. From that point on we have nothing but divergence, inconsistency and contradiction.

The Gospel of Mark is generally considered as the oldest of the Gospel accounts included in the New Testament. Mark was not one of the "Twelve Apostles." Christians usually claim that this account was written between approximately 50 and 65 A.D., or about 20 to 25 years after the events they depict, although we will visit the issue of the dates of the Gospel in a later chapter. Mark tells us that when the Sabbath was over (on Sunday), "Mary Magdalene, Mary the mother of *James,* and Salome" came to the tomb with spices to anoint him. The name "Mary the mother of James presumably refers to James the brother of Jesus as related in Mark 15:40, wherein she is described as "Mary the mother of James the Less and of *Joses* (same spelling as Jesus in Greek, and many claim it should be translated as *Jesus*, but that early efforts to preserve Roman Catholic traditions of the eternal virginity of Mary leave us with the English translation Joses). They came "early in the morning....when the sun had risen." (Mark 16:2). They found the stone rolled away, an empty tomb and a "young man in a long white robe sitting on the right side..."(16:3). The young man told them "He is risen!" showed them where he had laid and said "Go tell the disciples —and Peter- that he is going before you into Galilee; there you will see him, *as he said to you."* The women then fled the tomb "and they said nothing to anyone, for they were afraid." It is fairly amazing and incredible that they said *nothing to anyone.* To

The Resurrection: Part One

find the tomb of someone you know and love empty and a mysterious person at the tomb tells you he is risen from the dead, and to tell no one is simply beyond belief. How did the disciples find out then?

Well, there is more in the Gospel of Mark, but the overwhelming consensus, even among Christian scholars, is that the verses that follow- verses 9 through 16 were added later. One of the dead giveaways is that verse 9 contradicts the first part of chapter sixteen twice by telling us that Jesus appeared *first* to Mary Magdalene *alone*, who *told* the other disciples (rather than *telling no one because she was afraid*), and then by going on to tell us who Mary Magdalene was, even though she had just appeared in the first part of the chapter. In essence, we start getting another version starting at verse 9. The following verses appear to be a summary of other resurrection appearances of Jesus that are included in the other Gospels. It includes the two disciples on the road to Emmaus and the appearance to the eleven "as they sat at table." The section also includes the strange, discordant verse "And these signs will follow those who believe: In my name they will cast out demons; they will speak with new tongues; they will take up serpents; and if they drink anything deadly, it will not hurt them..."(verse 17). Picking up presumably venomous snakes and drinking poison has at no time been a part of the Christian mystique (other then the one episode with the Apostle Paul after being shipwrecked near Malta and then the antics of some of the West Virginia Pentecostal crowd). The fact that church father Ireneas, bishop of Lyon, at least *one hundred and thirty years* later refers to this section, is no help whatsoever in proving its authenticity. Even Christian apologist Frank Morrison, in *Who Moved the Stone*, concludes that this section is a later addition, and not a part of the original Gospel.[3] The purpose of this insertion is obvious — it is an attempt to fill in the blanks, and make the ending of the Gospel consistent with the other Gospels.

So other than these highly disputed concluding verses, the Gospel concludes with the three women finding an empty tomb; a mysterious man in a long, white robe, tells them he is resurrected and will meet the disciples in Galilee (He "goes before you", so presumably the implication is that they are to go to Galilee); and they run away "and said nothing to anyone, for they were afraid." This is the end of the Gospel. Frank Morrison contended that this was a "fragment" of the conclusion of the Gospel, and that there was more, but it had been lost. [4]The only basis for this belief seems to be that *there must be more*, or else this Gospel is insufficient to lend probative value to the resurrection, omits obviously crucial sightings of Jesus, and through these obvious omissions, renders the Gospel incompatible with the other, more substantive and detailed resurrection accounts. Other Christian apologists contend that verse 8 is deliberately meant to be the conclusion of the Gospel because the impression to be given is only that Jesus is alive.

So the proof of the resurrection in Mark is an empty tomb — period. But in all fairness, if the mysterious young man declares that Jesus will appear to the disciples in Galilee, "as he told you", then the implication is that Jesus *did* appear in Galilee — and this is another story, one that we are not told *here*. The Gospel of Mark has no ascension to heaven, and we are left with the impression that somewhere he stills walks the earth, which some apologists claim is exactly the impression desired, since they claim he does walk the earth through the Holy Spirit.

Then we have the Gospel account of the Gospel of Luke. Most Christian apologists contend that Luke was written about 62-64 A.D. Luke tells us that "It was Mary Magdalene, Joanna, Mary the mother of James and the other women with them" (24:10) who had come to the tomb "very early in the morning" (v. 1). They found the stone rolled away and the body gone. Then suddenly, while they stood perplexed, "two men stood by them in shining garments" and told them Jesus was risen. They went, and far from *saying nothing to anyone* they reported these things to the disciples "and to all the rest." But Peter ran to the tomb and saw the linen shroud in which Jesus had been buried, and Jesus gone.

That same day, two disciples were on their way to Emmaus, a village seven miles from Jerusalem. They came upon another person, who walked with them into town and who seemed very confident of Jesus' godly mission and very knowledgeable of the Scriptures concerning Messianic prophecies (at least more so than they were, and to the point that the two travelers were very impressed). Later the stranger left, and the two disciples experienced a certain epiphany, "their eyes were opened and they knew him…"(24:31). They *knew*

The Resurrection: Part One

him as Jesus! They were his disciples, but they supposedly did not recognize him on the road or during dinner. Why not? Apparently he was, as this narrative is related in the Gospel of Mark, "in another form" (16:12). What intriguing, mysterious language. So it was Jesus, but he looked like another, completely different person. Then how did they know it was really Jesus? Isn't it more likely that afterwards they were talking about how knowledgeable the man had been concerning Scripture and they decided that it must have really been Jesus they were talking to, because "Did not our hearts burn within us on the road, and while he opened the Scriptures to us?" (24:32) (This passage always reminds the author of the "burning heart test" used by the Mormons).

Part of the answer may be in the verses that follow. The disciples continue on to the disciples in Jerusalem and relate what happened. On meeting the disciples, they find the eleven disciples "gathered together saying, 'the Lord is risen *indeed* [in other words he really *has* risen] and has appeared to Simon!'"(referring to Simon Peter, whom we shall see referred to by the Apostle Paul as the first disciple that Jesus appeared to, although an appearance to Peter alone does not even appear anywhere in our New Testament Gospels). The two disciples who had arrived from Emmaus are told this before they even had time to tell their own story. We can only reasonably estimate how this information from these disciples would naturally serve to reinforce, if not to instill, the belief that it was in fact Jesus that they had met on the road, and in turn their tale reinforced the belief of the disciples that Jesus had *indeed* risen. Even more interestingly, if we read back in the *exact same* account that we just referred to, in Luke chapter 24, we discover the amazing fact that *Jesus did not appear to Peter at all!* Peter merely found the empty tomb and the grave clothes and he "departed, marveling to himself at what had happened" (Luke 24:12). So the only possible conclusion is that during the course of the day, Peter convinced himself that Jesus was resurrected and so related to other disciples *not that he had physically seen Jesus* but only that Jesus was resurrected, and the interpretation placed on this by the other disciples was that Peter had *actually seen* the risen Jesus, not just the empty tomb. In fact, it was not even necessary for Peter to declare Jesus resurrected, it was only necessary for Peter to relate that he had found the empty tomb, and the resulting gossip and second-hand distortion would fill in the blanks quickly until the story had become one of an actual sighting of Jesus.

And if in fact Peter was not convinced already, the story of the disciples on the road to Emmaus would have been enough to convince him, and for Peter to conclude, and proclaim, that Jesus was risen, and the Peter story quickly became Jesus "was seen by Cephas, then by the twelve" after his resurrection, as related by Paul (I Corinthians 15:5). This then is undoubtedly the somewhat awkward, disjointed origin of the appearance first to Peter before the others — Peter in reality having seen only the empty tomb. But this incident, combined with the story of the road to Emmaus, gives us a glimpse of the nature, origins, and workings of gossip and rumor which we as human beings are all too familiar with, and for which we do not need to consult an expert or read a book to become knowledgeable about. It is all too familiar a part of human experience and behavior. But to reach this conclusion we must decide if we are going to accept the conclusion which seems natural and reasonable from the facts — to accept the conclusion which "conforms to reality" as we know it and experience it in our daily lives, or demand *a priori* a conclusion which requires the supernatural in order to fit into the demands of our pre-existing belief system.

The Gospel of Luke goes on to relate how the disciples, already full of the Jesus sighting craze, were visited by Jesus and he ate with them. After eating, he then taught them the Scriptures and *"Then* [presumably referring to an event which immediately thereafter followed] *he led them out as far as Bethany, and he lifted up his hands and blessed them. Now it came to pass while he blessed them, that He parted from them and was carried off into heaven"* (24:51). The disciples go back to Jerusalem worshipping Jesus and were continually in the temple praising and blessing God. This is the end of this Gospel. The Gospel account is clear and unmistakable: **Jesus is ascended into heaven on Easter Sunday, after appearing to the eleven disciples one time in Jerusalem, and he ascends from Bethany, a mile from Jerusalem.** Interestingly enough, in the first chapter of Acts of the Apostles, presumably also written by Luke, Jesus remains with the disciples forty days and then ascends to heaven from the Mount of Olives in Jerusalem.

The Resurrection: Part One

Next we have the Gospel of Matthew. Forty percent of the Gospel of Matthew is almost verbatim the Gospel of Mark. It almost as though the Gospel of Mark is included in the Gospel of Matthew. It has been argued endlessly and fruitlessly whether Mark borrowed from Matthew, or whether Matthew borrowed from Mark, or if they both drew from a third source. The date therefore is unknown and indeterminable. It has been surmised that there was originally an Aramaic Matthew, written in the language of the Jews of Judea and therefore presumably older. Some have thought that the Gospel of the Hebrews, which we know was used by the Jewish Christians, referred to as the Ebionites, was actually another name for this Aramaic Matthew. What concerns us here is the resurrection sequence, which adds startlingly new claims.

In Matthew, "Mary Magdalene and *the other* Mary came to see the tomb"(Matthew 28:1), very similar to the other sequences except minus a woman or two. But then there is a radical departure. "And behold, there was a great earthquake; for an angel of the Lord descended from heaven, and came and rolled back the stone from the door and sat on it. His countenance was like lightning and his clothing as white as snow. And the guards shook for fear of him, "and became like dead men" (28:2-4). This narration adds many significant and vital facts and poses new questions. The women do not find the stone already rolled away as in Mark and Luke. An angel comes from heaven and rolls it back for them. Either they find the stone already rolled back or an angel comes from the sky and rolls it back for them. There is a large earthquake. Frankly, there is either an earthquake or there is not. One does not miss an earthquake. If for instance, right now it is October 5, 2011 at 5:11 p.m., there is either an earthquake at this spot at this moment, and let's say a large boulder is moved nearby, or there is not. It is a fairly significant question. The young man in white in Mark is now metamorphosized into an angel of the Lord who descends from the sky (and in Luke actually becomes variously two men in white or two angels).

Some have attempted to reconcile this by saying that this narrative is written in a form of the historical past tense, something like the historical present, but using the past tense to describe an event that was actually an action completed in the *then* past, best narrated in the past perfect, or completed past, and that these things had actually already occurred *before* the women arrived, in order to explain the situation of the empty tomb they encountered. For instance, they would claim that the passage *really* meant, and should have read, "there *had been* a great earthquake, and an angel of the Lord *had* descended", etc. But the historical past tense, the past tense used to express a completed action in the past, is used no where else in this Gospel, or any other for that matter. It is highly awkward, especially since the thought sequence it is a part of, which we have rendered a paragraph, begins in the past tense, i.e., "Now after the Sabbath, as the first day of the week began to dawn, Mary Magdalene and the other Mary came to see the tomb…"(v.1). As currently written the paragraph follows in the same past tense and appears to be deliberately and correctly written so. Further, Koine Greek, in which it is written, uses the imperfective, representing a continuous action in the past, or the aorist tense, which is an indefinite action in the past. The entire paragraph uses the aorist tense and there is no basis for distinction. Further, and more decisively, the subsequent narrative refutes this claim because it continues in the same tense, with the women as participants: "But the angel answered and said *to the women*…" (v.5). So to say these things happened before they arrived is absurd. This would be a completely different narrative.

Then the angel tells the women that he is risen and directs them to go and tell the disciples "He is going before you into Galilee; *there* you will see him." And so "they ran out quickly from the tomb with fear and great joy, and ran to bring his disciples word." These are women who were not so afraid that they *told no one*, as in Mark. And once again, the angel, as in Mark, says that the resurrection appearance to the disciples will definitely be in *Galilee*, not Jerusalem. But in Luke, since the sole resurrection appearance is in Jerusalem, as though by conscious effort to internally reconcile the narrative, we have a sleight of hand, and the angel does not say "He is going before you into Galilee; there you will see him" (implicitly "go to Galilee!"). Instead in Luke the angel says: "Remember *how he spoke you when he was still in Galilee…*" saying that he would rise from the dead.

Then, when the women run to tell the disciples, they suddenly run into Jesus himself and they held him by the feet and worshipped him. Jesus tells them to go and tell the disciples "to go to Galilee, and there they will see me" (v.10). In this narrative, the disciples actually

The Resurrection: Part One

go to Galilee and, lo and behold, Jesus actually appears to them on an unknown mountain in Galilee. He anoints them to go into all the world and make disciples and baptize them, and the Gospel suddenly comes to an end. It is the only appearance to the disciples narrated in this gospel. The impression left is that Jesus is still in the world, not ascended into heaven. And he appears to them once only, and only on a mountain in Galilee, not on the Mount of Olives, and not in Jerusalem at all.

What can we say about the rule of innocent misrecollection here? We have two dramatically conflicting accounts. If we compare it to something common, as for example an auto accident, it is not a question of whether a car was red or purple, or even whether the light was yellow or green. It is of one witness saying the accident occurred in Los Angeles, and another saying it happened in Chicago, and one saying the accident involved a big rig semi, and the other saying it involved two Volkswagons (or more like one saying it involved a jetliner that crashed). The accounts are so conflicting that we can only conclude that we are talking about two completely different events. Or more pungently, that we are dealing with lies. Not the material that lends itself to such a conviction upon which we would make major judgments of life and death, which morally we could do on nothing less than evidence beyond a reasonable doubt. Not the evidence upon which we would convict and consume the life of another, and not the evidence upon which we would commit our own lives, thoughts, desires, fortunes, destiny, actions, aspirations and future hopes, which is exactly and precisely what the Christian apologists, pastors, and evangelists openly seek and demand from us, and in fact will accept nothing less.

As previously mentioned, unique to Matthew is the account that the tomb was guarded and a "Roman seal" put on the tomb. We do not know the details of the "seal", although many Christian apologists have speculated that it was a frightening specter of death upon any who would dare tamper with the tomb. This claim of a Roman guard seems vital to the proof of any resurrection since we have the glaring weakness of the claim of resurrection consisting in the fact that the body is entrusted to Jesus' own disciples, the very ones who later claim he is resurrected. In fact the issue of a guard posted is so obviously

Conviction Overturned

vital and probative, that it is stupendous that three other evangelists, seeking to write a credible account to prove the resurrection, failed to include this crucial fact. It is therefore a highly doubtful, self-serving tale, and an afterthought. In any event, as the narrative of Matthew makes clear (27:62), it was *the next day* that a guard was asked for from Pilate, and so the guard would not have arrived until at least *the next day!* As related above, the most likely time that any disciples would have come to rescue or take the body would have been the first night, when the tomb, even by the account of the Gospel of Matthew, was unattended and "anyone or his brother" could have waltzed in and taken the body (I carefully say *some* disciples, not using the standard phrase *"the disciples"*, as though twelve, or seventy or more marched shoulder to shoulder to the task).

But, alas, we are not done. We have the "Gospel of John", also known as the Fourth Gospel, which the Christian churches claim as written 85-90 A.D., fifty to sixty years after the events. In John, Mary Magdalene comes alone to the tomb on Sunday morning "while it was still dark" (John 20:1). She finds no angels, no Jesus. There is no earthquake. She finds the stone rolled away from the entrance to the tomb. We may be getting closer to the truth in some respects. We have the lone figure of Mary Magdalene. She is a very interesting character. She is, we are told, the woman out of whom Jesus cast seven demons. There is absolutely no reason scripturally to indicate that she was the woman caught in adultery. The Bible's descriptions of maladies are framed with the point of view of the first century person's view in mind, including his medical and psychiatric knowledge. Afflictions were often seen as a matter of possession by powerful demons. The only modern day equivalent of a person, apparently with no physical disorder, being possessed by seven demons would be a psychotic state — schizophrenia. So fittingly, the first "sighting" of Jesus, which starts the trail of "appearances' running, is from a known schizophrenic, *apparently* now cured by a casting out of demons.

At that point, Mary runs to tell Simon Peter and "the other disciple, *whom Jesus loved*", who is identified for us as Lazarus by the use of the exact same manner in John 11:3, and 11:5. There is only one disciple in the entire New Testament who is described as "the disciple that Jesus loved." Only Lazarus is ever so described

The Resurrection: Part One

and named, a point that Christians have a hard time dealing with, for various reasons we will discuss later. These two disciples run to the tomb. They enter it and they find the linen clothes in which Jesus had been buried and the head covering laying apart from it. Lazarus, who had arrived at the tomb first, "saw and believed" (20:8). Then we are told, incredibly, that "For as yet *they did not know the Scripture*, that he must rise again from the dead" (20:9), despite the fact that they had supposedly been told this three times. Strangely enough, the *enemies* of Jesus, the Jewish leaders, were supposedly so familiar with these predictions that he would rise from the dead the third day, that they had gone to Pilate to ask that a guard be placed so the body could not be stolen (Matthew 27:62-64). Apparently we are to believe that they were paying better attention than the disciples were.

We are not told at this point, whether Peter yet believed Jesus resurrected. Based on the editorial comment of verse nine that "they did not yet know the Scripture, that he must rise again from the dead," we can only assume that this statement means that Peter had no reason to think at that time that Jesus was resurrected. Of course Peter is absolutely right, there *is* nothing about an empty tomb to suggest the supernatural. Now up to this point, this portion of the narrative, with Peter visiting the empty tomb, is close to the account of Luke, with the exception that Peter is now not alone. Lazarus appears to have been written out of the Lucan account, and he deliberately reinserts himself into this narrative, even claiming that he outran Peter and was actually the first to reach the tomb and look inside and see the linen shroud, but that Peter was the first to actually go inside (20:4-6). The significance of this portion is that there is no Jesus, and there are no angels, or anything else supernatural. The disciples visit an empty tomb. But more events happen.

In this narrative, after the disciples leave, Mary stays at the empty tomb. She then sees two angels that speak to her. They are described as angels, not men in white robes. Immediately thereafter she meets Jesus himself. But she doesn't recognize him and thinks it is the gardener. She asks him where the body is. Jesus says her name and she recognizes him. In a strange comment, Jesus tells Mary not to cling to him because he has not yet ascended to the Father. Mary then goes and informs the disciples of these events. Then, later on Sunday, Jesus

Conviction Overturned

appears to the disciples while they are assembled behind closed doors, presumably in Jerusalem, since if Peter is in Jerusalem on Sunday morning, as described in the other gospels, he could not have traveled 150 miles to be in Galilee in the evening. He then breathes on them and says "Receive the Holy Spirit..." (20:22) and presumably the Holy Spirit by this account is given here and not at Pentecost, as narrated in Acts, chapter 1, where it occurs on the first feast of Pentecost after Jesus' ascension. This discrepancy has led to doctrinal attempts to reconcile the accounts by, among other things, claiming that the real *power* of the Holy Spirit for casting out demons, healing the sick, and speaking in tongues occurred at Pentecost. Since the disciple Thomas is not present and does not believe, Jesus returns eight days later when Thomas is present, and he also believes. The Gospel ends at the end of chapter 20, but another story has been added as chapter 21, which includes an account of Jesus meeting seven of his disciples while they are fishing in Galilee at an unknown time.

These then are the Gospel accounts. None of them are primary accounts of persons who speak in the first person of seeing the risen Christ, but they are secondary accounts of those who presume to inform us of what their testimonies were. The Gospels are systematic accounts to describe the life of Jesus and prove his resurrection. In the first chapter of Acts of the Apostles, we have a continuation of that account, telling us that after the resurrection Jesus lived among the apostles for forty days, teaching them about the kingdom of God. He promised them that they would receive the gift of the Holy Spirit, which obviously they had up to that time not yet received, although we are told that they had *already* received this on Easter Sunday in John, chapter 20. After forty days he led them out from Jerusalem to the Mount of Olives, less than a mile away, and while they watched, he ascended into heaven.

TheApostle Paul, in chapter 15 of the First Letter to the Corinthians, gives us a summary account of Christ's resurrection appearances, stated apparently for instructional purposes. His account, presumed to be written about 53-57 A.D., or in other words about twenty to twenty five odd years after the events, provides a somewhat different version of the resurrection appearances of Jesus. Paul tells us that the resurrected Jesus "was seen by Cephas ['the rock', another name for Peter], then by the twelve..." (15:5). The "appearance" to Peter is undoubtedly nothing other, in reality, than the non-appearance that we have already seen in Luke and John. Peter merely sees the empty tomb, which becomes distorted through rumor into Peter actually seeing the resurrected Jesus. We do not have in the canonical Gospels an appearance alone to Peter before the other disciples.

The narrative of Paul continues, "After that he was seen by over five hundred brethren at once, of whom the greater part remain to the present, but some have fallen asleep" (15:6). We are not told if he was seen by over five hundred at the same *place* as well as the same time, but presumably this is so. We have no such reference to this in the Gospels. It would be a startling event, since all of the appearances, except the one Paul claims to himself, are to small groups of persons already disciples of Jesus. Once again, we are left to wonder at such a glaring omission, so much so that the truth of this must naturally stand as doubtful and suspect.

The narrative continues, "After that he was seen by James, then by all the apostles..." Once again, we do not have in the canonical gospels, those a part of our New Testament, an individual appearance to James, apart from the others, but we do have it in the Gospel of the Hebrews, an Aramaic Gospel — Aramaic and so presumably written by and for the Judean Christians, and therefore probably more closely approximating the viewpoint of early Christians in Judea. Only portions of this Gospel exist. It appears to parallel the Gospel of Matthew but with no supernatural birth and hence no nativity sequence. It is especially fascinating that the Apostle Paul was both familiar with and quotes from this source, which has been universally rejected by the orthodox Christian church because its doctrinal perspectives are deemed heretical. The early Jewish Christians, i.e., the first Christians, did not see Jesus as God, or as born of the Holy Spirit and therefore without a physical father, but rather saw Jesus as anointed as Messiah at the time of his baptism, receiving the Christ spirit from God, and believed the Christ personage departed from him on the cross at the time he uttered "My God, my God, why hast thou forsaken me?" We will see however that this doctrinal point of view is quite consistent with Pauline understanding of Christian doctrine and other early Christian teaching.

And last, according to Paul, Jesus was seen by himself, in the account already referred to. Paul, as Saul of Tarsus, merely experienced a light "brighter than the sun shining around [him]" (Acts 26:13) and heard a voice that identified himself as Jesus. There was no person or form. This hardly constitutes a resurrection appearance of Jesus, but Paul sees it as such and claims he encountered the resurrected Jesus. The men who accompanied Paul only heard a voice but saw no one (Acts 9:7). This account varies somewhat by the time Paul addresses the Sanhedrin, the Jewish ruling counsel, in Jerusalem many years later. There he says that the men with him "saw the light, but did not hear the voice of him who spoke to me" (Acts 22:9). When he speaks to King Agrippa, he adds substantially more to the message that he heard from the voice in the sky, which in that rendition includes considerable detail in the role which Paul is to play as an evangelist to the Gentiles (Acts 26:15 et seq.). Paul indeed becomes in a sense, both historically and doctrinally, the father of the Gentile church (this is not the author's hyperbole, but rather Paul himself, in a characteristically self-glorifying, boastful manner claims 'I am your father'). And yet the testimony of Paul, through whom the Gentile world is supposedly directed by God to receive the Gospel of salvation, is little different from that of various religious mystics throughout history, viz., "a funny thing happened on my way to the market, *I met God, who told me the meaning of life and told me to tell you...etc."* Such is a variation of Mohammed, Buddha, the prophet Joseph Smith, David Koresh, and countless others.

And so we have our record of *direct* testimony, such as it is. In summary, I would like to make some general observations:

General Observation Number One: The Drift from Clarity to Darkness—The Journey to the "F" Zone

The trend that seems most notable in the Gospel accounts is the following. We seem to have a solid historical core about an arrest, trial and crucifixion. The parallels in the accounts are compelling and largely believable. But the farther we get away from that core, and proceed beyond it, the more the accounts both diverge from each other, and also become more vague, disjointed, inconsistent and

The Resurrection: Part One

contradictory. This is of great significance to myself. The importance of this pattern to me, as a trial attorney, is the following. I have defended numerous criminal cases for several decades and dealt assiduously in the defense of the worst felons, working as closely, painstakingly and confidentially as possible in preparing their defenses, and rehearsing endlessly the smallest details of their defense. What I have often found, is that in their narratives, I frequently find *exactly* the same pattern. As to the lead-up to the crimes, the defendant can give me a thorough, detailed, coherent, trustworthy account, but there comes a threshold point, at which this breaks apart, and the narrative of the defendant starts to become vague, inconsistent or incoherent, often contradictory. The threshold point is when the defendant passes from the domain of truth into the domain of fantasy and lies, and begins to invent his or her own world of reality. It is the "L" zone — the lie zone. They have passed from historical reality into what they would like us to believe happened.

To look at this another way, what is the crucial historical fact of the Gospel of Jesus? The answer should be obvious (unless you skipped the introduction and the title of this chapter) - it is of course the resurrection. And yet, within the four Gospels, we have fairly detailed accounts of the life and teachings of Jesus, and of his arrest, trial and crucifixion. Yet as to the most important event of all, his resurrection, we have only a few disjointed, inconsistent summary chapters — to be exact, we have eight genuine lines in Mark, one short chapter in Matthew, one chapter in Luke, and two chapters in John, and all of them, as we have seen, confusing, sharply contradictory, vague, and self-serving. It is because the self-serving desperate authors have obviously passed into the "L" zone. We will find again the passage of the threshold into this obscure "L" zone when we deal with the two nativity accounts presented in the Gospels. And yet the Christian apologists and evangelists do not just want us to believe these historical facts, they want us to pledge our all — our very being and purpose — to the truth of these facts and be led by a book, the Bible; by a religion, Christianity; and, although this would be fiercely denied, by certain people - those who lead, interpret, and dominate the respective branches of Christendom, and tell us how we should think, act, and even vote.

Is this all in the "L" zone of lies? In our context, the word *lie* may not necessarily be the most appropriate, for the simple reason that the Gospel authors are secondary historians, not primary historians — they are not relating their personal experiences. Instead they are relating various stories that have sprung up and are in general circulation. I hesitate to use the term myth, although this is an appropriate term to use, and I could well term this the "M" zone. However, certain mythologists, such as the late Joseph Campbell, would take great exception to the use of that term. They would state that a myth, properly understood is not *false*, it is a true statement about the nature of life and represents the reality of our world put into a story form. They would state that a myth is a metaphor embodying ultimate reality. Indeed, this is one, but not the only, understanding of myth. Therefore, I will avoid so controversial a term and instead use the term *legend* to indicate a story which the teller merely relates, perhaps not knowing or caring as to the truth, but with an absence of mendacity. But nevertheless the story lacks a basis in truth and is false. Hence, we may still call this the "L" zone of legend. If you wish to be more exact about it, both lies and legends come under the rubric of falsehood. So, if you will, this is indisputably the "F" zone - of *falsehood*. As we move from truth to falsehood, we move from light to darkness, and from clarity, consistency and common sense into the realm of obscurity, confusion, contradiction *and* increasing, progressive embellishment.

General Observation Number Two: Progressive Embellishment

What I see most obviously in the Gospel accounts is a progressive development of the story from the earliest accounts to the latest. This is marked by progressive embellishment and exaggeration of accounts. This development is consistent with falsehood, not the truth. The truth remains the same — what happened *happened*, but what can, and often does change, is the telling of what happened. This is capable of gross distortion, to the point where lies and legends replace facts. The dead giveaway is the process of progressive embellishment. A young man in a white robe in Mark, regarded as the earliest account, turns into an angel in Matthew, and becomes two angels in Luke, and

The Resurrection: Part One

by John it isn't just two angels, who by now are relegated to a mere cameo appearance, but Jesus himself who appears. In Mark there is merely an empty tomb and a proclamation that Jesus will appear in Galilee, and we are left to surmise that he is alive; then there are appearances — to Mary, the schizophrenic; then in an arguably vague, indeterminable "other form" to two men on the road to Emmaus who never recognized him; then in a supposed appearance, which can be determined to be an actual non-appearance, to Peter; in an even more vague, unknown, unrecorded manner to James; to a flock of women; then to all the disciples on an unknown mountaintop in remote Galilee; then to the disciples in the heart of Jerusalem; then they go back and summarize these appearances and add these to the otherwise "*unfinished*" Gospel of Mark. Finally he appears to 500 disciples at once! All of this is nothing more than progressive development and embellishment of a story, which is a shameless hallmark of falsehood, and has no relationship to the truth.

Not only that, but when there exists such a history of progressive development and rank embellishment, we are left to ponder when the embellishment began and what the original facts really were. Is Mark the *original* story? If in fact, as the Christians claim, it was written twenty to twenty five years after the events it describes, not by an eyewitness, or even by one of the disciples, and it merely purports to summarize eyewitness accounts, then how de we now what the original account was? This leads us to believe the original events were even less than what is related in the original, truncated version of Mark, which itself may well have fit the pattern of embellishment.

And there is something even more alarming. We assume, based on the narrative of Acts of the Apostles, that Christian evangelization started immediately on the first Pentecost after Easter Sunday — precisely fifty days after Easter. But matching the events depicted in the Acts to known history reveals something else. In the book of Acts of the Apostles, Peter and John are the main movers and evangelists in Jerusalem. But very early on, presumably in not more than the first weeks or months after the first Pentecost, they are warned to stay out of the Temple and stop preaching (Acts chapter 4). But they return to the Temple preaching ("We must obey God and not men"). The Jewish Sanhedrin must decide what to do with them, and one of the

Conviction Overturned

greatest teachers of the day, Gamaliel, makes a speech to the Jewish Sanhedrin council suggesting that to persecute them will make the Christians grow even more. His remarks are very enlightening from the standpoint of historical chronology. He said *"Men of Israel, take heed to yourselves what you intend to do regarding these men. For some time ago Theudas rose up, claiming to be somebody. A number of men, about four hundred, joined him. He was slain, and all who obeyed him were scattered and came to nothing"* (Acts 5:34-36). He also mentions the rebellion of Judas the Galilean in 6 A.D. His conclusion is that they should leave the Christian movement alone and it will also come to nothing. But the significance of these remarks is that he cites the movement of Theudas, a messianic leader, as something that occurred in the past.

The movement of Theudas is recorded in the history of the era written by Josephus.[6] Theudas had followers and he led people out into the desert. There was some apparent attempt to dry up the Jordan River. They were put down by the Romans. But interestingly enough, this rebellion was in *44 A.D.!* Yet by what is apparently the beginning of the ministry of Peter and John, as recorded in the book of Acts, this has already taken place! The crucifixion of Jesus is regarded as having occurred in either 32 or 33 A.D., based on the New Testament chronology, determined as follows. John the Baptist's ministry is stated to have began in the fifteenth year of the reign of Tiberius (Luke 3:1), who came to power in 14 A.D., so the fifteenth year was the year 28 A.D., the entire first year of an emperor's reign always being included as the 'first year' in all Roman histories. Jesus is baptized, presumably soon after, and begins a ministry that explicitly passes three Passovers and he is crucified at the third Passover of his ministry, which would place it in either 32 or 33 A.D. So although it appears that the activities of John and Peter (for they are the only disciples whose activities are recorded in the early chapters of Acts despite the fact that apparently all of the other apostles are at this time still in Judea but apparently absent), while according to the text seeming to occur shortly after the crucifixion, in fact occur *at least ten to twelve years later, and possibly more.*

So the apostles, or at least those recorded as instigating the Christian movement, had over a decade to mull over what happened with Jesus. This means that far from the sudden Christian outburst of activity and Pentecostal energy that the book of Acts records as happening fifty days after the crucifixion, that in fact the Christian movement, if it existed at all, was virtually non-existent for a decade after Jesus' death. After a decade of study and thought they decided that Jesus' death was not the end, but that in fact his death was a actually a fulfillment of the messianic mission and that this Jesus would return again in the very near future to restore Israel to its glory and rule the world. The conversion of Saul of Tarsus occurs even *later than this*.

Now I would be both thoroughly remiss and unfair were I not to mention that the Christians have an answer to this Theudas controversy. Some have claimed that the Theudas rebellion referred to by Gamaliel was *some other* Theudas in *some other* rebellion, needless to say one absolutely lost to history (Nelson Study Bible, New King James Version, Thomas Nelson, Inc. 1997, footnote to Acts 5:36-37). Of course the very point of Gamaliel's remark is to establish an historical reference point from the then not too distant past that would be immediately very familiar to his listeners. The rebellion of Theudas was a major historical event, recorded by Josephus, and obviously well known to the Judeans of the fist century. *There is no other recorded rebellion of Theudas* and there are no grounds for this assertion. It is as though in the current age one referred to [the attack upon] Pearl Harbor, or the Korean War, or 9/11 to establish an historical point of reference which Americans of the Twentieth or Twenty First Century would be immediately familiar with, and up would jump the Christians and say this refers to *another* attack on Pearl Harbor, or *another* Korean War, not the one we are familiar with. But we will see that this is a very familiar tactic by the Christians, emphasizing their absolute lack of intellectual honesty.

Third Observation:
The Flawed Argument from Martyrdom

But all of this to one side, we are confronted with another argument made by the Christian apologists which is among the most strident. It goes something like this. Jesus' twelve apostles all saw the resurrected Jesus and firmly believed this. And they *all* went to their deaths affirming that Jesus was risen from the dead because they had seen it with their own eyes, and they would not *all unanimously* have died for something that was not true, or if you will, for a lie (except for the Apostle John whom we are told died of old age). This is on the surface a powerful argument. Here is that same argument, made powerfully by Christian apologist Simon Greenleaf:

"Propagating this new faith, even in the most inoffensive and peaceful manner, they could expect nothing but contempt, opposition, reviling, bitter persecutions, stripes, imprisonments, torments, and cruel deaths. Yet this faith they zealously did propagate; and all these miseries they endured undismayed, nay rejoicing. As one after another was put to death, the survivors only prosecuted their work with increased vigor and resolution. The annals of military warfare afford scarcely an example of like heroic constancy, patience and unblenching courage. They had every possible motive to review carefully the grounds of their faith, and the evidences of the great facts and truths which they asserted; and these motives were pressed upon their attention with the most melancholy and terrific frequency.

It was therefore impossible that they could have persisted in affirming the truths they have narrated, had not Jesus actually risen from the dead, and had they not known this fact as certainly as they knew any other fact. If it were morally possible for them to have been deceived in this manner, every human motive operated to lead them to discover and avow their error. To have persisted in so great a falsehood, after it was known to them, was not only to encounter, for life, all the evils which man could inflict, from without, but to endure all the pangs of inward and conscious guilt' with no hope of future peace; no testimony of a good conscience, no expectation of honor or esteem among men, no hope of happiness in this life, or in the world to come." [7]

This is very eloquent and heart-wrenchingly poignant. Only one problem: It simply isn't true. On examination, we find that this is specious and without foundation. The foundational facts upon which this claim rests are simply false.

We simply do not know what happened to the "twelve apostles" or whether there ever were twelve apostles. There is simply no evidence

The Resurrection: Part One

one way or the other. There are two contradictory lists given in the Gospels as to who the twelve apostles even were, although Christian apologists paste this over by saying that some Apostles were known by different names in the different Gospel accounts (a perfect, all-knowing God who specializes in giving us confusing, ambiguous accounts of world historical cosmic salvation events). There is a list of apostles in Luke 6:12, and another given in Matthew 10:1, which is typically identical with Mark chapter 3 (most of the Gospel of Mark is virtually incorporated verbatim into Matthew). Philip is classed alongside Bartholomew in both, possibly as a brother, but in Gospel of John, Philip's brother, presumably an apostle, is Nathaniel. In Acts 1:13 he is placed alongside Thomas, "Philip and Thomas", and that is followed by "Bartholomew and Matthew." Philip and Nathaniel are presented in the Fourth Gospel as the first two disciples converted. The accounts that are promoted by churches as to the fate of the apostles are based on questionable, late traditions, which are finally encapsulated in Fox's Book of Martyrs, written fifteen hundred years later. If Christians accept these remote, late traditions, why do they no accept the apparitions of the Blessed Virgin Mary, from the same period of time?

The book entitled "Acts of the Apostles" deals with *at the most* only five of the Apostles that it claims later spread the Gospel, and most probably as we will see, it really only deals with two — John and Peter. As to one, James the brother of John, "son of thunder" (apparently he must have had a boisterous, dominant personality — in other words, you would know if he *wasn't there)*, the account is so brief, saying only that King Herod II had him beheaded with a sword, that it seems more like the author of Acts wanted to cut him out of the story faster than King Herod did. This is possibly because the absence of James from the early church, who had been so prominent in the Gospels, was a source of embarrassment which had to be dealt with.

We have references in the book of Acts to Philip, starting in Acts 1:13, where he is in the list of apostles. Later, Philip is identified as the first to bring the Gospel to Samaria in Acts chapter 8. He later has the famous encounter with the Ethiopian eunuch in Acts chapter 8. So he has certainly earned the name "Philip the Evangelist." He is usually represented as the same Philip that is so prominent in the Gospel of

John. There are some problems with this view. In Acts chapter 6, the first church deacons are appointed to assist in food distribution. Among the first seven chosen to serve is Philip. There is no mention in this account of his being one of the twelve apostles and if he was, we do not know why he would be chosen as a deacon. Secondly, when he goes to Samaria to preach the Gospel, the Gospel is received by people in Samaria and many are converted. But although Philip can perform miracles, the Holy Spirit "had not yet fallen" on any converts. The apostles John and Peter had to come to Samaria and lay hands on the new converts in order for them to receive the Holy Spirit. If the baptism of the Holy Spirit promised in Acts chapter one, and delivered at Pentecost, meant anything, it must have meant the ability to cause the Holy Spirit to "fall upon" others as required in Samaria. And we would wonder why John and Peter, the old backbone of the church, possessed these powers and Philip did not, if in fact Philip was one of the apostles. So *this* Philip could not have been one of the apostles and hence is not Philip the apostle mentioned in the Gospels and in Acts 1:13. Or, alternatively, we simply have another tradition as to who the apostles even were.

Some claim that James the brother of Jesus, head of the Jerusalem church in Acts, is the same as James, son of Alpheus in the Gospels, or James the "lesser." However, James the brother of Jesus is problematic as being James the Lesser, apostle of Christ. Unlike the situation with Philip, most Christians vehemently reject the view that this is the same James. They generally refer to chapter 7:5 of the Gospel of John, where it is stated that Jesus' brothers do not believe in him, at least on the occasion of the Feast of Tabernacles about to take place therein. Hence the view that Jesus appeared to his brother James alone before he appeared to the other apostles, and that this meeting is presumably what led to the conversion of James, "the brother of the Lord." Of course since there are no "twelve apostles" named in the fourth Gospel, we do not know when the disbelief of his brothers, corporately, occurred in relation to the supposed naming of the twelve, or whether one of his brothers came to believe subsequent to this incident and became a follower, and later was named one of the twelve. This is not an illogical sequence of events. But of course even the time line we are talking about is obscure. Supposedly, based

The Resurrection: Part One

on the synoptic Gospels, the ministry of Jesus lasted three years, but in the fourth Gospel the narrative is written in such a way as to move from one Passover feast, in chapter 2, to the next one, at which he is crucified, and so it appears to be one year of ministry. In any event, the view that James the brother of Jesus is not the same James as James the Lesser is the traditional Christian view. If the view is true, then we simply do not know what happened to James "the Lesser", or what he was a "lesser" of. It would usually mean a younger brother of someone.

So then, we simply do not know what happened to between seven and nine of the apostles (who were really *eleven apostles* after Judas Iscariot). The figure is seven if we accept Philip and James the brother of Jesus as apostles. The brief excerpt of James the brother of John, son of Zebedee, in Acts is questionable. If true, we would wonder why we never hear of the preaching or activities of this James up to the point he is suddenly executed in Acts by King Herod II. Why was he not arrested along with John and Peter the several times they are arrested and brought before the Sanhedrin? Why was he not imprisoned with them? There is simply no mention of him until he is mentioned as beheaded by the King. It is almost as though this was a remedy to cover up for the embarrassment of his absence. But if we accept this as valid, then we only have eight other "apostles" to account for. If we do not accept this questionable narrative then there are nine to account for (if you do not accept James the Lord's brother and Philip the Evangelist; and this is accepting the account of Judas the Iscariot as dying).

But even accepting as true this questionable tale as to James, the brother of John, the Acts of the Apostles, dealing with the first thirty years of the church after Pentecost, tells us of the evangelistic careers of Paul, not even one of "the twelve" (or eleven), of Peter, John, possibly of Philip (if it is the same Philip as in the Gospels) and arguably, of James "the Lesser" if in fact James the Lesser is James, the brother of Jesus. So we are told of about between three and five Apostles. What happened to the rest? Certainly not the unfounded, often contradictory and incredible tales created by the Catholic church centuries later (which has "Saint James" dying in contradictory locations, such as in Spain, and we do not know which St. James we are talking about — James the brother of Jesus, bishop of Jerusalem, who was stoned thrown from the top of the temple in Jerusalem in 62 A.D. per Josephus — or James the brother of John, who was supposedly beheaded? Who was left to be martyred in Spain?). Succinctly put, if we are to believe beyond a reasonable doubt based vicariously on *their* belief, shouldn't we have some convincing evidence that this is true — that they both believed and that they died for those beliefs? Wouldn't the all knowing, all-powerful God, who cared enough to give his only son to a painful death to save us, and who desires that we believe, have moved heaven and earth to give us convincing accounts of the sacrifices of these claimed martyrs?

Well, we have an account. And sadly enough it is not what Christians claim, or what they need to support their case. In fact, it discredits the Christian case. In chapter 28 of Matthew, in the one time that Jesus is said to have appeared to his disciples, on a mountain in Galilee. *"Then the eleven disciples* [not ten or nine or eight, but all eleven] *went away into Galilee, to the mountain which Jesus had appointed for them. When they saw him, they worshiped him, but **some doubted**"* (Matthew 28:17). This is an amazing admission, which tends to undermine the entire import of this paragraph. All the disciples went to see Jesus, and *some doubted* even after supposedly seeing him resurrected. If they had actually seen him resurrected, why then would they doubt? They could only doubt if they had not *actually seen him*, which belies the entire resurrection claim. Even more cogently, we would query why the author would even bother informing us that after the resurrection of Jesus "some doubted." The only logical reason is that the author knew that some of the "twelve apostles" had abandoned the cause, that they were no longer followers of Jesus, or at least that they were not willing to accredit the resurrection of Jesus. This would have been indeed troubling. There is no other reasonable explanation for this glaring admission and inconsistency.

This is naturally a much more reasonable explanation of why the "Acts of the Apostles" only accounts for the histories of several of the Apostles and the rest are lost to history. It also explains why in the synoptic Gospels, at crucial events, such as the raising of Jairus' daughter, and the transfiguration on the mount, Jesus calls only three of his disciples — Peter, John and James — to accompany him. The

The Resurrection: Part One

other disciples are not witnesses. Isn't this because these three were the main leaders of the movement afterwards, and only *they* were testifying as to these events. And conceivably James, the brother of John, later backed out, and so a convincing account of his martyrdom had to be invented and inserted into the Acts of the Apostles in a one-liner in chapter 6. And so these two — Peter and John — became the "backbone" of the church, at least the Jewish church, according to the Apostle Paul. In the Jewish Talmud, Sanhedrin 43a, it states the "Yeshu [Jesus] had five disciples — Matti, Necki, Netsur, Burni and Toda." Despite a difference in names, this is relatively more consistent with Acts of the Apostles. If there were ever twelve Apostles, the overwhelming majority were unwilling to support, much less die for, the claim that Jesus was resurrected. The non-show of Jesus' own disciples is enough to cast doubt on the whole pretension, without even examining the details as we have above.

And if this conclusion be not true, then the obvious question is why the careers of the twelve apostles are not *all* represented in Acts, seeing that the very purpose of the book of Acts is to show how the Holy Spirit worked through the original apostles to found the church during the first roughly thirty years after the crucifixion. Indeed, although they will *never* admit it in a million years, the Christian apologists are universally dismayed at the lack of a reference to the other apostles in Acts, and the domination of events by John and Peter alone of the original apostles, at least until the arrival of the self- appointed apostle Paul. It is an omission tantamount to an admission — an admission that "the twelve" are simply lost to history and apparently to be consigned to the group classed under that clumsy but concise, pregnant and embarrassing Matthewan rubric of the "some [who] doubted." Apparently *eight to nine, and more likely nine,* "doubted" (i.e., they didn't believe, because they had experienced no resurrected Christ). Their disbelief was to the extent that they simply disappeared from sight. As to their proclaimed poverty because of the Gospels, that the two known apostles, Peter and John suffered, we would speculate that they were poor when they were fisherman of Galilee. Later they survived off of the tithes of the Christian world, a subject which so obsessed the writing of the apostle Paul, that he never lost a chance to shame those who were not contributing enough for the support of his ministry. It is a far cry from the poignant scene depicted by the Bible proponents and apologists.

The falsehood of this argument from supposed martyrdom notwithstanding, a more obvious observation lay at hand. Of what value is this argument in the first place? The world is full of examples of those who died for falsehoods, false beliefs, false religions, false teachers, false ideologies. There were plenty of Muslim martyrs and Mormon martyrs. There are plenty of Jonestown martyrs, David Koresh martyrs, Palestinian martyr bombers, 9/11 martyrs, etc. That humans will willingly die for falsehood or idiocy is not a virtue to be glorified. Gibbon, in his *Rise and Fall of the Roman Empire* devoted a chapter to pointing out that relatively few Christians were ever martyred in the brief and sporadic persecutions of the Roman Empire, that Christians have grossly exaggerated the facts to glorify themselves, and that many times more non-Christians were killed by the Christians when the Christians came to power than were the Christians ever martyred themselves (and that was just during their consolidation of power, not in the centuries to the present). Gibbon estimates that not more than approximately 2,000 Christians were ever martyred in the 300 years until they assumed power, whereas the Christians, once they assumed power, murdered hundreds of thousands in the name of Christ. [8]

And if some early Christian *did* go to their deaths believing, of what importance is it really? We have already pointed out that it was only necessary that *some* disciples retrieved the body of Jesus from the tomb. It does not follow, logically or factually, that this event was a conspiracy which every follower of Christ, or even the most intimate disciples, was involved in, or even aware of, or ever became aware of. For that matter, we have no reason to think that any, much less all, of "the twelve", had anything to do with it. With a certainty, any disciples who had taken the body were not going to stand up and admit it to the disciples and to the world. What would have been their motive to do so? To discredit Christianity? Why would they do that if they themselves were disciples? Wouldn't they face retaliation by the Jews and the Romans? This would have been an incentive for their silence, not for speaking out. So some may have died believing the resurrection was true. So what? Does that make a falsehood *true*? Does sacrifice for a lie, make the lie the truth? Is communism creditworthy

The Resurrection: Part One

or praiseworthy because so many have died for it? Is Nazism any more valid because Horst Wessel died for it? Or because millions died for it in W.W.II.? Is David Koresh, Jesus in the flesh because many died believing him so, and will he therefore come back in 2012 to judge those that judged him? Is Jim Jones a prophet of God because his followers were willing to die for him?

Or possibly there is a more significant legacy in those *"that doubted"* even after the supposed resurrection — the majority of the twelve apostles that simply disappeared from history because they ceased to believe. In the Nicodemuses and Josephs of Arimathea who simply disappeared from history after the Gospels. Are they among those that "doubted"? So, in summary, we do not know what happened to the "twelve apostles". We are certain that a decade after the crucifixion, a few of his former followers appeared to launch a new cult of Jesus, through the rivaled leadership of the newcomer Paul, to a world far distant and remote from the place where events occurred and the seeds were planted, and it became a worldwide religion.

The people who resided where the events occurred and were present when the events occurred, i.e., the known eyewitnesses, overwhelmingly continued to reject the truth of the resurrection, and even over one hundred years after the crucifixion, according to Justin Martyr in his *Dialogue with Trypho,* continued to insist that the disciples had stolen the body (which is of course semantically impossible, since they were *given* the body to keep by the Romans, so they couldn't have stolen it!) And yet the Christian apologist cry still rings out today: "If he was not resurrected, then *produce the body!"* I say, *"You took the body, you produce the body! The burden is on you to prove the resurrection. You had the body in your possession. You tell us what you did with it! How can the burden be on non-believers to prove what you did or didn't do with the body?"*

Fourth Observation: "People are the Same Everywhere" (Or, who were the Pentecostals before they were Pentecostals? Answer: The Pentecostals)

But this is surely an analysis that is not complete by any means. Our individual approach to common sense draws inescapably upon our own experiences of life, and the common experiences of mankind. In approaching the issue of why a group of human beings in the first century could arrive at such a view of what had happened in their recent past, whether it be days earlier, or decades earlier I cannot help to make what are really two observations, the first of which draws in upon personal experience, of myself and others, and the second of which draws upon what I consider the common experience of mankind. The first observation of mine is based upon my considerable personal experience and that of others with Pentecostals.

The narrow definition of Pentecostals is of Christians that believe that the spiritual gifts which the Bible says the Holy Spirit delivered to the early disciples at Pentecost in the book of Acts, such as healing, prophecy, speaking in tongues, are still current in our present day and that believers can receive these same gifts from the Holy Spirit, usually as a second anointing of the Holy Spirit some time after salvation, at which time they are said to be *filled* with the Holy Spirit, as opposed to merely *receiving* the Holy Spirit when they accepted Christ as their savior. But I tend to view the term in a larger sense, as appropriate to describe a category of human beings, of whatever religion, that are highly susceptible to obsession with the supernatural. They are most interested in, and receptive to, notions of divine power, of another world other than the one we see; of competing good and evil forces which can manipulate and dominate our world; and in particular with a divine being, or other spiritual forces, which they can personally communicate with and have a relationship with, and often receive power and authority from. I do not mean to represent them as a single, monolithic, or even identical, class of persons. There are many differences of degree and quality within their ranks. These are merely predispositions, which vary greatly within society at large, and so my remarks should be considered. I do not wish to paint all with the same brush. These are only generalizations — accurate ones, but still general.

These individuals are imbibed with a sense of wonderment and awe at what they sense as another world beyond the material world we experience in this life - another world which is just beyond their fingertips, or perhaps at their fingertips. There is with this "Pentecostal mind", if I might dare to name it such, a "spiritual sense" or spiritual

The Resurrection: Part One

"eyes" which allow them to "see" (to use a term of art, to *discern)* what the rest of us who are just too worldly do not see. They perceive a more ultimate reality of spiritual forces acting in the world and of God acting everywhere. To them, one must only be willing to open his or her mind or heart to gain access to this other world. They see the world around them as worldly, while they are otherworldly. Theirs is a world of daily miracles and unseen angels waiting in the wings. The miracles are often mundane — their car transmission is suddenly working, a tire that was flat now miraculously has air in it. The pain in their back, or the headache, is miraculously gone after a prayer. A line from an open book, or a discarded newspaper lying on the ground, could contain a message from God. God sends you a messenger, perhaps a colleague or a stranger, to suddenly give you a message. God suddenly speaks to you and tells you to deliver a message to a complete stranger you encounter on the street or in a supermarket. Life is a divine adventure. Such is the "Pentecostal" throughout history.

This is a brief summary of what I call the "Pentecostal personality." Admittedly there is a wide range of beliefs and doctrines, as well as quality and degree to which these predispositions apply to individual cases. The personality is roughly the same whether the person is Christian, Hindu, Cabbalistic Jew, or New Age. Many Roman Catholics, or non-Pentecostal evangelicals are just as much a part of this syndrome as the Pentecostals per se. Their outward manifestations simply take different forms because of overriding doctrinal limitations. The devotees of the mineral baths of Lourdes, or the wonder-working powers of Our Lady of Fatima, are no less convinced or fanatical than the American Pentecostals, whether they speak in tongues, have their fillings turn to gold, or can personally heal others or not — these are merely outward manifestations of a common mindset. I am not a psychologist — I am an attorney and evangelist, with considerable experience dealing with these persons — and I am convinced that my summary is correct.

America in particular, is no stranger to Pentecostals that make the most amazing proclamations and claims. Gold dust falls from the sky, fillings in teeth turn to gold, angels and demons appear and leave, cripples rise up and walk, the blind receive sight, and myriads of other miraculous events occur within their circles. I have personally spoken to many of these Pentecostals and they appear to me to be sincerely convinced of their claims, even when they are obviously false and foolhardy. I have had people tell me their fillings were turned to gold and that their dentist would verify it, that someone had touched the eyes of a person born blind from birth and the person had sight, and that persons who were clinically dead were revived to life, all of them absolutely false claims. It is always a queen size question mark in my mind as to whether they are *lying*. I am convinced that despite the sometimes obvious impossibility, foolishness or glaring falsehood of their claims that these people sincerely *believe* the things that they claim. In their minds they have somehow, some way brought themselves to believe in their own claims. I am sure that this statement is not without controversy and there are those who would insist that they are in fact lying, which is to say that the persons know that what they are saying is false.

My second observation, I hope less controversial, but more significant, is that the same kinds of people have always existed in history. There have always been those that possessed the religious or mystical mind. And yes, there have always been the *Pentecostals*, only under different names and involved in different activities. The same *people* that perform, experience, or witness healings, that have divine encounters with angels, that hear the voice of God, that receive divine instructions, that suddenly speak as an oracle of God, or speak in other, unknown languages, often those from outside of our world, existed in the first century just as much as they exist today. But one difference is that those that lived in Second Temple Israel lived with the background of a society obsessed with religion, controlled by its nation's priesthood, obsessed with religious law, and with Scripture that taught a world of the divine and the miraculous, a world surrounded by the immediate accessibility of the miraculous and of angel visitation. It was also a world increasingly dominated by messianism and apocalypticism, propelled by Israel's despair of foreign domination, lament of lost glory, and aspiration for eventual restoration to power, which would arrive after a cataclysmic period of world suffering and terror, and victory of Israel over its enemies under the leadership of a modern day David figure who would restore Israel to world greatness, world domination, and a time of unparalleled peace and serenity. [9]With such a cultural background the "Pentecostal" mindset was very much at home. They would have been cherished people living in all their glory. The ground was tilled for exactly what we saw start immediately upon that Sunday morning that we now call Easter, and which spread like wildfire, especially when that fire leaped into the pagan world where, unlike in Israel, men were frequently born of Gods, often through virgin mothers, and even died and resurrected and ascended into heaven. Alas, we have the makings of a *Bible.* In other words, **Who were the Pentecostals before Pentecost? Answer: The Pentecostals!**

When Does Rumor Become *Legend?*

As to the issue of the development of legends, we should note some controversy. A notable Christian apologist, William Lane Craig, has claimed that resurrection legends could not have possibly developed in the time periods we have discussed, based upon the opinion of A.N. Sherwin-White, a classical historian of Oxford University, who claimed that it would require at least two generations in the ancient world for legends to develop.[10] First, to refute such a preposterous claim requires little more than to look at our own history and the legends of such luminaries as Davey Crockett, where fantastic legends abounded *during his own lifetime.* And this, mind you, is in a fairly literate country by historical standards. This is America of the nineteenth century, not Israel in the first century, with an active and well-informed press, which was notably absent form the ancient world. Secondly, what is a *legend,* but merely exaggerated rumor and scuttlebutt that has gained great currency? To suggest that over a period of twenty or thirty years such accretion of rumor, exaggeration, and wishful thinking could not coalesce into fantastic tales that could not be penned by advocates reflects simple obstinacy. Even in our own era we have dedicated believers of everything from Elvis sightings, alien abductions, and multitudes of fantastic conspiracy theories (The U.S. government orchestrated the 9/11 attacks, etc.). The only difference is that the first century had a greater level of ignorance and gullibility. However it is reflective of the Christian apologists to seek high and low to foster result-oriented propositions, however fatuous and contrary to reality they may be.

In point of fact, the rumors and exaggerations surely started at the time of the crucifixion with such persons as Mary Magdalene. However, the appellation *legend* would seem to attach only after two things take place: the passage of some amount of time, the gaining of widespread currency. A third point to consider is the dating of the Gospels, and the obvious progressive embellishment that we have observed. Although the period of time that the Christians claimed elapsed until the Gospels were written, which they claim as twenty to thirty-five years as to the synoptic Gospels, is undoubtedly a much greater period of time, and some date our present Gospels well into the second century, the time period when even William Lane Craig admits that legend dominated.

A Criticism of the Christian Apologists' Critique of the Gospels

I have found it most notable that among the defenses of the Gospels written by many Christian apologists there seems to be a trend to refute any attacks upon the truth of the Gospel accounts by supposedly looking at the other side of the coin and asking, "How could they have lied about this?", which presupposes that the Gospel writers sat down and invented all of the resurrection accounts and then foisted them on an unaware public. This is a presupposition vital to their technique. The argument usually goes, in one form or another, that no sensible person could have sat down and lied about these things and thought they could convince people of these things, and no readers would have been expected to have believed such lies out of the blue. This is a straw man argument used by the vast majority of Christian apologists, including Simon Greenleaf, in *The Four Evangelists*, and others.

R.A. Torrey, in his T*alks with Men,* [11] looks at the differences in the Gospel accounts, and asserts the proposition that if they were false, then either the Gospel writers all worked together to create a false account in collaboration, or they all wrote separate accounts unaware of the work of the others. He asserts that if they had collaborated then the facts would have been the same. The different facts show that they were written individually. But if they were separate, then the commonalities show that they are all telling the truth. The first part of

The Resurrection: Part One

his claim is largely true. The Gospel accounts arise in part from largely different traditions, such as Jesus appearing on a mountain in Galilee, versus appearing to his disciples in a room in Jerusalem; an empty tomb being found versus a huge earthquake and an angel coming down and opening the tomb. These accounts are irreconcilable. But his second alternative, that the commonalities prove the truth of their accounts, is untenable because of those very same vast, irreconcilable differences in the accounts.

The more reasonable, likely series of events is one of secondary authors, themselves not eyewitnesses, who merely recorded what others were saying, or as we might imagine, what was being said that others had seen. So it is basically a summary of legends, not a systematic conspiracy to tell lies.

Chapter Four

THE NATIVITY

The next major area to be considered is the nativity of Jesus. It should be next considered, immediately after an examination of the resurrection, because the nativity and the resurrection bracket the life of Jesus as narrated in the gospels, and together are designed to show the supernatural origin and outcome of Jesus of Nazareth. Indeed, the significance of Jesus according to the Christian church is that he was the son of God, or if you will, the very God nature, conceived of a virgin through the Holy Spirit in order to be the substituted sacrifice, the propitiation of the wrath of God, for the sins of the world. So naturally, the miraculous birth is presented as essential to this case.

We find at the outset that there are two accounts of Jesus' nativity, those of the Gospel of Matthew and the Gospel of Luke. The Gospels of Mark and John contain no nativity accounts. They merely begin with a mature adult Jesus. Naturally enough, most Christians have heard the nativity account so many times, being recounted in particular in Christmas nativity scenes and pageants, that they have formed in their minds a composite story that embraces parts of both accounts. But a proper analysis involves separating the two accounts and comparing them.

In the Gospel of Matthew, Joseph is betrothed to Mary but she becomes pregnant by the Holy Spirit. Joseph intends to put her away, but an angel appears to him in a dream and tells him of the divine conception and tells him to name the child Jesus. So Joseph married Mary. Then the narrative tells us, "Now after Jesus was born in Bethlehem of Judea in the days of Herod the king", wise men came from the east seeking the child born King of the Jews because they saw "his star in the East" and came to worship him (2:1-2). King Herod hears of this and is perturbed. He inquires of the scribes and chief

The Nativity

priests where Jesus is to be born. They inform him of the prophecy of Micah that he is to be born in Bethlehem, in Judea. We are already informed in this account that Jesus was born in Bethlehem. There is no indication whatsoever in this account that Jesus and Mary were anything other than residents of Bethlehem. The "wise men", the magi from the East, come to Bethlehem following the star and find the parents and child, presenting him treasures. Then an angel appears to the wise men in a dream and tells them not to return to Herod as they had promised. "Now *when they had departed,* behold, an angel of the Lord appeared to Joseph in a dream" and directed Joseph to flee to Egypt to save the child from the wrath of Herod. So he "arose" and took Jesus and Mary "by night and departed for Egypt." We must presume that it was the same night and that it was when he arose from the dream. As phrased, it could certainly not be weeks or months later. Herod then sends soldiers to Bethlehem and they murder the children two years and under, not it would seem because the child had been born two years before, but only to ensure that all "babies" were killed. The gist of the foregoing narrative is that the star heralded the birth of Jesus and so it was a contemporaneous event.

So Joseph goes with his family to Egypt until an angel of the Lord tells him that Herod is dead and directs them to return to Israel. But on his return he hears that Archaleus, the son of Herod, is ruling in Judea and Joseph is "afraid to go there"[Judea being the *there*], indicating that on his return he was intending to return to Judea - proof that that was his home, i.e., Bethlehem. Why would he be intending to return to Judea unless his home was there, in Bethlehem? So instead he "turned aside" (went out of his way) into the region of Galilee, "And he came and dwelt in a city called Nazareth…" (2:22-23). In the very wording it is clear that he had not resided there before. It does not say *"a city named Nazareth, where [it just so happened] they had lived before"* or simply *"he returned to Nazareth, where they were from."* In Matthew, Jesus is presented in his genealogy, which we will discuss later, as the descendent of the kings of Israel, and there is no hint that he was born in surroundings of anything other than a normal birth in an established home.

In the Gospel of Luke, we have quite a different account. In Luke, Joseph and Mary both reside in Nazareth, in Galilee, at least 150 miles away. An angel appeared in person to Mary to announce that she would have a child from the Holy Spirit, whose name would be Jesus who would have "the throne of his father David." The only connection with Bethlehem is that Joseph's lineage is from Bethlehem, being of the house of David. We are told that a decree was issued by Caesar Augustus that "all the world should be registered" in a "census."(2:1-2) The census occurred while Quirinius was governor of Syria. "So all went to be registered, everyone to his own city"(2:3) Joseph traveled to Bethlehem while Mary was nine months pregnant to register "because he was of the house and lineage of David"(2:4). While they are there the child is born in a stable "because there was no room for them in the inn." So clearly they were not of this town, and Joseph did not even have family in Bethlehem or else he would not have sought a room in the inn, and would not have his wife give birth in a stable. So we are struck with the contradiction that in Matthew the family is undoubtedly from Bethlehem by the clear and unambiguous language, and they move to Nazareth, and in Luke they are from Nazareth, and by chance the child is born in Bethlehem after traveling 150 miles while Mary is nine months pregnant, presumably on a donkey or on foot. This is but the beginning of the discrepancies.

    What about this flight to Egypt in Matthew? How does it gibe with Luke's account? The wise men come. The wise men leave. Presumably they came for a reason, to worship the child, and after accomplishing their purpose they left. There is no indication, and no reason to think, that they stayed any length of time to reside in Bethlehem. As soon as they depart, the angel appears to Joseph and he departs for Egypt. The quickest route would have been to the coast, near Gaza, and thence by the coastal route, hugging the Mediterranean until arrival in northern Egypt. By this way it would have been 150 miles to the scarcely populated Wadi of Egypt, the dry riverbed across the Sinai Peninsula. It would have been 200 miles to any significant population centers on the edge of the Nile Valley. If they had chosen to go to the coast of the Dead Sea and follow the King's Highway south, through the Valley of Arabah to the Gulf of Akabah at Eilat, and then gone west to Egypt, it would have taken considerably longer. So this was a very substantial journey. Once again, the most expedient method of travel would have been donkey or horse-driven.

The Nativity

And yet we are told in the Gospel of Luke that 40 days after the birth, Mary was in the Temple for her Levitical purification ceremony required by Jewish Levitical law (Luke 2:22). This presents a problem on two fronts. One is, where does the flight to Egypt fit in? How could they take a long arduous journey that would take weeks and then be in the Temple forty days later? More importantly, were we not informed in the Gospel of Matthew how fearful Joseph and Mary were of Herod, whom they knew planned to kill the infant Jesus? Upon the return from Egypt, we are told in Matthew, they did not return to Judea, where Bethlehem was located, because Archelaus, the son of Herod, had acceded to the throne in Judea. Bethlehem is six miles from Jerusalem. We are told that Joseph "was afraid to go there" (Matthew 2:22). So instead they "turned aside" from Judea (2:22). We are even informed that an angel warned Joseph in a dream from returning to Judea (2:22). It is one thing when God tells you not to do something you really want to do. It is another things when God tells you not to do something that you are dreadfully afraid to do and do not want to do anyway. Interestingly, Joseph supposedly went against his own fear and disobeyed God at the same time.

Now Jerusalem was the chief city of Judea. In Jerusalem Herod had built a large palace immediately adjacent to and overlooking the Temple. If they were terrified of Herod's son, Jerusalem would have been the last place on earth they would have gone. Not only did they go there, they made a great impression on at least two persons in the Temple — Anna and Simeon, two people that literally couldn't keep their mouths shut about Jesus (Luke chapter 2). This makes no sense whatsoever and is completely contradictory. How can he "turn aside" from going to Judea because "he was afraid" to go there, and even an angel warned him not to go there, and at the same time he went to the Temple for a purification ceremony forty days after the child birth? These are absolutely irreconcilable accounts. Either one account of the other *cannot* be true. So which one is a falsification?

We are also told in Matthew that after Jesus was born and Joseph departed for Egypt that an irate Herod ordered the murder of all infants in Bethlehem. We are told nothing of this in Luke. Not only this, but the historian Josephus, no admirer of Herod, who loves to catalogue all of the barbarities of Herod, made no mention at all of this in his histories. Now the absence from Luke is somewhat puzzling. Christian scholars claim that Acts of the Apostles was also written by Luke, a claim which is based on the beginning of chapter one of Acts, where reference is made to a former work written by the author to one Theophilus, concerning the life of Christ. The Gospel of Luke is written to Theophilus. From chapter 16 onwards, the Book of Acts is written in the first person and the author describes himself as a traveling companion of the Apostle Paul on his journeys. Luke is described elsewhere in the Epistles as a companion of Paul in his journeys. Now Luke was a gentile physician from outside of Israel. It is very significant that when Paul visits Jerusalem in what appears to be about 57-58 A.D., Luke accompanies him. Then, as we know from Acts, Paul is imprisoned by the Romans at the behest of the Jewish leaders and he remains imprisoned in Israel two full years. When he finally is sent by ship to Rome to stand trial, the same Luke accompanies him. So presumably Luke has remained in Israel two years also. We have no reason to think he went anywhere else for those two years. Now Luke, or the author that wrote what we now know as the Gospel of Luke, may have indeed had much more experience in visiting Israel than we know, but assuming that the author of the Gospel of Luke is the same author of chapters 16 onwards of Acts, then we can ascertain that the author, our Luke, could indeed claim as he did to "have a perfect understanding of all things from the very first" (Luke 1:3), having resided at least two years in Jerusalem, form 57-59 A.D., or from 58-60 A.D. He also, according to the account in Acts, had full access to James, the brother of Jesus, who would have been familiar with the nativity of Jesus, and undoubtedly with countless others who knew Jesus. And he was in Jerusalem, six miles from Bethlehem. It is incredible that no one mentioned to him that so many innocent children were massacred only six miles away at the time of the birth of their Lord and Savior. It is so incredible that we simply cannot believe that this history ever happened. A more likely explanation is that what we have here is the same as what we have in the resurrection accounts. We have a Galilee tradition, in which Jesus is actually born in Bethlehem, and a major massacre takes places there, and later the family of Jesus moves to Galilee. Then we have a Jerusalem tradition. In Jerusalem, they *know* that no massacre took place in Bethlehem, and they know that Jesus' family was not from

The Nativity

Bethlehem, so these elements never become a part of that tradition. Instead we have an alternative account of how Jesus, whose family in this tradition is from Galilee, happened to be born in Bethlehem, namely a census.

Let us now examine this census which was the reason for Joseph being in the far away town of Bethlehem for his wife to give birth. The plain, undisputable fact of the matter is that *there was no census* as described in Luke. Qurinius was governor of Syria. In 6 A.D. the Romans made Judea a Roman province, under the jurisdiction of the province of Syria, where Quirinius was governor. As part of that Roman takeover of governance, there was naturally a need to develop a tax base to pay for the administration of Judea as a Roman province. So there was a census for tax purposes. But it was not a "census of the whole world" ordered by Caesar Augustus.

This census was not a matter of historical trivia, because the taxation led to a major revolt in 6 A.D. led by Judas the Galilean.[1] This census and the revolt receive considerable treatment by Josephus. So the reference by the author of Luke is a reference to an event that would have been known by the audience. It is intended to draw attention to a historical frame of reference and it does so. The first problem is, though, that the census is 6 A.D. We are told in Matthew that Jesus was born while Herod was the King. We know as a fact that Herod died at the Passover in 4 B.C. So we have a ten year difference in time. And Luke tells us that Jesus was "about thirty" when he began his ministry in the fifteenth year of the reign of Tiberius (who came to power in 14 A.D.), or in other words 28 A.D. The chronology does not fit, either internally, or as to Matthew's narrative.

But we have an even larger problem in that we have no record of *any census* in which persons had to travel to their ancestral homes. Josephus tells us nothing of so strange an event. Why would the Romans care about the ancestry of the persons being taxed or what their ancestral lineage was? This would seem, if anything, to be a Jewish concern, but this was not a Jewish census, and the Jews were prohibited in the law of Moses from taking a census anyway (David faced severe retribution for doing so in II Chronicles). Some Christian apologists have attempted to claim that this census was the census that Augustus ordered of the *whole* world in 8 B.C., described by the historian Suetonius. [2]However, that was a census of only Roman citizens in the empire in order to establish new Senatorial lists. It would not have included the family of Joseph, was not of "all the world", would not required the registration of the Jews in Israel, and would certainly not require anyone Jewish to return to his ancestral home. This narrative is pure fantasy.

And yet it is clear to any reasonable person that it was the census of Quirinius that is referred to in the narrative of Luke. Yet Christian apologists try to tell us that the reference is to *some other* census — a variant of an argument we have already heard and will hear again. And yet, as we have seen, there is no other census that fits the bill. The census of Quirinius, which led to a famous period of warfare, was a well-known historical landmark for listeners, such as today might be a reference to the attack on Pearl Harbor or 9/11. The reference is obvious. But the Christians try to essentially say, "*Well, it was another Pearl Harbor. It was another 9/11.*"They also try to tell us, naturally *without a shred of evidence* in support, that Quirinius was actually governor twice — that he was governor earlier. This is not only wrong, it is also pointless and irrelevant, since Israel undoubtedly changed from being a self-governing vassal state of Rome to come under direct Roman rule, as part of a Roman province, in 6 A.D. If Quirinius was governor of Syria before, he did not have authority over Judea and Galilee, and so did not tax those areas, and did not order a census of those areas. However, it highlights the aptitude of Christian apologists throughout history to invent history to support their often preposterous suppositions.

What the census narrative demonstrates is that the gospel author, and indeed the early Christians, were desperate to place Jesus' birth in Bethlehem, to fulfill perceived messianic pretensions, and to find a way to make it plausible that a person that everyone knew was from Galilee, was *actually* born in Bethlehem of Judea. It was especially compelling in the Jerusalem tradition because the people there knew that Jesus' family was not from the area. We will find out the reason for this desperation when we visit the issue of fulfillment of prophecy in the following chapter.

CHAPTER FIVE

FULFILLMENT OF PROPHECY IN THE LIFE OF JESUS

There is a cultural backdrop to the Christian obsession with prophecy that must be understood at the outset because it is foundational to that obsession. There was a pre-existing Jewish obsession with messianic prophecy in the Second Temple period. It arose out of a Second Temple cultural milieu of a politically emasculated Israel which dreamed of a past glory and nationhood, now reduced to subservience to successive world empires — the Persians, the Greek, and then the Romans. The glory of David and Solomon, a regional Hebrew Empire, the days of the prophets, were idealized, most notably in Scriptural history. It all remained a distant dream, but a very real and inspirational dream. In the midst of this hyper-idealized milieu arose the twin pillars of messianism and apocalypsism — the vision of the end of the national agony, to be replaced by Israel's victory over the oppressive, pagan world surrounding it under the leadership of a new David, anointed by God, as the original David was. Typically the victory of national Israel, of good over evil, would occur after a traumatic, harrowing end of times scenario. The book of Daniel was a classic of this genre of writing, and spawned many other similar writings of this apocalyptic, messianic genre, and even fanatical religious movements such as the Essenes. Typical to the genre were pseudonymous writings which posed as writings of earlier prophets such as Enoch and even Daniel.[1]

Now messianism was not a feature of the foundational Hebrew writings contained in the Pentateuch. What Bible apologists refer to as a messianic prophecy pronounced by Moses in Deuteronomy 18:15 ("The Lord will raise up for you a Prophet like me from your midst... him shall you hear...") is literally, by its very terms, a reference to the role of prophet, which was common to Israel during the royal period, and represents an attempt during the royal period to legitimize and validate a role in the Hebrew religious economy for figures such as Isaiah, Amos and the other prophets. It does not mention a future messiah of the Jews, although later Second Temple Jews and Christians could obviously apply their own brand of interpretations to infuse a messianic meaning. In fact that is exactly what occurred over and over during the Second Temple period and continued under the Christians, a process called isogesis, as opposed to exegesis, or taking out of the text only that which it reasonably contains. Various passages of Scripture were infused with messianic meanings and messages that were never a part of the original meaning. An entire series of messianic "prophecies" were originated, just waiting to be fulfilled. One Second Temple rabbi famously said "all Scripture speaks of the messiah." Nothing could better encapsulate the period than this statement, which is still quoted today by Bible proponents.

With such religious fervor, and even fanaticism, as existed in the Second Temple period, accentuated by the anxiety of foreign rule, and made all the more humiliating when Israel changed form a self-governing vassal state to become part of an actual Roman province ruled directly by Rome in 6 A.D., the opportunity for religious and social upheaval were obvious. All it would take would be the execution of a presumed end of times, apocalyptic messiah for some to seek to realize the fulfillment of myriads of presumed prophecies. This would be the largely unrecognized world historical legacy of this period of history. But for the majority of Jews, the more significant product was the Jewish revolt of 66 A.D. All of the foregoing is essential to the understanding of this cultural background of the Jesus movement, and many of the same messianic, apocalyptic writings are still the cornerstone, or at least the grinding stone, of modern evangelical Christianity, supplemented by the Christians' own apocalyptic supplement to the book of Daniel — the book of Revelation.

So considering this background, it is not at all surprising, that very early in its history, Christianity would seek to establish the primacy of Christ as Lord, savior, and in the Jewish context, messiah, based upon a fulfillment of prophecy. So important is this consideration that all the Gospels are replete with fulfilled prophecies. And needless to say, today every Christian evangelist that seeks to convince a wary prospective convert or a skeptic will begin his conversion talk by reference to the "miraculous fulfillment of prophecy." Frequently this is even adorned with mathematical equations stating the extreme mathematical impossibility that such prophecies could be fulfilled in a single life, as it was in the life of Jesus. So let us look at some of these prophecies objectively to test their accuracy.

Prophecy: The messiah would be born in Bethlehem. Fulfillment: Jesus was born in Bethlehem.

Bible proponents will say that a qualification to be messiah of the Jews would be birth in Bethlehem, in fulfillment of the proclaimed prophecy of Micah 5:2.

Reality: Jesus was not born in Bethlehem.

One of the main reasons why the Jewish leaders rejected Jesus' claim is that he was not born in Bethlehem. This is clearly laid bare and admitted in chapter 7 of the Gospel of John, beginning at verse 40:

"*Therefore many from the crowds, when they heard this saying* [concerning the pouring out of the Holy Spirit] *said 'Truly this is the Prophet* [who would appear before the coming of the messiah, as prophesied in Malachi]' *Others said 'This is the Christ.' But some said, 'Will the Christ come out of Galilee? Has not the Scripture said that the Christ will come from the seed of David and from the town of Bethlehem, where David was?'*" Later, when the Pharisees sought to have him arrested, Nicodemus asks that Jesus not be condemned before he is heard. The Pharisees reply to Nicodemus "Are you also from Galilee? Search and look, for no prophet has arisen from Galilee."(7:52). Based upon the expectations which the Jewish people at the time had, based on their Scriptures, this was a very meaningful question. These are not the objections of prejudiced, hateful, conceited, narrow-minded antagonists but of conscientious seekers after truth based upon Scriptural guidelines. They pose legitimate questions that deserve an answer. We would think that if not Jesus, at least the Gospel writer, would have a ready answer that would inform the people that Jesus *in fact was* born in Bethlehem and merely grew up in Galilee.

Conviction Overturned

It is notable that both the crowd and the Pharisees, masters of law and prophecy, are already convinced that they know where Jesus is from, and that it is Galilee. In fact, at the outset of this section, on a different note, we hear the crowds ask "Do the rulers know indeed that this is truly the Christ? However, **we know where this man is from,** [presumably, based on the gist of this section of Scripture it is clearly not Bethlehem that he is from, or else they would be saying that prophecy is fulfilled, based on verses 40 et seq.] **but when the Christ comes, no one will know where he is from"** (John 7:26-27). This is a very interesting comment, since we are told that first century Judaism was confirmed in the belief that the Christ would come from Bethlehem. There was obviously another, since lost, tradition.

What is Jesus' answer? What is the response of the Gospel of John? What is most important is that Jesus does in fact give his only response at the beginning of this section to this line of questioning as to where he was born and the accusation that he is a Galilean. He replies very glibly, "You both know me *and you know where I am from...*" (7:28) [in other words, "*You're right!*]. So much for birth in Bethlehem! Apparently nothing is said or known about the supposed Bethlehem birth. We would imagine the Christian response is that Jesus wished to keep it a secret at this time, for whatever reason. We would think that a merciful God would wish to bring others to knowledge of his only son, and not obscure the truth. But people are left in their misconceptions based upon their good faith adherence to Scripture and good faith belief in what they see as the facts. We would also expect the type of editorializing that we find so often in the Gospels (as we find for example only a few sentences away in v. 39, concerning the reference by Jesus to rivers of living water: "But he spoke this concerning the Holy Spirit, whom those believing in Him would receive; for the Holy Spirit was not yet given, because Jesus was not yet glorified." We would have expected a slight editorial comment here, such as for example, "*For they did not know that Jesus was born in Bethlehem of Judea, and believed that he was born in Galilee.*" There is nothing of the sort. Not only is there no response from Jesus and no editorial comment, but in fact the entire Gospel of John lacks any narrative concerning the birth of Jesus.

The Gospel of Mark is regarded as the oldest of the canonical

Fulfillment of Prophecy in the Life of Jesus

Gospels and the one that Christian apologist and author Frank Morrison essentially calls the only original account, implying later embellishment by the other Gospels, specifically in regard to the appearance of the angels at the tomb, which Morrison contends was only in fact one of the disciples [2]. This Gospel contains no nativity account and starts with the baptism of Jesus and the commencement of his ministry, which is where many think the original Matthew Gospel began. So the Gospel of Mark adds to the consensus that the early Gospel account had no birth in Bethlehem and no supernatural birth at all. In Mark he is all Galilean, and nothing else.

Now we have two nativity accounts, in Matthew and Luke, which we have already explored in depth in chapter 4. In summary, these are two accounts in serious, irreconcilable conflict. In Matthew the family is clearly *from* Bethlehem, and not Galilee. There is no indication that Jesus is born anywhere other than in a private residence, not in any stable "because there was no room at the inn." They flee to Egypt to escape Herod and on their return do not return to Judea because of fear of Herod's son on the throne, and because an angel directs Joseph to bypass Judea and so they move to Galilee, to a certain city named Nazareth, where they had not lived previously. An angry Herod, deceived by the wise men from the east, orders all the children in Bethlehem, a city six miles from Jerusalem, murdered, a fact which the citizens of Jerusalem, 25 years later, and Herod's arch-antagonist, the historian Josephus, are totally unaware of.

In Luke, the family is from Nazareth in Galilee, and Joseph takes his nine month pregnant wife to register for a non-existent census, which the author seems to explicitly relate to the famous census of Quirinius, which took place at a much later time (6 A.D) and does not fit with the chronology, and which did not require that people register at their ancestral homes. In fact the census of Quirinius, well-known to first century Judea because it engendered a famous armed rebellion, was a tax census, that would have been aimed at people's property and so would take place where they resided, not their ancestral homes. If reference is to the census of Quirinius, then all Israel was already under direct Roman rule, Herod had been dead for ten years already, and his son no longer ruled. Forty days after the birth of Jesus, far from avoiding Judea, Joseph and Mary travel to the Temple in Jerusalem, under the noses of Herod's family, for the purification ceremony, and they are very visible. There is no flight to Egypt and no massacre of infants in Bethlehem.

Far from establishing a firm foundation for a birth in Bethlehem, the two irreconcilable nativity accounts, add further evidence against the authenticity of the claim. *At least* one of them *must* of necessity be false. Joseph could not *both* have deliberately avoided going to Judea, and also gone to the Temple forty days after the birth; and Jesus could not have both been born at the census of Quirinius in 6 A.D., and been born when Herod (who died in 4 B.C.) was King in Judea; not to mention the preposterous notion that he traveled over 150 miles on a donkey with a woman nine months pregnant for a Roman census of the whole world requiring people to travel to their ancestral homes, which even conservative Bible proponents admit never took place; or that there was a massacre of the infants which not one in the locale ever even heard of. In point of fact, these fantastic accounts are obviously contrived and demonstrate only desperation to refute the very arguments being made in John chapter 7 by the Jews — that Jesus was not born in Bethlehem.

Prophecy: Born of a Virgin.
Fulfillment: Jesus was born of a virgin.

Christians refer to the passage of Isaiah 7:14, as a prophecy of a messianic virgin birth: "Therefore the Lord himself will give you a sign. Behold, the virgin shall conceive and bear a son, and shall call his name Immanuel."

Reality: There is no such prophecy. This is a passage taken completely out of context, which by no reasonable, objective means reflects prophecy of a virgin birth for any future messiah.

The Gospel of Matthew, after relating that Gospel's account of the virgin birth, concludes by relating this verse from Isaiah 7:14 as a prophecy of the virgin birth of Christ, stating *"So all this was done that it might be fulfilled which was spoken by the Lord through the prophet Isaiah...*[quoting the above verse]*"* (Matt. 1:23). Isaiah 7:14 can only be understood in the context of chapters 7 and 8 of Isaiah. The prophecy is part of the geo-political struggle then ensuing in the nation. Judah faces invasion from the Northern Kingdom, characterized as Ephraim, in alliance with Syria, called the Syro- Ephraimite war. King Ahaz is afraid. The year is 735 B.C. The Judean king, Ahaz, seeks foreign alliances to reinforce his kingdom. Isaiah assures him that the nation will be victorious and that Ephraim and Syria themselves face imminent collapse. But Ahaz needs assurance that God will save him and his kingdom. In fact "...the Lord spoke again to Ahaz, saying 'Ask a *sign* for yourself from the Lord your God; ask it either in the depth below or in the height above'" (Isaiah 7:11). Isaiah offers doubting Ahaz a *"sign"* from God that he will be victorious.

Now just what is a "sign"? We are literally surrounded by signs. Signs show us something, so necessarily we can see it. A policeman shows a badge. It is a sign of authority. We write a password for a computer program. It is a sign that we are the person authorized to use the program. The Bible is also full of signs. But signs are not prophecies. Signs are things that can presently, or contemporaneously, be seen. Now in the first place, how can a sign to Ahaz be something that will occur 700 years later? Ahaz says essentially, "Show me a sign that I will prevail in my upcoming battle," and Isaiah supposedly responds, "God will give you a sign — there will be a virgin birth 700 years from now." Obviously to be *sign* for the benefit of Ahaz it must be something which Ahaz can see in the immediate future since the enemy threat is immediately before him. To suggest that the *sign* is *solely* a birth over 700 years later seems preposterous under the circumstances. How could he see a sign when he has been dead seven hundred years, and what good is such a sign to him? The Christian suggestion, first stated in the Gospel of Matthew, and heralded for 2,000 years as an absolutely astounding prophecy, is far beyond mere isogesis, the infusion of material that simply does not exist in the text to affect its interpretation. We are now in the realm of sheer stupidity.

Evidence from Surrounding Narrative

And this observation is reinforced by the surrounding narrative, which explains in detail just what the *sign* was and proves that it was given to Ahaz, as promised, at the time. The so-called "prophecy" does not end above. It continues. "Behold, the virgin shall conceive and bear a son, and shall call his name Immanuel. *Curds and honey shall he eat, that he may know to refuse the evil and choose the good. For before the child shall know to refuse the evil and choose the good, the land you dread will be forsaken by both her kings. The Lord will bring the king of Assyria upon you and your people and your father's house — days that have not come since the day that Ephraim departed from Judah."* Most Christians do not even know that the passage actually continues. So we are told explicitly that before the child mentioned as a sign has attained the age of reason, to know good from evil, presumably we might suppose about seven years old, Ahaz would prevail. So before that time period had expired, both Israel (Ephraim) and Syria would themselves be conquered by a more powerful adversary, Assyria. The prophecy actually continues, "And it shall come to pass in that day that the Lord God will whistle for the fly that is in the farthest part of the rivers of Egypt, and for the bee that is the land of Assyria. They will come…" (v. 18 et seq.) referring to future Assyrian invasion of Judah.

Next, commencing in chapter 8, we have the fulfillment, or the actual production, of the *sign*. God tells Isaiah to take a scroll and write on it "Maher-Shalal-Hash-Baz" which means "Hasten the Booty", which seems a variation of 'To the victor, the spoils', clearly an inspirational rallying cry to the already predicted victory. He does this in front of two witnesses. The narrative continues, "Then I *went into* the *prophetess* and she conceived and bore a son"(8:3). Then God tells him to call the son "Maher-Shalal-Hash-Baz", the same name he had written down, and he is told that before the child can cry "My father, and my mother" that "the riches of Damascus [Syria] and Samaria [Northern Kingdom] will be taken away before the King of Syria." So the name refers to the imminent triumph predicted and is part and parcel of the *sign*. Before the child can discern right from wrong (7:16) or say "my mother" or "my father"(8:4), the enemies of Judah are roundly crushed, which in fact happened within two years of the prophecy , or from early 734 B.C. to 733 B.C. That he shall eat "curds and honey" could be a reference to a baby's first foods, or to a period of privation because of war while the child is an infant. This

Fulfillment of Prophecy in the Life of Jesus

is obviously a continuation and fulfillment of the same sign given to Ahaz. His enemies will be destroyed in short order.

Now the *prophetess* mentioned, who bears the child, can be none other than the wife of Isaiah. The use of the term does not necessarily mean that she was a prophet and the usage seems strange to us. The only modern comparison we could refer to would be traditional German usages, where a doctor's wife would be called, for example, *Frau Doctor Mueller* and her husband *Herr Doctor Mueller*. In fact, we might not know for sure which one is really the doctor, or they both could be.

Who is Immanuel?

But there are other issues raised by the texts. Christian apologists will make several more arguments. First, they will say that Isaiah 7:14 refers to a child that will be named Immanuel, and so this child of Isaiah could not be the child referred to in the *sign* given to Ahaz, it must be Jesus born 700 years later. They seem to forget the obvious — that the child born in Bethlehem was not given the name *Immanuel* either! As a matter of fact, the angel told Joseph specifically to name him *Jesus*, not Immanuel. The Christians later named him *Immanuel* as a metaphorical name, in part based upon, and erroneously referring to, *this passage*. So there is little merit in this argument.

Let us explore this issue of the name "Immanuel" in the context of the succeeding narrative. It has been argued by some Bible proponents that since a child can say "mother" and "father" long before they know right from wrong, that the child prophesied in 7:16 (Immanuel) is not the child identified in 8:4, and so likewise the "virgin" of 7:14 is not the woman in 8:3, rendering this a related, but different, sign, meant to possibly reinforce the original prophecy. This would mean that the father is not identified and the mother only vaguely. Then this Immanuel is suddenly the possessor of the land, with the announcement that the armies of Assyria "will fill the breadth of your land, O Immanuel" (v. 8) but they shall be broken "For God is with us" (which literally, and it appears not coincidentally, is an exact translation of "Immanuel" - "God with us") (v.10), leaving him at best a mystery.

Conviction Overturned

If the naming itself was the sign, then the identity of the mother and child is unimportant. Perhaps more importantly, if his mother is to name him "Immanuel", then why does Isaiah give the child a different name? The answer is that the entire sign is that the child signifies that "God is with us" [with them, Judah). "God with us" [or not with us] has tremendous Old Testament usage. Moses tells the stubborn tribes of Israel not to go into the promised land after their original reluctance to enter in, because "God is not with you" (Nu. 14:42). "You shall not be terrified of them; for the Lord your God, the great and awesome God, is among you" (Deut. 7:21). The promise now is that God is with them. So in chapter 8, Isaiah prophesies a coming Assyrian invasion will "go over all his banks. He will pass through Judah, he will overflow and pass over... will fill the breadth of your land, O Immanuel" (8:8).

Who is *Immanuel* here, who will be present when Assyria invades? Is he speaking of Jesus? No, he is speaking to Israel (whom God is with). And so "Take counsel together, but it will come to nothing. Speak the word, but it will not stand, *for God is with us!*" (v. 10), being a reference to the Immanuel in v. 8. The reference to Immanuel in 7:14 is the very same reference to "Immanuel" here in these passages. It is not the literal name, but the *designation* and fulfillment of the sign that God is with them and they shall be victorious. A *designation* in English is related to the word *design* and *sign*. It merely repeats the obvious, that the child is a sign that God is with them. It is metaphorically a name. It has been argued that the name Immanuel requires the child to be divine, but this does not seem to be implicit, since the essence of the *sign* given is that God is with Judah and so she need not fear defeat. We have already cited the Old Testament usages above (Nu. 14:42, Deut. 7:21).

Finally, the final proof that the child *is* the *sign* is confirmed definitively by no less than Isaiah himself in 8:18: "Here am I and the children whom the Lord has given me! *We are for signs and wonders in Israel...* " Not that there was any doubt by the context and narrative. But just to be sure, this is confirmed by Isaiah. The term "wonders" may not necessarily add a miraculous element to the birth of the children, since the *wonder* part is the prediction and fulfillment of the victory over the two enemy nations, which is the only purportedly prophetic part of this narrative (and we have no way of knowing if it is not truly *vaticinium ex eventu)*.

Evidence from Linguistic Background

But now what of this *virgin* issue? Was the *prophetess* a virgin? We are not told. We are told that Isaiah had a previous son. We do not know if he had a new wife or not. But a review of the terms used may be of help. By looking at the original languages we can determine that the term translated "virgin" is not the precise or exclusive translation of this passage, as used in the Gospel of Matthew. Matthew quotes from the Greek Septuagint version, which uses the name *Parthenos*, which usually, but does not always, mean "virgin" when used in the Septuagint. It does not mean such in the Septuagint's version of Genesis 34:3 referring to the "young woman" Dinah, who is raped. But the translation of "virgin" may be too narrow a meaning as compared to the original Hebrew. The term used in the Hebrew text is *Alma*, which is generally given the meaning of "young woman of marriageable age". It parallels the English word "maiden."

It is very significant that there is actually another more precise word in Hebrew, *Bethula*, which narrowly means "virgin." The writers of the Septuagint Greek translation in the third century B.C. translated this word as *Parthenos*, which usually means precisely "virgin." [3] Matthew therefore, writing in Greek, to an audience which more likely than not had the Septuagint translation, was not justified in his usage. On the other hand, it has also been argued that the LXX translation is often loose in its translation of Hebrew. [4] But in any event this does not settle the controversy of the original Hebrew passage and in particular of whom the proclamation refers to.

Why did Isaiah not use the more precise term *bethula* if he wished to stress virginity and a miraculous birth? It has been speculated that Isaiah did not want to stress the virginity but did not want to leave it aside, therefore he employed calculated ambiguity. In fact, the two terms correspond closely to the concepts of "maiden" and virgin" in English. "Maiden" in past times had a connotation including virginity because young unmarried women were assumed to be virgins. In English, why do we use the term "maiden voyage" and the term "virgin soil"? Is there really any difference? In those contexts there is an obvious identity of meaning.

The term *bethula* is used six times elsewhere in the O.T. and always seems to overlap with the idea of virginity, generally referring to a young woman of marriageable age (Rebecca is called both an *alma* and a *bethula)*[5]. There is a male form of the word, *alem*, used to refer to the young King David, and seems to bear no sexual connotation. It is used in Isaiah 54:4 to describe a rejected, barren wife, not necessarily a virgin [6]. Although conservative Bible scholar John Walton thinks this Isaiah 54 usage indicates something less than virginity[7], it seems that this reference would substantiate the usage as being of a woman who has never had a child. In this instance, the term would seem to overlap with the idea of a spinster, a woman who has never had a child or who is barren, which could well relate to the status of Isaiah's wife, at least if she is considered too old to bear children. We have already seen how the term could still apply, alternatively, if she is a new wife who has never had children.

Hebrew scholars often refer to the sister language of Ugaritic, of which a substantial library has been found. Ugaritic studies of the Ugaritic cognate of *alma* have also been made. Two instances are cited which render the Ugaritic cognate as a contrast to a married woman, including in the hymn to Nikkal, "Behold, an *alma* will bring forth a son." This suggests that the birth is not a virgin birth but only a young maiden having a child[8].

Is anything to be gained from the fact that *alma* is used with the definite article in Isaiah 7:14? Although it has been claimed that this renders the subject a special unmarried virgin, in fact it may also simply designate a particular person of the class of unmarried young women. The latter would seem to make no sense as forming any kind of a sign (i.e., "some woman somewhere will have a child")[9]. So does all of the above indicate that the *sign* given to Ahaz was of a virgin birth, meaning a miraculous birth? No, far from it. It only tells us that a particular woman — a maiden, perhaps as we see from above even an "old maid", will soon give birth.

In summary, the linguistic analysis of the use of the term *alma* does not prove that the sign is necessarily of a virgin birth. On the contrary, we can only determine that if Isaiah had wanted to emphasize a miraculous birth he could have easily used the term *bethula* instead of *alma*. Therefore, analysis has focused on the context as well for meaning. Isaiah tells King Ahaz that this will be a *sign* to him. Some conservative scholars have said that the birth must necessarily be miraculous to serve as a sign, and so *virgin* must be implied. However the Bible is full of signs from God that are not miraculous. The sign that Eli's family is finished as high priests is the death of his two sons on the same day (I Sam. 2:34); the sign that God is with the children of Israel is that they worship him on Mount Sinai (Exodus 3:12) ; the sign that Saul will be king is that he will find his lost donkeys the next day and that he will meet three men, one carrying three goats, another carrying three loaves of bread and the third carrying a skin of wine (I Sam. 10:2-3). Surely a sign can be an ordinary sign and so this adds nothing to our analysis.

So the context of the wider story must be looked to. Bible scholar Herbert Wolf claims that it must be an ordinary conception because the facts related in chapter 8 seem to portray a marriage, including the two witnesses, one of whom is a priest. Surely a priest could be at hand at the marriage of Isaiah and a *prophetess* (8:1-2)[10] However, they have also been interpreted as only witnesses to the fulfillment of the prophecy to be given concerning the names [11]. Also the term "went to" the prophetess in 8:3 always refers to sexual relations. The verb actually used is *qrb*, meaning "to draw near", which generally means a first act of intercourse (Gen. 20:4, Lev. 18:6,14,19: 20:16; Deut. 22:14, Ezek. 18:66). Another verb used in Scripture is *bw*, for "to go into her", which is always used for the first act of intercourse. So arguably the former term may be slightly ambiguous and so may refer to either the first or subsequent acts of intercourse, but it indicates that Isaiah was probably not previously married to the prophetess [12]. If it is the same wife, the woman is obviously not a virgin. But neither would she be called a "maiden." It has been argued also that Isaiah's prior wife was dead and he was marrying a prophetess, a young maiden, and Isaiah's wife is the young woman referred to.

Faced with all of the above, Christian apologists will often put their own *spin* on the above by saying that Isaiah 7:14 was a double "prophecy." That although it was fulfilled at the time, it was ultimately

Conviction Overturned

fulfilled in Christ. One of the problems with this is that there is not a shred of evidence in support of this. There is no wording, phrase, or anything else in the narrative to indicate this. In fact, the narrative shows a *complete* fulfillment at the time (the child is born, and within two years Ahaz' two enemies are destroyed, and they are later invaded by Assyria but survive). In fact, even Isaiah himself tells us *that the sign is fulfilled and completed!* Once again, desperation, imagination, wishful thinking, and fanciful invention seem to be commonplace characteristics of the Christian apologists' work ethic and *modus operandi*. There is an invariable penchant, beginning as early as the Gospel of Matthew, to use a huge, unwieldy sledgehammer to hammer square pegs into round holes and round pegs into square holes in order to have something to hang their hat on. But ultimately their hat rack proves to be awkward and insecure and ends up breaking into splinters upon the slightest testing.

What we see in the above linguistic analysis, the contextual analysis and the surrounding narrative is once again an attempt to rip a phrase out of both its text *and* its context, and to manufacture a prophecy. This "prophecy", as we have seen, was not even included in what is probably the original Aramaic Matthew, which is probably identical to the Gospel of the Nazareans, used by the original Palestinian Christians, and is the reason why the earliest Christians, the Jewish Christians, expressly rejected the teaching of the virgin birth. Likewise it was not in the Gospel of Mark, the oldest canonical Gospel. Neither is it in the Gospel of John. The doctrine of the virgin birth was not known, or at least not expressed, by the Apostle Paul, whose God-inspired duty we are told was to teach the world to embrace correct doctrine. It was not included in what he considered the essential early "creed" of I Corinthians 15, and in point of fact Paul made it clear that Jesus was a descendent of King David "after the flesh" (Romans 1:3). The doctrine of a virgin birth is actually very much a staple of pagan religious myth and represents a period of time when the Gospel was becoming a largely pagan affair because of the conversion of many pagans to the faith. A god becomes a man through a virgin birth no less than 80 times in the pagan world, including Hercules, Adonis, Atys, Mithras and many others. This is an adaptation and incorporation of pagan mythology into the story of Jesus.[13]

Prophecy: Messiah would come out of Egypt.
Fulfillment: The Egyptian sojourn of the infant Jesus.

This is based on the alleged prophecy of Hosea 11:2; *"Out of Egypt I have called my son."*

Reality: There is no such prophecy that the Messiah would come out of Egypt.

In narrating the flight to Egypt, the author of Gospel of Matthew states "When he [Joseph] arose, he took the young child and his mother by night and departed for Egypt, and was there until the death of Herod, that it might be fulfilled which was spoken by the Lord through the prophet, saying, *'Out of Egypt I have called my son.'"* (2:14-15).

The problem with this reference to Hosea 11:2 is that the verse in question is in no way, shape or form a reference to any Messiah coming to Israel from Egypt or by way of Egypt. Jacob, whose named was changed by God to Israel in the Old Testament, is often referred to as the "son" of God. "For I am a father to Israel" (Jeremiah 31:9). The children of Israel become the twelve tribes of Israel, and the progeny of Israel so become "Israel" — the nation of Israel. Corporate Israel, as a nation, is always the "son" of God in the Old Testament.

In fact, the phrase quoted from Hosea, the part never recited by Bible proponents, begins as follows:

> "When *Israel* was a child, I loved him, *and out of Egypt I have called my son* [Corporate Israel is explicitly referred to as the *son* in question]. As they called them, so they sacrificed to the Baals, and they burned incense to carved images [Did Jesus sacrifice to the Baals?] I taught Ephraim to walk, taking *them* [the plural corporate form, referring to the Northern Kingdom] by their arms, but they did not know that I healed them. I drew them with gentle cords, with bands of love, and was to them as those who take the yoke from their neck. I stooped and fed them. He shall not return to the land of Egypt; but the Assyrian shall be his king, because they refused to repent." (Hosea 11:1-5).

Conviction Overturned

The theme of Hosea, as many of the prophets, is that Israel, in this case the Northern Kingdom in particular, has turned from God and must return to God. In these passages quoted above, Hosea declares that God has rescued them from Egypt because he loved them, but unless they repent they shall become captives of the growing empire of Assyria, which in fact came to pass. Hosea mentions Israel by name in verse one, above, as the *son* that he calls from Egypt. But Matthew takes great liberties with our gullibility and uses absolute intellectual dishonesty in literally yanking this verse totally out of context to make a neat prophecy, supposedly fulfilled in the life of Jesus. Once again we see the penchant to punch round pegs into square holes and vice-versa.

Perhaps a more interesting question however, is why early Christian authors would have felt it was necessary to portray Jesus as coming from Egypt. One likely answer is found in the surrounding time period. In the book of Acts of the Apostles, the Apostle Paul returns to Jerusalem after a missionary journey in approximately the year 57 to 59 A.D. The book records how Paul is set upon by hostile Jews who turn him over to Roman authorities for punishment. An interesting encounter occurs in Acts chapter 21 when the Roman commander is about to have Paul led into the barracks. The Roman commander says to Paul "Are you not the Egyptian who some time ago stirred up a rebellion and led the four thousand assassins into the wilderness?' (21:38). The question evokes several important considerations. It reminds us that there were many messianic false starts and pretensions during this time period, all promising a coming triumphant new kingdom for Israel, often seeking to commence the same through violence. The questions refers to a leader from Egypt that came to Jerusalem in 54 A.D. to create such a rebellion. **[14]**

Now this notion of an Egyptian coming to save Israel seems at first blush odd. Why an Egyptian? But we can only imagine this false messiah's pretensions to leadership — that he was from Egypt, like Moses was. And so, naturally enough according to this line of thought, Israel's deliverer would come from Egypt, and so the phrase from Hosea 11:2 could be seen as prophetic by those eager to see it as such. Hence the pretension that the Messiah would be from Egypt would have had a start. It made a certain sense, from the historical standpoint.

But the argument can be made that this Egyptian individual, according to the commander's statement, was only a "prophet", not a messiah. This of course begs the question of the Roman commander's grasp of the theological significance of a messiah, or whether he would only use the term "prophet" as a catchall phrase. Remember also that Jesus' own followers referred to Jesus as a prophet (Luke 24:19: "... Jesus of Nazareth, a prophet mighty in deed and word before God and all the people..."), so the use of the term by the Roman does not his preclude "the Egyptian" claiming to be messiah or others claiming him the messiah. Whoever led a fight to free Israel from bondage was seen as a messiah, as Simon Bar Kochba would be a century after Jesus. There were many would-be messiahs.

But the supporters of Jesus, seeking to prove that their messiah was the true one, if we are to judge from what we have seen already in this section on fulfillment of prophecy, were not people to be outdone. Quite the contrary. They very soon had a ready answer: "Our Jesus was *also* from Egypt. He was taken there by his parents to escape the wrath of Herod and an angel of God called them back when it was safe to return." So like Moses, and like the entire nation of Israel, he *was called out of Egypt.* This scenario — competition with other messianic pretensions - is a much more likely explanation of this alleged fulfillment of prophecy. It also may establish a relative date of this portion of Matthew, as after the date when Paul was taken prisoner in Rome, so perhaps after 60 A.D.

Prophecy: He would grow up in Nazareth
Fulfillment: Jesus was raised in Nazareth and so was called "Jesus of Nazareth"

The prophecy is quoted by the author of Gospel of Matthew "and he came and dwelled in a city called Nazareth, that it might be fulfilled which was spoken by the prophets, *'He shall be called a Nazarene"* (2:23)

Reality: There is no such prophecy.

In fact, this is an easy one. Not only is there no such prophecy, this is not even a passage any where in Scripture or in any other writing. This is simply an invention by the author. "Jesus will grow up in Nazareth — we have to have a prophecy. So let's invent one." The only thing remotely, vaguely or arguably similar is the dedication of Samson to be a *Nazirite* in Judges chapter 13. The angel tells the mother that Samson "shall be a Nazirite to God from the womb..." But this is a different word entirely. The angel tells the mother of Samson that Samson shall be *Nazirite* from birth, *not* that he shall live in Nazareth and be a *Nazarene*. The Nazirites' vows are described in Number chapter six. They never touched wine. Jesus did touch wine. He was not a Nazirite and made no pretensions to be one. What does the Samson narrative have to do with the Jesus narrative? Absolutely nothing. It's just that somewhere, somehow, someone thought we would be very gullible, and *it sounded great on paper!* Matthew, or whoever wrote the Gospel, is a highly inventive, resourceful, imaginative individual, with very few scruples worth mentioning. But we still always hear it piously stated, "It was prophesied that Christ would be born in Bethlehem and grow up in Nazareth", usually followed by something like, "What are the odds of that happening?"

Prophecy: The infants would be massacred in Bethlehem. Fulfillment: The infants were murdered by Herod in search of the baby Jesus according to the narrative in the Gospel of Matthew (2:16).

This alleged prophecy is based entirely and exclusively on Matthew 2:17. Following a description of Herod's order to kill all infants in Bethlehem two years and under, the author writes, "Then was fulfilled what was spoken by Jeremiah the prophet, saying,

> *'A voice was heard in Ramah, Lamentation, weeping, and great mourning, Rachel weeping got her children, Refusing to be comforted, Because they are no more'"* (Jeremiah 31:15)

Reality: There is no such prophecy.

The context of the Jeremiah quote must be examined. This is another example of a mere phrase or sentence being ripped out of its surrounding context and simply summarily linked to a completely unrelated event with the declaration that this is a "fulfillment of prophecy." Jeremiah is a prophet to the Southern Kingdom of Judah after the Northern Kingdom has fallen captive to Assyria. Jeremiah's message is plain: The Northern Kingdom fell to captivity because it abandoned God. The Southern Kingdom has also abandoned God. Unless Judah repents and returns to God it also will fall captive to Babylon. Jeremiah fervently repeats his powerful and eloquent message to Judah (hence the term "Jeremiads"). In chapter 31 God reaffirms that he is a father to all Israel and that he will gather all the children of Israel and lead them back again. He states, "For I am a father to Israel, and Ephraim is my firstborn." (31:9). Now Ephraim was the second born of Joseph, but in Genesis 49, Jacob gives Ephraim pre-eminence and "Ephraim" becomes the rubric for the Northern Kingdom. He is the metaphorical Northern Kingdom of Israel. The entire Northern Kingdom was conquered and carried off captive to foreign lands by Assyria in 722 B.C. He continues, "Hear the word of the Lord, and declare it on the islands afar off, and say 'He who scattered Israel will gather him, and keep him as a shepherd does his flock.'"(31:10).

In this midst of this highly poetic and eloquent prediction of God's grace and love for Israel, the passage quoted by Matthew is given: *"A voice was heard in Ramah, lamentation, weeping, and great mourning, Rachel weeping got her children, refusing to be comforted, because they are no more"* (Jeremiah 31:15). Now just who is Rachel? She is the metaphorical mother of Israel, but more precisely and to the point, she is the wife of Jacob and the natural mother, not of all their children, but only of Joseph and Benjamin. And as the mother of Joseph, she is the grandmother, and the metaphorical mother, of Manasseh and *Ephraim*. Both are a part of the Northern Kingdom, which is called, it just so happens, *"Ephraim."* Hence, nothing is more understandable than the fact that the metaphorical mother (and actual grandmother) of Ephraim is crying for the loss of her children, because they are gone "and are no more." But alas, God tells her (them, the nation of Israel),

"Refrain your voice from weeping, and your eyes from

tears; for your work shall be rewarded, says the Lord, *and they shall come back from the land of the enemy.* There is hope in your future, says the Lord, *that your children shall come back to their own border."* (31:16-17)

Below, God continues,

"Is Ephraim my dear son? Is he a pleasant child? For though I have spoken against him, I earnestly remember him still; therefore my heart yearns for him; I will surely have mercy on him. "(31:20)

The message and context above is clear enough. There is no prediction of children being murdered in Bethlehem or anywhere else as a part of the ascendance of any messiah. The only children spoken of above are the metaphorical children of Ephraim, the Northern Kingdom. They are not murdered, they are taken captive. And the only *prophecy* that can be discerned is that they will come back from captivity (another failed biblical prophecy incidentally, since they never came back. We will deal with this topic later). The passage quoted in Matthew is not a messianic prophecy or any prophecy at all. Once again, just leave it to the author of the Matthew text to take a phrase completely out of context and just say, "Look, *this* is *that*!" But *this*, isn't *that*, and in fact has absolutely nothing to do with that, as even a cursory reading of the context will tell us.

It is of absolutely no merit whatsoever that some Christian apologists come along with their own *spin*, claiming, "Well this isn't really a prophecy, and it doesn't even claim to be a prophecy. This is only a correspondence with a *historical, metaphorical allegory* from Old Testament history. This is doubletalk and rubbish. They are only saying that certain historical events happened in order that they be obviously paralleled by the life of Christ. But the phrase from Jeremiah has nothing to do with the context of the narrative in Matthew, and neither does the narrative in Jeremiah, and the meaning which the author of Matthew intends to ascribe to his "fulfillment" is clear. By any interpretation he intends to quote this as a *prophecy* of his Jesus the messiah, and it lacks the least modicum of intellectual honesty.

Fulfillment of Prophecy in the Life of Jesus

Prophecy: The messiah would be a descendant of King David. Fulfillment: Jesus was a direct descendant of King David, the "son of David."

Text: This is based on the genealogies of Jesus in the Gospels of Matthew and Luke.

Reality: There are two contradictory, self-serving genealogies which prove nothing.

Anyone who wants a lesson in desperate *spin medicine,* intellectual shenanigans, literary distortion, and deliberate unashamed isogesis, should study the genealogies of Jesus in the New Testament. In the Second Temple, the dream of a messiah, although without firm basis in the Old Testament Scripture, grew to a fever pitch, and naturally devolved on the great figures and epochs of Israel's past. Naturally it came to settle on the figure of King David, greatest personage from the golden age of Israel, anointed of God, and presumed author of beautiful Psalms. The messiah naturally would be another David, and correspondingly would be the "son of David." It would seem that nothing would cement messiah's identity more than literal descendence, which in point of fact would also make him the heir to the throne of David, which would once again be a reality. So then, proof of this literal descendence would be of paramount importance. So the authors of the Gospels of Matthew and Luke went about doing just that. But what they came up with are two contradictory and irreconcilable genealogies which cause one to doubt the very claim in the first place; and which give the Bible proponents cause for considerable stretching to find a good *spin* for this embarrassing situation (which of course they will never admit is in the least bit troubling, for they will never admit that they wish the Bible only had *one* genealogy of Jesus).

Matthew's genealogy of Jesus is from Abraham. It is given in Matthew 1:2-16. Showing the Bible's commitment to symmetry, and the view that arithmetical symmetry shows the hand of God, the author tells us that "All the generations for Abraham to David are fourteen generations, from David until the captivity in Babylon are fourteen generations, and from the captivity in Babylon until the birth of Christ are fourteen generations" (1:17). So apparently this amazing generational symmetry is itself proof that Jesus is messiah. The problem is that from the Babylonian captivity until the birth of Christ only *thirteen* generations are listed: Shealtiel, Zerubbabel, Abiud, Eliakim, Azor, Zadok, Achim, Eliud, Eleazar, Matthan, Jacob, Joseph, and Jesus — thirteen generations. Apparently the Bible's inerrancy does not extend to mathematical inerrancy. A person whose mind is beyond the clouds cannot be expected to be concerned with such mundane things as arithmetic.

In this genealogy Jesus is the descendant of every single one of the kings of Judah from David to the captivity. This includes Jeconiah, against whose seed God put a curse saying that no one from his descendants would ever rule as king (Jeremiah 22:28-30). The Bible's proponents depict this as another biblical miracle. Since Jesus was born of the Holy Spirit, he was not of the "seed" of Jeconiah and so could rule as king (although the curse is expressly against Jeconiah's "descendants", arguably broader than his "seed", but it seems like the Christian apologists will have it both ways). In any event, this reckoning rather defeats the purpose of a genealogy in the first place. In other words, Jesus is not a descendant of *any* of them by this reckoning, is he? He is born of the Holy Spirit, of God, and so none of this is his genealogy in fact.

Next we have the genealogy of the Gospel of Luke, which is from Adam, in Luke 3:23-38. It is an absolutely distinct genealogy, coinciding with the other in only three genealogical entries — one being King David, another Zerrubabel, and another being Joseph, father of Jesus. In this genealogy Joseph's father was named Heli, the son of Matthat. In Matthews' genealogy, Joseph's father was Jacob, son of Matthan. Earlier than this the names are all different. These are two distinct, different and irreconcilable genealogies. Now, the Christian apologists have a ready, traditional answer for the different genealogies that deserves to be considered, for it is truly "one for the books." They tell us, quite sincerely, that the genealogy of Luke is *through Mary*, not Joseph. And that a genealogy is given through Mary in Luke because the Gospel of Luke stresses the humanity of Jesus, and also his humility (who need all those kings as ancestors when you are a man of the people?).

Fulfillment of Prophecy in the Life of Jesus

There are many problems with this approach. The biggest one is that there is not one shred of evidence for this. This genealogy is clearly stated through Joseph in the text. It begins, "Now Jesus himself began his ministry at about thirty years of age, being (as was supposed) *the son of Joseph, the son of Heli,*" etc., etc. Now Christian apologists would have you read *"Jesus...the son of Joseph, the son* [-in-law] *of Heli..."* etc. Now this is a very bold, in fact brazen, sleight of hand, and the very obvious rejoinder is that this *just isn't in the text*! There is no more amazing piece of isogesis, inserting one's own ideas and wishful thinking into the text, in all of hermeneutics, both biblical and extra-biblical, than this rather amazing piece of intellectual and literary dishonesty. But this answer is the only one that explains away two irreconcilable genealogies, starting with the problem that Joseph could only have had one father, not both Jacob and Heli.

Apart from the interlude about the intervention of the Holy Spirit in the birth process, which would only cut Jesus off from the natural lineage, such divine intervention does not affect the genealogy here given and has nothing to do with changing the genealogy from Joseph to Mary. Furthermore, in the entire Bible, genealogies are always given through the father, not the mother. Israel was a very patriarchal society, starting naturally with the Patriarchs and the Twelve Tribes of Israel (all named after the sons of Israel). Neither is this unique to Israel and the Bible, since we also find this in all histories throughout the world.

There is another problem with the genealogies. They do not both just intersect at Joseph and David. They both intersect also at Zerubbabel, the Jewish leader who led the Jews back from Babylon to Israel, and his father Shealtiel. So according to the Bible's proponents both Joseph and Mary were descended from King David, but also, in the same direct genealogy, both were also descended from Shealtiel and his son Zerubbabel. Now here is the kicker — in Luke, Shealtiel's father is Neri and before that there is a completely different genealogy back to Nathan, a son of David who did not become king. In Luke, Shealtiel's father was King Jeconiah! And before him all the kings of Judah back to David, naturally through his son Solomon. Now Shealtiel *could only have had one father!* He didn't have two fathers

— Neri *and* Jeconiah. (Just like, we might add, Joseph, whose father was either Jacob or Heli, not both). What are the Christians trying to do with us? Do they think we are absolute idiots? It is mind boggling in the first place, how two people, descended from a single ancestor, from different children of that ancestor, later on will have *another* common ancestor, from *the male line* of both. Just think of it! If you and I had a common ancestor, let's say our great-great-great grandfather, and we are each descended from two different sons of his, on a straight *male line*. Okay as far as it goes. But then, add in that we also have a common paternal *grandfather.* Who was the father of our grandfather? It means that both of our great-grandfathers had the same son. The problem is apparently not that difficult when you consider the Bible's method of reconciling this — a single person had *two different fathers* at the same time (why didn't I think of that?).

The result of seeing two such irreconcilable genealogies side by side is to sense the sheer desperation of the authors and should cause us to distrust the sources all the more, and as well the conclusion sought to be reached, that Jesus was a direct descendant of David. He is not a direct descendant of King David in any event if he is born of the Holy Spirit and has no human father. These genealogies clearly exist in the realm of nonsense.

We have reached a milestone in our review of fulfillment of prophecy in the life of Christ. Thus far all of the prophecies we have considered are those given us by the author of Matthew. These alleged prophecies have for 2,000 years been the mainstay of Christian messianic prophetic claims as to Jesus, and are still heralded as proof that Jesus was God made man to save men. Let us look at some others, even some of more recent origin.

The Bible Correctly Foretold the Exact Time of Jesus' Ministry and Crucifixion Hundreds of Years Before

This is based on Daniel's "70 Weeks of Years" prophecy in Daniel 9:24-27.

Reality: Daniel's 70 Weeks of years prophecy is a failed biblical prophecy.

The Christian Argument

This is an argument that has been popularized in recent times, most notably and famously about a century ago in the book *The Coming Prince* by Sir Robert Anderson.[15] This argument is based on the "Seventy Weeks" prophecy contained in the book of Daniel in chapter seven. The book of Daniel is alleged to be written by the prophet Daniel in Babylon during Israel's captivity there. Part of the book is a series of prophecies concerning the future state of Israel and of future geo-political events. It is the first book of the Bible that has messianic overtones. The book was especially popular among apocalyptic and messianic elements during the late Second Temple period (exactly the milieu from which Jesus arose) and it is especially popular today among the modern day counterpart — the apocalyptic end-of-times Christians, who are waiting to be raptured before the coming to power of anti-Christ.

At the outset of chapter nine, the prophet Daniel notes that the captivity of the Jews in Babylon is approaching seventy years duration, and that the prophet Jeremiah prophesied that the desolations of Jerusalem should last seventy years. So understanding this, he is praying to God to have mercy on Jerusalem, which is now a desolation, and to forgive it of its former disobedience of God. While he is praying, the angel Gabriel appears and delivers a prophecy concerning Jerusalem to Daniel:

> *"Seventy weeks are determined*
> *For your people and for your holy city,*
> *To finish the transgression,*
> *To make an end of sins,*
> *To make reconciliation for iniquity,*
> *To bring in everlasting righteousness,*
> *To seal up vision and prophecy,*
> *And to anoint the Most Holy.*
>
> *Know therefore and understand,*
> *That from the going forth of the command*
> *To restore and build Jerusalem*
> *Until Messiah the Prince,*

Conviction Overturned

There shall be seven weeks and sixty-two weeks;
The street shall be built again, and the wall,
Even in troublesome times.

And after the sixty-two weeks
Messiah shall be cut off, but not for Himself;
And the people of the prince who is to come
Shall destroy the city and the sanctuary.
The end of it shall be with a flood,
And till the end of the war desolations are determined.

Then he shall confirm a covenant with many for one
week; But in the middle of the week
He shall bring an end to sacrifice and offering.
And on the wing of abominations shall be one who makes desolate,
Even until the consummation, which is determined,
Is poured out on the desolate."
Daniel 9:24-27 (NKJV)

The prophecy is based on the Hebrew system of a week of years (7 years) which of course was central also to the jubilee system, which was every fifty years. The prophecy is of a future seventy weeks of years. Now the context alluded to is vital to an understanding of the prophecy. Daniel has referred to prophecy from the prophet Jeremiah, who prophesied up to the time of the fall of Jerusalem to Babylon, that Jerusalem would be desolated for seventy years. Daniel refers to this fact at the outset of his prayer and essentially asks God, as part of his supplication, to be true to his word. Now the angel Gabriel informs Daniel that the seventy years desolation and captivity of Israel is not the end of the matter with God. Israel's punishment is not merely the seventy years desolation of Jerusalem. Daniel has it wrong! It is "seventy weeks" of years that "are determined for your people and for your holy city, to finish the transgression, to make an end of sins, to make reconciliation for iniquity," [i.e., to pay for Israel's disobedience in former times], and "To bring in everlasting righteousness…"(v.24). So there is much more to come. Seventy weeks of years are 490 years.

Fulfillment of Prophecy in the Life of Jesus

Now the key to when this period begins and ends is essential to the Christian understanding. Christian apologists find this answer in chapter one of the book of Nehemiah. Nehemiah is a Hebrew cup bearer for the Persian King Artaxerxes. In the twentieth year of the reign of Artaxerxes, Nehemiah is extremely sad over the state of Jerusalem. Seeing his distress King Artaxerxes inquires of Nehemiah. The king is so taken at Nehemiah's travail that he orders the city of Jerusalem to be rebuilt. Now this is an order recorded in secular history as the month of Nisan, first month of the calendar, at the spring equinox (March-April), in the twentieth year of the reign of Artaxerxes. This is estimated at 444 or 445 B.C., depending on when in the month of Nissan it may have occurred and how this would correspond to our modern calendar system (in other words it may have been at the beginning or end of the twentieth year of Artaxerxes).

Verse 25 makes it clear "That from the going forth of the command to restore and build Jerusalem until messiah the prince, there shall be seven weeks and sixty two weeks..." Sixty two and seven equal sixty nine. So Christians depict this as a prophecy that Jesus will come 483 years after the starting point. So the calculation would seem that this would be 483 years after 445-444 B.C. But there is a catch.

These apologist claim that in the Bible Hebrew prophecies are always in "prophetic years" based upon the lunar calendar, or "lunar year", which they claim is 360 days. This claim is based on the fact that the Hebrew calendar supposedly only had lunar months of thirty days, which they claim is shown in numerous scriptures, such as the 150 days that it rained in the Great Flood of Genesis, which is depicted as five months; or the 1,260 days of the Great Tribulation in the book of Revelation, which is meant to correspond with three and a half years. So they claim that this prophecy is based on twelve months of thirty days, or 360 day years. The total number of days (365.25 x 483 = 173,880 days) must be divided by 365.25 to render this prophecy in our years. So 173,880 days equals 476.0575 *solar* years, or 476 years and 21 days. The argument of Sir Robert Anderson is that since we passed from 1 B.C. to 1 A.D directly, with no zero year, we add on one year, and so the date can be accurately reckoned to Sunday of Passover week in the year 32 A.D., to be exact April 6, 32 A.D., the supposed day of Jesus' triumphal entry into Jerusalem. Other conservative Christian scholars, while believing in the weeks of years prophecy as related to Jesus, have taken issue with the pinpointing of the date that Anderson gave. The date Anderson gave was shown not to be the week of Passover. Others have said it corresponds to the year 33 A.D., instead of 32 A.D. But in any event, the above calculations surely put the result in about the spring of 32 or 33 A.D., the time Jesus was believed to be crucified.

"Prophetic Years" v. Solar Years

But before we go further in out observations, let us review the methodology employed, The above translation of the prophecy into "lunar *prophetic* years" is quite a self-serving sleight of hand, which shows some amazing ignorance or naiveté. There is no such thing as a "prophetic year." This is a mere invention of the Christian apologists. The Hebrew year was not a lunar year — it was a luni-solar year. Despite the importance of the phases of the moon for all ancient peoples, no nation of antiquity could maintain a true lunar year (which is 354 days, the time it takes for the moon to go through twelve cycles of phases, not 360 days). In fact, from time immemorial, human beings were able to determine that there was a pattern or course to the seasons and that after approximately 365 days that pattern began again. The pattern exists because that is how long it takes the earth to orbit the sun. However, it is not necessary for men to know that the earth is in fact orbiting the sun. Men have been adept from very early periods of history at following the course of the sun and stars. So the solar year became a prime method of calibrating time, alongside the lunar months. A year is a *year*: the length of time it takes for the earth to complete a circuit of the sun. Otherwise you have a mess of the calendar system - especially the agricultural system ends up entirely out of order. From ancient times it was known that you cannot take twelve cycles of the moon and call it a year — it isn't. You cannot have a viable calendar system which is eleven days out of sync every year. There is no such thing as a true lunar year. There are only lunar months, which vary from 28 to 30 days, not a standard 30 days.

Ancient Israel was no exception. So the Hebrews went to great lengths to bring their calendar into synchronization with the real,

Fulfillment of Prophecy in the Life of Jesus

solar year. They added an intercalary month every third, sixth, and eighth year. It was an extra month of Adair. They would add an extra month to these after many decades. Various modifications were used for the insertion of the third month of Adair. So although they could count months in the short term by the completed phases of the moon, over an extended period of time any accounting of years, such as any prediction like the one we have here, will correspond to solar years, i.e., our years, by the introduction of intercalary (catch up, or "leap" months). We do the same thing by leap years every four years to make up for the extra one fourth of a day each year. It would be ludicrous to imagine it otherwise.

As to the examples they use to support their argument, let us look at them. They claim that Genesis says the waters of the flood rose for 150 days, which is depicted as five months. So, their argument goes, since there are twelve months in the year, they must have had 360 day years! Frequently, even in law, there are deadlines given for things to be done - of 120 days, 150 days, and 180 days. We frequently say that this is four, five or six months, and think nothing of it. A default judgment must be set aside, for instance, in 180 days. We commonly *call it six months.* Does that mean the legal system uses a 360 day year? This is what the Christian apologists would have us believe. By saying this then, when we later look at a statute of limitations requiring an action to be filed within *two years*, do we say, "Oh, it must be filed really in 720 days, or ten days before the two years expires!?" Of course we do not. When we see *two years,* we know it means two years. So 100 years ago is the same length of time as *100 years hence.* There is no difference in the system of calibration. According to their so-called prophetic year system, one hundred years ago was 1910, but one hundred from now will be *2108!* This would be ludicrous. But this is exactly the ridiculous result we are asked to reach.

As to the second source that they use to postulate a "prophetic year" that is shorter than the solar year, they use the book of Revelation. It is interesting that they use a New Testament book to retrospectively ascribe a supposed "prophetic year" to the Old Testament. The last chapter of Daniel spoke of the daily sacrifice in the Temple being taken away for 1,260 days. Revelation, using the apocalyptic prophecies of Daniel as basis and inspiration, sees the anti-Christ as ruling the earth three and a half years. Christians say this corroborates the concept of the prophetic year because 1,260 days here, or 30 months, equals three and a half years, when three and one half years would really be *1,278 days!* So, they say, there is such a thing as a "prophetic year" which must be carried out no matter how long the projection is for. So what about Jeremiah's seventy years captivity? Is it is really only 69 years? Just calculate it: If you lose five days per year, it is 350 days less than 70 years. Add in the one fourth day of leap year for each year and you get 368 days, exactly one year behind. Seventy "prophetic years" is almost exactly 69 years. But the Bible makes it clear it was *seventy years*, not 69. In the book of Haggai we are told the Second Temple was dedicated the first day after the completion of exactly seventy years. Must all biblical prophecies that employ time be recalculated?

Since we have seen above the genuine Hebrew method of calibrating time, why wouldn't a Hebrew prophecy or prediction based on time, use the Hebrew method of reckoning time? Why would they use something else? The purpose of communicating is to transmit ideas and concepts to your audience. That is why common language and meaning are important. If I told you that something would happen in 35 years, you would understand it. But if I then said that it would be in 35 *Kangaroo* years, you would be lost. We failed to communicate. What is a kangaroo year? Who knows? What we do know is that this is sheer stupidity. Why would a prophet, or God, be so moronic, as to make a time prediction using a calibration of time that the audience, either then or now, does not use or understand, and what is worse, which they would misinterpret to mean what they understand as a *year*, which is a solar year, which all human being from the beginning of time have known and understood, and therefore confuse the audience into missing the point of the prediction? Why does God put the prediction into a format where you must do a mathematical calculation just to see how much time he is really saying?

In point of fact, during the Second Temple period, there was an ongoing debate over the calendar, but it was not over a "lunar" year versus a solar year, it was between having the then current luni-solar year with intercalary months, and having a straight 365 solar year, advocated by the *Book of Jublilees,* the book of *Enoch,* and by the

Fulfillment of Prophecy in the Life of Jesus

Essene community. Nobody wanted a 354 day "year" or a 360 day "year", because nobody was stupid enough to want it.[16]

But the Christian apologists ignore all of this. Why would a prophecy be made which, in the first place, does not correspond with the Hebrews' own reckoning of time (the solar year that we use); and which in the second place is otherwise absolutely unintelligible and incomprehensible both by the way the Hebrews told time and we tell time? But we are meant to suppose that "God works in mysterious ways" and apparently likes to pester us with unintelligible ambiguity. Apparently that is part of the mystery. There is no such thing as a "prophetic year" in the Bible. This is simply more baloney for your Christian baloney sandwich. This is sheer invention.

And incidentally, without the "prophetic years" calculation, using their formulation and starting date of the prophecy, their messiah would have arrived in 483 solar, i.e., *real* years, which would be 39 or 40 A.D. Pontius Pilate was only governor until 36 A.D. So it looks like their messiah may have jumped the gun.

Observations: Starting Point and Bifurcation of Prophecy

Despite this absurdity, we should proceed with our observations. First, when does this prophecy point to? Better put, when does it begin? When is "the going forth of the command to restore and build Jerusalem…?" Secondly, why is the prophecy divided into two parts of "seven weeks" (49 years) and of "sixty-two weeks?" Christians say the only significance of this is to make a total of sixty-nine weeks of years. But this does not answer the question of why the obvious division between seven first, followed by sixty- two. This is a deliberately bifurcated prophecy. Why? We will find the two issues of when the starting point is, and the bifurcation of this prophecy, to be connected. Let us start with the first question, that of the starting point.

Historically, it is a matter of undisputed fact that there are several attested possibilities. The first is immediately upon the destruction of Jerusalem in 587 B.C. Even before this event, after the second deportation, in the fourth year of Zedekiah, in 593 B.C., the prophet

Jeremiah writes to those in exile, and God promises to restore them. *"For behold, the days are coming, says the Lord, 'that I will bring back from captivity my people Israel and Judah', says the Lord, 'and I will cause them to return to the land that I gave to their fathers, and they shall possess it'"* (Jer. 30:3). Later, the Lord says, *"Behold. I will bring back the captivity of Jacob's tents, and have mercy on his dwelling places,* **the city shall be built upon its own mound***, and the palace shall remain according to its own plan."*(30:18). Jerusalem had not yet been destroyed, but it would be. This declaration from God can be seen as an order to restore and rebuild the desolated city.

But more pointedly, a clear decree to rebuild was issued by the Persian Emperor Cyrus when he granted liberty to the captive Jews in Babylon in 538 B.C. Now the significance is that this is what *the Bible* sees as the decree to rebuild the temple in Jerusalem and is quoted at Ezra 1:2. *"Thus says Cyrus king of Persia: All the kingdoms of the earth the Lord God has given me. And he has commanded me to build him a house in Jerusalem which is in Judah."* Now the temple was at the heart of the cultural and national life of Jerusalem. If there was a temple there was a Jerusalem. We know that this decree in fact led to the rebuilding of Jerusalem under Ezra and Nehemiah. This decree is the beginning of the fulfillment of the prophecy made by Jeremiah quoted above. This decree of Cyrus restored national Israel, and led to a return of the Jews to their homeland and opened the Second Temple period.

Isaiah the prophet clearly saw this pronouncement by Cyrus as *the decree* to rebuild Jerusalem: *"Thus says the Lord your redeemer… Who says to Jerusalem, 'you shall be inhabited', To the cities of Judah, 'you shall be built…'" Who says of Cyrus, 'he is my shepherd, and he shall perform all my pleasure, Saying to Jerusalem 'You shall be built, And to the Temple 'Your foundation shall be laid…"*(Isaiah 44:24-28).

Later there was another decree from the Emperor Darius in 520 B.C., which merely reconfirmed the decree of Cyrus allowing the restarting of the construction of the Second Temple after it had stalled for eighteen years (Ezra 6:3-12). However this later decree was only a ratification of what was earlier decreed.

Fulfillment of Prophecy in the Life of Jesus

Now at this point we have rather naturally glided into the second question: that of the prophecy being bifurcated into two parts. Let us step back and look at the big picture of what we have before us staring us in the face. This decree of Cyrus which ended the captivity and restored national Israel was in 538 B.C. What is the time period between the destruction of the Temple and Jerusalem in 587 B.C. and the decree in 538 B.C.? If you have guessed (or if you are good at math, *calculated*) 49 years, then this proves that you are an able mathematician. Now let us see how good your memory is? When did we encounter the number *49*? That is correct — the first part of the prophecy is seven weeks of years — 49 years. Now in the texts that are among the oldest of the Hebrew Masoretic text developed by the Jews in the Middle Ages, and upon which all of our Christian Old Testaments are based, there is an *athnach*, the equivalent of a semi-colon, between the seven weeks and the sixty-two weeks [14], which indicates only one thing — two anointed ones. The Jewish translation of their own Scripture, devoid of the isogetical Christian influence, reads as follows:

> *"Seventy weeks have been decreed for your people and your holy city until the measure of transgression is filled and that of sin complete, until iniquity is expiated, and eternal righteousness ushered in; and prophetic vision ratified, and the Holy of Holies anointed. You must know and understand: From the going forth of the word to rebuild and restore Jerusalem until the [time of the] anointed leader is seven weeks; and for sixty-two weeks it will be rebuilt, square and moat, but in a time of distress. And after those sixty-two weeks, the anointed one will disappear and vanish."* (Daniel 9:34-25). ."(JPS, Tanakh translation).

Several differences are notable. There are clearly two anointed leaders. And unlike the Christian version, "There shall be seven weeks and sixty-two weeks; The street shall be built again, and the wall, Even in troublesome times…" which leaves an ambiguity as to when the rebuilding shall take place, whether after the seven weeks, or after the sixty-two weeks. Christians obviously interpret this to mean the latter, after the arrival of the Christian messiah. The Jewish translation makes it clear that the rebuilding occurs after the seven weeks, i.e., 49 years. Is it only coincidental that the period of 49 years corresponds with the actual decree of Cyrus to rebuild 49 years after the destruction? Hardly so. This would be an unreasonable conclusion. The answer is that this is written as requiring a double fulfillment, with only the first part fulfilled and the second part prophetic, to be fulfilled in the future. This is the way it is written. The first part, of 49 years, is already fulfilled at the time the prophecy is made, in 538 B.C., when the order to rebuild is issued. The sixty-two weeks then commences at the time of the decree of Cyrus, in 538 B.C. We can also now understand the phrase, "the street shall be built again, and the wall, even in troublesome times" (Daniel 9:25), as referring to the troubled rebuilding, in particular of the walls of Jerusalem, against hostile opposition from the local population, recounted in the book of Nehemiah.

Now it is most notable, that the Christian apologists are quite devoid of any explanation as to the meaning of the seven weeks, except that that they do not think it is important. In fact, unless you consider the 49 years of captivity from the destruction of the temple until the decree of Cyrus — "the going forth of the order to rebuild" — then the seven week part of the prophecy in fact has no meaning. Only considering that interval as a vital part of the prophecy does it have meaning. It cannot be coincidental and it is obviously the first part of the prophetical formulation — an event and a passage of time that has already occurred.

Now the balance of this paragraph is instructive, both the Jewish and Christian translations:

"The army of a leader who is to come will destroy the city and the sanctuary, but its end will come through a flood. Desolation is decreed until the end of the war."(JPS, Tanakh translation).

"And the people of the prince who is to come shall destroy the city and the sanctuary. The end of it shall be with a flood, and till the end of the war desolations are determined." (NKJV).

Fulfillment of Prophecy in the Life of Jesus

How could the Temple (sanctuary) and city be there to be destroyed unless it had been built in the interval, after the seven weeks and the sixty two weeks? So the traditional Jewish translation must necessarily be correct.

Now the word translated "messiah" is *mashiach* in Hebrew, which means *anointed*. It is never used as a title in the Old Testament, but is used as such by Christians [15]. We can see that the first anointing of what the Christian Bible calls the "Most Holy" is correctly translated by the Jewish version as the anointing of the Holy of Holies after the seven weeks, not of the messiah. This is correct, since the term the Most Holy [place] always refers to the inner Temple, translated also as Holy of Holies. So after 49 years the Temple can be rebuilt [or start to be] — exactly what happened.

But the more important question is — who is the anointed leader who comes after 49 years. The answer is indisputable. It is Cyrus himself. You might ask, "How can this be? A foreign, pagan ruler! He cannot be an 'anointed one', a 'messiah.'" But that is exactly what Cyrus is in the Old Testament. He is so termed in Isaiah chapter 44-45:

> *"Thus says the Lord your redeemer... Who says to Jerusalem, 'you shall be inhabited', To the cities of Judah, 'you shall be built...'"* Who says of Cyrus, 'he is my shepherd, and he shall perform all my pleasure, saying to Jerusalem 'You shall be built, And to the Temple 'Your foundation shall be laid...''* (So Cyrus is clearly seen as ordering the rebuilding of Jerusalem and so 538 is the going forth of the order to rebuild)(24-28). *"Thus says the Lord to his anointed* (mashiach is the term translated - no guess work involved here at all), *To Cyrus, whose right hand I have held — to subdue nations before him and loose the armor of kings..."* (Isaiah 44:24-45:1).

Also in chapter 42, v.1:

> *"Behold! My servant whom I uphold, My elect one in whom my soul delights!*

I have put my spirit upon him {he is anointed of God though the Holy Spirit};

He will bring forth justice to the Gentiles."

There is no question but that Cyrus is the first anointed one — the messiah if you will — of Israel, being in fact the deliverer and restorer of Israel. There is also no question but that Isaiah sees Cyrus as the one who has given the order that Jerusalem be rebuilt ("...He shall perform all my pleasure, saying to Jerusalem, 'you shall be built...'"), and so this is unquestionably the order referred to in the prophecy of Gabriel in Daniel — the beginning of the sixty-two weeks.

We can also see in the Jewish translation the message of Gabriel in light of his correction of Daniel — that seventy years is not the full punishment for Israel. A purging is necessary of seventy weeks of years "until the measure of transgression is filled and that of sin complete, until iniquity is expiated, and eternal righteousness ushered in..." In the Christian translation these are the things which the anointed leader is understood to do, presumably after the sixty-nine weeks have transpired: "Seventy weeks are determined for your people and for your holy city, to finish the transgression, to make an end of sins, to make reconciliation for iniquity, to bring in everlasting righteousness..." Presumably this will be done not *by means of the seventy weeks* by way of purging, but rather after the seventy weeks are concluded by means of the propitiatory blood sacrifice in atonement for sin by Jesus. So Christians have interpolated their later distinctly Christian theology, their *spin,* into the text.

So then, where is the fulfillment, now that we understand the meaning of the bifurcation, and the starting point? Sixty two weeks of years is 434 years. 434 years from 538 B.C. is 104 B.C. Many Jewish scholars have depicted this prophecy as referring to the period of Alexander Janneus, the arch-enemy of the Pharisees, who condemned many Pharisees to crucifixion. But this is a far-fetched fulfillment during a tumultuous period of time, and the actions of Alexander seem minor compared to the brutal reign of Antiochus Epiphanies sixty years before, which seem much more dark and apocalyptic. In any event the reign of Alexander Janneus was not followed by the destruction of Jerusalem, so cannot be a fulfillment.

Fulfillment of Prophecy in the Life of Jesus

What we have here, quite clearly, is the phenomenon of the *failed prophecy*. Although Christians claim that all Bible prophecies are proven true and that a biblical prophecy has never failed, in fact the Bible is full of bogus prophecies, as we will see in the next chapter. However, the failure of the prophecy, stemming from Cyrus's decree, led to more than consternation. It led to a reanalysis and recapitulation of that prophecy, basing it instead on the decree of Artaxerxes referred to in Nehemiah. And now that momentous apocalyptic period of an anointed leader was drastically shifted to the first century A.D. As we will see, such a strategy eventually leads to attempted self-fulfillment. And what occurred was actually a plethora of messianic pretensions, beginning about the time of Judas the Galilean in 6 A.D. and continuing at least until Simon Bar-Kochba and the Jewish revolt of 132 A.D. The difference of the Jesus claim is the successful crossover into the Gentile world, engineered by the Apostle Paul, combined with the claim of resurrection, and with the Gentilization of the Gospel message, replete with elements of classical pagan mythology such as the virgin birth, and God becoming man, which made the new religion both compatible with pagan religious views, and comprehensible and appealing to pre-existing pagan sentiments.

Of course neither is the ministry of Jesus followed immediately by the destruction of Jerusalem, even assuming the truth of their so-called prophetical year calculation. But they have an answer. Evangelical Christians have developed the doctrine of dispensationalism, which includes the "postponement theory." A necessarily very brief, superficial digression into this arcane philosophy of biblical history is warranted here. Dispensationalism is a theory developed to bridge irreconcilable elements of the Bible, most importantly the God of the Old Testament from the God of the New, and the unique covenant with Israel based on the Law of Moses versus the universal covenant made by Christ's sacrifice based on faith and centered on the Gentile world and its church. It postulates God's successive dispensations in his dealings with man, of which the New Testament dispensation is the final one, but which succeeds, without nullifying, the covenant with Israel, which is eternal and unbreakable. God deals with Israel and the Gentiles differently. Among some, but not all, adherents of this view even much of Jesus' own ministry is seen as not directly relevant to the church. The apostle Paul called Jesus "the minister to the circumcision" (Romans 15:9), claiming himself to carry God's message to the Gentiles.

In the present dispensation God is dealing with the Gentiles through the new covenant. The church will eventually be raptured to heaven and God will deal once again with the nation of Israel. The postponement theory postulates that the seventieth week was postponed, much as someone uses a stopwatch, and that the last apocalyptic week will occur at a later time, before the postulated return of Christ in glory, and God will deal once again with his chosen nation, Israel.

A school within dispensationalism further postulates that God left the door open for Israel's salvation for a generation — roughly forty years — after the crucifixion, but that Israel's continuing rejection of Christ led God to turn away from that relationship, causing God to unleash the destruction of Jerusalem and the temple in 70 A.D. as a reprisal. According to the latter school, if Israel had responded and accepted Christ as king he would have returned in glory as King of Israel within forty years. But presumably, and inexplicably, the seventieth week was programmed to come *anyway* before Christ's return, if we are to believe the Daniel prophecy, even though the Jewish War and the destruction of Jerusalem was only the result of Israel's rejection. So how could it be both a programmed fulfillment of prophecy but also an elective, conditional punishment that Israel could have avoided?

But the relevant matter for our analysis of the Christian point of view is a gap between the sixty-ninth and the seventieth week, which is no where even remotely stated in the prophecy, but which clever Christian biblical scholars intuited almost two thousand years later. So it is as though you told someone in all sincerity that it is 100 miles from New York to Sidney, Australia. But, we should add as a matter of significance, that there is a huge gap between the ninety-ninth and the one hundredth mile that is real doozey! Welcome to baloneyland! Once again, great liberties are taken to invent bridges from one side of an irreconcilable chasm to another.

A Prophecy that Begs Self Fulfillment: Jesus Proclaimed self as the Son of Man Described in Daniel

One obvious observation is that a prophecy as to the time something will happen will tend to lead to its own fulfillment, or at least attempted fulfillment. The failure of the prophecy of Daniel 9:24-28, seen in its true and obvious light, led to a necessary modification of its terms, at least necessary to those who insist on seeing Scripture as true, and so must do a *spin*, to use the modern vernacular, on the text. And so the prophecy comes to be seen as dating from the decree of Artaxerxes referred to in Nehemiah. And so the prophecy is dated from the year 445 or 444 B.C. And so what we have is attempts at self-fulfillment, including a plethora of would-be messiahs starting in the first century A.D. Many we have already encountered — Judas the Galilean in 6 A.D.; Theudas; the Egyptian; and eventually Simon Bar-Kochba, declared by the high priest at the time to be the messiah.

It is obvious that this is exactly what Jesus attempted to do. Jesus apparently proclaimed himself to be the messiah predicted in Daniel chapter 9! Referring to the destruction of Jerusalem, Jesus said, "For days will come upon you when your enemies will build an embankment around you...and level you, and your children within you, to the ground; and they will not leave one stone upon another, *because you did not know the time of your visitation"*(Luke 19:43-44). Visitation always refers in the Bible to a spectacular intervention by God in human affairs to render salvation or punishment. So Jesus' ministry, according to him, represented a visitation by God.

In character with this, he refers to himself as the "son of man', the term assigned to the one who assumes power over the whole earth under the authority of the Ancient of Days in Daniel 7:13, and the name of the angelic personage who appeared to Daniel in chapters 10-12, who both prophesied exactly the history of wars in Israel after the division of Alexander the Great's Empire and also of an apocalyptic end of times and "time of troubles", remarkably similar to the prophecies of Jesus, which will come upon the world. His vision of the end times tribulation refers to the abomination of desolation (the desecration of the Holy of holies) referred to in Daniel and culminates with the "son of man will come in the clouds with great power and glory" (Mark 143:26). When asked by the high priest if he was "the Christ, the son of God", Jesus' answer was that they would next see him "coming in the clouds of heaven", an exact reference to Daniel 7:13 ("And behold, one like the son of man, coming with the clouds of heaven"!). The high priest naturally tore his clothes in distress, the deliberate reference being evident. Jesus' preaching of the Kingdom of God, especially in Mark and Luke, illustrate his role as the son of man, the messenger of Daniel and Malachi, who would set aright the world on behalf of God and usher in a new age.

Jesus' preaching is highly apocalyptic, a trait increasingly common in the Second Temple period, especially the latter end of it the time of Jesus. We know the full extent of such obsessiveness on the part of some Jews during this period from the Dead Sea Scrolls a product of the Essene community — a monastic, apocalyptic, messianic ultra-religious fringe movement, thoroughly obsessed with the book of Daniel and its end of days theme, and with ideas strikingly similar to Jesus and the early Christians. So there is no question but that Jesus referred to himself as that person represented in Daniel as "the messenger", the end of times "prophet" or the messiah by late Second Temple apocalyptic/messianic Jews.

The obsession with the end of times, the coming of a savior, and a coming kingdom, so similar to many in our own times, should not come as a surprise. This was chronologically the last desperate grab by apocalyptic, messianic Jews to prove the truth of prophecy (Idea: "If no one is around to be the messiah, then it must be that I am!"). If it was not Jesus, it would be someone. So why not resurrect a failed prophecy and fulfill it? If this was in any way, shape or form, a prophecy of the arrival of Jesus, it was a deliberately self- fulfilling one. This is to say that anyone could make the arithmetical calculation, determine the correct time, and proclaim himself the "son of man." His death would be a product of the offensiveness of his preaching.

Prophecy: The messiah would have to come before Israel became a Roman province in 6 A.D.
Fulfillment: Jesus was born before 6 A.D.

Text: This is based on Genesis 49:10, *"The scepter shall not pass from Judah, nor a lawgiver from beneath his feet, until Shiloh comes."* *Reality: This is a failed prophecy.*

Christian commentators point to the scepter as a symbol of the power of life and death and point out the legal incapacity of the Jewish Sanhedrin to condemn Jesus to death at his trial. This authority was reserved to the Roman governor. Hence, the scepter had passed from Judah.

In Genesis 49, Jacob gives a prophetic overview to the destinies of his twelve sons. In the prophecy to Judah in verse 10, the "scepter" and "lawgiver" are obvious references to a ruler, a king. *Shiloh* is an obscure term that is taken to mean a deliverer, savior, or *messiah*. The prophecy is that there will always be a ruler from the tribe of Judah. The Christian interpretation is that the *nation* of Judah will always have a king over it. The distinction is not necessary in any event because in 587 B.C. Jerusalem was captured by the Babylonians and destroyed, and its people taken away into captivity. So there ceased to be a king from Judah, there ceased to be any king at all in Judah, and Israel ceased to be a sovereign nation. *And no deliverer, savior, or shiloh ever came.* The prophecy utterly failed, as many biblical prophecies have. We will review this phenomenon more in a later chapter.

Although the captives returned after the decree of Cyrus, Israel remained a subject province of the Persian Empire. After the conquest by Alexander the Great it became a part of the Hellenistic Empires that replaced Alexander's rule, shifting between the rule of Egypt and Syria. Only in 167-162 B.C., over four hundred years after the destruction of Jerusalem and the scepter passing from Judah, the revolt of the Maccabees eventually secured for Israel its own kingship under the Hasmonean dynasty in 141 B.C.

If the prophecy was not already failed, it would have been failed again in 43 B.C., when an Idumean foreigner, Herod, became King. In point of fact, when Judea and Galilee became administratively a part of the province of Syria in 6 A.D. and came under the direct rule of a Roman governor, the Herod family continued to preside in Galilee, and so we have the encounter between Jesus and Herod depicted in the Gospels. Pilate supposedly deferred to Herod in the issue of Jesus' fate — "I found no fault in this man... and neither did Herod."

Unlike other passages that the Bible proponents have attempted to quote as prophecies, this *is* a prophecy, but it is a failed one. It is a failed one which has been pulled out of the closet, dusted off, and reinvigorated with new life and meaning for those who are either ignorant of, or willing to ignore, history. The square pegs are getting harder and harder to drive into round holes.

Christ would be crucified—Psalm 22

Text: Psalm 22, seen as a predictive prophecy of the suffering of Jesus on the cross, i.e., *"They have pierced my hands and my feet."*

This is the Psalm that Jesus is portrayed as reciting while on the cross, *"My God, my God, why have you forsaken me?"* (Psalm 22, vs. 1). It is portrayed as having enormous theological implications for Cristology, the study of Christ's divine and human nature, both by Trinitarians and also by Adoptionists and Docetists.

Christians claim that this Psalm, supposed to be written by King David, portrays in part a person suffering death from crucifixion, and so is prophetic. As much of the Old Testament, not to mention the Psalms, is highly poetic, its passages are often obscure. It depicts human misery, uncertainty, torment, and a feeling of alienation from God, and ends in deliverance and joy. It depicts a person confused, who believes God has abandoned him; not the cool, calculating Lamb of God, resigned to his fate, depicted in the Gospel of John, but perhaps closer to the man who sweated blood and begged that he be spared the crucifixion in Luke, chapter 22. Most of the Psalm could depict anyone suffering agony or in the throes of death, and surrounded by enemies. The key passage, that causes Christians to use it so widely, *"they have pierced my hands and my feet"*, is a highly controversial translation from the Hebrew text. The Hebrew translation states *"Dogs surround me, a pack of evil ones closes in on me, like lions they maul my hands*

Fulfillment of Prophecy in the Life of Jesus

and my feet..." (JPS, Tanakh Translation). The image is of someone fighting off a pack of savage dogs or beasts that bite and claw at your hands and feet while you fight and kick at them. That the image is of lions is reinforced by verse 14, where the protagonist's tormenters are likened to lions: *"They open their mouths at me like tearing, roaring lions..."* In his life, David had felt the torment and despair of rejection and betrayal, even being ejected from his throne and chased out of Jerusalem. Even the term *pierced,* however, is equally consistent with the imagery of being attacked by dogs and lions and fending off the attack.

Isaiah Chapter 53

Isaiah chapter 53 has the distinction of being one of the Scriptures used in the book of Acts as an example of fulfillment prophecy for purposes of evangelism. In chapter 8 of Acts, an Ethiopian eunuch is reading Isaiah 53, the depiction of the "suffering servant", and is wondering aloud who it refers to. Along comes Philip the evangelist and supplies the answer — he delivers the Gospel of Jesus. This portion of Scripture, it actually begins at Isaiah 52:13 and continues to the end of chapter 53, is claimed by Christian apologists to be a portrayal of the life, ministry and death of Jesus.

These passages admittedly bear a convincing resemblance superficially to the Gospel account of Jesus and the theology of atonement. Christian apologists will especially cite references to the Gospel account of the trial and execution of Jesus. *"He was oppressed and afflicted, yet he opened not his mouth...And as a sheep before its shearers is silent..."* is claimed to refer to Jesus as silent before his accusers (as he is portrayed in Matthew, and before Herod in Luke. In the Gospel of John he appears much more vocal). *"And they made his grave with the wicked - but with the rich at his death, because he had done no violence, nor was there any deceit in his mouth... He was numbered with the transgressors..."* being cited as a referring to his crucifixion among criminals, but his burial in the tomb of Joseph of Arimathea. He had *"no form or comeliness...there is no beauty that we should desire him",* a reference to his lowly estate (although the lowliness of his estate is not established by any means in Mark or Matthew. In Matthew he is the direct descendant of every king of Judah, and there is no indication that he was born anywhere other than in a private residence - no stable or manger, no visits by shepherds — this is exclusively Lucan territory).

Equally important, are not just the factual, but the theological comparison as the vicarious sin-bearer: *"But he was wounded for our transgression, he was bruised for our iniquities, the chastisement for our peace was upon him, and by his stripes we are healed...the Lord has laid on him the iniquity of us all." "By his knowledge my righteous servant shall justify many, for he shall bear their iniquities." "He bore the sin of many, and made intercession for the transgressors."* We are told a biblical seven times that he will apparently die, and we are told seven times that he shall bear the sins of others.

There is also a clear reference to resurrection in these passages. *"When you make his soul an offering for sin, he shall see his seed, he shall prolong his days...He shall see the labor of his soul and be satisfied..."* These verses imply a resurrection after being slain for the sins of others and actually bearing the sins of others by his death.

The theory of the atonement for sin by the intercessory death of Jesus is held to be established by Christians. Clearly intercessory atonement for sin by *someone* can be established in these verses. Whether in fact this was accomplished by Jesus of Nazareth would depend on the validity of the other evidence we have reviewed to first establish the truth of the Gospel accounts. In other words, the theological comparison is valid only if the other factual assertions of the Gospel are valid.

The comparison of this portion of Scripture to Jesus was not lost on early Christians, starting with the author of Second Peter. This would naturally be so, considering the messianic cultural milieu and obsession of the late Second Temple period and hence the natural inclination of many Jews to see these verses as messianic.

When we look more carefully however, there are other likely interpretations of these passages. The more traditional Jewish interpretation is that this is a reference to an idealized Israel, or to the "righteous remnant" who returned from Babylon and maintained the Mosaic Law, typified as an individual. This is consistent with the Jews

Fulfillment of Prophecy in the Life of Jesus

as a people who would serve as a "light to the Gentiles" (Is. 49:6) and spread the knowledge of God throughout the world. The reference to the "righteous remnant" within Israel is especially compelling, in light of the historical background portrayed in the book of Nehemiah, which portrays a righteous remnant intent on restoration of Jerusalem as a religious base being opposed by other Hebrews who had remained on the land during the captivity and did not share the religious idealism of the righteous remnant.

This view is bolstered by other references to who "the servant" is. *"Behold! My servant whom I uphold, my elect one in whom my soul delights! I have put my spirit upon him; he will bring forth justice to the Gentiles..."* (Is. 42:1-2). In chapter 49, the "servant" is also idealized as an individual, and it later appears that the individual described is *actually the entire nation of Israel.*

"Listen, o coastlands, to me, and take heed, you peoples from afar! The Lord has called me from the womb; from the matrix of my mother he has made mention of my name. And he has made my mouth like a sharp sword; and in the shadow of his hand he has hidden me, and made me a polished shaft; in his quiver he has hidden me.

And he said to __me__, you are my servant, __O Israel__, in whom I will be glorified. Then I said 'I have labored in vain; I have spent my strength for nothing and in vain; yet surely my just reward is with the Lord, and my work with my God.'" (Is. 49:1-4).

"And now the Lord says, who formed me from the womb to be his Servant [clearly not the pre-eternally existing, co-equal with the father, Trinitarian Christian God made flesh, who created the earth] *to bring Jacob back to him* [the function of the "righteous remnant"], *so that Israel is gathered to him (For I shall be glorious in the eyes of the Lord, and my God shall be my strength). Indeed he says, It is too small a thing that you should be my servant, to raise up the tribes of Jacob...I will give you as a light to the Gentiles, that you should be my salvation to the ends of the earth."* (Is. 49:5-6).

Chapter 49 continues with a remarkable similarity to the language of 52:12-15: *"Thus says the Lord, The redeemer of Israel, their holy one, To him whom man despises, to him whom the nation abhors, to the **servant** of rulers: Kings shall see and arise, Princes also shall* *worship..."* (Is. 49:7). This is clearly the same servant alluded to in chapter 53, and it is just as clearly the nation Israel or at least the "righteous remnant" who is abhorred by the nation and despised. These will be given *"as a covenant to the people, to restore the earth..."* (v.8). Subsequent verses depict this righteous remnant in foreign lands after "waste" and "destruction", for the land will *"even now be too small for its inhabitants; and those who swallowed you up will be far away."* (v. 19). But the Jews abroad in foreign lands will eventually prosper and *"Kings shall be your foster fathers, and queens your nursing mothers; they shall bow down to you with their faces to the earth, and lick up the dust of your feet."* (49:23). This is strikingly similar to the language of 52:13-15; *"He shall be exalted and extolled and be very high...So shall he sprinkle many nations* [light or blessing to the Gentiles], *kings shall shut their mouths at him..."*

If these passages clearly refer to the righteous remnant of Israel, or the nation of Israel, what is the justification of reading Isaiah chapter 53 (or more exactly 52:13 to the end of chapter 53) as something different? Why isn't the typified, idealized individual, Israel, who is often idealized in the Old Testament as a person and referred to as a "he", not also seen as the subject of these passages? This is clearly the only reasonable interpretation of this passage.

But what about the apparent references to resurrection. We must remember the same resurrection analogy arises famously in Ezekiel chapter 37 — expressly referring to the resurrection of the nation Israel from its ruins after the Babylonian destruction.

As to the apparent factual similarities, a more likely explanation is that the Gospel accounts, written decades after the death of Jesus, tend to portray an idealized account of his death that are heavily influenced and shaded by biblical passages, such as this one, and such as the "Shepherd" portions of Zechariah, chapters 11-13, passages which in the Second Temple messianic milieu came to be seen as messianic. This is the old story of the person walking in the woods that keeps noticing arrows fired right in the middle of circles drawn on the trees. No arrows have missed their marks. He finds it remarkable that anyone is such a good archer that he hits the mark every time. But then he comes upon a person drawing circles around arrows *already* fired into the trees! Anything can be *read into* an account if the order of events appears to be prescribed beforehand by divine pre-ordination.

Jesus Rides into Jerusalem on a Donkey

"Behold, your king is coming to you...lowly and riding on a donkey, a colt, the foal of a donkey... '(Zechariah 9:9)

Response: According to the Gospel accounts this was a deliberately staged event

We even see the above described attempt to deliberately fulfill prophecy happening in the Gospel accounts themselves. Jesus makes his triumphal entry into Jerusalem riding on a donkey. Christians still use this as an example of fulfillment of prophecy. *"Behold, your king is coming to you...lowly and riding on a donkey, a colt, the foal of a donkey... '*(Zechariah 9:9). But in the Gospel, Jesus tells his disciples directly and specifically to go and fetch a donkey so he can ride into town on it! (Matthew 21:1-7). How much of a "fulfillment of prophecy" is this? If he had arrived on a lightning bolt it might have been spectacular. As it is, it is a very deliberate and calculated fulfillment which really has no value as predictive fulfillment, since anyone can fetch a donkey and ride on it.

Sold for thirty pieces of silver—Zechariah 11:13

"Then I said to them, if it is agreeable to you, give me my wages; and if not refrain. So they weighed out for my wages thirty pieces of silver. And the Lord said to me, 'Throw it to the potter' — that princely price they set on me. So I took the thirty pieces of silver and threw them into the house of the Lord for the potter." (Zech. 11:12-13.)

So likewise, the idealized "Shepherd of the Lord" in Zechariah chapter 11, who despises the obsession with riches and commercialism of Israel's present shepherds, is rejected by the nation and angrily asks for his wages, which they value at thirty pieces of silver, which in turn is "[thrown] to the potter — that princely price they set on me."(Zech. 11:13). Naturally, in the Gospel accounts, Jesus the "good shepherd" must clear the moneychangers from the temple and later Judas betrays

Jesus in return for thirty pieces of silver. This sum ends up being used to buy a potter's field - a mixture of deliberate fulfillment, such as Jesus' Danielesque "time of visitation" or the ostentatious riding of a donkey into Jerusalem the week of Passover in fulfillment of Zechariah 9:9, and a memory and recording of events framed by prophetic guidelines.

In Matthew, a remorseful Judas returns the thirty pieces of silver to the temple, then went and hanged himself. The chief priests did not want the *blood money* in the temple treasury so they used it to buy *"the potter's filed, to bury strangers in. Therefore that field has been called the Field of Blood to this day."*(Matt. 27:3-8). The author then goes on to inform us *'Then was fulfilled what was spoken by Jeremiah* (sic) *the prophet, saying 'And they took the thirty pieces of silver, the value of him who was priced, whom they of the children of Israel priced, and gave them for the potter's field."*(27:9). In addition to a very loose and errant translation, since it was Zechariah and not *they* (the children of Israel) who gave it to the potter's field, the author is also obviously confused, since he quoted Zechariah 11:13, but referred to Jeremiah. At Jeremiah 32:6-9 there is an account of Jeremiah buying a field in order to show a confidence in the future, but he buys it for *seventeen* shekels of silver, not thirty, and the passage is nothing like the wording quoted.

Now curiously, and embarrassingly for the Christian apologists, the author of the Gospel of Luke has no knowledge of this incident of such purported prophetic fulfillment. In Acts chapter one, Judas used the thirty pieces of silver to buy a field *"and falling headlong, he burst open in the middle and all his entrails gushed out. And it became known to all those dwelling in Jerusalem, so that the field is called in their own language, Akel Dama, that is Field of Blood"* (Acts 1:18-19). At least they agree as to the name of the field, and that it was purchased by the thirty pieces of silver. It was not given to the temple for the potter, nor used to purchase a burial place for strangers; Judas did not hang himself; and just where does "the potter" fit in anyway? So much for this fulfillment of prophecy. However, as a choice example of the imaginativeness of Bible proponents, the genuinely magnificent explanation has been given that Judas *did* buy the field, and then he *did* hang himself, but then the rope broke and he fell down the side of a cliff and his insides gushed out (Depending on your point of view this gem may come under the heading 'The glory of the human imagination", or "The hermeneutics of lunacy." You decide the best title. In any event, it is a choice and fortuitous parenthesis to end a discussion of the fulfillment of prophecy in the life of Jesus).

Chapter Six

FAILED BIBLE PROPHECIES

One of the most effective tools for evangelistic ministry has been the claim that is made as to the Bible's purported perfect record for fulfillment of prophecy. The argument is made that biblical prophecies have *always* proven true, unlike any other book in the world. The argument usually is made that the only one that can accurately predict the future is one that can control the future to ensure what happens. The only one that can completely control the future any time he chooses is God. This is the proof that God has written, or at least inspired, the Bible. All other claimed holy books, say Bible proponents, contain failed prophecies. Since only the Bible is inspired by God, only the Bible's prophecies are correct 100% of the time. Naturally some leeway is given for prophecies that have not yet been fulfilled. But future prophecies, especially those interpreted as "end times" prophecies are emphasized because of the Bible's claimed perfect track record. Prophecy seminars are always a popular, well-attended attraction for the faithful in evangelical churches. Prophecy Bible studies, especially in the book of Revelation, are also a popular draw. There is no lack of fascination with biblical eschatology, the study of the end times, in evangelical churches.

To write a chapter on *failed* biblical prophecies would seem to be a useful and necessary counterweight to balance these claims. However, it is one that comes with an abundance of prefaces as to some obvious problems inherent in the endeavor. It is necessary to review the literary territory first before we can commence. Finding obviously failed biblical prophecies, by the very nature of the endeavor, should not be terribly easy. This is so because of several problems, which we must first appreciate.

Biblical Editing

First, and most obviously, even conservative biblical proponents will admit there is editing of the Bible, at least the Old Testament, across centuries. Moses did not write of his own death in Deuteronomy — the ever useful Joshua, we are told, edited and added this. Being God's anointed successor he was entitled to add to a document inspired word for word by God to Moses, despite Deuteronomy's own curse on all who would add to or detract from the words of the book (Deut. 4:2). Since there is an editing process, we would expect that any prophecy that did not come true can be spotted and be edited out. Why would an obviously failed prophecy be kept in the Bible? The prophet's very failure would mean he was not a prophet and so he would not be one of the Bible's prophets that we would be reading today. The Bible itself harshly rejects any prophet who prophecies falsely: *"...when a prophet speaks in the name of the Lord, if the thing does not happen to come to pass, that is the thing which the Lord has not spoken; the prophet has spoken it presumptuously; you shall not be afraid of him."* (Deut. 18:22). In point of fact the penalty for a false prophecy was to be put to death: *"But the prophet who presumes to speak a word in my name...that prophet shall die"*(Deut. 18:20). With such a strict standard we should naturally only *expect* to see *fulfilled* prophecies in the Bible. This is the first reality we face.

Functionally Conditional Prophecies

But we have a second obstacle to claiming the term *failed* prophecy. This is the phenomenon, although Bible proponents vehemently reject the idea, of God changing his mind and *repenting* of proposed actions, or of relenting from carrying out his stated and *prophesied* plans. Many Bible proponents are emphatic that God *cannot* and *will not* by his very nature as God ever change his mind, just as he is incapable of regretting action he has taken, or of repenting. The Bible proponent will recite fervently the verse *"God is not a man, that he should lie, nor a son of man, that he should repent* [or change his mind, which as every evangelist knows is at least the translation of *repent* from New Testament Greek]. *Has he not said, and he will not do? Or has he not spoken and he will not make it good?"*(Numbers 23:19, according to

Balaam's oracle to Balak, king of Moab regarding the blessing God had ordered for Israel). Thousands of volumes have been written over the issue of God changing his mind or not, of the concept of divine impassivity, and the concept of divine predetermination of events versus randomness and human decision-making in history, and of the related issue of predestination versus free will. I would not dare dwell on these issues at this time, except that the Bible *does* clearly demonstrate that God can relent (or repent, to use biblical jargon) and change his plans to avert events that God has already inspired his prophets to foretell, which relates to failed prophecies. We will deal with the complications of the issue of divine omniscience later.

The most obvious example is that of the prophet Jonah, who is the most classic example of failed biblical prophecy, the fierce protests of Bible proponents to one side. Jonah prophesied the doom of ancient Nineveh, against his own will and inclinations, at the insistent and express demands of God. The wording of his prophecy of doom is unconditional and unequivocal.

The destruction prophesied did not come to pass. But that doesn't count, say the bible proponents — Nineveh repented, and God will always have mercy upon one who repents. That was the very purpose of God's mission to Jonah — to bring about repentance. Some others will go a step further: God, in his infinite foreknowledge and omniscience, *knew* that Nineveh would repent, so God knew he would never bring the destruction to pass. So what about God's declarations that they would come to pass? Were those lies or the truth?

So the issue then is that God's prophecies are sometimes conditional, even when not stated to be such, and so conceivably not prophecies at all, unless we term them *conditional* prophecies, i.e., threats. The texts often leave nothing to indicate that the prophecies are conditional. About the middle of the eighth century B.C., the prophet Micah prophesied doom and destruction to the nation of Judah because of the sins and greed of its leaders. *"Zion for your sake shall be plowed as a field and Jerusalem shall become heaps of ruins, and the mountain of the temple like the bare hills of the forest"* (Micah 3:12). He was one of the first of a series of prophets to do so. The strength of a prophecy would seem to be the fulfillment within the lifetime of the hearer. And indeed, such a destruction did come to pass

— but in 587 B.C., over 150-170 years later —approximately the time period from the present to the American Civil War or the Mexican War. A prophecy made for America's destruction made at the time of the Civil War might seem like something far-fetched, grasping, and desperate. Compounded with this, we have almost all subsequent prophets, as well as those in the Northern Kingdom, consistently prophesying doom of their kingdoms, generation after generation. It would seem to be just a matter of time until they are right, although we could just as correctly say that as to each generation, they are failed prophecies. What is significant, however, is the explanation given that Israel continued to repent, and therefore put off its destruction. The reigns of Hezekiah and Josiah are the most significant cases in point. Josiah's reforms and return to righteousness leads to God expressly exempting him from destruction during his lifetime, but with a promise of destruction during the lifetimes of his heirs.

Vaticinium Ex Eventu—Prophecy After the Fact

The third reality we must confront is the phenomenon of *vaticinium ex eventu* — purported prophecies made before events which in fact were written long after the events, and sometimes pseudonymously, by those claiming to be the prophet writing. At first glance this would seem to us preposterous, but such activity has a long religious history, leading even the present time. In the present day and age, alleged prophecy has continued within and without religious circles. The most famous of recent times involve the prophecies of Fatima — or to be exact, those associated with "Our Lady of Fatima", the appearances of the Blessed Virgin in Fatima, Portugal in 1917. The Blessed Virgin was claimed to have appeared to three children. The oldest child, Lucia Santos, then only ten, became the virtual spokesperson for all three. Within the next two years the two other children died of the flu epidemic, leaving Lucia the only witness to conversations with the Blessed Virgin — "Our Lady of Fatima." [1]Many in the crowd that gathered on the day of the last appearance had claimed to have seen phenomena related to the sun, but only Lucia, and presumably the other two children, had heard the Blessed Virgin speak. There had been prophecies uttered to Lucia by the Blessed Virgin. Among the prophecies spoken by the Blessed Virgin, and told to the world by Lucia Santos, was the rise of communism in Russia and World War II. These prophecies would seem rather astounding. But when was the world told of these prophecies? It was in *1941!* Now *that* is astounding! It does not seem at all difficult to predict the rise of the Soviet Union and World War II in 1941. But of course the point is that Lucia Santos said that the Blessed Virgin had told her these things *in 1917!* This is not all. Even more astoundingly, the Blessed Virgin granted Lucia Santos the privilege of a vision of the attempted assassination of Pope John Paul II, which occurred in 1981. When did she have the vision? In 1917 of course. When did she report this to the world? In 1997! Lucia's visions have been validated and authenticated by the Roman Catholic Church. Lucia herself has been beatified while still alive, a very rare occurrence, which is the last step before sainthood. She was staunchly admired by the late Pope John Paul II, who was a dedicated devotee of Our Lady of Fatima. Curiously, previous to her visitation by the Blessed Virgin, Lucia was known as the town fibber, and had previous alleged paranormal encounters with angelic beings which were regarded as fanciful, and she was known to dream of sainthood. After the visions, she was virtually locked away in convents, and continued to have frequent encounters with "the Lady", who appeared to her at random, but these encounters were hidden from the public, who were led to believe that the only appearances of the Virgin had been those of Fatima in 1917. It is ironic that the late Mother Theresa, an intelligent, learned, and dedicated servant of mankind, is precluded and damned from ever receiving sainthood because of her honesty in revealing her doubts about her faith, and even the existence of God, but that a person who was considered a liar by her own relatives and neighbors, and exhibited symptoms of classic schizophrenia, is made a saint.

This is an example of *vaticinium ex eventu* (assuming that you are convinced that Lucia did not genuinely receive the prophecies in 1917, as she claimed). Why is the above history important? Because even though the above history of Lucia Santos leaves Bible Christians howling derisively with laughter at what they see as the stupidity of Roman Catholicism, Bible Christians have their own Lucia Santos'. One of them is the "prophet" Daniel in the Old Testament, upon whom

Failed Bible Prophecies

much of their eschatology depends. A review of this book of the Old Testament is in order not because its characteristics are exclusive, but because it is illustrative of the practice of prophecy after the fact in the Bible.

We would expect that with the preceding three techniques, or safeguards in place — biblical editing, the propensity to view prophecies as conditional after the fact if not fulfilled, and prophecies after the fact packaged to look like prior documents, that we would find no obvious failures at all. Yet in the prime example of prophecy after the fact, we will find a record of failure. Only if you dare, let us go for a wild ride on the "prophet" Daniel's time machine.

A Wild Ride on Daniel's Time Machine — through the past, present and future

There is a Canaanite site that bears the name *Danel*. In the book of Ezekiel, which is from the period of early captivity, a certain Daniel is referred to as a very righteous person, along with Noah and Job (Ezekiel 14:4; 28:3), so there was a wise person or legend from Jewish history known as Daniel, who is depicted as the author of the Old Testament book in his name. Now the setting of Daniel is as follows. Daniel was supposedly taken captive as a very young man or boy from Jerusalem during the second deportation of Hebrews to Babylon in 597 B.C. He serves, along with other young Hebrews, as a servant in the royal court, and rises to be known as an esteemed prophet and counselor to the king. There are two parts to the book one details various stories in the life of Daniel, wherein he suffers for his dedication to his faith, and the second part where Daniel has, or interprets, visions and dreams, thereby becoming a prophet per se. His life as a prophet, and hence the writings, scan a period from shortly after his captivity until the time of the conquest of Babylon by Persia and the subsequent liberation of the Jews from captivity by the Persian Emperor Cyrus in 538 B.C. Therefore, the Bible proponents believe that this book and its prophecies date to the sixth century B.C.

Much research has been done on the book of Daniel. It would be fair to say that all reasonable biblical scholars, without exception, date the book of Daniel to the mid-second century, clearly within the late

Second Temple period. Robert Driver [2] has thoroughly reviewed and undermined the traditional view of the Bible proponents and his work is highly recommended. The book of Daniel is written in two languages. The opening portion is written in Hebrew, but it quickly switches to Aramaic, which is the common language of Second Temple Judaism. It is the language of the return from captivity. And the Aramaic is the Aramaic of the late Second Temple period as spoken in Israel, not that of Babylon in the sixth century B.C. It is interspersed with Greek words and constructions, even the names of the musical instruments used, which did not exist in Israel until well into the Second Temple period. Neither would Babylon have had access to the Greek names of musical instruments in the sixth century B.C.

Israel came under Alexander the Great's rule in 331 B.C. Thereafter it remained under the rule of Alexander's successor empires — the Hellenic Egyptian Ptomelaic empire and the Hellenic Seleucid empire ruled from Syria. More than just in political association, Israel became increasingly Hellenized, and the common Greek language, *Koine Greek,* became the language of the eastern Mediterranean, and also a common language of Israel. *Koine Greek* is a dialect distinct from Classical Greek, which arose in the Hellenized world after the time of Alexander the Great spread his Macedonian Empire throughout the Mideast and Mediterranean. This language would not, and could not, have been known or spoken in sixth century B.C. Babylon, the setting of Daniel. Linguistically, this is a work that *could not* have been written before 300 B.C. As we will see, the actual writing can be almost pinpointed with accuracy. So the book of Daniel is not written by any Daniel of the sixth century B.C. Someone borrowed the identity and composed a fictional account set in sixth century Babylon. It is genuinely "pseudo-Daniel" who gives us this account.

The book of Daniel is very important to Christians. Together with Revelation and Jesus' Olivet Discourse, it forms a definitive eschatology of the end times and the coming of the Kingdom of God to earth under Christ. Daniel presumably tells the future history of the world and the coming of the Kingdom of God, the Ancient of Days, and of the majestic "son of man", to commence an eternal rule of righteousness over mankind. And yet at the outset we see that Daniel is a very poor historian. He describes the succession of kings during the captivity of the Jews. He describes them as Nebuchadnezzar; then Belshazzar, son of Nebuchadnezzar, who reigned until the conquest of Babylon, that according to Daniel was accomplished by Darius the Mede, who is stated as being the son of Ahasueras, the Persian Emperor. Darius was succeeded by the Emperor Cyrus of Persia. We know that in fact Nebuchadnezzar was succeeded by Evil-Merodoch, followed by Neriglassar, followed by Nabonidus, followed by Belshazzar (the son of Nabonidus, not Nebuchadnezzar), who was the king at the time of the Persian conquest of Babylon by Cyrus. Many of Daniel's descriptions of Nebuchadnezzar are actually events from the life of Nabonidus. So although Daniel purports to present us with no less grandiose a task than the future history of the world, he seems to be very weak on the history of what is supposedly his own times. This is the equivalent, in modern terms, of a person reciting the order of recent presidents of the United States and saying Kennedy, Nixon, and Clinton (and leaving Clinton as the current president). What would you think of the political sagacity of such a person? You would certainly question the person's political awareness and would not expect any useful political knowledge or wisdom from such a person. And yet such a person, Daniel, purports to foretell the political future when he does not even know the present. And the world view of thousands of otherwise intelligent Christians is informed in part by his prognostications.

    A favorite of evangelical end of times devotees is the story of Nebuchadnezzar's statue dream in chapter 2. Nebuchadnezzar has had a troubling dream and he seeks someone who will tell him what the dream was and give the interpretation of it. Daniel is able to do both. Nebuchadnezzar has dreamed of a huge, magnificent image. The image's head was of gold, the chest and arms were of silver, its belly and thighs were of bronze, its legs were of iron, and its feet were partly of iron and partly of clay. *Then "a stone was cut without hands, which struck the image on its feet of iron and clay, and broke them in pieces."* Then all of the elements in the image were crushed together and became like chaff from a threshing floor and the wind carried them away. *"And the stone that struck the image became a great mountain and filled the whole earth"* (2:34-35). Daniel interprets this dream as outlining the future empires that would rule the world, with Babylon, Nebuchadnezzar, being the head of gold. Each successive empire would be inferior. Very significantly, *"the fourth kingdom shall be as strong of iron, inasmuch as iron breaks in pieces and shatters everything; and like iron that crushes, that kingdom will break in pieces and crush all the others. Whereas you saw the feet and toes, partly of potter's clay and partly of iron, so that kingdom shall be divided; yet the strength of the iron shall be in it, just as you saw the iron mixed with ceramic clay"* (2:40-41). So the fourth kingdom would be originally as strong as iron but would become weakened when it is figuratively divided and mixed with clay. This kingdom is replaced when *"the God of heaven will set up a kingdom which will never be destroyed; and the kingdom shall not be left to other people; it will break in pieces and consume all these kingdoms and it shall stand forever."*(3:44) This is explained as the stone made without hands which destroyed all these other elements.

Now these four kingdoms, or empires, are described again in Daniel, chapter 7, in the context of a vision. In chapter 7 they appear as animals, and undoubtedly correspond to the same world kingdoms of chapter 2. The first, corresponding to Babylon, was a lion with wings of an eagle. The second beast was a bear with three ribs in its mouth. The third empire was represented as a leopard with four wings and four heads. The fourth, as in chapter 2, receives the greatest emphasis and its role is described in almost the exact, same words. This beast is *"dreadful and terrible, exceedingly strong. It had huge iron teeth; it was devouring, breaking in pieces, and trampling the residue within its feet. It was different from all the beasts that were before it, and it had ten horns. I was considering the horns, and there was another horn, a little one, coming up among them, before whom three of the first horns were plucked out by the roots. And there, in this horn, were eyes like the eyes of a man, and a mouth speaking pompous words."*(7:7-8). After this reign, according to Daniel, comes the Ancient of Days, whose eternal kingdom destroys the fourth beast - the fourth empire. It shall be ushered in by *"One like the Son of Man, coming with the clouds of heaven! He came to the Ancient of Days, and they brought him near before him. Then to him was given dominion and glory and a kingdom."*(7:13-14). This kingdom "shall not pass away."This kingdom is unquestionably the same as the stone not cut by hands that establishes its kingdom on the earth in chapter 2. So the representations of both of these chapters must be taken into consideration to interpret the identity of the empires.

The identity of these four kingdoms is crucial to the Christian eschatology. The first is stated as Babylon, seen as the contemporaneous kingdom of sixth century Daniel; the second, that of silver, is interpreted as that of the Medo-Persian Empire; the third, of bronze, as the Greek Empire of Alexander the Great; and the fourth as the Roman Empire. The mixture of iron and clay is the divided kingdom of the later Roman Empire, divided after Diocletian and increasingly weak and unstable. Daniel is given credit in this interpretation with, among other things, having foreseen prophetically the rise of the Roman Empire. In this scenario, this empire is replaced by the coming of the Kingdom of God to reign on earth. But what of the fact that the Roman Empire, at least in the west, was dissolved in 476 A.D., and even the eastern empire, in Byzantium, fell to the Muslims Turks in 1453? To the Christian fundamentalists the answer is easy — the Roman Empire will be reconstituted, only to be replaced by the Second Coming of Christ and the institution of the eternal kingdom. Hence, the intense interest in the Treaty of Rome that created the European Monetary Union, seen as the precursor of such a reconstituted Roman Empire. To follow along in this nonsense, Cardinal Ratzinger, now Pope Benedict XVI, is sometimes cited as the false prophet of Revelation, who will assist the rise of a worldwide anti-Christ, who will rule this demonic world super state. To many, the news is incessantly searched for any tidbit to be interpreted into this end times scenario. Many seriously think that Barack "Hussein" Obama, supposedly a closet Muslim, is in fact the biblical anti-Christ.

But what if their interpretation of the order of the empires is not correct? What if there is another interpretation of the succession of empires? What if Daniel did not foresee the Roman Empire? More in point, what if the fourth empire was not Rome, but really pseudo-Daniel's contemporary world empire of Greece, by the third and second centuries B.C. divided into competing sub-empires under the generals of Alexander the Great? In fact, this is what can be clearly demonstrated, and not by liberal Bible critics, but rather by credentialed, conservative Bible scholar, John H. Walton. In "The Four

Kingdoms of Daniel" in *The Journal of the Evangelical Theological Society*, v. 29, N.1, p.25 (March 1985), Walton has carefully reviewed the arguments on behalf of the Roman Empire and the Macedonian Greek Empire as being the fourth empire. His conclusions, drawn heavily on research from Robert Gurney [3], are very convincing and incontrovertible.

One of the most glaring errors in the Christian view is the omission of the Median Empire from the four empire scheme. What did other non-biblical contemporary sources see as the succession of recent empires? Herodotus, writing in the fifth century B.C., described preceding world empires as the Assyrians, *the Medes*, and the Persians. Polybius, writing later, cited Assyria, *Media*, Persia and Macedonia. The fourth Sibyl, like *Daniel*, was a Jewish document dating from about 140 B.C. It cites the four world empires as Assyria, *Media*, Persia, and Macedonia. This would have been exactly the same view of history embraced by Daniel's Jewish audience to whom the prophecies were addressed and who were meant to interpret and understand them. Without exception, all historical accounts view the Median Empire as a principle world empire to be counted in any succession of world empires. That Daniel's account would not include Media after Babylon and before Persia is practically impossible and not realistic. But the Christian view has merged Media with Persia as the "Medo-Persian" Empire, whereas the consolidation was later than the earlier Median Empire itself, which deserved and always received its own standing in history. Only the self-serving Christian *interpretation* of Daniel ignores this and proceeds as though it didn't exist. Once again, we see a quick sleight of hand which skips over a significant piece of history to obtain a pre-conceived result. So the second empire in Daniel chapter 2 and 7, is Media; the third is Persia; and the fourth is the Macedonian Greek Empire of Alexander the Great and his successor empires. But this is not all.

In Daniel chapter 7, the second beast, the bear, has three ribs in his mouth. There is no explanation for the three ribs in the Christian view. But in Jeremiah 51:27-29, three nations came against Babylon along with the Medes — whom he describes as Ararat, Minni, and Ashkenaz. Significantly, exactly as in Daniel, after Nebuchadnezzar, Media began to impinge on the Neo-Babylonian Empire. And as with a bear, the Median Empire was slow and ponderous, especially in comparison with its successor, the Persians. The Persians, the third beast, are depicted as a fast-moving leopard with four wings, representing the four corners of the world, in other worlds representing a more genuinely worldwide empire, and four heads, representing four Persian kings - four who dominated during the height of Persian expansion.

Now here is a point of contention regarding who the four heads represent. In the Christian view, the four heads represent the four generals of Alexander the Great that after his death divided the empire. However, the four generals of Alexander represent dilution, division and dissolution of power, closer to the divided power - and the union of iron and clay - seen in the feet of the image in Daniel chapter 2; whereas the four heads of the leopard represent strength. Also, the fourth empire of Daniel starts as solid iron in chapter 2's image and later is diluted and divided into a union of iron with clay. This subsequent dissolution closely resembles what happened to Alexander's single, powerful empire stretching from the Mediterranean to India later collapsing into smaller, warring empires that could not cohere.

Further, the fact that the four heads represent four Persian kings is confirmed later in Daniel 11:2. Writing in the time of "Darius the Mede", whom the author portrays as a Persian king, Daniel says, *"And now I will tell you the truth. Behold, three more kings will arise in Persia, and the fourth shall be far richer than them all; by his strength, through his riches, he shall stir up all against the realm of Greece."* These are undoubtedly the same four kings represented by the four heads of the leopard in Daniel chapter 7. Hence the third beast, and the third empire, is Persia, not the Greek Empire of Alexander.

We have not yet reviewed the information on the fourth empire in these two chapters of Daniel. When we do, we find even further confirmation that the fourth empire described is that of Greece, and not Rome. The greatest attention is given to this empire. The fourth empire is "different from the others" and is more powerful than all the others. It is iron that destroys and shatters all before it. The empire created by the rapid conquests of Alexander the Great as a world historical event clearly fulfills this role. Even today, this empire is remembered much more than the Persian or Assyrian and Neo-Babylonian Empire.

It is "different from the others" because it is western. The same could not be said for Rome, which was also westernized and during most of its history also Hellenized and increasingly centered on the Greek, Hellenized eastern part of its empire (hence, not "different" from its predecessor). Even more convincingly, in Daniel the *fourth empire crushed the first three.* Greece conquered Babylon, Media, and Persia. But Rome did not conquer these three areas. The famous defeats of Crassus and Mark Antony when they attempted to move east against the Parthian Empire forever attest to this failure (In point of fact, Trajan did extend the Roman Empire all the way to the Persian Gulf for approximately twenty years, but did not conquer Persia. However, this brief, incomplete interlude, years after the golden age of Augustus, would not justify the claims made for the fourth empire).

But what of the ten horns of the last beast? Does this fit with the Greek Empire? They do. Alexander's four generals were not successful at holding their territories intact. By the late third century B.C. (close, as we shall see, to the time of writing) there were ten independent states existing within what was Alexander's empire. In chapter 7, Antiochus Epiphanes, the nemesis and persecutor of the Jews and their religion, is unquestionably seen as the pompous little horn, the tenth horn. This horn is said to have defeated three other horns. This corresponds entirely with Antiochus the Great, Antiochus Epiphanes' father, having conquered Cappadocia and Armenia, and having acquired Palestine from the Ptolemaic kingdom in Egypt.

Even more express, the pompous little horn of chapter 7 is undoubtedly the exact, same "little horn" of chapter 8:9. In chapter 8, a male goat "came from the west, swept across the whole earth, without touching the ground..." and destroys a ram. The goat has a large horn, which was broken and four horns grew in its place. The one "little horn" grew great toward the south and east and *"exalted himself as high as the Prince of the Host, and by him the daily sacrifices were taken away, and the place of his sanctuary was cast down"* (v8:11). Lest there be the slightest bit of doubt, the Scripture tells us that the ram is the kings of Media and Persia and the goat is Greece. "The large horn between its eyes is the first king. As for the broken horn and the four little horns that shall arise in its place, four kingdoms shall arise out of that nation, but not with its power"(v.22). So the Bible itself identifies the little horn as Antiochus Epiphanes, and the little horn is unquestionably a part of the fourth kingdom, or empire, in chapter 7. So the fourth empire is the Greek in chapter 7, and therefore chapter 2 also. We shall see the reign of Antiochus Epiphanes as contemporary with the writing.

So unquestionably, the fourth kingdom is Greece, not Rome. Not only did Daniel not foresee the Roman Empire, he only wrote about contemporary events at his time — the mid-second century, the time of the persecution of Antiochus Epiphanes and the revolt of the Maccabees. More importantly, the Greek Empire came to an end and the Kingdom of God did not come — only another human empire came, and went. Unless, Christians might ingeniously add, it is *the Greek* Empire that will be reconstituted, and then Christ will return. But then, what of the Roman Empire missing from the scheme, and not mentioned as coming in between? How do you explain that when the very point of the prophecy is that the fourth world empire is the last one and will be replaced by the Kingdom of God? Did we lose 500 years or more of history somewhere? Can such a large event in history be neglected? We are getting into even more far-fetched territory. The result of this inquiry is clear — this is plain and simply a failed prophecy. The Greek empire, the fourth empire, was to be replaced by the *Kingdom of God*, not by the *Roman* Empire. There was to be no other world empire in between. Daniel is no prophet at all. But we will see that this is not the only failure of Daniel. The story continues, but Daniel has somewhat more success as he records the history of his own days as they unfold, falsely purporting it to be prophecy.

As will see by the close parallel with its contemporaneous history, which will be demonstrated herein, the events surrounding the writing of Daniel is the time of the Maccabean Revolt. Antiochus Epiphanes attempted to conquer the Ptolemaic Empire in Egypt in 168 B.C. He was rebuffed and humiliated by the threat of Roman power. While he was returning from Egypt, Israel revolted. Antiochus Epiphanes exercised his wrath against Israel, banning the temple sacrifices (the "abomination of desolation", referred to in Jesus' end times Olivet Discourse, and hence a principle landmark in Christian eschatology since it is believed that this will occur again), banning circumcision, and requiring Jews to worship pagan gods and eat pork. The result was a Jewish revolt led by the Maccabeus family, which in 164 B.C. liberated Jerusalem and restored the temple cult. Soon thereafter an independent nation of Israel was virtually acknowledged by the Seleucid Empire.

The author of Daniel carefully follows these events through the prism of several successive visions, all of which describe current events and give prophecies as to where these events will supposedly lead. We have several prophecies with successively more, and differing details, because the details changed as events unfolded in a manner different from the manner prophesied in the previous vision. What we have is after the fact fine-tuning of prophecy. So the result is a series of overlapping visions with conspicuously different and conflicting details. In chapter 7, the vision of the four beasts, God arrives and kills the pompous tenth little horn, who has persecuted the Jews, Antiochus Epiphanes. There is no mention of his banning of the temple cult, which occurred in December, 167, B.C., so this account was presumably written in 168, after his arrival from the Egypt campaign and before the attack on the temple cult. This was when the suffering of Israel began and the author predicted "three years and a half" or "three times and a half" of suffering until the arrival of the Kingdom, when God would kill Antiochus Epiphanes. This would bring the death of Antiochus Epiphanes and the liberation of Israel in mid-164 B.C.

So Daniel had another vision in chapter 8, which modified the period of suffering. New visions were necessary to the author because by mid-164 Antiochus was not dead, and the persecution and suffering were not over. So it was necessary that God and his angels got to work again to supply some more visions. So the new vision in chapter 8 clearly identifies Antiochus Epiphanes as the little horn that *"exalted himself as high as the Prince of the Host, and by him the daily sacrifices were taken away, and the place of his sanctuary was cast down"*(8:9). He predicted that the desecration of the temple would last 2300 days,*"then the sanctuary shall be cleansed."*(8:14). This would be a bit over six years from December, 167 B.C. or until mid-161 B.C. In fact the temple was "cleansed" and the temple cult restored in Chislev (December) 163, celebrated ever since by the feast of Hanukah. So some further work had yet to be done. Not one to allow angels to sleep on the job, the author of Daniel puts the angels to work again. In chapter 9, the angel Gabriel arrives to tell Daniel that "half a week", that is half a "week of years", or three and a half years, remain from the ending of the temple cult, which would bring liberation in the middle of 163. So the suffering was shortened by two years from one vision to the other. [4]

In chapter 11, a most amazing chapter, Daniel is supposedly given a lengthy vision of very detailed and accurate history, much more so than any other purported prophecy in the Bible. Other than stating proper names in a symbolic or coded fashion, it reads like a standard work of history. It starts with the empire of Alexander the Great, its subsequent division, and the events that followed as they concern the nation Israel. Israel is a part of the Ptolemaic Empire, then of the Seleucid, then the "King of the North" (Antiochus Epiphanes) attempts to defeat the "King of the South", the Ptolemaic king, is turned back, and begins persecuting the saints and desecrating the temple. The saints resist and a war commences. This exact same history can be read in any history of the period, in the historian Josephus, or in the book of I Maccabees in the Jewish Apocrypha. This history provided by Daniel is very accurate in describing the period of Antiochus Epiphanes and the Maccabean revolt except for the very end of the history, regarding the future and the end of Antiochus Epiphanes. He predicted that Antiochus would return and conquer Egypt, which he did not, and effectively *could not,* do because of Roman power, and he predicted that he would turn eastwards and northwards and in Syria be defeated by Michael the Archangel. He created a new time line — 1,290 days (three and a half years again), which seems to be lengthened immediately thereafter to 1,335 days, to final liberation. Antiochus Epiphanes in fact died of a sickness, and was not killed in a battle with Michael the Archangel, and he died in 164, not mid-165. So once again, even with post-event editing and sloppy *vaticinium ex eventu* - prophecy after the fact, we have failed prophecy. "Daniel" is no prophet. He is a failed prophet and cannot correctly teach us the past, the present or the future. He does however unwittingly teach us of one thing — he teaches us what the word *sheister* means for all times. And yet thousands have formed their view of our world and of the future from the pen of this charlatan and fake.

Egypt would suffer Depopulation and Captivity for Forty Years

In the Bible there are multiple prophecies concerning the fates of other nations, in particular the enemies of Israel. They are usually prophecies of doom. One of the most common is that Egypt will not only be conquered by its enemies, but that the entire nation will be taken into exile, much as happened to Israel, and that in fact it land shall be completely depopulated for forty years. Through the prophet Jeremiah, God was angry with the Jews who had migrated to Egypt after the capture of Jerusalem. God predicts that Nebuchadnezzar will capture Egypt. *"When he comes, he shall strike the land of Egypt and deliver to death those appointed for death, and to captivity those appointed for captivity, and to the sword those appointed for the sword. I will kindle a fire in the houses of the gods of Egypt and will carry them away captive...He shall also break the sacred pillars of Beth Shemesh* (literally, the House of the Sun, in On)*that are in the land of Egypt, and the houses of the gods of the Egyptians he shall burn with fire"* (43:11-13). Later Jeremiah writes, *"'As I live', says the King, whose name is the Lord of hosts, 'Surely as Tabor is among the mountains and as Carmel is by the sea, so shall he come. O you daughter dwelling in Egypt, prepare yourself to go into captivity! For Noph* (Memphis) *shall be laid waste and desolate, without inhabitant'"* (46:18-19). All Egypt will be delivered into the hands of its enemies, Babylon, *"but afterward it shall be inhabited as in the days of old."*(v. 26). Jeremiah actually goes to Egypt to set up some rocks and piled them on the pavement in front of a house of pharaoh in the town of Tehaphnehes, where the Jews resided, to symbolize that the Babylonians would "set his throne upon these stones that I have hid"(43:9-10). He prophesied the destruction of the Jewish community in Egypt (chapter 44).

The prophet Ezekiel is even more severe in his prophecy concerning Egypt. *"And the land of Egypt shall become desolate and waste...I will make the land of Egypt utterly waste and desolate, from Migdol to Syene, as far as the border of Ethiopia. Neither foot of man shall pass through it nor foot of beast shall pass through it and it shall be uninhabited **forty years...her cities shall be desolate forty years**; and I will scatter the Egyptians among the nations and disperse them throughout the countries. Yet says the Lord God, '**At the end of forty*** *years I will gather the Egyptians from the peoples among whom they were scattered. I will bring back the captives of Egypt and cause them to return to the land of Pathros, to the land of their origin... '"* (Ezekiel 29:9-14).

"'From Migdol to Syene [all Egypt] those within her shall fall by the sword', says the Lord God. 'They shall be desolate in the midst of the desolate countries, and her cities shall be in the midst of the cities that are laid waste. Then they will know that I am the Lord, when I have set a fire in Egypt and all her helpers are destroyed'"...(Ezekiel 30:6-8)

"Thus says the Lord God: 'I will also make a multitude of Egypt to cease by the hand of Nebuchadnezzar king of Babylon...They shall draw their swords against Egypt, and fill the land with the slain. I will make the rivers dry, and sell the land into the hand of the wicked; I will make the land waste, and all that is in it, by the hand of the aliens. I, the Lord, have spoken.'"(30:9-12).

"Thus says the Lord God: 'I will also destroy the idols, and cause the images to cease from Noph [Memphis]; *There shall no longer be princes from the land of Egypt; I will put fear in the land of Egypt. I will make Pathros desolate, Set fire to Zoan, and execute judgment on No [Memphis]. I will pour out my fury on Sin [Thebes], the strength of Egypt; I will cut off the multitude of No, and set a fire in Egypt"...* (30:10-16). *The young men of* Aven [On, or Heliopolis] *and Pi Beseth shall fall by the sword, and these cities shall go into captivity...At Tehaphnehes* [where the Jewish community resided] *the day shall also be darkened...And her daughters shall go into captivity. Thus I will execute judgment on Egypt, and they shall known that I am the Lord"*(30:18-19). *"I shall scatter the Egyptians among the nations, and disperse them throughout the countries. Then they shall know that I am the Lord.'"*(30:23, 26).

Over a century before the time of Jeremiah and Ezekiel, the prophet Isaiah also had his say on Egypt. *"And the Egyptians I will give into the hand of a cruel master, and a fierce king will rule over them' says the Lord of Hosts. The waters will fail from the sea, and the river will be wasted and dried up. The rivers will turn foul; the brooks of defense will be emptied and dried up; the reeds and rushes will wither, the papyrus reeds by the river, by the mouth of the river, and everything sown by the river, will wither, be driven away, and will be no more. The fishermen will also mourn..."* However, Isaiah also goes on to prophesy that "in that day" Egypt will cry out to the Lord and *"he will send them a savior and a mighty one, and he will deliver them."* Then *"the Lord shall be known I Egypt, and the Egyptians shall know the Lord in that day, and Egypt will make sacrifice and offering"* to the God of Israel and... *"they will return to the Lord"* (19:20-22).

These prophecies are fearsome and unequivocal. They are also entirely wrong. Egypt was not captured by Babylon under Nebuchadnezzar. It did not suffer the depredations described above at the hand of Nebuchadnezzar. Neither did Egypt, or any portion of it, ever go into captivity for forty years or any other length of time. No portion of Egypt was depopulated or desolate for forty years. The Jewish community continued to thrive and was a dominant and influential portion of world Judaism. It was not taken captive. At one point they even had an Egyptian temple in competition with the one at Jerusalem. The Nile River has never dried up and devastated the country. They cannot use the standard argument of Bible proponents that it hasn't happened yet but will happen, because it was supposed to happen under Nebuchadnezzar. What is this then? *This is pure fantasy and fiction.* These prophecies are products of anger against Egypt, and against Jews that had supposedly disobeyed God by fleeing to Egypt, and not the product of any God who inspired the prophets to predict the future. They are not inspired by God, they are inspired by the prophet's own vitriol (and perhaps by some good Israeli wine!). These are obviously and unquestionably failed prophecies.

The Ten Northern Tribes Would be Reunited in Israel

Nothing is more clear than the prophecy that God would reunite not just the southern tribes of Judah and Benjamin (the Kingdom of Judah), but all twelve tribes to the land of Israel, including those of Samaria and the Northern Kingdom (the Kingdom of Israel). The Northern Kingdom had gone into captivity first, in 722 B.C., to the Kingdom of Assyria. It would not be until 587 B.C, that the Southern

Kingdom would be taken captive by Babylon. The prophecies are clear. Hosea, from Samaria, brought a harsh indictment from God against the backsliding Northern Kingdom, also known as Ephraim: *"Ephraim has encircled me with lies..."* (Hosea 12:1); *"Ephraim is also like a silly dove without sense... "(*7:11). As most prophets, his is a prophecy of doom and gloom, predicting catastrophe for Ephraim and captivity. As punishment *"he shall not return to the land of Egypt; but the Assyrian shall be his King..."* (11:5). But God still loves Ephraim, *:"How can I give you up, Ephraim?"* (11:8). *"'They will return to him: they shall walk after the Lord. He will roar like a lion, when he roars, then his sons shall come trembling from the west; they shall come trembling like a bird from Egypt, like a dove from the land of Assyria, and I will let them dwell in their houses' says the Lord."* (11:10-11).

There is still the unqualified promise of restoration: *"Then the children of Judah and the children of Israel shall be gathered together, and appoint for themselves one head..."*(Hosea 1:11). Hosea, of the Northern Kingdom, in its final days prophesies that the Northern Kingdom will return to God and will also return to the southern monarchy of the house of David: *"For the children of Israel shall abide many days without king or prince, without sacrifice or sacred pillar, without ephod or teraphim. Then the children of Israel shall return and seek the Lord the God and David their king."* (Hosea 3:4-5). Jeremiah was equally clear: *"And I will cause the captives of Judah and the captives of Israel to return and will rebuild the places as at the first"*(Jer. 33:7). Jeremiah has God saying, *"I am a father to Israel, and Ephraim is my firstborn"*, so he will not forsake the Northern Kingdom, but *"they shall come back from the land of the enemy"* and *"come back to their own border"* for God will *""surely have mercy on him."*(Jer. 331:9-12).

Ezekiel also, writing after the exile of the Southern Kingdom to Babylon, prophesies the rejoining of "Joseph, the stick of Ephraim" together with Judah and they shall together become one nation. *"Thus says the Lord God, 'Surely I will take the stick of Joseph, in the hand of Ephraim, and the tribes of Israel, his companions, and I will join them with it, with the stick of Judah, and make them one stick, and they will be one in my hand...I will make them one nation in the land...and one king shall be king over them all; they shall no longer be two nations, nor shall they be divided into two kingdoms again.'"* (Ezekiel 36:19-22). The first part was true — they lost their kingdom, but they never returned to worship the God of the Bible and never regained loyalty to the royal line of David. However poignant, it is a failed prophecy.

The children of the ten tribes, Ephraim, were distributed throughout the Assyrian Empire. Already religiously syncretized with pagan religion, according to the Bible, they did not remain a cohesive group, as the Hebrews in Babylon. They were acculturated with the native peoples and their identity totally lost. They have long ceased to be an identifiable people, They are lost to history. And they *never returned to the land of Israel.* The book of Ezra (1:5) makes it clear that it was "the heads of the fathers' houses of Judah and Benjamin" and "the men of Judah and Benjamin" (10:9) who returned to the land from Babylon. This is a failed prophecy.

The Christian response is that at the time of the division of the kingdoms, there were some in the North who remained loyal to the Temple cult in Jerusalem, and so they left the Northern Kingdom and went south to live, presumably becoming a virtual part of the tribe of Benjamin. So the argument is that they were all represented and ultimately some descendants returned from captivity in Babylon, so therefore the prophecy is fulfilled. Not only does the claim lack historical support that this migration ever occurred in any significant form whatsoever, but any miniscule remainder of the ten tribes in the south could in no way constitute fulfillment of such unequivocal, unlimited and grandiose prophecies as we have seen above. The promise is that *all* the tribes of Israel, not just a tiny residue of some, would return to the land of Israel. This never happened. And it never will because it never can. First, find them!

The Death of Jehoiakim

Anger seems to be a not uncommon inspiration for prophecies of doom, not the anger of God but the anger of man, as we saw with Jeremiah's prophecies over Egypt after some of the Jews sought refuge there. Jeremiah seems to have also gone over the edge in his reaction to King Jehoiakim. After all, Jehoiakim had the audacity to take out a

Failed Bible Prophecies

knife and rip up Jeremiah's scroll and throw it in the fire. Jehoiakim shall be "buried with the burial of an ass, drawn and cast forth beyond the gates of Jerusalem" (Jeremiah 22:19) It was prophesied that "he shall have no one to sit on the throne of David and his dead body shall be cast out in the day to the heat, and in the night to the frost" (36:30). Naturally, Jehoiakim's greatest offense was in wounding the self-pride of the temperamental Jeremiah, inducing the foregoing tirade (literally a "Jeremiad"), of which no one wants to be at the receiving end. But in point of fact, II Kings, a history of the kings of Israel and Judah, would certainly notify us if the king's end was so spectacularly ignoble as predicted. Such a ceremony of desecration of a king's body could not go unnoticed. If his body was dragged out of the city and dumped unburied like a piece of trash we would hear about it. In fact, nothing of the sort happened. Jehoiakim simply "slept with his fathers", an indication of a normal and natural death (II Kings 24:6).

Jeconiah would be childless; Jehoiakim would have no heir to the throne

It was also prophesied that Jehoiakim would "have no one to sit on the throne of David"(Jer.36:30) , and as to his son, Jehoiachin, also known as Jeconiah, that he would be childless. ""Thus says the Lord: 'Write this man down as childless, a man who shall not prosper in his days; For none of his descendants shall prosper, Sitting on the throne of David, and ruling anymore in Judah" (Jer. 22:30). Jeconiah reigned three months in Judah and was taken captive to Babylon. But the Gospel of Matthew states that "Jeconiah begat Shealtiel, and Shealtiel begat Zerrubabel" who returned to Israel from the captivity and was in truth regarded by the Jews at the time as the rightful successor to the throne of David (Matthew 1:12; Haggai 2:23). According to the same Bible, Jeconiah indeed had a child and descendants, who were heirs to the throne, including Zerrubabel, and even Jesus, if you accept the Matthew genealogy.

Destruction of Tyre by Babylon

The prophet Ezekiel prophesied expressly that Nebuchadnezzar, king of Babylon, would destroy the city of Tyre, and would scrape it clean like the top of a rock, and that "fishing nets would be spread over it" (Ezekiel 26:7-14). This never came to pass. Nebuchadnezzar failed to capture Tyre. Tyre was destroyed by Alexander the Great in 332 B.C., over 250 years after Ezekiel's prophecy. Many Bible proponents hail this as an amazing fulfillment of prophecy. But the prophecy was to be fulfilled by Nebuchadnezzar, the reigning Babylonian monarch and to be fulfilled in the then current time of Ezekiel, not 250 years later by another nation. This is a failed prophecy, which was inspired by Ezekiel's obvious anger at Tyre, not by any God who existed and acted in dimensions beyond our own.

Judah (i.e., the House of David) would always provide a king of Israel until the Kingdom of God Arrived (Gen.49:10)

We should not be unmindful that under the rubric of *failed prophecies* there are many prophecies that we have already addressed at length. Among them is Genesis 49:10, that Judah would always supply a "lawgiver" and a "scepter"[king or ruler] for Israel until "Shiloh comes", i.e., the same eternal kingdom, later typified as "Ancient of Days" or "son of man coming on the clouds of heaven", to establish a universal, eternal kingdom. That Judah would supply such a ruler is an express reference to a king from the tribe of Judah and implicitly, considering the rest of Jewish and Bible history, from the house of David. When Judah went into captivity in 587 B.C. Judah ceased to have a "lawgiver from between his feet" and "the scepter passed from Judah", without the Kingdom of God coming. This is a failed biblical prophecy of monumental proportions. Although Israel became virtually independent, under primarily Hasmonean and later Herodian rule, from 162 B.C. until 6 A.D. (in Judea, Herodians continued to rule in Galilee), there was no ruler from the house of David ever again. The Hasmoneans were not descendants of David. Neither was the family of Herod. Even if you assume the Bible proponents' argument that Jesus was a descendant of David, and therefore rightful king, and

Failed Bible Prophecies

also that he was "Shiloh", you still have a 600 year gap that *cannot exist under the terms of the prophecy*. And what's more, Jesus never ruled Judea as king. And even if you accept the Herodian kingdom as a legitimate biblical kingship over Judah, you still have greater than four hundred year gap in which lawgiving and the scepter had definitely passed, *and no Kingdom of God came*. And in fact, this latter argument is complicated by the fact that according to none less than church father Origen, under the Jewish Patriarchate in the second and third centuries A.D., the Jewish patriarchate was given the power of capital punishment — the "scepter." So Judah had a lawgiver and had the scepter again. Is this to be included under the prophecy of Genesis 49:10? **[6]** And what of the restored nation of Israel since 1948? Is this included? Is this an extension of the prophecy? The scepter of Israel seems to come and go for hundreds of years, but no Kingdom of God ever commences on the earth.

Jesus Would Return to the World in Glory within a Generation

Oh, yes Christian, he did say this! It is as clear and unequivocal as the bells on Easter Sunday. And it is a prediction and prophecy that most Bible proponents wish was not there. In Mark, as he faced the Sanhedrin, the high priest asked him, *"Are you the Christ, the Son of the Blessed?"* Jesus replied, *"I am. And you will see the son of man sitting on the right hand of the power, and coming in the clouds of heaven"*, directly paraphrasing Daniel 9, the vision of the coming of the son of man to take power. This would certainly appear to be prediction that his return would be so soon that even the high priest Caiaphas would live to see it. Now Bible apologists would say that he is only referring to Caiaphas metaphorically as a representative of the Jewish people, and that he really means that the Jews will still be around when he returns.

But this passage does not stand alone. Just before the transfiguration on the mount, Jesus told his disciples, *"Assuredly I say to you that there are some standing here who will not taste death till they see the son of man coming in his kingdom."(Matt. 16:28)*. This statement is clear and unequivocal, and his message to Caiaphas, if not already clear, is made all the more clear by this declaration. Obviously the coming of the kingdom is one and the same event as the son of man returning on the clouds of heaven. There is no doubt but that this is a prophecy: Jesus will return within one generation. By Luke, which is written much later, Jesus' statement to Caiaphas is toned down some. He merely says. *'Hereafter the son of man will sit on the right hand of the power of God".*(Luke 22:69). It is no wonder then that the early church, in the age of the apostles, were so convinced that the end was extremely near. This is why the Apostle Paul told people to stay as they were in life, and to not even bother to marry or have children, because the end could come at any moment. *"But this I say, brethren, the time is short, so that from now on even those who have wives should be as though they had none, those who weep as though they did not weep, those who rejoice as though they did not rejoice, those who buy as though they did not possess, and those who use this world as though not misusing it. For the form of this world is passing away"* (I. Cor. 7:29). This passage makes it eloquently clear that Paul expects "the end" of this world and the return of Christ immediately. He would never have imagined people reading these passages two thousand years later and Jesus had not returned.

Now the dispensationalists will have their own explanation. They will admit that Jesus meant exactly what he said — he did indeed intend to return in glory in one generation. But the Jews rejected him, and so his return was delayed at least two thousand years, and in the meantime, the message would go out to the gentiles. *If* the Jews had accepted Jesus as Messiah, the argument goes, Jesus *would* have returned at the time of the Jewish War in 66-70 A.D. and would have saved Israel and ruled over a worldwide millennial kingdom. However, God supposedly knew that the Jews would reject Jesus at that time, and so God's plan the whole time was to have an opening of at least presumably two thousand years in which God would save the Gentiles. So only in theory, or in principle, could the Jews have accepted Jesus. So then, if I might be so brazen to ask, why was the promise, and *prophecy*, made in the first place?

Now, even more interestingly, we have another side to this argument, or should I really say *the* other side — that the Kingdom of God *already came*. This is the Roman Catholic argument: That the institution of the church, and in particular the alleged consecration of Peter as the see of Rome (alleged institution of the papacy), constituted the coming of Christ and the kingdom of God in glory. I will simply state this argument for the record and not belabor a response. The arguments of Luther, Calvin, and centuries of Protestant adherents have, I believe, sufficiently addressed this claim. I will only add one small observation that I am sure of, which is that there are undoubtedly thousands of childhood victims of priestly sodomy who do not feel that they experienced the coming of the kingdom.

Conclusion

We began this survey on a number of lengthy prefaces concerning techniques and practices of biblical authors, in which some would say the author was backing off his claims of showing failed biblical prophecies before he even started. We end the survey very succinctly. The Bible is not a book of 100% perfect prophecy. It is not a book of prophecy at all. How many of the Bible's prophecies are false? All of them are. Because there are no genuine prophecies which have been fulfilled. There is only human diatribe, bias, and wishful thinking, pasted over with fake prophecies, mindless excuses, and self-serving equivocation.

Chapter Seven

JESUS OF NAZARETH: SAVIOR AND SODOMIST

It is rather remarkable, and has also been frequently remarked, how Jesus has been portrayed in art work throughout history. As we almost all know, Jesus has generally been portrayed in a very effeminate light. He normally has long, flowing, apparently perfectly groomed and combed hair. It is not the long hair of the "long hairs", such as your rock stars — unkempt, disordered, rough, "manly" — but rather the meticulous, soft look we more readily indentify as a woman's hair. In fact, as we all know, there is usually, but not always, a difference between a man's hair when long, and a woman's hair. Any cosmetologist or barber will tell you this. He also has a perfect, white, and often rosy complexion. Such is often the traditional "look" we associate with Jesus from youth. We have seen it in a thousand paintings and murals.

And yet in point of fact, to be totally frank, the Christian conception of Jesus is one of absolute *a*sexuality. What do I mean by this? Do I mean he was sexless? Well, in one sense yes. He is definitely considered to be a man. But in terms of sexuality, meaning sexual instinct, desire, and orientation, he is considered to be *a*sexual. There is no church doctrine that has ever been developed or promulgated on this point. No church council or papal encyclical ever addressed this issue in all church history. But such is *practically*, but not doctrinally, the case.

The early, preeminent church father St. Augustine probably vocalized openly what the church generally has always in its heart of hearts believed to be true: "Christ had no strife of flesh and spirit which came upon human nature from the transgression of the first man inasmuch as he was born of the Spirit and the virgin, not through fleshly desire." This meant that he was void of any sexual desire. So much for "tempted in all points just as we are." [1]

Christians have always regarded Jesus as asexual, and beyond the grasp of genuine sexuality. For all practical purposes, he is seen as sexless. Anyone care to argue the point? Ever seen anything written on the sexuality of Jesus? It is scarce. There is *The Sexuality of Jesus*, by William E. Phipps; and more infamously, the book and film *The Last Temptation of Christ*, not even slightly a "Christian" movie. There is very little extant on the point.

This disposition on the part of Christians is actually quite unusual. The church eventually roundly condemned *docetism* — the doctrine that Jesus was *only* a divine figure in the form of a human being, but that he was never actually a human being. Clement of Alexandria, one of the great thinkers of the early church — was harshly corrected for his opinion that Jesus did not tire as a human being. This was seen as a form of docetism. Jesus was held to be as fully human as he was fully God at all times. As a human, Jesus tired, he grew hungry, he sweated and bled, and yes he urinated and defecated. To deny these things is heresy, according to the church. And yet, in regard to his sexuality, western culture, or at least Christianity, is absolutely and fundamentally docetist. Do not get me wrong — there is absolutely nothing stated doctrinally in this regard and there never will be either, because it is simply not an issue. It is something assumed. No one will call it an article of faith, but it is implicitly assumed as a matter of faith never questioned, never reviewed, never contemplated. Why bother?

And if Jesus was in fact virtually asexual, then in what manner was he *"in all points tempted as we are"?* (Hebrews 4:15). Does the gay preacher's son in Fort Worth think that Jesus was tempted in the same manner he is? Does the gay altar boy in Boston? Or, for that matter, the straight preacher's son and altar boy? But does the Bible present us with any information? Have Christians read the Bible through a cultural and doctrinal lens, that filters out unwanted information, just as they do in regard to the many factual, historical, and doctrinal incongruities and discrepancies discussed in this book? Let us search further.

Conviction Overturned

Jesus was a Jewish rabbi, who began his career at about the age of thirty, and may have continued his career for about three years. Jewish culture of the first century was highly traditional, and conventional, or in other words "orthodox." Men were expected to marry and to have children. A man would be married by age thirty. For a man to not marry and to have no interest, or make no efforts, toward marriage was unusual. For a rabbi it was especially expected of him. For a rabbi to not be married was unheard of. It was actually a father's duty to see that his son was married and to wait more than ten years beyond puberty was prohibited. After marriage the duty to "be fruitful and multiply" was an absolute duty. Celibacy was condemned. **[2]**

Yet we think nothing of the fact because of our presumption of asexuality. To the Christian, Jesus was God, so of course he did not marry, did not share any male interest toward women, and never performed or even thought about sexuality. So this does not seem at all strange. In fact, this is what we would expect. But our Jesus of Nazareth has some other strange quirks that *should* raise some eyebrows.

Jesus on Transsexualism

Our Jesus had some rather pronounced views on transsexualism. They are views that most Christians outright ignore, or minimize, and for very good reasons. Read the following:

"But he [Jesus] *said to them, 'All cannot accept this saying, but only those to whom it has been given: For there are eunuchs who were born thus from their mother's womb, and there are eunuchs were made eunuchs by men, and there are eunuchs who have made themselves eunuchs for the kingdom of heaven's sake. He who is able to accept it, let him accept it'"* (Matt. 19:11-12).

He who is able to "accept" what? He was certainly right about the first statement — not everyone could accept it, especially in his environment. Of course, as we will see, for some people it came quite easy, just like the "sacrifice" of many young men in giving up the pleasures of women to become Roman Catholic priests. But let us look at this revealing statement more carefully.

Now the term "eunuch" confuses people. *Supposedly,* the Christian apologists will tell you, a eunuch is a castrated male, and that is all they will say. Why is the man castrated? Well, they will say, they were castrated by oriental despots to take care of harems, because the eunuchs themselves *could* not have sexual relations with the women in the harem. Although there are instances where this was true, how many harems were there in priest-dominated Second Temple Jewry? Maybe one or two among the Herodian royalty. For that matter, how many existed in the Hellenistic Greek culture in the eastern Mediterranean? And just who castrated these men? Were they slaves that the owners deliberately ordered castrated at birth, or as boys? We are back to the Socratic method again.

How about some real answers? Eunuchs are nothing less than what we know as transsexuals today. They are exactly the same thing. They have always existed in history, and at times and places in history they have been more prominent and more influential than they are today, to say the least. They were dominant in the royal court of Rome after the third century A.D. according to Gibbon in *The Decline and Fall of the Roman Empire*. They were highly influential, and had a prominent place in society, in Pakistan of all places (Northwestern Hindustan) before the British Christian Raj came and declared them distasteful and unclean. [3]. And just as Jesus stated, the origin of their transsexuality was varied. Some "were born that way." Now this is a most unusual statement for some people. Most people, including Christians, are unaware of this concept. Jesus certainly was not. This seems like hermaphroditism — the natural bearing of physical attributes of both sexes. When I was in high school biology class I was told that this simply did not exist in nature. Why should I have ever believed differently? But the living word of God knew better.

Others made themselves that way "for the sake for the kingdom of God" and that was very commendable, according to Jesus. Jesus finding it commendable actually led the early Christian father Origen to go out and castrate himself in the third century A.D. Why shouldn't he, if Jesus said it was a commendable and holy act? Now all Christians will tell you that Jesus did not *really* or *literally* mean it was a good thing. Why do they say that? How do they know that? How they will fight and quarrel to insist that other things of the savior are to be taken literally, except where they would rather not accept it and would rather ignore it. Jesus was not speaking to twenty-first century Omaha. He was speaking at a time in the world when men were frequently and regularly castrated in order to perform a female role model. These persons were highly visible in society and often held high and influential positions in government and society, including advisors to kings (such as the Ethiopian eunuch in Acts chapter 8). So why would we think that he was not speaking literally and frankly? If it was not literal, what was it? Was it "shock talk"? I am sure some were shocked, but what were they supposed to be shocked into, or out of? Was he trying to make another point? If so, what point? That you should do anything for the kingdom of God? Wouldn't there be some other examples to choose to show this? Once again, the Christian apologists' explanations are as preposterous as they are desperate.

What is especially surprising, and actually startling, about these remarks, however, is the time and place where they are made. Orthodox Jewish sentiments during the Second Temple period are very clear. They are evident in Scripture, and they are clearly homophobic and puritanical. The Law of Moses leaves no doubt about the attitudes of the Jews at this time. Leviticus states, *"If a man lies with a male as he lies with a woman, both of them have committed an abomination. They shall surely be put to death"* (Lev. 20:13). It is short, unambiguous, and definitive. Likewise, we are told that *"A woman shall not put on anything that pertains to a man, nor shall a man put on a woman's garment, for all who do so are an abomination to the Lord your God"*(Deut. 22:5). An "abomination" is a term reserved for the most hideous of offenses to God. A man who is castrated is not even allowed to worship God with others: *"He who is emasculated by crushing or mutilation shall not enter the assembly of the Lord"* (Deut. 23:1). Needless to say, this was not a society where transsexualism, under the name of eunuchs, or any other name, would have any sanction. If it was an abomination to put on a woman's clothes, what about becoming a woman?

And let us be clear about this process we are speaking of. The point is that "emasculation", and that is the process of becoming a eunuch if one is not born that way, is done to render a man *un*-masculine, as the term indicates. So his sexuality is *trans*cended —

he overcomes it, and becomes something else. In any event, he is regarded as effeminate. So what we are talking about, I submit, are effeminate men. But, you might add, there are effeminate men who are not transsexuals. That is very true, and this brings up another line of inquiry. How is transsexualism related to homosexuality and how is homosexuality related to effeminacy?

I would not begin to attempt to explain this, for a number of very good reasons. In the first place, it is not necessary for our present purposes to explain this. Secondly, much has been written on the topic. Suffice it to say, there is an obvious relationship between transsexualism and effeminacy (a man having notable female characteristics in his behavior can be compared to a man physically having female characteristics). So transsexualsim is physical and effeminacy is behavioral. Yet when we come to the issue of homosexuality we find more issues at play. A person with homosexual orientation may not be effeminate at all. And a man who is effeminate may not be gay at all. And yet effeminate behavior has to do with female role playing by a man, the same as cross-dressing, which is a more obvious and extreme form of effeminate behavior. And transsexualism is a more active, physical role-playing. Are these then not a matter of degree? Are there some men who are effeminate in their behavior and desire to be women? Are they sometimes "born that way", with physical characteristics of women? Or are they sometimes only "born that way" with a desire to become women, but they are not. Obviously some men born with a desire to be women, actually make themselves like women, or "are made that way by men," as Jesus says (because usually they do not do it themselves, and someone else does it, albeit at their behest).

I do not mean to suggest a continuum between gay men, cross-dressers, and transsexuals, because some gay men have no desire to be effeminate, much less to be women. And, as we said, there are effeminate men that are not gay. However, there are *some,* but not all, effeminate men that *are* gay, that might fit the norm of a continuum. They may wish to be women so fervently (or believe that they really are) that they may dress themselves as women as a form of making themselves women, and may eventually literally make that transformation into women.

Conviction Overturned

Enough said on this point. We could leave this subject matter as only a bizarre, inexplicable statement by Jesus. But we find more related, bizarre information in the Gospel accounts. First, let us see who we are dealing with in the Gospel account of "John."

Who Wrote the "Gospel of John"?

This is actually a question that is easily answered, at least if the Gospel itself is to be believed. The Gospel says who wrote it. It claims to be written by "the disciple that Jesus loved." The following makes it expressly clear: *"Then Peter, turning around, saw the disciple **whom Jesus loved** following, who had also leaned on his breast at the supper, and said, "Lord, who is the one who betrays you?' Peter, seeing him, said to Jesus, 'But Lord, what about this man?'"* Jesus then intimates, but does not say directly, that the disciple that Jesus loves just might live until his return, which is very consistent with prophecies Jesus made elsewhere (see chapter 6, "Failed Bible Prophecies"). Then the Gospel tells us, *"This is the disciple who testifies of these things, and wrote these things; and we know that his testimony is true"* (John 21:23-24). So unquestionably, according to this, "the disciple whom Jesus loved" is the one who "testified" of these things, and others who presumably heard him wrote it down. He is the "author" of the fourth Gospel. So who was "the disciple whom Jesus loved"?

The narrative itself also supplies that answer. Only one man *in all of the Gospels* is ever called *"the disciple whom Jesus loved."* In John chapter 11, twice Lazarus is called that. In 11:1-3, we are told, *"Now a certain man was sick, Lazarus of Bethany, the town of Mary and her sister Martha. It was that Mary who anointed the Lord with fragrant oil and wiped his feet with her hair, whose brother Lazarus was sick. Therefore the sisters sent to him, saying 'Lord, behold, **he whom you love is sick.**"* Jesus then goes to Bethany. In the meantime Lazarus, who was sick, has died. Jesus raises Lazarus from the dead. Now is there any question but that in this narrative Lazarus was "the disciple whom Jesus loved", or as Christians are fond of paraphrasing "the beloved disciple?"(a phrase which actually no where appears in Scripture). Right after the announcement above, Jesus tells his disciples that the sickness of Lazarus "is not unto death" (it appears from the narrative that it actually was, unless Jesus was right and Lazarus was not dead) and says it is for the glory of God. Then, in the next verse, we are told, *"Now Jesus loved Martha and her sister and Lazarus"* (v.5). We have it again.

These are the only three individuals we are told that Jesus loved, at least loved in particular. Of these, only one is a man — Lazarus. We are not told about any other man, that Jesus loved him. We see this person again at the dinner table, the night that Jesus is betrayed. In John 13, Jesus has announced, while at dinner, that he will be betrayed (There is never indication of twelve disciple in the fourth Gospel, for reasons we shall see). The narrative continues, *"Now there was leaning on Jesus' bosom one of his disciples,* **whom Jesus loved.** *Simon Peter therefore motioned to him to ask who it was of whom he spoke. Then, leaning back on Jesus' breast, he said to him, 'Lord, who is it?'"* (John 13:23). This is the same narrative referred to in chapter 21.

So there is no reasonable doubt but that Lazarus is the "disciple whom Jesus loved" and "the disciple whom Jesus loved" is the author. It is amazing how some things that are very easy and straightforward to comprehend, are so incredibly difficult for Christians to grasp. The title is not a part of the work. We have all been told that it is "The Gospel of John" and this is traditional. But tradition is not necessarily truth. No less a conservative biblical scholar as Ben Witherington has declared that this Gospel is unequivocally written by Lazarus [4]

There are other factors to consider which only corroborate this conclusion. Eighty percent of the Gospel of John takes place in the environs of Jerusalem and fifty percent the last week before the crucifixion. This suggests a person from the vicinity of Jerusalem, such as Lazarus (Bethany is only two miles from Jerusalem) and someone who became a solid, committed "disciple", or camp follower, the last week of Jesus' life. This would be the probable situation of Lazarus, since the raising of Lazarus is shortly before the Passion Week. Right after the raising is the plot to kill Jesus, when we are told "the Passover of the Jews was near"(11:55) and next comes a supper at Bethany, given by Martha and Mary, at which Lazarus attended, which was "six days before the Passover"(12:1-2). There is no other explanation for the above distribution of the Gospel account.

Conviction Overturned

More troubling for the theory that the disciple John wrote it, is the absolute absence of critical events that would be in a narrative written by John, the son of Zebedee. John was one of the inner three, consisting of John, his brother James, and Peter, who alone were at such events as the raising of Jairus' daughter and the transfiguration of Jesus on the mount. That he was an eyewitness to such events as Jesus taking on a divine, otherworldly aspect and aura, in the transfiguration, and meeting with Elijah and Moses, and did not tell us about it, is just incredible. Only the author of II Peter, regarded as a second century forgery, and even regarded as suspect in the day of church historian Eusebius, and not written by the same person as I Peter, claims to have been an eyewitness of the transfiguration. So this testimony would be vital. And to see Jesus raise a person from the dead is an astounding event. If it were John, he would not be able to contain himself from writing about the raising of Jairus' daughter. And yet this author *does* describe the raising of Lazarus. Yet in this narrative of the raising of Lazarus the disciples are not mentioned. We hear of them not wanting to go with Jesus to Bethany when they get the news of Lazarus' sickness: *"Rabbi, lately the Jews sought to stone you, and you are going there again"* (John11:8). Finally Thomas says, sarcastically however, *"Let us also go that we may die with him"* (11:16). Whether they really went, at least at that moment, is unknown, but appears doubtful. But as we will see below, there may be other reasons why the synoptic Gospels do not include the raising of Lazarus. The fact that the raising of Lazarus should appear in a Gospel written by Lazarus is to be expected however. Needless to say, it was an important event for Lazarus.

An Evening at Dinner

This brings us to the last night before the resurrection, called by some "the last supper." We have already taken note of this evening dinner Jesus took with his disciples. The synoptic Gospels indicate Jesus had dinner with "the twelve." There is no indication of how many disciples were with him in the fourth Gospel, and in fact the term "the twelve", and the concept of "the twelve apostles", does not exist in the fourth Gospel. We do not know how many disciples Jesus had, and so there is

Jesus of Nazareth: Savior and Sodomist

no notion of some of the foremost disciples becoming "apostles." We only know that his disciples were commissioned *after* the resurrection, in John chapter 20.

What is so peculiar about this supper is the position of Lazarus, in relation to Jesus. We are told that, *"Now there was **leaning on Jesus' bosom** one of his disciples, **whom Jesus loved.**"* After Jesus announces that someone at dinner will betray him, *"Simon Peter therefore motioned to him to ask who it was of whom he spoke. Then, **leaning back on Jesus' breast**, he said to him, 'Lord, who is it?'"* (John 13:23). That this person was Lazarus and not John, son of Zebedee, has already been shown by the testimony of Peter himself (John 21:20, compare to 11:3, 5). Now this is a curious physical position to be in — leaning on someone's breast, or chest. It brings to mind Bing Crosby's famous lyrics, *"Cuddled on my shoulder, nestled in my arms... Oh, this is paradise..."* Crosby's lyrics seem to correspond exactly.

Christian apologists have a very ready response. They claim that this is not at all unusual. They claim that this type of behavior was very customary among men in the contemporary first century Jewish culture. The problem with this argument is that *they do not have the slightest shred of evidence in support of their claim, either inside the Bible or outside the Bible!* There is absolutely no example, or reference, anywhere in Hebrew or Jewish literature, history, documents, or writings to suggest that men just affectionately leaned on each other's breasts at dinner. We have absolutely no reason to suggest that the bounds of propriety regarding display of affection between men were any different in Second Temple Jewish culture than they would be today. Naturally, I must qualify that word "today." Today, in twenty-first century New York, or Los Angeles, it would not be at all unusual to walk into a restaurant and see a man cuddling another man, leaning on his chest during supper. But this was not twenty-first century New York or Los Angeles. This was a priest-dominated, religion-based society grounded in the kind of homophobia that we reviewed above, as codified in Leviticus and Deuteronomy. Anything other than conventional gender models was not only frowned upon, it was condemned at the point of death. In such a culture, behavior such as what is depicted here is outlandish.

Curiously, this situation is not portrayed at all in the synoptic

Gospels, even though Jesus' announcement of his betrayal is, and in fact Jesus' identification of who the betrayer is, is stated in almost identical language. In the fourth Gospel, it is "he to whom I shall give a piece of bread when I have dipped it" (13:26). In Matthew, after Jesus' announcement *"each of them began to ask him 'Lord is it I?'"* And Jesus says, *"He who dipped his hand with me in the dish will betray me."*(Matt. 26:22-23; Mark 14:20 is almost the same). Suspiciously omitted is the interlude with Peter asking Lazarus, who is laying on Jesus' breast, and whom apparently Peter thinks Jesus will pay greater heed to than to him, to ask Jesus who will betray him. This interlude tends to show Lazarus as the greatest confidant of Jesus and the one closest to his heart, metaphorically and physically. Peter appears more as an outsider. But of course this would only be natural of "the disciple Jesus loved." And this is all the more reason, not only why this tidbit is not in the synoptics, but why *Lazarus himself* is also omitted — not just at the last supper, but in each and every one of *the entire Gospels* - and not even mentioned. He is *persona non grata* to somebody, for some reason. And yet, in Luke, we have a large role for Mary and Martha of Bethany, who are *Lazarus' sisters*, but no Lazarus! We even have the large dinner put on by Mary and Martha, depicted in John chapter 12, but no reference to the fact that their brother Lazarus had *just been raised from the dead!* (Luke 10:38-41).

And just coincidentally, the fourth Gospel is distinct from the others because it relates mostly long, private conversations of Jesus, sometimes in the midst of personal encounters, without the other disciples present, such as the meeting with Nicodemus, and with the Samarian woman at the well, whereas the synoptics relate mostly Jesus speaking to the crowds, or to the disciples as a group. This type of intimacy with Jesus, just like the intimacy portrayed above at the "last supper", is precisely the type of thing that would have been resented by the other disciples. These same disciples would naturally tend to draw a circle around themselves, and to claim that they — the "twelve", just like the twelve tribes of Israel — were the only true disciples, soon to be transformed into "the twelve apostles."

Jesus of Nazareth: Savior and Sodomist

An Embarrassing Incident in a Garden

Everyone knows the story. Jesus goes with his disciples to the Garden of Gethsemane, at the foot of the Mount of Olives, where he and his disciples had been staying in the nighttime to sleep. Since Judas, Jesus' betrayer, was one of the twelve, he had also been sleeping there also, and he knew exactly where Jesus would be in the nighttime. When they arrive at the garden, Jesus leaves his disciples and goes off alone to pray. Judas has been paid by the chief priests in the Temple to lead a crowd sent by them to arrest Jesus. Judas then betrays him with a kiss, his signal to the crowd identifying Jesus (We fail to understand, if the crowd was immediately present with Judas, why he would need to kiss Jesus as a signal, when he could simply say, "That's him right there!").

Virtually every single Bible scholar, conservative or critical alike, believes that the Gospel of Mark is the oldest of the four canonical gospels. It is rare that there is such uniform agreement over anything concerning the Gospel. This is in part because much of Mark is included in Matthew, and also in Luke, and sometimes different parts of Mark are in one or the other. Also, there are more "hard" saying in Mark, that seem inconsistent with the tenor of the Gospels and its message, and which are eliminated or smoothed over in the other Gospels, such as the statement that in Nazareth Jesus *"could do no mighty work there… because of their unbelief"*(Mark 6:5-6). This is regarded as being at least rather awkwardly or inartfully phrased, since Jesus, as God, in Christian theology could not be *unable* to do mighty works, and in any event his power to do miracles cannot be dependent on the belief of his audience. He looks more like a magician in this narrative. We have some versions of Mark 2:4 that say Jesus was moved with anger at a leper when he cleanses him (changed to "moved with compassion" in our versions). In Mark, Jesus is especially concerned to hush anyone who would declare him to be the messiah of God, including the demons (1:34), perhaps to explain to a Palestinian contemporary audience why this was not proclaimed until long after his death. Also, the resurrection in Mark is very barebones and lacks the elaboration in the other Gospels, which as we mentioned in chapter three, is pure progressive embellishment. In what is regarded as the original ending of the Gospel of Mark, we have only an empty tomb and a stranger in white announcing that he is risen. This is obviously the first version of what would later be a more elaborate story. But another reason why the Gospel of Mark is considered to be first in time is because of the frequent inclusion of details in the narratives that are missing in the other gospels. For instance, Jesus meeting the rich, young ruler who asks Jesus how to "inherit eternal life" and Jesus ultimately tells him to sell all that he has and give it to the poor. This is in all three synoptic gospels. But oddly enough, it is only in Mark that he is called "young", in addition to being a person "with many possessions" and a "ruler" in Luke and Matthew (Mark 10:17-22). Not very much, but an additional detail the author knows, that the others missed. There are many more details in Jesus' encounter with a demoniac possessed by a "legion" of demons on the other side of the Sea of Galilee, when he sends the demons into a herd of pigs. This is a lengthier and more complete version of the story. (Mark 5:1-20).

It is because the Gospel of Mark is the earliest, the closest in time to the events portrayed, and the relative completeness and accuracy compared to the other accounts, that its portrayal of the arrest of Jesus is so important. It is especially the last point covered, that of additional details lacking in the other accounts, that concerns us so much here. We have an additional, strange, and bizarre occurrence in the Gospel of Mark account of Jesus' arrest in the garden that is omitted in the others. Mark tells us something else that occurred immediately after he tells of the arrival of Judas and the crowd. He first tells us that the disciples fled. Then he says *"Now a certain young man followed him, having a linen cloth thrown around his naked body. And the young men laid hold of him, and he left the linen cloth and fled from them naked"* (Mark 14: 51-52). We never hear about the naked, young man again, and he was indeed naked, except for a linen cloth. The situation is at least curious. Jerusalem is at a very high altitude, and we are talking about this area at about the time of the spring equinox, in late March or possible early April. Nights are cold in the vicinity of Jerusalem. This is deliberately translated in all versions as a "cloth", not a linen overcoat, tunic, or other linen clothing. Why is a man naked, except for a linen cloth — not even clothing, and why is he with Jesus in a garden? Even more curious, we are told that Jesus went to the garden with "his disciples" (14:32) after having dinner "with the twelve" (14:17). So where did the young man come from? He is obviously not one of

Jesus of Nazareth: Savior and Sodomist

the twelve. He is only "a certain young man." Did another person join them at dinner? Even though he was not one of the "twelve", was he another person considered a disciple, who joined them later and went with them to the Garden of Gethsemane? It almost appears that this section must be, or should be, related to another section of Scripture, which may have been excised.

Well there is an obvious answer. Who did the Jewish authorities go to the Garden of Gethsemane that night to arrest? Jesus? Yes, to arrest Jesus. But not only Jesus. No, we told in the Gospel of John that they went there to arrest Jesus *and Lazarus!* This itself is a surprise. They did not go to arrest Peter, the leader of the disciples, or the "sons of thunder" - the two sons of Zebedee — they went to arrest Lazarus, the one person in their minds the most linked to Jesus. The Bible makes it clear, *"But the chief priests plotted to put Lazarus to death **also**, because on account of him many of the Jews went away and believed in Jesus"* (John 11:10-11). So the plot was to seize and kill two people — Jesus and Lazarus. So they go to the garden to arrest *two people*, right? When they arrive at the garden, they in fact *do* seize two people, right? The first person was Jesus, who was the first person they intended to arrest, right? So who was the second person they "laid hold of"? It was the naked, young man. If the first person they seized was in fact the first person they went there to seize, why should we not think that the second person they seized *was* the second person *they went there to seize?* This only makes sense. The naked young man was the same person hanging on Jesus at dinner — Lazarus. So why does the author of Mark not just say it was Lazarus? For the very same reason that there is no mention of Lazarus in our canonical versions of the other three Gospels — Lazarus, the person the closest to Jesus, and the "disciple whom Jesus loved" could only have been resented by the exclusive club of "the twelve." There was every reason, human nature not the least, to exclude, omit, and marginalize this person who would have been seen as an interloper. He was a Jerusalemite who was not even with Jesus since the early days at the shores of the Sea of Galilee and in the region of Galilee, as they were, and which is where all of the twelve were from. The fact that he was "the disciple whom Jesus loved" made the matter all the worse. Knowledge of the relationship between Jesus and Lazarus is something they would have wanted to suppress.

Just what was that relationship? Just what happened in the garden? In twenty first century New York, it would not be uncommon for a man to be caught with a "naked, young man" in the nighttime in, let's say, Central Park, the modern day equivalent of the Garden of Gethsemane. Or for that matter, in any other large city, especially if the same young man was cuddling affectionately on his chest over supper in a restaurant a couple hours earlier.

But of course Christian apologists will tell us to not jump to conclusions. And of course, let's not jump to conclusions. There may be other, alternative explanations, and in all fairness we must explore other options. Maybe Jesus asked him to disrobe so he could examine the quality of his clothing. Maybe Jesus wanted to switch clothing with him. Maybe Jesus asked him to disrobe because he wanted to give him a physical examination (play doctor). Certainly there exist other hypothetical possibilities — as usual the question is the reasonableness of them. Then there exists the obvious explanation — Lazarus was "the disciple that Jesus loved."

This may not be unheard of. In the story of the early life of David, in the books of Samuel, we are told that David said that Jonathan, the son of King Saul, shared a love with him that was *"surpassing the love of women"* (II Samuel 1:26). We are told that *"the soul of Jonathan was knot with the soul of David, and Jonathan loved him as his own soul"* (I Sam. 18:1). David also *"loved him as his own soul"* (18:3). It is in the context of describing this emerging great love that we learn that, *"Saul took him that day and would not let him go home to his* [Jonathan's] *father's house anymore"* (18:2). Saul comes to resent David and eventually throws him out of the house and then tries to kill him. The Bible presents this as a result of Saul's jealousy of David's popularity. We would be led to wonder if there was not another reason why Saul resents David — the relationship with his son Jonathan, of which Saul does not approve and which humiliates him. We see a corroboration of this in the words of Saul when he rebukes Jonathan: *"Then Saul's anger was aroused against Jonathan, and he said to him, 'You son of a perverse, rebellious woman! Do I not know that you have chosen the son of Jesse to your own shame **and to the shame of your mother's nakedness?**'"* (I Sam. 20:30). Why is his relationship with David one of "shame"? At this point David was not a competitor for the throne, and David had nothing against Saul. On the contrary, the Bible makes it clear that the antagonism and ill-feeling was entirely one-sided, of Saul against David, so there should have been no shame in Jonathan's "befriending" of David. Unless, of course, there was more than friendship. And why, of all things, is it "to the same of your mother's nakedness?" In the Bible, the phrase "someone's nakedness" always refers to sexual promiscuity (Lev. 20:19 et seq.). What does the sexuality of Jonathan's mother have to do with it? As a matter of fact, why does the issue of sex even enter into his rebuke of Jonathan? And why the reference to "perverseness"? Once again, unless of course *perversion* went to the heart of Saul's rebuke. A person would be very naïve not to see a homosexual relationship as existing between David and Jonathan. But of course, Bible proponents will say, David could not have been a homosexual because he was watching Bathsheba take a bath and then became madly desirous of her and married her. Does this sound like a homosexual, they will ask? No, it does not. It sounds like a bisexual. Perhaps Jesus is "Son of David" in more ways than one.

The Secret Gospel of Mark

Bible scholar Morton Smith had spent part of W.W.II in Israel, unable to return because of the war. While there, he visited the small Eastern Orthodox monastery at Mar Saba, which had been an active monastery since the fifth century. At the monastery he studied many ancient manuscripts of which the monastery was the repository. He returned there in 1958 for the purpose of cataloguing the vast library. While there, Smith found a singularly remarkable manuscript.[5] It was a manuscript from a monk in the seventeenth century, in which he had hand-copied what purported to be a letter from Clement of Alexandria, the eminent, early bishop of Alexandria Egypt, in about 200 A.D. The monk had copied the letter in a blank spot at the end of an early edition of a work by Ignatius of Antioch, a second century bishop and church father. In the letter, which is addressed to someone named Theodore, Clement refutes an early Christian sect called the Carpocratians. The Carpocratians are known from the writings of Ireneas, later second century bishop of Lyons, who was one of the

Conviction Overturned

original "heresiologists" of the church. In his work *Against Heresies* he condemned them for sexual promiscuity of all kinds practiced under the guise of Christianity.

Now in the letter, purportedly from Clement of Alexandria, which the monk copied, Clement rebukes the Carpocratians for basing their teachings on a portion of the Gospel of Mark. It appears from the letter that Clement claims that the Carpocratians are using what was in fact a genuine version of the Gospel of Mark, but which was a later version, which Mark composed in Alexandria, which contained some additional teachings not included in the earlier gospel. In the letter, Clement claims familiarity with this gospel, but only claims that the Carpocratians have misinterpreted it. Clement quotes the section which he claims that the Carpocrations are misusing. He states that this section should be inserted in our version of the Gospel of Mark after 10:34:

"*They came to Bethany, and a woman was there whose brother had died* [No identities given, but we know the incident exactly from the fourth gospel]. *She came and prostrated herself before Jesus, saying to him, 'Son of David, have mercy on me.' But his disciples rebuked her. Jesus became angry* [very curiously like the controversy concerning the same language in Mark 1:41; see chapter 8, "Progressive Development of Scripture"] *and went off with her to the garden where the tomb was.*

Immediately a loud voice was heard from the tomb. Jesus approached and rolled the stone away from the entrance to the tomb. Immediately he went in where the young man was, stretched out his hand, and raised him by seizing his hand.

The young man looked at him intently and loved him; and he began pleading with him that he might be with him. When they came out of the tomb they went to the young man's house, for he was wealthy.

And after six days Jesus gave him a command. And when it was evening the young man came to him, wearing a linen cloth over his naked body. He stayed with him for the night, for Jesus was teaching him the mystery of the Kingdom of God. When he got up from there, he returned to the other side of the Jordan."

It is a curious passage indeed. It surely appears to be a second version, or retelling, of the Lazarus story. And if it a forgery, an issue that immediately comes to mind, why would the author not just insert the names of the persons from the "Gospel of John" — Mary and Lazarus? And why would some of the facts be changed? Why does Jesus personally roll back the stone instead of simply calling to the deceased, as in "John's" gospel? Wouldn't the forgerer want to be sure that his story is identifiable and the details parallel the other account?

The letter of Clement goes on to reject as inauthentic some of the sayings the Carpocratians attributed to the gospel, which were definitely sexual in nature, such as the purported quotation "naked body on naked body." Clement only quoted one more line from the "secret gospel". It was a sentence which Clement claimed to follow Mark 10:46: *"And the sister of the young man Jesus loved was there, along with his mother and Salome. And Jesus did not receive them."* Strangely enough, our present version of Mark 10:46 is awkwardly written, and it appears that something has been deleted. It reads, *"Now they came to Jericho. As he went out of Jericho with all his disciples and a great multitude, blind Bartimaeus, the son of Timaeus sat in the road begging."* Apparently something happened in Jericho. Why did they go to Jericho in the first place? If nothing happened there, why is it mentioned?

Morton Smith believed that the text was authentic. However, he did not accept Clement's conclusion that this was a later, different version of the Gospel of Mark. He believed that this was part of the original, authentic version, and that these passages were deleted. In fact, this is not unlikely, since there are various extant variations of Mark from ancient manuscripts. Very famously, verses 9 though 16 of chapter 16 have been added, and do not occur in the earliest, reliable manuscripts. Then there is the change already referred to of Jesus being angry in 1:41. Smith believed that these verses were deleted because they were scandalous. Smith believed that the linen cloth was related to the rite of baptism. In the ancient world adult converts were baptized by full body immersion and were fully nude. They probably wore a white linen cloth until the moment of immersion. But Smith believed there was also a homo-erotic contingent of Jesus' ceremony, where Jesus would have sexual relations with the initiates to "the mysteries of the kingdom." This does not seem to be an entirely outlandish idea. The Apostle Paul always stressed the act of baptism as the achievement of a union with Christ. Smith believed that in the private rite of Jesus this included a physical union as well, through sexual intercourse. This would seem to be in the tradition of Elmer Gantry pounding the "love of God" into impressionable, weak-willed young women, or of Catholic priests catechistically sodomizing young boys in bringing them closer to God. " Give me that old time religion!"

In addition to the above obvious internal and circumstantial evidences of genuineness, the world's foremost authority on the writings of Clement of Alexandria, Otto Stahlin, has concurred that the writing style and diction match that of Clement exactly, to the point where it would be impossible to decipher any difference between this writing and any others of Clement.[6] This is no small task for anyone. To believe it is a forgery requires that a person existed, long before the age when ancient manuscripts were readily made available, who had such a grasp not only of the eighteenth century Greek handwriting in which the monk wrote, but also of the Koine Greek of Clement, as well as the nuances and style of Clement, to have composed this work. Nevertheless, there have been attacks on the genuineness of this manuscript.

The attacks have focused around a few objections. One is that the letter, written remember on blank pages at the end of a work by Ignatius of Antioch, happens to be written in a part of the work that warns against forgeries. Hence, the theory goes, maybe this is a forgery itself. However, a reasonable response to this is that the monk who transcribed it just so happened to have found some blank pages at that spot in the work. Further, if he were a forgerer, why would he write it near a text that warns of forgeries? It would appear to be something the monk seemed to innocently ignore, which is an indicator of good faith. In point of fact, it might be added, the monk that found this must have been aware of the potentially scandalous importance of this work. He must have also been aware of the desire that many would have in the church to destroy it, just as surely as they had deleted this text from the canonical Gospel of Mark. So it would behoove him both to copy it, and to copy it in a place where it would be hidden, but could be retrieved by a person who knew where to look.

It is also claimed that the work is *too much* like the writings of Clement, and such close similitude should be suspect. This seems like a rather difficult and unwieldy hypothesis to either support or refute. This reminds me of Dr. Henry Higgins in *My Fair Lady* telling someone that their English accent was too good, therefore they must be a fraud. It is also objected that Smith dedicated his book on the subject cryptically "To the one who knows." This reference is so cryptic and ambiguous that nothing of positive merit can ever be drawn from this.

In further defense of the genuineness of this document, we could look to some other internal factors. If the document is a forgery, it is forged for some purpose. What would be the purpose? The only purpose could be to write a work that has the effect that this text does, which as I see it, is the obvious depiction of Jesus as a homosexual. And if that is the purpose of the forgerer, to embarrass the church by depicting Jesus as gay, then why the great efforts by the purported author, Clement, to condemn as false and not genuine certain phrases that he cites the Carpocratians as quoting, such as "naked man on naked man." It would seem that these phrases would be exactly the kinds of phrases the forgerer would wish to represent as those of the Gospel, rather than repudiating them. This is inconsistent and inexplicable, except as a mark of genuineness. Also, this letter is suddenly cut off in mid-sentence at the end of the blank spaces, for no explicable reason. Could it be that the only reason is that this was all that was available to the monk? Wouldn't a forgerer have left a neat ending?

These are interesting issues. The only real bottom line is that the case of the genuineness of the "Secret Gospel of Mark", itself a misnomer if it is only a text deleted from the original, cannot be conclusively proven one way or another. Smith was only allowed to take photographs of the letter, and not the volume itself. This was sufficient for most analysis, but ultimately more information as to authenticity could be obtained from the document itself.

Conclusion

Fortunately, the case as to Jesus' homosexuality does not depend on the authenticity of this purportedly deleted scene from the Gospel of Mark. It depends instead on the canonical, accepted Gospel of Mark, on the so-called Gospel of John, and on the natural, reasonable conclusions to be drawn there from. In light of this, we might be led to wonder if perhaps the theological charge against Jesus highlighted in the Gospel accounts, of blasphemy in proclaiming himself son of God, was the sole reason for the haste and determination of the Sanhedrin in putting him to death. Was there another reason that we are not being let in on? Was there another reason, of which the puritanical Jewish leaders were even too ashamed to proclaim publicly, or even charge? Perhaps we can also draw from this a potentially new perspective on Judas. Did he betray Jesus for thirty pieces of silver, as he has been demonized, or is he simply another instance of a true believer disillusioned with a phony religious leader that is engaged in what he sees as perversion. These are all matters for speculation and can never be answered.

The Gospel of Thomas

The Gospel of Thomas is a controversial document that has been universally discredited by mainstreams biblical scholars, which has been historically dominated by believers. The several centuries after Jesus saw a plethora of fraudulent and often eponymous literature purporting to be sacred texts. Opponents of the Gospel of Thomas relegated the texts to this category. In recent decades it has been more widely accredited. The attacks on its authenticity have been largely twofold. It has been depicted as a late text and therefore too remote from the teachings of the historical Jesus. It has also been attacked substantively as containing claimed statements of Jesus, in particular in regard to gender and sexuality, as so inconsistent with the teachings of Jesus in the canonical gospels as to constitute obvious forgeries. The nature of these claimed inconsistencies and their correlation with the canonical statements of Jesus will be examined below.

First, as to the historicity of the gospel. The complete text, in Coptic language was discovered at Nag Hammadi, Egypt in 1945, along with a hidden library of other texts. However, there were portions of a Greek text of the same discovered in the late nineteenth and early twentieth century at Oxyrhynchus, Egypt, dated from 130 A.D to 250 A.D. The gospel had also been referenced by earlier church authorities. So early versions of the extant texts are believed to be dated to at the most about 200 A.D. The dating of an original text is debated. Christians are quick to rebut the authenticity of a writing based on the lateness of known or extant versions of the documents. And yet there are no extant early versions of the accepted canonical gospels (i.e., the New Testament). Indeed, the earliest portion of a piece of the New Testament gospels is a piece of the Gospel of John the size of a credit card from approximately 125 A.D., a hundred years after Jesus and a good 30-35 years after the gospel was written.

However, the nature of the Gospel of Thomas is a collection of sayings of Jesus, purportedly written by Jesus' twin brother, Dydimus Thomas, with no miraculous birth narratives, no miracles, no messiahship, no resurrection, no end times predictions, and in fact no biographical information whatsoever. Also, the sayings almost all have a counterpart in the synoptic gospels, although sometimes with different wording, showing that it is an independent tradition and not merely a copy of the synoptic gospels. In point of fact, this difference of wording is part of the proof offered that this collection of sayings pre-exists the canonical, synoptic gospels. It is precisely a collection of sayings of Jesus which is considered to be an antecedent to the creation of the later, formal gospels. As a source of Jesus' sayings, the form and content of this gospel has much in common with what is called the *Q* gospel, a source preceding our synoptic gospels of Matthew, Mark and Luke and which each drew information from. And it is also the very lack of the progressive embellishment of miraculous birth, miracles, messiahship, end times predictions, and resurrection that we find in the other gospels that attests to its authenticity. It is literally written before those traditions had crept into the narrative. The most important thing about Jesus to its presumed author, and to its audience, was his message. It is wisdom literature. Bible scholar John Dominick Crossan, a chief scholar of the Gospel of Thomas, considers it to have been written approximately 50 A.D., carefully explaining his methodology of dating in his work *The Historical Jesus*, and reaffirmed in his introduction to *The Gospel of Thomas: The Lost Sayings of Jesus*, by Dart and Riegert (Seastone Press, 2000). Bible scholar Helmut Koester, in an exhaustive and authoritative study of the history of early Christian writings, including the gospels, determined this gospel to mark the earliest strata of sayings literature of Jesus, predating the canonical gospels (*Ancient Christian Gospels: Their History and Development*, Trinity Press International). Far from being farfetched later documents, they have all the hallmarks of original Jesus history. There is even evidence the original may have been written in a dialect of Aramaic, the language of Jesus, which would make it one of the few original Christian writings to have had that distinction, almost all early Christian writing, including our New Testament Gospels, having been in Koine Greek, the literal common world language of the western world at the time.

The supposed inconsistent teachings of Jesus contained in the gospel are quite surprising, but in no way are they inconsonant with the teachings or behavior we have already identified in the canonical, "mainline" gospels. However, to Christians they are shocking, and so offensive that they deserve the brand of heresy which the church has long branded them with.

In saying paragraph (logia) 22 he sees children being suckled and compares them to those entering the Kingdom of heaven. He is asked "Shall we then, as children, enter the Kingdom?" He replies, "When you make the two one…and when you make the male and the female one and the same, so that the male be not male nor the female female…then you will enter the Kingdom."

These passages are often alluded to as promoting "unisex" or certainly asexuality. But to even postulate this conclusion implies a transcendence of one's biological gender or sexual roles. And this is the offense to Christians, who proudly herald their God as the creator of biological gender, who does not create or instill any such thing as gender confusion. They see their Jesus as only going to the bathroom appropriate to his biological birth gender (kudos to Mike Johnson and the Maga Republicans!). The asexuality is certainly akin to the teaching that one must become as a child to enter the kingdom of heaven, since a child has presumably no sexual desires. It is also a direct extension of his praise of men who castrate themselves to enter the Kingdom of Heaven in the canonical gospels, the design of which is perfectly consistent with these verses.

There is unmistakable support of at least *female* transgenderism as well as unmistakable misogyny. A woman must become a man to be saved. In logia 114, Simon Peter suggests "Let Mary leave us, for women are not worthy of life." Jesus replies "I myself shall lead her

Jesus of Nazareth: Savior and Sodomist

in order to make her male, so that she too may become a living spirit resembling you males. For every woman who will make herself male will enter the Kingdom of Heaven." This seems like an impossible task. Not so impossible in the twenty-first century, and perhaps bizarrely not so difficult for Jesus of Nazareth in the first century if he himself had aspects of both sexes in his character. But this is all fully consistent with the mainline, accepted gospels. In fact, the woman becoming a man is merely a mirror counterpart to a man castrating himself to enter the kingdom of heaven, so easily sanctioned by Jesus in the synoptic gospels.

In the bizarre world of this first century "great teacher" (or *God man*) men castrate themselves to become effeminate, and women transform into men. It is only a short skip and a hop to his extended live-in stay with Lazarus, whom Jesus "loved", in the excised "Secret Gospel of Mark"; or to Lazarus shamelessly snuggling on his shoulder at the Last Supper; or to his being caught with a naked young man in the woods the night of his arrest that ran away. It is a strange world indeed for this young Jewish rabbi "great teacher", and a far cry from the homophobic bathroom politics of his ardent contemporary Maga followers. This is the LGBT Jesus we never knew.

Postscript and Apology

I should apologize for the use of the term "sodomist" in the title to this chapter. My intention was to utilize the language used by Christian evangelicals to refer to gays, with such epithets as "sodomists" and "buggerers", used by church luminaries such as the late Jerry Falwell and the ever versatile Ted Haggard (who converted church funds to pay male prostitutes). It only seemed fair to me to use the same epithets in referring to their savior. No offense was intended to gays, and although not politically correct, I do also have a number of legal codes in support of the term being legally correct, such as the Uniform Code of Military Justice, the Texas Penal Code, and the old Indictable Offenses Act in effect in most of the British Caribbean Commonwealth, which define sodomy as *consensual* sexual relations between two males. Although I know that many Bible proponents also feel the term is offensive, I feel no need to apologize to them.

CHAPTER EIGHT

THE PROGRESSIVE DEVELOPMENT OF DOCTRINE IN THE BIBLE — ORTHODOXY SPRINGING FROM DIVERSITY IN THE NEW TESTAMENT

As we previously discussed, one of the Bible proponents' self-defense weapons to explain what could potentially be seen as inconsistent teachings is the doctrine of progressive revelation: God gave us what we needed, or what we could understand and digest, at various epics of human history. He also gave us what we otherwise needed at each stage of history to form us into the people and society we would need to become for the succeeding epic. Abraham did not need to know about the Holy Trinity, so it wasn't disclosed to him. Later, humans would need to know this. I call this approach the "A,B,C's" of Biblical understanding. In this approach God, in dealing with humans throughout history, at least before the present era, dealt with humans on the basis of **accommodation** (it is no use forcing too much on stubborn, wayward humans all at once, so let's give in to their whims and habits), which might justify God condoning what we would see as horrendous violence, abuse and genocide, things which in this view were really not the things of God, but the things of humans that God merely condoned for a season; **borrowing** from pre-existing human institutions and practices to make himself understood and more readily obeyed, such as perhaps borrowing what may appear to be a far-fetched ritual, or genocidal violence, or a prevalent but erroneous understanding of something in nature; and **condescension** — God explains things in a manner that people can understand, like dealing with children, and gives in to some of their fancies. As can be seen, these concepts overlap.

God uses these approaches to gradually bring humans from one place, the place God finds them, to another, loftier place, that God wants them to be. He does so throughout history, always having in mind the ultimate sacrifice of Christ and a New Covenant through the blood, in which his Holy Spirit would be united with his people, and they would no longer need to rely on cumbersome ritual structures of the Law of Moses, but they would have the indwelling Spirit to guide them. We can interpret much of Scripture in the light of this approach. The teaching that mold is a form of leprosy in Leviticus chapter 13, and the remedies given for "leprosy in a building", can be seen as incorporating (borrowing) foolish pre-existing human understanding into the law in order to satisfy (accommodate) deficient human understanding of something that people thought was important. Why attempt to correct them? It could only lead to distrust of God's law and to rebellion, so God talks to them in a way they will appreciate (condescension). Some, although it seems an increasing minority among evangelicals, would even say God tells people stories that may not be literally factual, but which are allegories of the human condition, such as the Garden of Eden, or the seven days creation. Hence, discrepancies can be explained and harmonized. God has gradually revealed more and more truth in history.

In truth, when studied more closely, what we really find is not progressive revelation, but progressive development of doctrine. The Bible is not a unity. It is fundamentally a disunity. It is a disunified conglomeration of diverse, often contradictory and inconsistent points of view. All of the biblical editing in the world cannot cover this up. This is so because the Bible, both the Old and New Testaments, grew out of historical diversity and progressive change. Different points of view — theological and cultural — predominated at different points of time, and the authors expressed those views. The world of the Old Testament eventually grew into an orthodoxy, in which variant views from Israel's past were gradually smothered, often accompanied by awkward assimilation, reinterpretation and editing. Something very similar happened in the world of the New Testament, as Christianity became what we know as Christianity today.

The Progressive Development of Doctrine in the Bible

New Testament Development of Doctrine

The orthodox view is that there was one single Christian theology since 32-33 A.D., the presumed time of the resurrection of Christ and Pentecost. This orthodoxy was absolute, universal, and wholly consistent. In this view, under the unifying force of the Holy Spirit —a single mind—the apostles promulgated a single, unified faith throughout the world, which faith, with the same central doctrines, is carried on today in the mainstream church (the Catholics would agree with this but say it is preserved in the Catholic church; the protestants would say it is the protestant churches generally; the Eastern Orthodox would say obviously that it is *their* doctrine). As opposed to this apostolic orthodoxy, heretics would arise and challenge the *correct*, orthodox teachings, and attempt to deliberately change and distort the well-established doctrines laid down by the apostles. But they were obviously not biblical teachings, most Christians realized that, and these heretics were repudiated by mainstream, orthodox bishops and the church hierarchy, the successors of the apostles and upholders of true, orthodox doctrine. Sometimes these heresies would grow large, and suppression would be arduous and difficult, such as those that rejected the doctrine of the Holy Trinity, necessitating a major, world- wide church council, such as the Council of Nicea in 325 A.D., which was necessary to get everyone on board for orthodoxy in order to formally repudiate and drum out the heretics. In fact, this view is based on the idea of a universal, uniform church that we see emerge after the Council of Nicea, called by the Emperor Constantine, himself a convert, and immediately the temporal figurehead, enforcer, and therefore the most decisively influential person in the church.

We now know that this is not the correct view. The early Christian world, before the Council of Nicea, from the first century to the fourth, was an amazingly diverse group, with distinctive, conflicting views of such basic things as who, or what, Jesus was, and what he did for us. We can only give a thumbnail sketch here. Early in the last century, Walther Bauer wrote a book called *Orthodoxy and Heresy in the Early Church*. Bauer studied early Christianity in all areas of the ancient world. He studied all reports available to him as to what Christians believed, starting with the Apostle Paul and his contemporaries. Although there have been some refinements of his findings, his results have been generally accepted by scholars. Prior to the Council of Nicea in 325 A.D. there was generally a great diversity of beliefs within the church.

There were adoptionists. This is perhaps the most interesting group in many respects because it is most associated with the early *Jewish* Christians, who were obviously the *first* Christians, before, or in the very infant stages, of the evangelization of the Gentile world. Therefore it has the logical distinction of claiming to be early Christianity itself, or at least the early Christology — the study of who and what Christ really was — God or man or both? The Jewish Christians were the nascent Christians [1]. Adoptionists believed that Jesus was not God. He was a man of natural birth, He was adopted as the son of God at his baptism, at which time he was anointed by God and received the Holy Spirit in a manner never before experienced by a mortal man.

There were docetists, who believed that Jesus was strictly God, only taking the form of man, with no real humanity. So he did not suffer on the cross, he only appeared to suffer, because God cannot suffer. There were Gnostics, who had more exotic beliefs — there were many Gods; that some persons were beings that had fallen from heaven and now trapped in human bodies, but retained a divine spark. They only needed knowledge to return to heaven. Jesus provided that special, secret knowledge that they could attain by having a relationship with him. There were separationists, generally a doctrine held by many Gnostics and docetists - but by all rights logically closely analogous to adoptionism — that the Christ spirit, the divine being in Jesus, which some believed he had received at his baptism, left Jesus at his crucifixion and only the man Jesus died on the cross.

What happened is that one point of view won out. It was the Roman point of view. Rome was the center of the empire, the center of the literate world, the administrative center of the world, the center of the political world, and it became the administrative center of the church. In its midst were many great propagandists. Its views, which before 325 A.D. we refer to as proto-orthodox, gained dominance and became Christian orthodoxy after the conversion and ascendency of Constantine. Under the Emperor Theodotius, in 390 A.D. it became the exclusive state religion of the Roman Empire, its edicts enforced by the sword. Heresy was viciously suppressed. Then we move into the realm of medieval, state-sponsored religious terrorism that we are much more familiar with in Christian history. All conflicting views were branded as heresies. [2]

Now part of the problem we have in understanding the heretics' point of view is the scarcity of their documents. Scriptures were copied handwritten by scribes. Once the other views were branded heretical, they were not copied. Then they were destroyed. So we know of the views of the heretics mostly from the rebuttal of the heresies by such persons as Ireneas, second century bishop of Lyon, Gaul (now France) and Origen. Bart D. Ehrman, an original colleague of master conservative Bible scholar Bruce Metzger, and now the Chair of Religious Studies at he University of North Carolina, Chapel Hill, in *Misquoting Jesus,* has shown the frequent incompetence, ineptitude and illiteracy common among the scribes of the first through the fourth centuries, the seed time of our New Testament. [3] What is most important for purposes of this chapter, and of this book, is the effect on the transcription of the Bible and the Bible's reliability. Most importantly, in addition to the problems of error in transcription, it is a proven fact that there are numerous theologically- oriented, deliberate changes in the Bible to affect the wording and the meaning of portions of the New Testament, *i.e., even if you believe in the Bible, there are numerous forgeries you must account for.* Below are some of these deliberate, intentional changes.

Baptism of Jesus: *"This is my beloved son in you I am well pleased."* Luke 3:22.

In chapter one of the book of Hebrews, the author of that work provides us an interesting apologetic designed to show us the uniqueness of Jesus (according to Christians demonstrating his divinity). The chapter is designed to show that God *"has in these last days spoken to us through his son, whom he has **appointed** heir of all things* [not that he already was], *through whom also he made the worlds; who being the brightness of his glory and the **express image** of his person",* he purged us of sin and *"having **become** much better than the angels* [not that he was before]*, as he has by inheritance **obtained** a more excellent name than they"* [not that he necessarily always had a higher name than they] (Hebrews 1:2-4). There is plenty of room for argument within this preface as to whether the following section is designed to show that Jesus was God, and even this introductory paragraph seems as though the author is wedded to an adoptionist view of Jesus' "sonship." But be that as it may, the author wishes to show Jesus higher than the angels, and what is of interest to us is the following passage: *"For to which of his angels did he ever say: 'You are my son, today I have begotten you?"* (Heb. 1:5, being a quote from Psalm 2, referring to the anointment of King David). The author goes on to cite a number of verses from the Psalms, mostly written in reference to King David, such as Psalm 2 itself, or in reference to the rulers of the house of David. An interesting question, however, is when in the New Testament did God ever *say* this to Jesus? Verse 5 indicates that God really did *say* this to Jesus. This quote from Psalm 2 is repeated in Hebrews 5:5. Bible proponents have a ready answer: God said this to Jesus in Psalm 2, of course, and at no other time.

However, in Luke 3:22, Matthew 3:17, and Mark 1:9, at his baptism, the Holy Spirit appears in the form of a dove and a voice from heaven declares, *"You are my beloved son, in whom* [or you, Luke] *I am well pleased."* Yet in what appears to be a very early from of the Gospel of Luke, which Bart Ehrman has determined, based upon legitimate and accepted standards of biblical interpretation, to be the oldest form of the Gospel, God cites psalm 2 at the baptism of Jesus: *""You are my beloved son, today I have begotten you."* The conclusion that this is the authentic version is mostly a matter of pure logic. It is much more highly likely, especially given the victory, predominance, and tenacity of the Trinitarian view within church history, even to the point of burning at the stake all who would dare question the doctrine, that scribes made this change, deleting *"today I have begotten you"*, than it is that a scribe somewhere dared to add Psalm 2 to the text. It is more likely that they made the change so that the Gospel of Luke corresponded with existing versions of Matthew and Mark. **[4]** This is a highly adoptionist narrative. Why? In what manner has God ever begotten Jesus? If so, how can he be a co-equal, eternally pre-existent oneness in being with the father? Is he not then a subordinate being? Once again, volumes have been written for and against this position, and for most of the past seventeen hundred years there has been an overwhelming number of volumes written of Christian *spins* on this verse. The most popular is that Jesus was "eternally begotten of the father" or "begotten not made" (Nicean Creed) — a nice, ambiguous way of saying that Jesus could be both *begotten,* coming into existence at some point in time, and also be eternal. So *begotten* is apparently different from being made. If you have a baby, you and your spouse did not *make* the baby. The baby was always *somewhere, somehow, in some manner* a part of you (?!)

This is enough of theology. Although it is fascinating, the mind-boggling machinations of biblical Christology, as advanced by Bible advocates, are about as infinite as our Universe, but far less orderly and logical than our Universe is. Gaze at the night sky and you will find peace and solace. Concentrate on the biblical theology of Bible proponents and you are on the way to a straight jacket. My point is not the theological ramifications, but rather the literary trustworthiness. It just so happens that this original rendition of the baptism in Luke, and the obvious adoptionist slant of it, conforms to much else in Luke. After his baptism, *"Jesus,* **being filled with the Holy Spirit***, returned from the Jordan and* **was led by the Spirit** *into the wilderness, being tempted for forty days by the devil."* (Luke 4:1). Now wait a minute! These are troubling verses for the Christian apologist. How could Jesus (other name: God) be filled with the Holy Spirit? I thought *we* were supposed to get filled with the Holy Spirit? How can God fill God? And when was he filled with the Holy Spirit? As written, right after his baptism he is observed *then* "filled with the Holy Spirit." So presumably he was not always filled with the Holy Spirit. It appears that his "being filled with the Holy Spirit" happened when he was baptized, doesn't it? So the baptism takes on more than symbolism. It is an actual anointing, such as was done with the kings of Israel.

And what about this Jesus being "led by the Spirit?" How and why can the Holy Spirit *lead* Jesus anywhere? Isn't Jesus a co-equal member of the Holy Trinity, not in any way subordinate? John Wesley naturally had his Christian *spin.* The Holy Spirit's sphere of activity is God's contact with man, so while incarnated in the world, Christ is temporarily under the tutelage and direction of the Holy Spirit, although not always so. This is the art, or the doctrine, of *kenosis,* or emptying of Jesus, referred to in Philippians 2:5, where the son temporarily gives up his power and authority. A very neat, tidy explanation of the matter. We will not even get into the temptation in the desert. Was Jesus really "in all points tempted as we are?" (Hebrews 4:15). Does that mean that he not only could be tempted (How can God be tempted by the devil, his creation?), but that he was also *capable of giving in to temptation?* Could God commit sin? If he constitutionally *could* not sin, then how can he be said to have been tempted in the same manner we are, if we definitely *are* constitutionally capable of giving in to sin? Christian apologists have answers. They have answers for everything. They have had two thousand years to do nothing but think up answers to render the absurd seemingly logical. But the logic only satisfies those that already have faith and so *want* to believe, and are looking for something to hang their hat on. ("You must have faith in order to understand", not the opposite — paraphrasing St. Augustine). What we are seeing here - really in all of this section of Luke, especially in the original, Psalm 2 version of the baptism of Jesus, as well as the preface to Hebrews — is original, nascent Christianity. Jesus was a man, adopted by God at his baptism, endowed with the Holy Spirit as no man before, who was anointed to die for sin, and only after was he made higher than the angels and took his place as celestial ruler of humanity. Deliberate, calculated church-orchestrated corruption and suppression of texts followed.

Hebrew 2:9

Hebrews 2:8-9, in its current version, states , *"For when [God] subjects to him[Christ] all things, he leaves nothing that is not subjected to him. But we do not yet see all things subjected to him. But we do see Jesus, who, having been made for a little while lower than the angels, was crowned with glory and honor on account of his suffering and death, so that* **by the grace of God** *he might taste death for everyone."* However, there exists another ancient translation which states that Jesus died, not *"by the grace of God",* but *"apart from God."* Although our earliest existing manuscript is from the tenth century, one of the later manuscripts is copied from a second century manuscript, which bears this alternative version, *"apart from God."* More importantly, Origen, in the third century, verifies that this was the majority reading at that time, and it is quoted by a large number of churchmen, including Ambrose and Jerome, in the early centuries. [5]

That this is undoubtedly the original phrase in the Epistle to the Hebrews is clear from the accepted, standard rules of biblical hermeneutics. Here is why: "*Apart* from God" is the "harder" saying harder in terms of reconciling this with the rest of Christian theology. It seems mysterious as it stands, and much more likely a scribe would change it to something more suitable and understandable. Not only is "*apart from God*", finds Ehrman, consistent with the diction and style of Hebrews, but it is also more consistent with the theology of Hebrews. That theology is evident in the preface to chapter one of Hebrews, quoted above, which emphasizes the humanity of Jesus — he was "*appointed heir of all things*" and he "*became much better than the angels*" through his sacrifice. Hebrews also tells us how Jesus prayed "*with vehement cries and tears to him who was able to save him from death...yet he learned obedience by the things which the suffered...*" (Hebrews 5:7-8), seeming as though he did not want to fulfill the mission assigned to him, but learned obedience and did it anyway. And curiously this passage goes on, "*...having been perfected, he became the author of eternal salvation to all who obey him...*" (5:9). Indeed, we are told that , "*For it was fitting for him, for whom are all things and by whom are all things, in bringing many sons to glory, to make the captain of their salvation **perfect through sufferings***" (2:10). Only in Hebrews does Jesus become perfect through his death. We are left wondering how *he* was *imperfect* prior to his death on the cross. He is presented as very human, being "*in all points tempted*" just as we are (Heb. 4:15). So this theology — to be exact, this Christology — can be seen as compatible with the now heretical adoptionist approach. Under this approach, as well as under a separationist model, Jesus dies cut off from God.

In fact, the wording "apart from God" seems to fully complement Jesus' own words on the cross in the Gospels of Mark and Matthew: "*My God, My God, why have you forsaken me*" (Mark 15:34). In doing so he quotes the beginning of Psalm 22, which is King David in despair. This portrays a man that at least at that time, is not God. However, Bible proponents have once again put their *spin* on this phrase. It goes like this: God cannot tolerate sin — he hates it. Jesus, God the Son, just took all of the sins of the world — past, present and future - by God's judicial act, onto *himself* and they became *his* sins. So God *the father* cannot by his nature, as the embodiment of goodness, bear to see this, so he turns his back on the Son suffering on the cross (who somehow mysteriously, even though he is also the very same God nature, can and does bear it). And for that moment, Jesus experiences separation from the father, something he has never experienced because he is one with God. How *God* can be *separated* from *God* we are only left to try to wonder and imagine as we contemplate the arcane mystery of the Holy Trinity. Although he was *separated,* this is not the damnably heretical *separationist* doctrine — because he was *still* God and never separated from the God nature. Got that? I hope someone, somewhere does. I do not know how many hundreds of times I have made the above speech, and used the above explanation as a teaching point. Each time I made the above argument something inside of me just shuddered. But the point is this: If he is forsaken by God, then he is truly dying *"apart from God."*

I Timothy 3:16

Also to resist adoptionist tendencies in Scripture, there were theologically inspired changes to the text of I Timothy 3:16. Our Bibles say, *"God was manifested in the flesh..."* But in the Codex Alexandrinus, another very early text, the original text had the subject not as God, but as Christ, *"who was made manifest in the flesh"*, not implying that God was made manifest in the flesh in the person of Christ, which is the current implication. This text was obviously changed by a scribe by the slight change in Greek of a single letter — changing the theta to an omicron, which are two letters which look very much alike. So it no longer said "who was made manifest in the flesh" but now said "God made manifest in the flesh..." i.e., Jesus was now God, not what the original author said at all, but "good enough for Bible work." It turned out that the same forgery had occurred in four other early manuscripts. Eventually this forged translation became the majority translation. **[6]**

John 1:18

Likewise, in the Alexandrian version of John 1:18, Jesus is referred to as the "unique God" rather than the "unique son." This translation only appears in the Alexandrian version, which immediately causes suspicion. It did not become the majority version, and so it is not even in the King James Version and the versions derived from it. This is a deliberate scribal attempt to make Jesus God. It is not a very controversial one, since many Bible proponents do not believe it belongs in the Bible and admit it is a corruption by well-meaning scribes.

Gospel of Luke, and Joseph as "father"

In Luke 2:33 we have the story of the baby Jesus in the Temple, where he was blessed by Simeon, who makes a long oracle over the future savior. Many early versions state that "his father and his mother were marveling at what was said to him." This is later changed by scribes to make a universally, consistent rendition: "Joseph and his mother were marveling..." The reasons are obvious: Joseph has now ceased to be the father of Jesus — God is his father now. Later, twelve year old Jesus disappears from his parents and their group when they leave and he stays behind in the Temple. Older texts state that *"his parents* did not know it." Scribes transform this to say "Joseph and his mother did not know it." Later he is found in the Temple, speaking with prominent persons. Mary scolds Jesus saying *"Your father* and I have been looking for you!" Naturally, this is later changed to the uncontroversial *"We* have been looking for you."

I Corinthians 14:34-35.

First Corinthians chapter 14, an epistle of the apostle Paul, has been changed to affect the role of women in the church. This section *"Let your women keep silent in the churches, for they are not permitted to speak; but they are to be submissive, as the law also says. And if they want to learn something, let them ask their own husbands at home; for it is shameful for women to speak in church."* This is obviously a forgery for the following reasons. It appears in different places in the chapter in different early manuscripts; and where it appears in our Bibles, it

Conviction Overturned

is out of place, intruding and interrupting a discussion of prophesying and speaking in tongues, and then afterwards the discussion reverts to the discussion about prophesying. It was obviously inserted by a later misogynist who felt the issue had to be addressed.

But more importantly, it completely contradicts other teachings of Paul, who, for instance, just got done saying that women should "pray and prophesy" with their head covered. Now how can women prophesy in church and be silent at the same time? That is ridiculous. In I Corinthians 12:13 he stresses the equality of all in Christ. In Galatians 3:28 he declares without reservation, *"...There is neither male nor female, for you are all one in Christ Jesus."* Does this sound like the person who wrote the above section in I Corinthians 14? He always extolls women in ministry, especially in Romans 16, where he commends one "Junia" whom he calls an "apostle" (16:7; although some Bible proponents have deliberately and with absolutely no textual support changed the translation to Junius, a man's name, in order to avoid the apparent designation of her as an "apostle", which is a contradiction with I Corinthians 14). An apostle spreads the word, which is hard to do if you are always silent — the tricks go on, even after 2,000 years! And he says: "Greet Priscilla and Aquila, my *fellow workers* in Christ", terms used to depict those preaching the Gospel, and of course we know from Acts that this Priscilla and Aquila took it upon themselves to correct the errors of a Gospel preacher, Apollo. [7]

Objection will be taken that the section in I Corinthians corresponds with the tenor and teaching of I Timothy 2:11-15, which also demands silence from women. However, in the case of the Pastoral epistles — I and II Timothy and Titus, what is undermined is not the passage, but these works in their entirety. There are no credible biblical scholars that are not convinced that these works are second century forgeries. Marcion, who developed the first New Testament canon in approximately 140 A.D., believed in only the writings of Paul as authentically from Christ and sought to include everything from Paul in his canon. He had never heard of I or II Timothy, nor Titus. Additionally, the subject matter of subjection to a church hierarchy is from a later time period of church history.

Mark 1:41

Ehrman cites more examples. In early versions of Mark 1:41 Jesus is quoted as being "angry" when he heals a leper. But since Jesus must be portrayed as Godlike, he cannot be angry. The other three Gospels, written later than Mark, and in the case of Matthew and Luke, being based partially on Mark, always portray Jesus as compassionate. In fact, they tell the same story and say that Jesus had compassion when he healed the leper. So this verse is undoubtedly later changed by scribes to say, in conformity with the other two Gospels, that Jesus, "feeling compassion", healed the man. However, our current version still retains the phrase that after healing him, Jesus "severely rebuk[ed]" the man and then "cast him out", which seems more consistent with his anger, and less consistent with compassion. Someone has clearly "monkeyed" with the text (I now wonder if that expression is derived from something scribal "monks" do).

Luke 22:44: Jesus "sweating blood"

Likewise, in our present Gospel of Luke, we are told that in the garden of Gethsemane Jesus "sweated blood" (Luke 22:44), but this is absent from many early texts. It is highly unlikely, for very obvious reasons, that ancient scribes would ever deliberately take out of the text something so important. It is much more likely they would have added this to show the emotional suffering of Jesus alongside his physical suffering. However, it is inconsistent with the demeanor of Jesus portrayed throughout the rest of the arrest, trial and execution narratives. Jesus is by no means "silent before his executioners" in the Gospel of Luke. He addresses the Sanhedrin and proclaims himself the son of God, he talks to women on the way to the cross, and on the cross has a self-assured, upbeat, inspirational talk to the robbers dying with him. Unlike Mark and Matthew, there is no anguished protest of being "forsaken" by God at the moment of death. So the original reading, without the sweating blood, is unquestionably the correct one — this is a Jesus that accepted his role.

Mark 16:9-10

We have already considered this in the issues of the resurrection. It is the summary of Jesus' resurrection appearances, which is a condensation of the other Gospel narratives. Few Bible scholars consider these passages genuine. For one thing, it begins by telling us who Mary Magdalen was, even though she has just appeared in the preceding section. It is the only portion of the Gospels that talks about Jesus' disciples being enabled to speak in strange tongues, pick up snakes or drink poison. It is not in many early versions, and if it were genuine, Christian scribes would surely not have excised these portions. It is much more probable that scribes attempted to summarize the resurrection accounts from the other Gospels, which is exactly what has occurred here. The original Gospel ended with an open tomb as proof of the resurrection.

There are many more examples to be considered. What is the net effect of this faulty record of transmission? Bart Ehrman best summarizes it when he describes his journey into the intricacies of Bible study. He relates how he "began seeing the new Testament as a very human book...This stood very much at odds with how I had regarded the text in my late teens as a newly minted 'born again' Christian, convinced that the Bible was the inerrant Word of God and that the biblical words had come to us by the inspiration of the Holy Spirit. As I realized in graduate school, even if God had inspired the original words, we don't have the original words...For the only reason (I came to think) for God to inspire the Bible would be so that his people would have his actual words; but if he really wanted people to have his actual words, surely he would have miraculously preserved those words, just as he had miraculously inspired them in the first place. Given the circumstances that he didn't preserve the words, the conclusion seemed inescapable to me that he hadn't gone to the trouble of inspiring them." **[8]**

Although it took centuries for the Christian west to see what had occurred, the phenomenon of Bible distortion and self-serving re-writing was known to the ancients. In the second century, Christian opponent Porphyry wrote, *"Some believers, as though from a drinking bout, go so far as to oppose themselves and alter the original text of the gospel three or four or several times over, and change its character to enable them to deny difficulties in the face of criticism."* **[9]**

So far we have only reviewed obvious alterations of the text. There were also entire alternative Gospels, other writings that were suppressed, such as the *Gospel of Peter*, once accepted and read by at least some churches in Asia Minor as late as the third century A.D. In this Gospel, in a twist on the Matthew *"My God, my God, why have you forsaken me?"*, we have Jesus at the point of death saying instead, *"My power has left me..."* The narration then intimates that the Christ left the body of Jesus on the cross. This is clear separationism.

Acceptable Heresy: That which "made it" into our New Testament

We have discussed deliberate corruption of the New Testament. But even without the corrupted passages, what we have left is an incongruous, inconsistent and doctrinally incoherent set of writings, ready-made for the baloney shelf. On issues of doctrine, the Bible has the same degree of inconsistency and incoherence that we saw on the factual level. In truth and in fact, all the editing and corruption of Scripture cannot overturn the doctrinal irregularities and incongruities that are still obvious in the New Testament and which attest to earlier alternative historical-factual narratives and alternative doctrines, which later were made heretical and suppressed.

The first ten chapters of the book of Acts describe the earlier, pre-Pauline days of the Jewish Christian church in Judea. The church is headed by Peter and he is the dominant person in the narratives. The book attempts to relate some of his early sermons. In terms of what we know of early Jewish Christianity — the Ebionites, or the Nazareans — it is amazing how some of Peter's utterances parallel those doctrines later decried as heretical by the church.

In Acts chapter 2, the day of Pentecost, Peter gives the first sermon by the newly anointed disciples. He is freshly "full of the Holy Spirit", having just been anointed, accompanied by a rushing wind and cloven tongues of fire over his head, and those of the disciples. He proclaims *"that God has made this Jesus, whom you crucified, both Lord and*

Christ." (Acts 2:36). When did God *make him* [Jesus] *the Christ?* If he was God in the flesh, wasn't he the Christ from birth, destined to save man? As God in the flesh, wasn't he always *the Lord* of all creation? This has a definite and unmistakable adoptionist overtone.

Later, when Peter preaches the Gospel to Cornelius, a gentile, and so begins the ministry to the gentile world, he says that *"God anointed Jesus of Nazareth with* **the Holy Spirit and with power,** *who went about doing good and healing all who were oppressed by the devil, for* **God was with him.**"(Acts 10:38). This is an auspicious beginning to Peter's version of the early Jewish Gospel. Did Jesus' powers come with his anointing at his baptism? This is what is unequivocally implied. If not, when did this "anointing" occur"? Jesus was anointed *by* the Holy Spirit, in Christian theology, at his baptism, but was he anointed *with* [receipt of] the Holy Spirit? Wasn't he always one of the three persons of the Godhead, and therefore always one with the Holy Spirit and the father? And was "God with him" or was God *in him?* (Or was he just *God*?).

To the apostle Paul, there is little question over who Jesus is. There is always a distinction between God and Jesus — they are not one, and not the same thing: *",,,yet for us there is one God, the father, of whom are all things, and we for him, and one Lord, Jesus Christ, through whom are all things, and through whom we live."* (I. Cor. 8:9). Even in the pseudo-Pauline II Timothy, probably written by Paul's disciples, *"There is one God and one Mediator between God and men, the man Jesus Christ..."*(I Timothy 2:5). In Philippians 2:5-11, Paul famously proclaims the emptying process of Jesus, who *"being in the form of God"* (NKJV), a vague expression from the Greek word *morphe* that could mean being "Godlike", *"did not consider it robbery to be equal with God"* (NKJV), or *"did not consider equality with God something to be grasped"* (NIV) — all equally vague phrases, but clearly expressing that Jesus was something less than God. How can Jesus "rob" something he *already* had? How can he grasp, or grasp for, something he already had as the very substance of his being? But we are told that because he *"humbled himself and became obedient to the point of death...God has also highly exalted him..."*(2:8-9). So it is a matter not of an eternal plan that God — Father, Son, and Holy Spirit — have fashioned and predestined, but rather of a subordinate person, apart from God, who is "obedient" and only later is "exalted" to be the most high. "God has...exalted him..."- he hasn't exalted himself. He is not God — he is an appointed, anointed sacrifice for sin, and a mediator.

And so it is, likewise in all of Paul's writings that God raised Jesus from the dead, the same as in Peter's Pentecost sermon (Acts 2:32). Only much later, in the Johannine writings, do we read that Jesus raised himself from the dead. By the time of the Gospel of John, at the end of the first century, or about sixty years after the crucifixion, Jesus has become God. That is why this is the work that every Christian apologist will cite to you (John 1:1; 8:58; 10:30; 10:33). So the fight between mainline Christians and Jehovah's Witnesses will go on forever, because both have their proof texts from a Bible that contradicts itself, being knotted together from different authors, with different views, who contradict each other.

In Matthew 5:18, written to the Jews, and probably an augmented Greek version of the original Aramaic Gospel, but with many additions, such as the virgin birth, Jesus says, *"Do not think that I have come to destroy the Law or the prophets. I did not come to destroy but to fulfill. For assuredly I say to you, till heaven and earth pass away, one jot or tittle will by no means pass from the law till all is fulfilled. Whoever breaks one of the least of these commandments and teaches others to do so shall be called least in the kingdom of heaven, but whoever does and teaches them shall be called great in the kingdom of heaven. For I say to you unless your righteousness exceeds that of the scribes and Pharisees, you will be no means enter the kingdom of heaven."*

Now any good Bible teacher worth his salt will quickly give you the Christian spin on this passage. He will tell you that Jesus is *certainly* not saying what he appears in simple English (or simple Koine Greek) to be saying. They will teach you, just as I did hundreds of times, that Jesus fulfilled the law through his death for all people for all time, and so terminated the law. So by trusting in *his* righteousness, *his* righteousness is *imputed* to you. So to them, this passage treats of the doctrine of imputation and is not what it appears to be — an admonition that the Law remain in effect, with all of its ritual, dietary and other requirements. A more sophisticated, dispensationalist approach would be that Jesus was speaking to those still rightfully under the law — the Jews — because his sacrifice had not yet occurred. Judge for yourself! The least said about this self-serving hypothesis the better. We can certainly see where the Ebionites were coming from; and if a Christian, we could wish in our heart of hearts that God could just be *a little* more clear and less ambiguous — it's these seemingly straightforward, direct, unequivocal and forceful pronouncements that get you every time. It takes a calm, dispassionate, calculating, and clever theologian to unravel these hyperbolic statements and tell us what that Jesus fellow (son of God though he may be, praise the Lord) *really* meant.

Nothing is more clear than the duel between the writings of Paul, and James, the bishop of Jerusalem and the head of the Jewish Christians, over the issue of faith and works. This is highlighted in the Epistle to the Romans and to the Galatians by Paul on the one hand, and the Epistle of James, on the other. The Jewish Christians seem to have believed that the law was still in effect — at least the Ebionites we know of. Paul insisted that it was faith alone in Christ that led to one's salvation, apart from works.

The Epistle of James was written in direct rebuttal to the message of Romans (and Galatians), or vice-verse. Why else does James use the same example of Abraham sacrificing his son Isaac, and quotes the same verse, *"Abraham believed God and it was accounted to him for righteousness"* (Gen. 15:6, quoted in James 2:23) to demonstrate the need for faith plus works, which just so happens to be the same, exact example *and citation* given by Paul to demonstrate salvation by faith alone (Romans 4:1-4; Galatians 3:6). One uses the same example in order to refute the argument of the other. Despite all the elaborate arguments in the world given by Christians, these passages contradict each other and, it should be added, *deliberately* contradict each other, as the inspired authors themselves battle it out with each other. Just read Romans, chapter 4, and then James, chapter 2, and the contest is glaring to all but those who want to believe in the inerrancy of the Bible in the first place. James says *"faith without works is dead."* *"Even the demons believe"*, we are told. *"Was not Abraham our father justified by works when he offered his son Isaac on the altar? Do you see that faith was acting together with his works and by works faith was made perfect. And the Scripture was fulfilled which* says that *'Abraham believed God and it was accounted to him for righteousness.'"*(2:22).... *"You see that a man is justified by works, and **not by faith only**"*(2:24). This is written because Paul uses the example of Abraham and quotes the same Genesis passage, but he uses it to prove that man is saved "by faith alone." *"Therefore we conclude that a man is justified by faith apart from the works of the law"*(Rom. 3:28). These thoughts, and these passages, are irreconcilable. Perhaps Bible proponents should have just opted for Martin Luther's opinion that James is just, plain not inspired and wrong, and should be deleted from the Bible.

There are other doctrinal irregularities from modern evangelical beliefs. We need only look at the role of the "the laying on of hands" and the role of baptism in the New Testament. The protestant Christian church has traditionally seen the sacrament, or ordinance, of baptism as something symbolical only — representing an outward commitment to enter into the death, burial, and resurrection of Jesus, not as an act which actually imparts the grace of God. The person being baptized is already saved by his faith. This is unlike Roman Catholic doctrine, in which the act of baptism is a sacrament which literally washes away sin and saves the infant from hell should he die. Evangelicals harshly deride a practice in which salvation is premised on a physical act, a ritual, in which the person supposedly is saved without the knowledge, belief and commitment, i.e. the faith, that the Bible says is necessary for salvation. Likewise, in the Roman Catholic tradition, a person receives the Holy Spirit by means of another sacrament when the bishop, a person in apostolic succession to the apostles, lays hands on him or her and confers the Holy Spirit. In the evangelical scenario, a person hears the Gospel, believes on Jesus as his savior, and receives the Holy Spirit.

But the New Testament is not consistent on these points. After the author of I Peter describes the salvation of Noah and his family on the ark, he informs us *"eight souls were **saved** through water. There is also an antitype* [which means a fulfillment of a pre-existing *type,* an historical prefigurement of something that will occur in the future, i.e., if you will, a proto-type and anti-type) *which now **saves us** — baptism..."* (I Peter 3:21). Paul tells us that *"As many of you as were baptized into Christ have put on Christ."*(Galatians 3:27; presumably those not baptized *have not* put on Christ yet). *"Or do you not know that as many of us as were baptized into Christ Jesus were baptized into his death? Therefore we were buried with him through baptism into death, that just as Christ was raised from the dead by the glory of the father, even so we should walk in a newness of life"* (Romans 6:3). Presumably those not baptized have not entered into his death and resurrection, have no newness of life, and still walk under the condemnation of sin. In the book of Acts, after Paul's miraculous conversion on the road to Damascus, he arrives in Damascus and makes contact with disciples, who urge him *"Arise and be baptized that your sins may be washed away, calling on the name of the Lord!"* (Acts 22:16). You will never walk into a Baptist church today and hear anyone say "Arise and be baptized so your sins can be washed away!" And yet in the early church it was universally believed that the act of baptism literally was the physical act that removed sin, and *saved* a person. **[10]** The *Didache* is a mid-second century church instructional document that implies that baptism is necessary for salvation.

When it comes to receipt of the Holy Spirit, the book of Acts seems to be out on its own exclusive terrain, which matches the Roman Catholic model more than the evangelical one. In Acts chapter 8, the evangelist Philip, arguably the same one who is an apostle in the Gospels (see chapter 3) has gone to Samaria to preach the Gospel. Many believed the Gospel and were baptized. When Peter and John heard this they went to Samaria and *"prayed for them that they might receive the Holy Spirit. For as yet He had fallen upon none of them. They had only been baptized in the name of the Lord Jesus. Then they laid hands on them, and they received the Holy Spirit."* (Acts 8:15-17). This is a curious statement. Acts seems to have its own theology of receipt of the Holy Spirit. You can believe and be baptized and not have the Holy Spirit. Can you be a *saved* Christian and not have the Holy Spirit? Apparently so. Philip, who we are told cast out evil spirits, performed miracles, and healed people (8:5-7), could not effectuate the receipt of the Holy Spirit by others. The apostles had to come from Jerusalem to lay hands on them to accomplish this. All the Christian arguments in the world cannot erase this anomaly. And this anomaly is not only in this section of Acts. In Chapter 19, Paul meets believers in Ephesus. He asks them, *"Did you receive the Holy Spirit when you believed?" So they said to him, 'We have not so much as heard whether there is a Holy Spirit."* (19:1-2). It turned out that they had only been baptized with a baptism *of repentance* of John the Baptist. So they were baptized into Jesus and Paul *"laid hands on them, and they spoke with tongues and prophesied"*(19:6). This emphasis on the need for an intermediary and the laying on of hands to receive the Holy Spirit is the reason many scholars have believed that this document is from a later period of time, such as the second century.

What we can see in the New Testament is a documentary history that parallels the surrounding early church history. It is a church with doctrine that developed out of diversity and clashes of opinion. The documentary trail merely mirrors that diversity of thought. Is it any wonder then, that a church "father" such as Origen, of the second century, the most outstanding theologian of his day, the principal spokesman and apologist for his faith against opponents, and who wrote the first comprehensive Christian commentary of Scripture, was condemned as a heretic, after he rejected the concept of the Holy Trinity, formulating his own doctrine concerning the divine status of Jesus? Or that Tertullian, a principle church father and theologian, was condemned as a heretic for supporting the Montanist doctrine, which claimed that God continued to inspire persons to declare his will (diminishing the importance of a set canon of Scripture)? Or that Clement of Alexandria, another cherished church father, espoused the openly docetist view that Jesus could not have grown tired because he was God? All of the persons above are highly regarded in the church to this day and their writings are diligently preserved and studied. Yet all held views which would be rejected by historical Christianity and views which would cause them to be sometimes marginalized from evangelical circles even today. Christianity is a bizarre club indeed. But considering the background of the New Testament, it is understandable. The same degree of incoherence and inconsistency that we saw in the factual allegations of the New Testament, in chapters 2-4, we naturally find in the attempt to form doctrinal assertions in the New Testament.

Chapter Nine

THE PROGRESSIVE DEVELOPMENT OF DOCTRINE — THE OLD TESTAMENT

With the Old Testament, we see a process similar in many respects to what we saw with the New Testament, but taking place over a very long period of time, with persons who were not contemporaries of each other, but rather with people from various stages of history and with vastly different views of God. Through a strange but obvious process of editing, these views became part of a single set of writing we know as the Old Testament, or the Jews know as the Tanakh. The most genuinely fascinating feature of this collection, is the internal self-history which it implicitly incorporates and which tradition proclaims as the Old Testament's true historical outline. And therein lays the root of the Old Testament problem, and the subject-matter of historical inquiry.

The Old Testament is intimately bound up with the history of the nation of Israel. A study of the Old Testament is a study of Hebrew history. The manner in which that history is truly reflected in the history which the Bible itself tells us is debated. The traditional, orthodox view of the history of the Bible is clear. The Old Testament, and the nation of Israel, grew from the crucible of 400 years, or alternatively four generations, of Hebrew slavery in Egypt. Moses, an Egyptian official, but born a Hebrew, is sent by God to rescue the Hebrews through signs and wonders. This occurs either in the fifteenth century B.C., or else in the thirteenth century B.C. He leads them from slavery to wander forty years in the wilderness. During the wanderings, the people of Israel have an extended stay at Mount Sinai, at which point Moses receives the Ten Commandments and volumes of other requirements from God. This is the pivotal moment in Hebrew religious history — it is the covenant with God upon which the nation of Israel and its religion is founded. During the wanderings, Moses pens the history of the exodus from Egypt and the receipt of the Law — the Book of Exodus; the Law of Moses itself given him at Mount Sinai — Leviticus; the history of the wanderings in the desert — known to us as Numbers; and another book of the origins of the world and of the Hebrews — known to us as Genesis, containing the lives of the Patriarchs up to the arrival in Egypt. Just before entering the Promised Land that would be Israel, on the plains of Moab, Moses gives a second reading of the law, known to us as Deuteronomy. These five books are the Torah, or the Pentateuch, providing all of the Law of Moses which became the cornerstone of the civil and religious system of Israel and the basis of their covenant with God. To break the Law is to turn against God. This is the traditional view of what Moses wrote. The Bible itself does not claim that Moses wrote all five books. The Bible itself claims only that Moses wrote Exodus chapters 20 through 23, the "Book of the Covenant", and Deuteronomy. Tradition, and most Christians, claim more for the Bible than the Bible does for itself. But no traditionalist rejects the principle that the Law was given to Moses, as we see it today in the Bible, and that the Torah , or Law, was written during this period.

Upon the arrival in the land, there is a period of the conquest under Joshua, and Joshua writes the book of Joshua. Later there is another history of the period of the Judges which followed, called the Book of Judges, which some claim was written by the prophet Samuel in approximately the eleventh century B.C. Then we enter the royal period of Jewish history, starting with the kings Saul, David and Solomon. After Solomon the kingdom is divided in two — the Northern Kingdom of Israel, and the Southern Kingdom of Judah. In this period we see the histories of Samuel and other historical writings — some argue the book of Kings - as a chronicle of events, started during this period. But also in this period we see the emergence of the prophets.

The prophets are "covenant enforcers", who admonish the people of Israel to remain true to the covenant and the Law of Moses. We have the non-writing prophets, who are designated as such because they have not left writings. These are all in the early royal period and their exploits are covered in the books of Kings and Chronicles. The non-writing prophets, principle among them Elijah and Elisha, are miracle workers who engage in many divine signs and wonders. The later prophets — the writing prophets, such as Isaiah, Amos, Hosea, Jeremiah — do no miracles, but leave abundant writings. The Northern Kingdom goes into captivity in 722 B.C., never to reappear again. The southern Kingdom of Judah goes into captivity in 587 B.C., the times of Jeremiah and Ezekiel. Judah returns from captivity in 538 B.C. and thus commences the era of the Second Temple. We have a few prophets from this period — Zechariah, Haggai, and later Malachi. Then the prophets cease, and we have only the "word of God" in Scripture. There are various other writings and histories, such as the histories in the book of Chronicles; such poetry as Song of Solomon, and prose such as Ecclesiastes, Ruth, and Job, which many conservative scholars, Jewish and Christian, trace to the late royal or Second Temple period. The Psalms may cover a lengthy period of time, some being held to be written by David or Solomon, but most are from the Second Temple Period. This is the traditional, orthodox view of the history of the Old Testament. It is the view adamantly held by orthodox Jews and Christians alike. In this view, the Jews have had the Law of Moses, as it exists today, from the fifteenth century B.C. (or in an alternative dating, from the thirteenth century B.C.). The prophets came later and sought to force the backsliding children of Israel to return to the covenant and the Law.

This view is challenged by another approach. This approach to the history of the Old Testament is often referred to as the "Documentary Hypothesis." This is a very poor, inaccurate, and imprecise designation. A better designation would be the "historical approach" or the "historical-literary approach." It is anything but a hypothesis, since it is based on overwhelming historical fact, starting with a common sense approach to the documents themselves and what its authors say. A great part of that process therefore involves a review of the documents themselves in order to determine order, authorship, background, and historical and theological perspective. Hence it is at the outset a "documentary" approach. From this approach we can determine conclusively that the Old Testament was written by different authors with distinctly different historical circumstances, in

The Progressive Development of Doctrine — The Old Testament

different time periods, inculcated with differing views of God, and of God's relationship with man. The Bible was not written in the order the orthodox view holds, and naturally it was edited to fit the orthodox view of God, the world, and history.

The historical approach establishes that a literary tradition commenced somewhere in the royal period. Some would say the early royal period — the time of David and Solomon. Others would claim that all literature commenced in the late royal period. Most importantly in this period, the book of Deuteronomy is traced to the late royal period, probably during the reign of Josiah, in the late seventh century B.C. In the book of Kings (II Kings 22), Josiah is presented as a devout religious reformer that restores the Temple of Solomon and the Temple cult and represses pagan religious practices. While the Temple is being refurbished in the eighteenth year of Josiah (622 B.C), Hilkiah, the high priest "finds" the "book of the Law" in the Temple and brings it to Josiah. Josiah is exhilarated, and apparently also agitated at the find. He rents his garments, a sign of extreme anguish. He reads the book and realizes how the nation has transgressed God's law, and he orders the book to be read, followed, and honored. We are led to believe by this dubious narrative that the entire Law of Moses had apparently just been lost, ignored and forgotten until they recover this book which everyone had forgotten about. The historical approach believes that this book was the book of Deuteronomy, which was probably not truly found, but rather written, at this time. But since it purports to be written by the hand of Moses, naturally it must have a purported previous history, hence the account of its recovery. Additionally, the Torah, or Pentateuch - the five books of Moses, i.e., "the Law of Moses" — is no where characterized as *the* "book of the Law." It is always regarded as five books. A single book of the law is exactly what Deuteronomy is. Yet if they already had the first four books, then how could Deuteronomy have become lost? And if lost and then found, why is it so disturbing and exhilarating to find it when they *already had* the substance of the same laws in their possession, in fact in even greater detail and scope?

The prophets write at the times that each generally indicates as the reigns during which they prophesy — Isaiah for example (at least the first 39 chapters) in the mid-eighth century to the early seventh century; Jeremiah before and at the time of the Babylonian captivity; Ezekiel shortly after (There are some exceptions. Daniel is a separate case we have already discussed. The second part of Isaiah is regarded, and practically self-authenticated, as being in the early Second Temple period).

The single most important determination for our purposes here is the advent of the Law of Moses. When did the Mosaic Law come into being — that cult which today we identify as Judaism? We see it first in the book of Deuteronomy in the late seventh century B.C., discussed above. But the final formulation of the law, as we know it today, was after the return from captivity, with most of the first four books "of Moses", and certainly the portions we know as "the law" itself, being written, or at least memorialized in the form we know it today, at the time of the scribe Ezra (and many would claim by Ezra himself) in the mid-fifth century B.C. The most common view is that Ezra's public reading of the entire law in Nehemiah chapter 8 to an astounded and moved populace, that obviously had never heard anything like it before, was nothing less than the reading of a new work — the just completed Torah that we now know. Otherwise, just as with the finding of the "book of the Law" under Josiah, it is hard to imagine that the whole nation had forgotten, or never knew about, the books that Moses composed (or better said, that God dictated word for word to Moses) and by which their nation was supposed to be governed, and apparently at some time in their history had been governed by. And supposedly the entire Temple cult and practices, and the Aaronite priesthood, had been built on the premise of these books, but nobody knew about them. This is quite hard to believe.

As to the diversity of authorship, especially in historical narratives, there are identifiable groups of writers, or "schools" of authors if you will. They are not formal associations, but rather reflect different geographic, historical, and theological settings. They are known generally as the Jahwist, Elohist, Deuteronomist, and Priestly writings. The Jahwists and Elohists predominate the writing of early history, in particular Genesis, and are distinguishable by their designation of God — as Elohim, meaning literally "the gods", a more distant and amorphous god ("El" being the principle Canaanite god); or as Yahweh, the anthropomorphic, interventionist god that Moses met on Mount Sinai and who is the God of Covenants. Within the Elohim writings there is a Priestly addition and overlay.

Bible proponents have a typically neat but ineffective rejoinder, contending that God calls himself Yahweh only when he makes covenants, otherwise he calls himself Elohim, a plural name, when not relating anything concerning his covenants, which is really an end run around the entire issue. It does not take into account that in the Elohist versions, God takes the name Yahweh after his encounter with Moses in Exodus 6, when he reveals his name, which is but another method by which the Elohist promotes Moses and the Covenant with Moses at Mount Sinai as paramount, whereas the Yahwist sees all of God's covenants as major encounters; or that the Yahwist always elevates Aaron and the Aaronid priesthood while denigrating Moses, while the Elohist denigrates Aaron repeatedly while advancing the Levites generally as a means of promoting the Shiloh priesthood.

Nor does it account for the Elohist's continuous references to places and cities in the North, which are familiar in its narrative, while the Yahwist narrative concentrates on Judah and the south, being a southern, Judahite perspective; or why in Genesis 49, the Yahwist version establishes Jacob's blessing giving supremacy to Judah, and in the Elohist supremacy is given to Ephraim; or why Joshua, an Ephraimite, is successor to Moses in the Elohist version, but has no role in the Yahwist version; or for that matter, the Yahwist obsession with the supremacy of Judah and the rule of the house of David, not shared by the Northern-oriented Elohist. Or the fact that the Yahwist narratives are full of anthropomorphisms and the direct, active intervention of Yahweh; whereas the Priestly writers, portray a more abstract, less personalized God. [1]This is only a very brief, thumbnail sketch of a few of the differences. There are many more.

So, as Shakespeare said, "What's in a name?" Hundreds of years of history, tradition and rivalry can be in a name. The point is, that the Christian answer is about as absurd as saying that the Republican Party in America is the exact, same party as the Democratic Party — there are not two parties, only one - except that they call themselves Republicans when they oppose taxes, and Democrats when they do not. It is a typically absurd response, which is obviously a foolish non-response.

Conviction Overturned

The Deuteronomist starts with Deuteronomy but continues with historical works which echo the theme of Deuteronomy — follow the Law and there will be success, violate the law and there will be punishment. All History is then a moral lesson in which we can follow Israel's success or failures in terms of their loyalty to the covenants.

The priestly authorship is the easiest to identify, and arguably the most important for our purposes, for this is the period of priestly hegemony. It is the Second Temple period. Israel, for several centuries not a sovereign nation, with no kingship, evolves into a theocratic state. There is no king who is "anointed" by God to look to. In the void, the priests dominate society, a process that began during the captivity, when nationality is enforced by religion and their commitment to their national God, to hold a people together who would one day, at least as a remnant, return to their ancestral homes. The standard claim for whatever rule, ordinance, teaching, or doctrine the priests wanted to impose on society was the same: God said it to Moses on Mount Sinai. Eventually, even apart from the Torah, there developed a substantial, voluminous "second Torah", or "oral Torah", of what God told Moses that was not written down. But the justification for tradition, and the basis for obedience, was always and everywhere the same — God said it to Moses on Mount Sinai.

Now, the Bible proponents will say: "Anyone can develop any theory they want. There is no reason for us to abandon our view of the Bible's history. Where is the proof of this obnoxious, far-fetched theory anyway?" The proof, as usual, is in the Bible itself. Let's let the Bible speak for itself. We will see that reading the Bible causes us to ask many questions in order to arrive at understanding. The answer to those many questions will tell the story. The following represents only a very few of these questions.

Who made the ark?

In Deuteronomy (handwritten by Moses as it claims to be) Moses says, *"At that time the Lord said to me, 'Hew for yourself two tablets of stone like the first, and come up to me on the mountain and make yourself an ark of acacia wood...So I made an ark of acacia wood, hewed two tablets like the first, and went up the mountain, having the* *two stone tablets in my hand....Then I turned and came down from the mountain, and put the two stone tablets in the ark **which I** had made; and **there they are**, just as the Lord commanded me."* (Deut. 10:1-5). This statement is purportedly made forty years after the fact, and just to be sure there is no mistake, Moses insists that it is *the same* ark that is still with them and not another ("there they are").

Yet in the book of Exodus, God has chosen two artisans, Bezalel and Aholiab, and imbued them with his spirit in order to make the tabernacle of God and its furnishings, including "the ark of the testimony and the mercy seat that is on it" according to meticulously prescribed detail (Ex. 31:1-7). We are informed that the two gifted artisans in fact carried out the work of building the ark exactly as ordered by God (37:1-9). These are the orders and instructions that God gave Moses at Mount Sinai, some forty years before Moses' speech on the plains of Moab before crossing into the promised land. So Moses did not go up the mountain carrying the ark that he had made, and *there they sit today,* forty years later. According to this version, God gave the orders to Moses on Mount Sinai that only these two artisans were to build it, which they did *afterwards*.

These versions are obviously contradictory and irreconcilable. But our inquiry cannot cease here. This matter requires and deserves some thought. First, if they are written by the same author, why would the author contradict himself? The answer is obvious: they were not written by the same author because a single author would know what he wrote before. But this answer leaves a second question. Both of these books have presumably long been held as deeply revered by the Hebrew people — presented and believed upon as the sacred word of God. That being the case, why would one author write something that is diametrically opposed to the other? Now is when our minds must truly work. Think about it? There are only two possible answers. Either one of the two, or both, didn't know that the other work existed; or, the second author knew it existed but followed a separate tradition which the author regarded as superior to the other tradition embodied in the first work. In other words, he didn't think the other story was true. In either event, we have two differing traditions, not a single coherent tradition.

Conviction Overturned

Why does Ezra ignore the Day of Atonement (Yom Kippur)?

In Nehemiah, chapter 8, which takes places in the middle of the fifth century B.C., after the return from the Babylonian captivity, Ezra the scribe, the unquestioned religious authority and leader of his day, publicly reads the "Book of the Law of Moses" (Heard this expression before? The book that Hilkiah "found" in the Temple, apparently Deuteronomy) to the assembled people. He began reading on the first day of the seventh month, standing on a wooden platform, and addressing the crowd. On the second day *"they found written in the Law, which the Lord had commanded by Moses, that the children of Israel should dwell in booths during the feast of the seventh month..."*(Nehemiah 8:13) Then the Israeli's went out and put up booths and lived in them as directed *"And they kept the feast seven days; and on the eighth day there was a sacred assembly, according to prescribed manner."*(8:18). In chapter 9 we are immediately told that on the twenty-fourth day of the seventh month they assembled in sackcloth, with dust on their heads, and fasting, and stood and confessed their sins (9:1-2).

What is so surprising from this passage is not just that the people had no clue about the Feast of Tabernacles ever existing previously, but especially puzzling is the question: where is the Day of Atonement — the most solemn day in Judaism, established by God at Mount Sinai under penalty of death?! And if they had "found" the Feast of Tabernacles, why wouldn't they have found the Day of Atonement also? And why perform what appears to be an equivalent of the Day of Atonement on the twenty-fourth of the month? Just as a little refresher, Leviticus chapter 23 promulgates the required feast days. On the first day of the seventh month is the Feast of Trumpets in which trumpets are blown and an offering of fire is made to the Lord. There is no reference to it on the day Ezra begins to speak. And on the tenth day of the seventh month is the Day of Atonement in which every person is required to "afflict your souls" and anyone not doing shall *"be cut off from his people...it shall be a statute forever throughout your generations."* It is *"a Sabbath of solemn rest"* (23:26-32). There is no reference to this most important and solemn day, the most solemn day

The Progressive Development of Doctrine — The Old Testament

of the Jewish year, being observed in the book of Nehemiah, despite the fact that they have "found" the Feast of Tabernacles and celebrate a festival similar to Yom Kippur the twenty-fourth. It is unthinkable that such a holy and observant person such as Ezra would not obey the solemn Law of Moses in the book of Leviticus, and even more unlikely that he had not read it. The only answer of course is that he had never heard of it because the Day of Atonement had not been created yet. So Ezra could not be expected to know about it or observe it. The priestly code of Leviticus and related sections was still being processed. It is more likely that it was decided later that the *ad hoc* ceremony of atonement on the twenty-fourth was just a terrific idea, and that it would be commemorated each year right after the New Year, which became Rosh Hashanah. The Feast of Tabernacles was to be the fifteenth day of the seventh month for seven days, followed on the eighth day by a Sabbath and holy convocation (although in the time of Solomon we are told the festival was only seven days and the people were dismissed on the eighth,[I Kings 8:66]). For whatever reason, in the year that Ezra commenced the process, the actual "day of atonement" occurred *after* the Feast of Tabernacles, but not even on the eighth day, but on the *ninth* day of the feast.

The above reasoning is consistent with the fact that in the book of Deuteronomy there is *no Day of Atonement at all!* Chapter 16 of Deuteronomy prescribes the Feast days, and passes from Pentecost to Tabernacles. If Deuteronomy is written after Leviticus, and written on the plains of Moab, just before the Israelites come into their land, why doesn't this "second reading" of the Law refer to the Day of Atonement? Did God change his mind? Did God think it was necessary for Israel to do this forty years in the wilderness but it would not be important for Israel in their own country? Did God forget? Or had Israel been so good in the wilderness that God didn't think it was necessary anymore? Or, in the historical-literary approach, as it appears, Ezra had only Deuteronomy in front of him and this is the "book of the Law" that he is reading from. The Law of Moses is nowhere referred to as the book of the Law, for the Torah is always regarded as five books — the Pentateuch. The "book of the Law" is referred to here and in II Kings, when it is "found" by Hilkiah, and as we see here, it is obviously Deuteronomy that is being referred to.

That no Day of Atonement existed at this time is corroborated by the prophets Zechariah and Ezekiel. Zechariah 7:5 refers to the fasts of the fourth and seventh months during the exile, with the former, the ninth of Av, for the destruction of Jerusalem, and the latter for the slaying of the administrator Gedaliah (II Kings 25:25). There is a similar reciting of fast days at 8:19. There is no mention of the Day of Atonement. Ezekiel also recites the feast days and ignores the Day of Atonement, passing from Passover to the feast of the fifteenth day of the seventh month, which shall last seven days, the same feast Ezra refers to (Ezekiel 45:18-25).

Similar problems with the practice of the Passover

The fact that the Day of Atonement did not exist and was not prescribed is entirely consistent with what we are told in II Kings 23:21 about the Passover. We are told that in the eighteenth year of King Josiah (late seventh century) the Feast of *the Passover* was held *for the first time since the days of the Judges!* It is difficult to conceive of a people in covenant with God not commemorating the Passover each year as commanded in Exodus chapter 12, even though the original Passover was commanded by God to be done in the home. In Deuteronomy, the "book of the Law" that was "found" in the Temple by Hilkiah and delivered to Josiah, the Passover could only be observed at a central location, where God would put his name, i.e., the Temple in Jerusalem. As to other regulations for Passover, Leviticus requires that "for seven days you shall eat no unleavened breads" (Lev. 23:60) and Deuteronomy says "for six days you shall eat no unleavened bread" (De. 16:8). Did Moses change his mind? Did God? Or is someone confused? Are there two traditions, from different authors at different times? I suppose it didn't matter much if no one ever observed the Passover from shortly after it was instituted until the time of Josiah. The dates of Pentecost and Tabernacles are even more confusing in Deuteronomy, because they are dated from the agricultural cycle — Pentecost seven weeks from "the time you begin to put the sickle to the grain" and Tabernacles "when you have gathered from your threshing floor and from your winepress", making them appear very similar to pagan agricultural ingathering and harvest festivals (Deut. 16:9,13), whereas in Leviticus they are strictly based on the lunar cycle. All of the foregoing shows later priestly editing.

Why do people in the Old Testament consistently violate the solemn injunction to worship and sacrifice to God only at the Temple in Jerusalem, and that sacrifices can only be offered by the priests?

All feasts and sacrifices to God are required to be performed only in Jerusalem and only by the priests. (Deut. 12:5-27; 16:1-16). The priests are to administer the sacrifices (Leviticus 1-8). Yet throughout Scripture we see a different picture. Manoah, the father of Samson, makes an offering of fire to God, which God accepts (Judges 13:19). Gideon makes sacrifices to God wherever and whenever he chooses (Judges 6:19, 25). So does Saul, God's anointed, and the prophet Samuel takes no issue with this, only with Saul's impetuousness (I Samuel 14: 9-10, 34-35). Likewise Naaman (II Kings 5:18). Samuel makes offerings at Mizpah (I Sam. 7:9) and he builds an altar to God at his home in Ramah (I Sam. 7:17; at this time altars are only to make sacrifices upon). Even in the time of King David, Adonijah sacrifices wherever he pleases (I Kings 1:9).

Originally, in Exodus, chapters 20-23, considered to be a part of the Elohist early royal or pre-royal, writings, Israel is ordered to perform its sacrifices to God "in every place where I record my name..." (Exodus 20:24). This wording implies various places. Now the answer of the Bible proponents is that God's plan was that he be worshipped only at the Temple in Jerusalem, and that since Jerusalem was not captured until the time of King David, they could not have been able to fulfill the requirements of Deuteronomy, and so presumably were excused. But this is not any answer, because the books of Judges and Samuel make it clear that according to these histories the Hebrews always had the Tabernacle which they had in the wilderness, bearing within it the Holy of Holies and the Ark of the Covenant with its mercy seat, usually kept in Bethel or Shiloh. So there is no reason why the centralized worship under the auspices of the priest, as prescribed in Deuteronomy and Leviticus, would not be practiced there. The frequent, blatant, and unextenuated violations of this supposed rule are simply passed over by the Bible. In the book of Judges and I Samuel, centralized worship conducted by the priests, simply does not exist. Could it be because these people in fact did nothing violative of the Law as they knew it? Could it be because, as in the case of the Day of Atonement, there simply was no such requirement at that time? Could it be because these events, in the early history of Israel, were before the reign of Josiah, when the book of Deuteronomy came into being, telling the people what God had supposedly told Moses on Mount Sinai, and what Moses had allegedly relayed to the people on the plains of Moab?

The language of Isaiah, probably the greatest prophet of Israel, condemns the use of sacrifices, and leads one to question whether Isaiah was in any way familiar with the system of sacrifices ordained in the books attributed to Moses. He has God tell Israel, *"'To what purpose is the multitude of your sacrifices to me?' says the Lord.' I have had enough of burnt offerings of rams and the fat of fed cattle. I do not delight in the blood of bulls, or of lambs or goats'"*(Isaiah 1:11). This is a person who is unfamiliar with the written Levitical code of priestly sacrifices, supposedly given by God to Moses on Mount Sinai, and made incumbent upon Israel, because they had not been written yet (not even Deuteronomy in the case of Isaiah).

The manner of worship and sacrifice, as depicted in the book of Judges and I Samuel, is very different from the manner prescribed by the "Law of Moses." In I Samuel, chapter 1, we are told that Elkanah, father of Samuel and a godly man, *"went up from his city yearly to worship and sacrifice to the Lord of hosts in Shiloh"*(I Sam. 1:3). When Samuel was learning to be a priest in the tabernacle, his mother Hannah would make him a linen robe and *"bring it to him year by year when she came up with her husband **to offer the yearly sacrifice**"* (3:19). The Law of Moses requires persons to go three times per year, for Unleavened Bread/Passover; Pentecost; Feast of Trumpets/Day of Atonement/Tabernacles (Lev. 23; Deut. 16). There is no explanation for this discrepancy and this apparent willful failure on the part of Elkanah, except that it is no failure at all — Elkanah performed what was required of him at the time, *and whoever wrote this book was equally unaware of any duty to go before the Lord three times a year for feasts.*

So Elkanah and Hannah are at the yearly feast, and *"Hannah arose after they had finished eating and drinking in Shiloh. Now Eli the priest was sitting on the seat by the doorpost of the tabernacle of the Lord"* (I Sam. 1:9-10). What's this? At the feast in Shiloh they are eating and drinking immediately adjacent to the tabernacle? This is unlike the solemn priests-only ceremonies depicted in Leviticus. The feast was genuinely a feast before the Lord. Hannah, a woman no less, just gets up from the table and walks over to pray at the Tabernacle — the "Most Holy" priests-only abode.

Just as surprisingly, at the tabernacle at Shiloh, the Israelites would come and offer their own sacrifices and boil it themselves, without the assistance of any priest (I Sam. 2:13). This violates the Law of Moses according to Deuteronomy and Leviticus, assigning the making of offerings and sacrifices exclusively to the priests — the sons of Aaron (Lev. 1-8; Deut. 16). Additionally, the priestly sons of Eli, the high priest, are condemned for the offense of approaching people making sacrifices and then reaching in with a three-pronged flesh hook and taking the best of the meat. And yet, in Leviticus, this was the priest's due. The priests were always entitled to a portion of the sacrifice (Lev. 7:26-36; Numbers 18:8-20). So why is this an offense when the sons of Eli do it? And why is it such an offense that Eli and his family forfeit the high priesthood? (I Sam. 2:13-14, 27). The only answer is that the law of sacrifices and offerings contained in the book of Leviticus, and the endowments to the priests, were unknown. Leviticus had not been written yet.

In Judges chapter 21, we are told that the "house of God" was in Bethel "in those days." They lamented the near destruction of the tribe of Benjamin, so in remorse *"the people rose early and built an altar there, and offered burnt offerings and peace offerings."* (21:4). Where is the brazen altar, so carefully prescribed and built in the wilderness, that always accompanied the tabernacle (Exodus 27)? It did not exist yet. In chapter 20 of the same book, the children of Israel inquired of God at Bethel if they should go to war against Benjamin, because *"the ark of the covenant was there in those days"* (20:27). Why wouldn't the author just say "the tabernacle was there in those days"? (Unless of course it didn't exist yet, and only the ark was there). The questions that develop are numerous. How could the ark of the covenant be under the strictest requirements to be kept in the Holy of Holies all the time, with only the high priest entering, and then only once a year, as required in Leviticus, and yet we see the ark taken into battle, and actually captured in battle? (I Sam. 4-6). Why in the Greek Septuagint version of I Samuel does it state that the child Samuel slept beside the ark? (I Sam 3, Sept. version). If he slept beside the ark that means he would have either slept in the Holy of Holies, where only the high priest supposedly could enter; or that the ark was not kept in the Holy of Holies (no wonder this was corrected and edited out in the Masoretic version in the Middle Ages). We will see more related problems ahead.

Why was the Second Temple a copy of the tabernacle, in its dimensions, features and furnishings, but the first Temple—the Temple of Solomon—was not?

We know from extra-biblical Jewish writings, such as Josephus, that the Second Temple was based on the exact same dimensions as the tabernacle of the wilderness depicted in the book of Exodus. God gave explicitly detailed directions which were carefully followed in every detail for the construction of the Tabernacle (Exodus chs.25- 27; 36-38).

The Second Temple, other than the fact that it was not a tent but rather a permanent, stationary structure, was based on the tabernacle design, with the interior divided into two sections, the Holy of Holies being the section in back divided by a veil. In front of the Holy of Holies were the furnishings as described in the book of Exodus, such as the altar of incense, the candlesticks, the table of showbread. Within the Holy of Holies was the ark of the covenant, and over it the mercy seat with the statutes of the two cherubim on either side, at which the high priest alone could enter and make supplication on behalf of the people once a year. The furnishings of the temple were supposedly the same ones, or at least the same as the ones, made by the artisans of God in the wilderness during the time Israel was camped in front of Mount Sinai (although we shall see a major discrepancy concerning this later).

The Progressive Development of Doctrine — The Old Testament

But what of the first temple, the Temple of Solomon, why wouldn't the Hebrews, as endowed as they supposedly were with an Aaronite priesthood and an army of Levites dedicated to the Tabernacle, have built a temple which matched the Tabernacle, built according to the exquisite details of God's own plan? If it was good enough for God, why not follow it? Now most Christians today believe, erroneously, that Solomon's Temple did in fact match the wilderness Tabernacle, at least in the interior dimensions and furnishings. Oh sure, it was much more elegant, but only on the outside - the inside was supposedly the same, with a veil in front of the Holy of Holies, and the ark and mercy seat carefully cut off from view of all but the high priest, and then only once per year. What we find in the record is something quite different.

Most Christians would be shocked to know that at least in the book of Kings, written while the Temple of Solomon still existed, there was no veil. There was a wall separating the inner sanctuary and there were two folding olive wood doors to the inner sanctuary, made of two panels each, overlaid with gold, covering one-fifth of the wall, carved with figures of cherubim, palm trees and flowers overlaid with gold. Chronicles, written admittedly during the Second Temple period, omits the folding doors and only says *"And he made the veil of blue, purple, crimson, and fine linen, and wove cherubim into it"* (II Chron. 3:14; describing exactly the veil that was there in the Second Temple. Whatever happened to the exquisite, and exquisitely described, gold doors?). There were gold chains across the front of the inner sanctuary. The walls of the inner sanctuary were carved with images of cherubim, palm trees and flowers (So much for a prohibition of graven images existing at the time of Solomon). There were adjoining chambers all around the temple on the outside of it. There were two large pillars erected at the front of the temple with a wreath of gold chainwork on top and one hundred gold pomegranates (I Kings 6:14-35; II Chron. 3:1-17). This is not based on the Tabernacle of God. We would think that the nation of Israel would naturally wish to follow the designs handed down by God at Sinai. Is this merely an example of human self- wilfulness and lack of esteem for the designs of God? Is this merely early apostasy on the part of Israel? We might think so if we only had the book of Kings at our disposal. But, lo and behold, later biblical writers supplied a justification.

Kings was written during the late royal period. During the post-exilic period, a parallel history was written — the book of Chronicles. The author or authors of Chronicles were in a position to see the then existing differences between the desert Tabernacle and its counterpart, the Second Temple, and the earlier Temple of Solomon. And so the book of Chronicles has a ready-made answer which Kings lacks. In Chronicles we are told that the plans for the temple were given directly by God to David and he passed them along to his son Solomon (I Chron. 28:11-13). The author of Kings seems unaware of that fact. But naturally this fact justifies Solomon building the temple the way that he did.

But if that is the case, we have a similar problem. Why then, would the nation of Israel not rebuild the temple according to the plans which God laid down to King David? Wouldn't it seem natural that God would tell them if he wished them to change the design? Are people of the generations of Zerrubabel, himself a direct descendant of David, and of the prophets Haggai and Zechariah, guilty of such cavalier, reckless impiety and willful impudence? If they looked the plans of God in the face and thought they could do better, then they certainly were. Or is there another explanation? Is it possible the Hebrews, in the royal period, were not familiar with the Tabernacle, because this history had not been written yet? Perhaps we are beginning, through this process of questioning, to find an answer.

When Solomon built his temple, what happened to the furnishings that were in the tabernacle? What ever happened to the gold cherubim that were built in the desert?

God's directions to Moses on Mount Sinai, not just for the tabernacles but also for its furnishings, were explicit. He ordered the artisans of God to make a "brazen altar" in front of the tabernacle for sacrifices, made of bronze (Ex. 27:1-8); a bronze laver (Ex. 30:17-21); a table of showbread made of acacia wood overlaid with gold for inside the most holy place, as well as its dishes, pans, pitchers and bowls for the table, all of gold (Ex. 25:23-28); a gold lampstand (Ex. 25:31); and an altar of incense (Ex. 30). Inside the Holy of Holies he ordered to be made a mercy seat of gold and *"two cherubim of gold; of hammered work you shall make them at the two ends of the mercy seat, Make one cherub at one end and the other cherub at the other end; you shall make the cherubim at the two ends of it of one piece with the mercy seat. And the cherubim shall stretch out their wings above, covering the mercy seat with their wings, and they shall face one another"* (Ex. 25:18-20). These were not merely planned, they were built by God's chosen artisans, Bezalel and Aholiab, and installed in the Tabernacle, exactly as ordered (Ex. 37-40).

Now when Solomon built his temple, he also had the furnishings built. He made ten lavers of bronze (I Kings 7:38), an "altar of gold" (In Hebrew the word altar is *mizbeach*, which according to Strong's dictionary #4196 always denotes "a place of slaughtering" from the verb for "to kill for sacrifice"), which is described in Chronicles as a bronze altar (II Chron. 4:1); a gold table of showbread, gold lampstands, basins, trimmers, bowls, ladles and censers of gold for the temple (I K. 7:48-50). For the Holy of Holies, the inner sanctuary, he had made two cherubim, overlaid with gold, each with a wingspan of five cubits, to stand wingtip to wingtip, with a wingtip of each touching the wall on either side (I K. 6:23-28). *"Then the priests brought in the ark of the covenant of the Lord to its place, into the inner sanctuary of the temple, to the Most Holy Place, under the wings of the cherubim, For the cherubim spread their wings over the place of the ark and the cherubim overshadowed the ark and its poles* (I K. 8:6-7).

Now the question is, when Solomon built all these furnishings, what happened to the furnishings that were so carefully made at the express order of God and that had supposedly existed in the tabernacle for what is described as almost 480 years? An even more obvious corollary question is the following: Why would Solomon have had to have these things made if they already existed? The problem is compounded by the rather cryptic comment, possibly an editor's attempt to reconcile an awkward situation (just like the change from the gold folding doors to the inner sanctuary in Kings to the veil in Chronicles) in I Kings 8:3-4: *"So all the elders of Israel came, and the priests took up the ark. Then they brought up the ark of the Lord,* **the tabernacle of meeting, and all the holy furnishings that were in the tabernacle.***"* The author literally repeats himself as to the fact that "they took up the ark", presumably to the temple. Then he repeats

Conviction Overturned

the fact in verse four, and this time adds the tabernacle "and all the holy furnishings", as though in the editors time, people would think it strange that they brought up the ark and not the furnishing in the tabernacle and the tabernacle itself.

But be that as it may, let us continue the thread of our inquiry. So, they brought up the "furnishings" of the tabernacle, presumably those meticulously ordered by God and built to specification in the wilderness, as described in the book of Exodus, namely the brazen altar, the gold table of showbread, the gold candlesticks, the altar of incense, the gold cherubim statues and the gold mercy seat. And then what? They already had all those items in the Temple of Solomon — the ones Solomon built. Did they put them in a museum? Did they auction them off? Did they put them in storage? Did they bury them? Even more, why wouldn't some holy, pious king, such as Hezekiah, or Josiah, have said, "Hey, I want the cherubim over the mercy seat that God ordered Moses to build and put there in the desert, not the ones that interloper decided to build and put there! Get Solomon's cherubim out and put God's cherubim back in there!" I am of course only being half-facetious. Only half! The facetiousness is derived from the narrative itself, and easily lends itself to be a subject of fun.

This narrative makes no sense at all from a historical standpoint - any more than the equally mystifying statements that while "the ark" was at Bethel in Judges 21 the people built an altar there for burnt offerings, when they supposedly already had the brazen altar from the wilderness tabernacle. Let's get to the conclusion. There is only one realistic conclusion. There never was a wilderness tabernacle, nor any of the implements and furnishings associated with the wilderness tabernacle. The tabernacle was a fictionalized, idealized version of the Second Temple, dating from the Second Temple period, and projected back into history. The idealized tabernacle was a copy of the Second Temple and not vice-versa. It became not merely the product of the imagination of the zealous, pious Second Temple priestly hierocracy, but rather something "God told Moses on Mount Sinai", which became the rock solid mythical foundation of Jewish theocracy. The idealized formula "God said it to Moses on Mount Sinai" became incorporated in the creation of the largest "pious fraud" in history — the writing of the "priestly code" that became at least the lion's share of Exodus, all of Leviticus, and a large portion of Numbers, as well as substantial portions of other Hebrew Scriptures.

Why do the prophets not refer to the Law of Moses?

If the prophets came hundreds of years after God's giving of the Law to Moses at Mount Sinai, and their mission was to enforce God's covenant on backsliding Israel, then why do the prophets never refer to the Law of Moses, quoting the very texts we know? Malachi, writing in the mid-fifth century B.C., after we have the priestly code we now know, very broadly tells his hearers to "Remember the Law of Moses…"(Mal. 4:4), with no further elaboration. And it is the lack of specification and elaboration which perturbs us. If anything, prophets such as Isaiah seem to repudiate the Hebrew sacrificial system that today we see written into the heart of the Law of Moses: *"Give ear to the law of our God..."To what purpose is the multitude of your sacrifices to me?' says the Lord...'I do not delight in the blood of bulls, or of lamb or goats.'"* (Isaiah 1:10-11). Jeremiah is even more vociferous in declaring that the sacrificial system employed by the priests is not part of the law of God at all! He declares, *"For I did not speak to your fathers, or command them in the day that I brought them out of the land of Egypt, concerning burnt offerings or sacrifices"*(Jer. 7:11*)*. Hosea is equally clear, *"I desire mercy and not sacrifice, and the knowledge of God more than burnt offerings"* (Hosea 6:6 - oddly enough, the only passage of Old Testament Scripture that Jesus quoted two times. This shows something of Jesus' critical theology, and where he stood with the priesthood and its rituals). The prophets were no friends of the ritual sacrificial system of the priests.

What stands out in the prophets is quoting the word of the Lord according to their own prophecies, but never quoting from the Law of Moses that we know in Exodus, Leviticus and Numbers. Almost the only exception is the law of the Sabbath, the violations of which Jeremiah and Ezekiel decry (Jer. 17:21-23; Ezekiel 20:12). But the Sabbath may be an institution even more ancient than the Law of Moses (according to Genesis it is, dating to the creation of the world). Ezekiel, writing around 593-571 B.C., is the first prophet to give detailed prophecies concerning the temple and a sacrificial and feast system, and his prophecies are still a mystery for Orthodox

Jews and Christians alike. He is entirely off on his own tangent — his conceptions of the temple and sacrifice do not correspond to the Law of Moses as we know it in our Scriptures.

If the Law of Moses played the part that we know it did in the Second Temple period, and which it actually has played for over two thousand years in Orthodox Judaism, then we would naturally expect that Israel's prophets be very conversant with it and to widely cite it. In fact, we see the opposite. We see a dynamic period where Israel is dominated by the prophets and their prophecies — the living and fresh word of God, being followed by the end of prophecy and the beginning of an established, written-for-all-time law, serviced by a body of professional scribes and priests ("God said it to Moses on Mount Sinai"), and no need for any prophets to add anything new or challenge anything that exists. This progression seems so natural to human society and human nature, innately characteristic of universal religious development, and consistent with all the evidence we see of Jewish religious development. It is also consistent with the advance of religious hierarchy — of a priesthood - so common to all religious movements.

This change is also in great part a product of the advancement in world literacy. This was the era of an enormous leap in the world's literary content — the age of Plato, of Aristotle, and of Herodotus, the "grandfather" of historians, in Greek culture — all in the fifth through the early fourth century B.C. The advent of substantial literary works had actually begun in about the seventh century B.C., or about the time Hilkiah "found" the "book of the Law" (Deuteronomy) in the temple. The advances were not limited to Greek culture, although Israel was a part of the Hellenistic Greek world itself after 331 B.C. In fact it would be anomalous if something as detailed, lengthy, and comprehensive as the Pentateuch, the first five books of the Bible, and Joshua, had been written in the second millennium B.C. (in either the fifteenth century or the thirteenth century B.C.),as much as a thousand years before Herodotus, or if the works of Judges and Samuel had been written in the twelfth or eleventh centuries B.C., seven hundred years before Herodotus.

In all fairness, there have been attempts to undermine this simple proposition that the prophets do not refer to the law. These attempts are very unpersuasive. This has mainly been an effort to demonstrate

The Progressive Development of Doctrine — The Old Testament

that the prophets Jeremiah and Ezekiel have employed phrases that are the same phrases as those used in parts of "the priestly code." For instance, it has been pointed out that Ezekiel has God use the phrase "I have lifted up my hand…to bring you to the land…" (Ezek. 20:28; compared to Exodus 6:8); and Jeremiah, in his doomsday portrayal of a devastated earth (often seen by evangelicals of a vision of a pre-Adamic earth), uses the phrase "the earth was void and without form" (Jer. 4:23), which has been claimed as a quote from Genesis chapter 1. Ezekiel ascribes Judah's exile to the fact that they did not walk according to God's "statutes" and "judgments" (Ezek. 5:7), which is compared to the same language as Lev.26:15 (Even though almost identical language is used in Deuteronomy, 28:15: the "commandments and statutes"). Ezekiel also talks of people eating their children as a result of disobedience (Ezek. 5:10 compared to Lev. 26:29) Ezekiel also talks of the horrors of wild beasts, the sword, bereavement and pestilence upon the land, as comparisons with the priestly code (Ezek. 5:17 compared to Lev. 26 22,25).

However, as a first observation and objection, I can point out that anyone who has been involved in hyper-religious settings knows the tendencyofmemberstoconformtothecommondictionutilizedbyothers (and not just in religious circles, in anything from law to horticulture). Diction is learned behavior. We commonly use phrases different from those who lived in 1800. Jeremiah and Ezekiel were both priests and a part of the nucleus of the faithful in Jerusalem, among whom certain shared phraseology would have been commonplace. The "raised arm" or "uplifted arm" of the Lord was a common anthropomorphism. It is used extensively by Isaiah. It is used in Deuteronomy 11:2 in the same context — God brings the nation out of Egypt to the promised land, and if anything this is the origin of the phrase. The earth being "void and without form" may have been a popular conception, and for all we know it was such a graphic, poetically enthralling imagery, from such a prominent and influential prophet as Jeremiah, that this well could have been the origin of the phrase in Genesis, rather than vice-versa. And this is the second major objection to this line of reasoning. When dealing with such dominant prophets as Jeremiah and Ezekiel, who themselves were powerful and eloquent men, it is more likely that the Second Temple priests and scribes copied them, rather than the other way around.

And the third, and more obvious objection, is that these prophets do not cite, or even refer to, *the law,* as set out in the priestly code. The law is, above all, *the law* — it is a set of requirements for conduct that are incumbent upon the Jewish people. Referring to the "upraised arm" of God or the earth as "void and without form" is not the same thing as referring to a particular ordinance of the law that has been violated and upbraiding the people for its violation. This *absolutely no where* occurs among the prophets (with the exception of a reference by Jeremiah noted below, which we will see is a quote of Deuteronomy, not the "priestly code").

Also, much of the Priestly Code, in particular Leviticus chapter 26, which is the only part of Leviticus claimed as bearing the same language and phrases as Ezekiel and Jeremiah, may have been part of an earlier, independent source, later incorporated into Leviticus. The "priestly code" itself may not have been a single, unitary production, but rather may itself have been an amalgamation of different sources. Ezekiel himself was an Aaronite priest from the same time period, the exilic period. This writing may indeed have existed in the time of Ezekiel. For that matter, we have no reason to believe or not believe that it may have even been written by Ezekiel. Lastly, we cannot accept the proposition that Ezekiel was familiar with the priestly code of Exodus through Numbers, without considering all of the other relevant evidence. That Ezekiel, for example, is unfamiliar with the priestly code (our "Law of Moses"), is evidenced by the fact that he prescribes a temple, and a system of feasts and sacrifices, in chapters 40-45, which do not correspond to the exacting requirements of the Law of Moses. The only possible reason for this is that Ezekiel was not familiar with them, because they were not written yet.

Now one of the exceptions to the sweeping observations that the prophets do not quote the Law is Jeremiah quoting the law of slavery from the Law of Moses. Bible proponents will be quick to point this out (Don't go there Christian!). Jeremiah actually ascribes Judah's coming captivity to it's violations of the law of slavery and it's failure to free the slaves (even though we are later told in the Bible that it was Israel's failure to observe the Sabbath that led to the captivity): *"Therefore the word of the Lord came to Jeremiah from the Lord, saying 'Thus says the Lord, the God of Israel: "I made a covenant with you the day I brought you out of the land of Egypt, out of the house of bondage, saying 'At the end of seven years let every man set his Hebrew brother, who has been sold to him; and when he has served you six years, you shall let him go free from you.' But your fathers did not obey me nor incline their ear"* (Jeremiah 34:12-16). Jeremiah then tells us how Israel made a commitment to free the slaves after seven years but then reneged and brought the Hebrew slaves back into subjection, and because of this transgression they would go into captivity (34:18-20). But interestingly enough, this ordinance, in the book of Deuteronomy, chapter 15, and Exodus chapter 21 (an early section of Exodus from the Royal or Pre-Royal 'Elohist' period), would have been in existence at the time of this prophecy, being about 587 B.C., since he is addressing King Zedekiah just before the fall of Jerusalem. So Jeremiah should have been familiar with this part of the Law.

But Leviticus chapter 25:39-46 prohibits Hebrew from ever becoming slaves at all: *"You shall not compel him to serve as a slave... they shall not be sold as slaves. You shall not rule over him with rigor..."* They could only serve *"as a hired servant and a sojourner"*, not as a slave. Israel could gather slaves from the surrounding peoples, *"But regarding your brethren, the children of Israel, you shall not rule over them with rigor."* This is a prohibition of Hebrew slavery, which Jeremiah was *unfamiliar* with. Why wouldn't God, through Jeremiah, have just condemned Israel *for having any slaves at all?* Why wouldn't God just say, *"You have violated my law by having your Hebrew brothers as slaves? I am sending you into captivity for this!"* Which lead us to another question.

Why are there two laws of slavery?

Why is slavery prohibited for Hebrews in Leviticus, chapter 25, but Hebrews can be slaves for six years in Deuteronomy chapter 15 and Exodus 21? In particular, if Leviticus was given by God to Moses at Mount Sinai, and Deuteronomy is the "second reading of the law", given on the plains of Moab just before going into the promised land, some 38 years later, what caused the difference? Did God realize how difficult it would be for people to keep his law and so he condescended and accommodated their greed for slaves? But we would think that coming out of slavery themselves, the Hebrew people would have had no slaves themselves at that time. So this regulation to have no Hebrew slaves should have been easier to enforce at the beginning, before the institution ever began, than later, after people had slaves. Conversely, it would seem natural, once the institution of slavery exists, that it is easier to place a time limit on slavery first, and then later prohibit Hebrew slavery entirely. Surely this is what happened, which explains why Jeremiah was unfamiliar with the Leviticus passages. Leviticus had not been written yet. Leviticus was written after the return from the Babylonian captivity. We shall see that there are at least two versions of many things in the Old Testament, including narrative histories.

If God directed that only the sons of Aaron be priests, why are the priests of Shiloh descendants of Moses? And why are the Aaronite priests, and even the high priest, not mentioned in Deuteronomy? And why did David, a "man after God's own mind", choose two high priests, with only one a son of Aaron?

God made it clear that *only* the sons of Aaron could be priests (Exodus 28-29; Leviticus 8-9). In I Samuel, we learn that Eli and his sons, and presumably all of the priests of Shiloh, are descendants of Moses. Because of the corruption of his sons, an unnamed man of God tells Eli, "*Thus says the Lord: 'Did I not clearly reveal myself to the house of your father when they were in Egypt in pharaoh's house?* [The "house" of his father can only be Levi? We remember God's admonition to Moses "Is not Aaron, **the Levite,** your brother?"(Exodus 4:14)]. *Did I not choose him out of all the* **tribes** [only Levi is a "tribe", not the sons of Aaron] *in Israel to be my priest, to offer upon my altar, to burn incense, and to wear an ephod before me? And did I not give the house of your father all the offerings of the children of Israel made by fire?*" (I Sam. 2:27-28). These are meant to be among the Bible's classic rhetorical questions. But if you read Exodus and Leviticus, however, the answer to the above questions of God is unequivocally "no" as to each question. They were not chosen, according to what "God told Moses on Mount Sinai." How did this come to be, and why is this requirement of the Law of Moses not even mentioned in I Samuel?

Amazingly, in Deuteronomy, which we have seen as a document from the royal period, before the exile, there is no reference to any priesthood apart from the Levites as a whole. *"The priests, the Levites — all the tribe of Levi — shall have no part of inheritance with Israel; they shall eat the offerings of the Lord made with fire, and his portion'"* (18:1). In accord is Deuteronomy 10:8, *"At that time the Lord separated the tribe of Levi to bear the ark of the covenant of the Lord, to stand before the Lord to minister to him, and to bless in his name, to this day"* (no mention of any tabernacle *"to this day"* because there is no tabernacle at the time of Deuteronomy. We see here how all of these issues are interrelated). In accord is also Deut.12:12,18, 14:27,29; 16:11,14; 17:9,18; 24:8; 33:9) This is the common designation - "the Levites, the priests" — the term Levite is synonymous and interchangeable with priest. There is no mention of a position of high priest, and Aaron is only mentioned because he died and because of his heresy in the golden calf incident. We have requirements for the tithing to the Levites and their responsibilities. But there is no mention of any priesthood that the Levites must serve. In Deuteronomy, the Levites *are* the priests. In Joshua 18:7, the appointment of all Levites as exclusive priests is even more clear: *"But the Levites have no part among you, for **the priesthood of the Lord is their inheritance.**"* As a matter of fact, in all early historical works the term "Levite" and "priest" is synonymous (Ex. 4:14; Ex. 32:26-28; Josh. 3:3,8:14,33, 14:3, Judges 19, 20; Jer. 33:17- 22; Ezekiel 44:8 et seq.; Isaiah 46:2). In the historical books, only in Ezra, Nehemiah, and Chronicles, all written in the Second Temple period, is there an Aaronite priesthood functioning.

What we have opened the door to is the clear priestly rivalry. This portion of Scripture in I Samuel is by no means the sole evidence of this. In this passage we see not the Aaronite priesthood, but another priesthood which is descended from Moses and his son Mushi — often referred to as the Mushite priesthood. As a result of their disobedience, Eli and his descendants are banned from ever being priests. According to Exodus and Leviticus they should never have been priests in the first place. There is also a rivalry between the Levites and the Aaronite priesthood, which may or may not be a part of the same struggle.

In the book of Ezekiel, we read that the Levites are being punished for their disobedience and errors by losing their priestly functions!

*"'And the Levites who went far from me, when Israel went astray from me after their idols, they shall bear their iniquity. Yet they shall be ministers in my sanctuary, as gatekeepers of the house and ministers of the house; they shall slay the burnt offering offerings and sacrifices for the people and they shall stand before them to minister to them. Because they ministered to them before their idols and caused the house of Israel to fall into iniquity, therefore I have raised my hand in an oath against them' says the Lord God, 'that they shall bear their iniquity. And they shall not come near me to minister to me **as priest, nor come near to any of my holy things, nor into the most holy place…** Nevertheless I shall make them keep charge of the temple, for all its work, and for all that has to be done in it"* (Ezek. 44:10- 16). How can they be punished by losing something that, according to Exodus and Leviticus, they never had in the first place! They are now being relegated to the very functions which supposedly, in the Law of Moses contained in the "priestly code" (See Numbers 8: 5-28), they always had in the first place. This makes no sense. The phrasing of God's punishment in Ezekiel makes it clear that before the punishment they *were* entering the most holy place, which according to Exodus only the high priest could do and only once a year, and they *were* serving as priests. But it *does* make sense if we see the "priestly code", the last half of Exodus, all of Leviticus, and the first part of Numbers, as written later, in order to justify the position, authority, ordinances, and ritual system of the Second Temple priesthood by means of a standard, unchallengeable rubric — "God said it to Moses on Mount Sinai." Ezekiel is the mark of the final phase of that priestly *coup d'etat* - the replacement of one priesthood by another, and so the Jerusalem Aaronite priesthood, dominated by the high priest, comes to impose itself over Hebrew national life.

This is why we see the anomaly of King David actually appointing two high priests — Zadok, supposedly a son of Aaron, and Abiathar (I Sam. 23:6; II Sam. 20:25;15:35), the last survivor of the Shiloh priesthood, which we have seen was Mushite. Why was this done? The Bible does not say, but we can certainly surmise that this was a way to appease both factions. Later, Solomon expels Abiathar and he is exiled in Anathoth, a city of Aaronite priests (I Kings 2:35).

Why are there two versions of so many things?

The incidence of multiple versions of the same events, sometimes occurring at different times, called doublets, and sometimes intertwined into an attempt to form a single narrative, is bizarre and mystifying, unless one sees in the occurrence the existence of multiple traditions concerning the same events. There are two creation accounts. In Genesis chapter one is the standard seven day creation account. Genesis 2:4, a second account begins with the standard introductory phrase : *"**This** is the history of the heavens and the earth when they were created..."* The earth is created in one day: *"...in the day that the Lord God made the heaven and the earth..."* (using the same word for day that the creationists fight so fervently over as a twenty-four hour day in chapter one, insisting that it is not synonymous with "age"). God forms man from the dust of the ground *"before any plant of the field was in the earth and before any herb of the field had grown..."* (2:5). He *then* planted his garden in Eden and *"there he put the man that he had [already] formed"* (2:8). In chapter one, plant life began on the third day and man *and woman* were created the sixth day. In chapter two woman is created later, from the rib of man.

In chapters 7 and 8 of Genesis there are two flood accounts intertwined. *Elohim* causes the flood in chapter 6, but *Yahweh* makes a covenant with Noah in chapter 7, the first use of *berit*, a covenant, in the Bible. We are told the water rose 150 days, also that it rained only forty days and nights. Two of each kind of animals came to the ark in chapter 6. Yet we are told in chapter 7 that Noah brought seven pairs of "clean animals" to order to make sacrifices after the flood was over (we do not know how he distinguished between clean and unclean without the Law), an obvious effort of priestly editing.

God makes his covenant with Abraham in chapter 12, and again in chapter15, based on cutting animals in half, a very Mesopotamian ritual, and then makes it again in chapter 17, based on the ritual of circumcision, considered the priestly codes' version. Hagar, the slave woman, and mother of Ishmael is cast out into the desert twice and saved by God twice, in Genesis chapter 16 and chapter 21, in similar stories, except that in chapter 16, *Yahweh* [the Lord, or Jehovah] saves them, and in chapter 21 it is *Elohim* [God]. In Genesis chapter 21, Abimelech of Gerar seized a well of Abraham and is reproached

Conviction Overturned

by Abraham. The two meet, along with Phicol, commander of Abimelech's army. They make a pact, and Abraham called the place Beersheba, and the well is acknowledged as that of Abraham. Later, his son Isaac has a quarrel with Abimelech over wells. They meet, along with Phicol, commander of Abimelech's army, and make a pact. Isaac finds water in that place and names the well Beersheba, which became the name of the city "to this day" (even though the well was already there and named Beersheba by Abraham a generation earlier in the first narrative, which dealt with the same adversaries, who must have been very long-lived) (Gen. 26:17-33).

In another story Abraham, because of a famine, goes to Egypt and passes off his wife as his sister, for fear of the men there, because his wife Sarah was so beautiful. The pharaoh takes Sarah into his house and God plagues pharaoh's house. Pharaoh finds out and rebukes Abraham. (Gen. ch. 12). Later, he goes to Gerar and does the same thing with Abimelech, king of Gerar. But God comes to Abimelech and threatens him because of Sarah and plagues his house. So Abimelech rebukes Abraham and returns Sarah to him (Gen. ch. 20). To top off this bizarre string of events, later Isaac, his son, goes to live in Gerar, also because of a "famine in the land" and because of the beauty of his wife, Rebecca, goes through just the same series of events, also with *Abimelech!*(Gen. 26:1-11). This is obviously a series of traditions of the same story which took different forms. The Hebrews did not know if the story really concerned Isaac or Abraham, or whether it was about the pharaoh, or King Abimelech of Gerar, so the humorous result is simply three different stories with overlapping persons and events (Abimelech, Phicol, Beersheba, etc.).

Jacob goes to Bethel and has an encounter with God twice. God changes his name from Jacob to Israel in Genesis 32:28, and then apparently forgot that he had done so and changed Jacob's name to Israel again in 35:10.

In the wilderness wanderings, Moses draws out water from a rock twice (Exodus 17 and Numbers 20). Both places are called "Meribah", but one incident is before Mount Sinai, and the other is after, and in the second he strikes the rock rather than speaking to it as God ordered, and so is prohibited from ever personally entering the promised land. Moses chooses the seventy elders two times (Exodus 18 and Numbers

11). And he even goes up Mount Sinai and brings down the two stone tablets containing the ten commandments two times (Exodus 20 and 34). There are actually two markedly different sets of ten commandments in Exodus 20 and 34, with the first set being that we are readily familiar with, and the second a very ritualistic one. Only the second set are actually called "the ten commandments" and only the second set are expressly called by God the basis of the covenant with God (Ex. 34:10,27-28). These second set of commandments, expressly designated "The Ten Commandments" include observing the Feast of Unleavened Bread and the Feast of Weeks (Pentecost); appearing three times a year before God for feasts; the redemption of all firstborn; the ban on graven images; the Sabbath; the ban on blood left in offering sacrifices, or leaving the sacrifice of the Passover until morning; the offering of first fruits to God; and the ban on boiling a kid goat in his mother's milk (considered the basis of kashrut - kosher laws). This is an obvious attempt to blend two traditions into one narrative. In one tradition, Moses' father-in-law is Jethro. In the other he is called Reuel.

In I Samuel, there are two distinct versions of the anointment of Saul as king. In one, he is anointed by the prophet Samuel, while out looking for his father's lost mules. Samuel anoints his head with oil (I Sam. 10:1). He is ordered to go to Gilgal and wait seven days to be inaugurated, and in I Samuel 11:14, apparently an interrupted continuation of this narrative, he is made king at Gilgal and offered sacrifices there. In the second, the people of Israel demand a king and lots are drawn. Saul, supposedly already anointed king, is selected, but he is hiding in the baggage (I Sam. 10:17-27). Then he is brought in and acclaimed king. Samuel then records in a document "the rules of the monarchy" (which they supposedly already had in Deuteronomy chapter 17, which if true, would make this gesture gratuitous). In this narrative, Saul goes to Gilgal but begins the sacrifices before Samuel gets there, and so is condemned by Samuel to lose his throne (13:8-14).

In one narrative, God is infuriated and insulted at the demand of the people for a king because God is the king of Israel, who are his specially chosen, his "peculiar" people. God tells Samuel, *"It is not you they have rejected; it is me they have rejected as their king"* (8:7). In the other version, consistent with Deuteronomy chapter 17, there is no hint that royalty is anything out of the ordinary. God tells Samuel that he will send him a man from the territory of Benjamin whom Samuel shall anoint ruler of Israel and he will *"deliver my people from the hands of the Philistines; for I have taken note of my people; their outcry has come to me"* (9:16). God has decided to choose a king to save his people. Yet in chapter 12, the other narrative, Samuel roundly rebukes the people for choosing a king, and he calls down fearful thunder and lightning such as to frighten the people in order that they *"realize what a wicked thing you did in the sight of the Lord when you asked for a king"* (12:17). The people are afraid for their lives and they repent and beg that they not be killed for they *"have added to their sins the wickedness of asking for a king."* It is clear that not only are there at least two narratives, but one dates from the royal period, and so the change to royalty is certainly not condemned. The other narrative is from a later priestly version that repudiates royalty and sees God as Israel's only king, ruling through the priests.

The foregoing is by no means a comprehensive summary of the "doublets" and parallel accounts in the Old Testament. It is merely an introduction. It demonstrates a changing world view, a changing view of God, and hence changing doctrine.

Why does God condemn a monarchy for Israel if he has specifically allowed it in Deuteronomy?

As at least one of the above narratives from I Samuel demonstrates, regarding the institution of the monarchy under Saul, God is offended and insulted by Israel's turn to a monarchy. It is the Bible's plan that only God is the king of Israel, at least according to the attitude of the religious hierarchy of the Second Temple period. If that is the case, why does the book of Deuteronomy, in chapter 17, provide a complete code for Israel's monarch to live by? There is not a word of disapproval, much less condemnation. It only admonishes that when Israel decides to have a king *"you shall surely set a king over you whom the Lord your God chooses"* (Deut. 17:15). The king is prohibited from "multiplying" horses or wives for himself and ordered to write for himself *"a copy of this law in a book"* and read it daily all the days of his life and to fear the Lord and observe *"all the words*

The Progressive Development of Doctrine — The Old Testament

of this law and these statutes..."(17:19). Now the argument of the Bible proponents is an easy one. God always hated monarchy for Israel. However, in God's infinite foresight, he knew that one day, hundreds of years after their arrival in the land, the people would want a king, so knowing that they would disobey him anyway, he *accommodated* them by providing a law of royalty in advance. But when he promulgated the law of royalty, why did God not also tell them at the same time that if they *did* decide to have a king that they would "have rejected me [God]?"(I Sam. 8:7). Did he tell them that they would not only be committing a "sin, but a "great wickedness" (I Sam. 12:17) and that he would send such terrific thunder and lightning and rain upon them that they would fear for their lives and cry out in fear and repent what they had done and beg for their lives? (I Sam. 12:16-20). Did he tell them, as he later told Samuel, that the king they would choose *"will take your sons and appoint them for his own chariots and to be his horsemen"*; force people to plow his fields and make his weapons; *"take your daughters to be perfumers, cooks and bakers. And he will take the best of your fields, your vineyards, your olive groves and give them to his servants. He will take a tenth of your grain and your vintage, and give it to his officers and servants. And he will take your male servants, your female servants, and your finest young men, and your donkeys, and put them to his work."*? Did he tell them that they would *"cry out in that day because of your king whom you have chosen for yourselves..."*? (I Sam. 8:10-18). No, we do not hear a hint of these sentiments in Deuteronomy 17. We hear nothing to inform us that God in any way, shape or form is even remotely annoyed at Israel choosing a king for itself. It appears to be a normal, natural, perfectly sanctioned act.

Bible proponents would argue that God did not express his true sentiments and condemn the practice at the same time he promulgated the royalty code, because presumably (ho-hum) they would just ignore it anyway, so why even bother? A rather untidy argument indeed. If your meat shelf does not already have enough baloney on it, here is more baloney for you. The real answer: Deuteronomy was written (code word "found") in the eighteenth year of the reign of King Josiah (622 B.C.), probably written by his high priest Hilkiah, or the scribe Shaphan. This explains also why Samuel the prophet did not have it when he anointed Saul, but rather recorded his own law of royalty.

Hence, in many of the Psalms, the king is the *"anointed of God"* (the adjective *meshiach,* rendered as a noun, "Messiah" in Christian tradition), and is *"the Holy One of Israel."* In Christian interpretation, both the phrase "holy one of Israel" and "anointed one of God" (or Messiah) would be incorrectly seen as referring to Jesus, a person and designation never remotely contemplated by the authors.

Why do Isaiah, Job, and the Psalmists, multiple times refer to the Canaanite creation account, and never refer to the Genesis creation account?

Isaiah, in the late eighth century B.C., is probably the most revered and the most quoted of the Old Testament prophets. He is especially beloved of the Christians, because they see many of his prophecies as predicting Christ. His language is highly poetic and elegant. He refers at least two times to creation accounts, but always those of the surrounding Canaanite culture, which relate the battle of El, the chief god of the Canaanites, against the sea serpent Leviathan (the serpent is the figure of primordial evil in literally dozens of ancient religions). The Psalmists do the same. It is never in a didactic fashion, but rather occurs in the midst of extolling God for his power and grandeur. Isaiah, and the Psalmists, use the accounts as a point of reference — rather than teaching his audience something about the creation that they didn't know, he employs the accounts as something his Hebrew audience was readily familiar with and could relate to. And that is exactly the problem for the historicity and authenticity of the Genesis creation accounts — something so dear to the hearts of millions of evangelicals and "creationists" in America.

"For behold the Lord comes out of his place to punish the inhabitants of the earth for their iniquity; the earth will also disclose her blood, and will no more cover her slain.

*In that day the Lord with his severe sword, great and strong, **will punish Leviathan the fleeing serpent, Leviathan that twisted serpent; and he will slay the reptile in the sea.**"* (Is. 26:21-27:1, NKJV).

How the Bible proponents can carry on over these so-called "mystery" verses of the Bible. Who or what is Leviathan, they ask? These are only mystery verses to them, and only because they

The Progressive Development of Doctrine — The Old Testament

deliberately close their eyes to the facts, and stubbornly deny that their great prophet, the harbinger of their Lord, could ever refer to pagan cosmogonies. In fact, the identity of Leviathan is well known. It is a part of the Cannaanite mythology of the origin of the earth. El, their chief God (who is also the Hebrew god, at least of the Elohists — El, Eloy, Elohim [the gods]), defeats the forces of primordial chaos, represented by a huge sea monster — Leviathan. Today's Bible proponents may not know this, because of self-imposed ignorance and stubbornness, but Isaiah's eighth century B.C. Hebrew audience knew it very well and, as we shall see, they did not know the seven day Genesis account. This former account states that at the end of time God will defeat the "serpent", or sea monster, as he did at the beginning (Countless pagan cosmogonies portray a serpent as a primordial bearer of evil, who opposes the "good" god, and whose contest with God in some manner creates the world we now know. In the Persian cosmogony, and religions influenced by it, such as Judaism, the influence of the serpent upon man leads to the "fall of man" from his primordial paradise. In the original Persian solar-based cosmogony, and in solar - and hence agricultural/fertility religious schemes - this "fall of man" occurred at the time of the autumnal equinox, when things begin to be corrupted and die. Hence, the "Fall", in English).[2]

Again we hear, *"O arm of the Lord! Awake as in the ancient days, in the generations of old!! Are you not the arm that hacked Rahab apart, and wounded the serpent?* [or "dragon". Jewish Publication Society, Tanakh translation] . *Are you not the one that dried up the Sea, the waters of the great deep, that made the depths of the sea a road for the redeemed to cross over?..."*(Is. 51: 10-11, NKJV).

Rahab is again another name for the primeval mythological monster. In this instance, *God's* (that is to say *El's)* victory over the sea monster and creation of the world, is paralleled and compared to *his* later deliverance of the Hebrews from slavery in Egypt. Christian apologists use this verse to claim that Rahab is merely another name for Egypt. But this is not the case except in a metaphorical sense, in that Egypt to the Hebrews normally is meant to connote worldliness and bondage to the world. Hence the comparison to Rahab. But this misses the very point. There is an original entity Rahab, which is such a well known mythological character, of distinct attributes and quality, that the metaphor can be aptly made and comprehended. This is like someone calling San Francisco or New York , "Sodom and Gomorrah", and so some one will claim that there never were such places, either historically or mythologically, that those terms are just other names for San Francisco and New York. We would think such a misunderstanding constitutes gross ignorance.

This latter section of Isaiah is termed "Deutero-Isaiah" or second Isaiah, and is regarded by all credible biblical scholars as written by a different author, with distinct diction and style from the original prophet Isaiah, and dating to the late sixth century B.C. This author refers to the sanctuary as destroyed (63:18; 64:10), and refers to the liberation by Cyrus (ch. 45), so he is deemed to be writing between 538 B.C., and approximately 516 B.C., the inauguration of the Second Temple. Whether one accepts the second Isaiah or not, our "Isaiah" as a literary work, cites as factual, without discrediting or disparaging, the Canaanite creation myth, and shows no familiarity with the Genesis seven day creation account.

Psalm 74, one of the most famous of the Psalms, is self-dated from the time of the exile (587-538 B.C). It laments the destruction of Jerusalem and longs for a return to the land. The Psalmist asks God to rise up as in days of old, *"For God is my King from of old, working salvation in the midst of the earth. You divided the sea by your strength;* **You broke the heads of the sea serpents in the waters. You broke the heads of Leviathan in pieces, and gave him as food to the people inhabiting the wilderness."* (v.12-14). The famous psalm 89, glorifying the Davidic Covenant, is exilic or post-exilic, longing for the restoration of a then defunct Davidic monarchy. It states, *"You have broken Rahab in pieces, as one who is slain..."*(v.10).*

Job also, is extremely familiar with this cosmogony, and accepts it as true: *"His hand pierced the fleeing serpent..."*(Job 26:13) The Bible proponent wonders in consternation, "When did all this occur?", "What is he talking about?" Job refers to the Canaanite "genesis" account, which is the only one he knows at this time.

*[Footnote:. Psalm 89, of course, presents many more problems for the traditional, orthodox approach. The English Christian Bible has played free and fancy with the translation of verses 6-8. Compare the English Christian Bible translation with the Jewish Bible translation:

The Progressive Development of Doctrine — The Old Testament

*"For who in the heavens can be compared to the Lord? Who among the **sons of the mighty** can be likened to the Lord?*

*God is greatly to be feared in the assembly of the **saints**, and to be held in reverence by all those around him. (NKJV)*

Compare the more accurate translation of the Jewish Publication Society:

*"Your wonders, O Lord, are praised by the heavens, Your faithfulness, too, in the **assembly of holy beings**. For who in the skies can equal the Lord, can compare with the Lord among divine beings, a God greatly dreaded in the **council of holy beings**, held in awe by all around him?* This is pure Canaanite religion, that there is a council of gods, hence - "Elohim." This parallels Psalm 82, *"God stands in the congregation of the mighty; he judges among the gods..."(Ps. 82:1).* So we have the original conception of the First Commandment, *"I am the Lord God Almighty ("El Shaddai"). I will have no other gods before me",* {not, incidentally, "I am the only God."}].

Absolutely nowhere, do any of the biblical authors express the slightest awareness of the creation accounts of genesis chapters one and two. They *are* however both familiar with, and believe, the pre-existing regional Canaanite creation myths. This is because our Genesis creation account did not exist yet. It was written as part of the Priestly Code by scribes and priests (i.e., Ezra and the boys) in the Second Temple period.

****

The above short sampling of only a few illustrative questions is by no means meant to be comprehensive. That the above questions demonstrate contradictions is self-evident. That is not the point. Biblical apologists earnestly wish that contradictions were the only point of this. The point is that the resolution of every, single question is *inconsistent* with, and cannot be explained by, the traditional, biblical view; and in every, single case, the questions are consistent with, and explainable by, the historical-literary approach, the so-called Documentary Hypothesis. The reason why all of the above questions are posed is to show that these foregoing questions cannot be resolved within the framework of the traditional, orthodox view - the biblical view, meaning the Bible's own representation of itself. A massive amount of the Old Testament was written by priests and scribes in the Second Temple period, who forged documents, such as the book of Leviticus, most of Exodus and Numbers, and the Genesis creation account, and presented them as documents over a thousand years old depicting what God told to Moses on Mount Sinai. These priests and scribes wrote the works with the intention of justifying and promoting their own influence, control, and practices in a theocratic hierocracy.

What comes most to mind is the traditional jury instruction in regard to the role of circumstantial evidence in criminal cases. It is appropriate here because most assuredly we are discussing circumstances, and also most assuredly, as we stated at the beginning, the Bible proponents have the burden of establishing the truth of their charge — which is nothing less than the genuineness and truth of the Bible. Likewise, they do not deny that it is we, the readers and "hearers of the good news", who are the ones that will be asked to give up our lives and liberty to the God of the Bible in order to receive the salvation promised thereby. We are asked to "give our lives for and to Christ." The only analogy with a criminal case therefore is that it is our lives in the figurative noose. The Bible proponents are the prosecutors that must prove their case. The law of circumstantial evidence, below, has been modified to fit our inquiry and set of facts, replacing the term *"crime"* and the terms *"guilt or innocence of the defendant"* with *"the truth of the claim"*, [the claim being that that Bible is true] . The jury instruction, as modified, states:

> **However, a finding of [the truth of the claim] ...may not be based on circumstantial evidence unless the proved circumstances are not only (1) consistent with the theory that the [claim is true], but (2) cannot be reconciled with any other rational conclusion. Further, each fact which is essential to complete a set of circumstances necessary to establish the [truth of the claim] must be proved beyond a reasonable doubt. In other words, before an inference essential to establish [the truth of the claim]may be found to have been proved beyond a reasonable doubt, each**

fact or circumstance on which the inference necessarily rests must be proved beyond a reasonable doubt.

Also, if the circumstantial evidence [as to any particular claim] permits two reasonable interpretations, one of which points to the [the truth of the claim] and the other to [the claim not being true] you must adopt that interpretation that points to the [claim not being true] and reject that interpretation that points to [the truth of the claim]. If, on the other hand, one interpretation of this evidence appears to you to be reasonable and the other interpretation to be unreasonable, you must accept the reasonable interpretation and reject the unreasonable.

Apply the above rule of law to the fact situations above. Which side has the reasonable argument? Are the Bible proponents' arguments reasonable? Are the facts and circumstances consistent with their theory? The answer is obvious.

I find it amazing that in my lifetime a person went to prison for writing a forged autobiography of Howard Hughes. Yet the biggest forgery in history has dominated, and continues to dominate, our western civilization. And to question it is considered by many, even by those who do not believe in the Bible, to be irreverent, disrespectful and poor taste. And in "the year of our Lord" 2010, persons suffering from terminal diseases who can be saved, instead die, because someone who believes in this book files a court action to suspend stem cell research needed to find a cure. And he or she does so because the Bible supposedly "teaches the sanctity of human life", except for the unfortunate men, women, children, invalids, infants, oxen, goats, sheep, mules, and every living "thing that breathes" in places like Jericho and Midian, whose lives the Bible finds anything but sacred and that God would sooner slaughter on the spot than he would to break wind. Their lives are ordered to be snuffed out at will. But more on this point later.

Chapter Ten

THE BIBLE AND THE ORIGIN OF RELIGION

There are at least two very good reasons to address the broader issue of the Bible in the context of the origin of worldwide religion generally. The first is a fairly obvious corollary to all we have discussed thus far. If there are questions in regard to the reliability or credibility of the text, then we naturally look to alternative explanations and origins. When a stated motive or explanation proves faulty, the good trial attorney begins examining alternative theories. In science, a theory explains and predicts. If a theory utterly fails, we begin testing others. In regard to the origins of the Old Testament, the original *Bible*, in chapter 9, *The Progressive Development of Doctrine: The Old Testament*, what we saw was a fascinating, tortuous history of the Bible's origins from differing and discordant sources which were eventually synthesized into the Bible we know today. However, the sewing, hemming, and ironing process that was necessary to accomplish this synthesis left us with a few rough edges, which could be seen with varying levels of scrutiny.

But the next logical step in this process should take us back ever further in history, even back further than the *Genesis* we now have in the Bible. The book of *Genesis* we possess, although it purports to depict primarily the early second millennium B.C., and although based on legends and stories that are very ancient, is a document written much later, at least in the later royal period in the seventh to eight centuries B.C.**[1]**, and more likely, at least in the form we know it, in the post-exilic period in the fifth century B.C., as claimed by Julius Wellhausen in his *Prolegomena to the History of Israel*.**[2]** But regardless, the later origins would necessarily entail a tendency, if not a conscious effort, to project back into history the rudiments of the Hebrew religion that was current at the time of the authors. So naturally, we would

The Bible and the Origin of Religion

wish to know, on whatever evidence may exist, the true origins and outlines of the beliefs of the ancestors of the Hebrew nation. And I do not mean to suggest only the time of the Patriarchs, but what of the considerable period of the Egyptian sojourn? This period is variously estimated between four hundred years (Gen. 15:13), as the Apostle Paul believed, and at about 150 years, or four generations, as also indicated in Genesis 15:16 and Exodus 6 (the genealogy from Levi to Moses). What religion did the Hebrews possess at that time? Was there an *established* religion as such? And if so, was there a religious leadership with doctrine and rituals? Was Yahweh their God? All of these are but a few of the questions that naturally arise and which should attract our keen interest.

Another reason for this inquiry is because an entire field of Christian apologetics has arisen, garnering enormous enthusiasm and dedication among some Christians, which seeks to corroborate Christian doctrine by delineating parallels of the Bible story with the myths of ancient pagan religions, particularly myths related to or explaining the Zodiac. The purpose of this field of Christian apologetics is to demonstrate that these myths frequently contain elements of truth that date from the origins of our world, but that these myths represent a human distortion over time of original, divinely inspired truth, of which only the Bible contains a true, accurate and complete version. Furthermore, according to this view, the Zodiac *itself*, and the stars comprising it, were created by a divine being, in the form it exists, in order to tell the story of the Gospel, as would be later narrated in the Bible. The Zodiac then, according to this school, is in fact the Bible graphically portrayed in the stars, and then ultimately influencing the spawning of multitudes of ancient pagan myths and religions. A person need only read the Gospel, and then gaze over head at the night sky, to see the truth of the Bible's propositions.

The first endeavors in this area were from early Christian apologists, such as Justin Martyr, and revived in modern times by Ethelbert Bullinger, a Christian theologian, but these ideas have recently been popularized in Christian circles by Chuck Missler. If a divine being wrote the spiritual history of the world in the heavens, including the propitiatory sacrifice of Christ in atonement for sin, millions of years before our era, in order that when these events occurred, and when they came to be written in the Bible, the message in the heavens would serve as a corroboration of the Bible, then an investigation of these claims is in order. Even beyond the Zodiac itself, the idea is advanced that the religions of the ancient world also contained biblical ideas and concepts — the reason being that God *planted* Bible concepts in human minds, such as for example, that God impregnated a virgin and she gave birth to a man-god, *a la* Hercules, in order that when the Gospel came to our world people would be already familiar with, and embrace, these ideas. So these ancient religious myths were deliberate Gospel precursors promulgated by a God bent on world salvation. We will examine these claims at length later.

The Origin of Religion

The origin of religion and its study delivers some initial problems to us. Since it involves the beginnings of civilization, it is necessarily pre-history and we have few written records, except those which exist in later religions, where we may only have a partial glimpse into mankind's past. We can also gain much insight from primitive peoples in the modern world. Much of our analysis must be suppositional, based on our knowledge of the human mind, the human environment, and common human experience. And yet we have fascinating clues. Indeed, in our world we experience some unusual, ubiquitous commonalities.

Why do we always buy twelve eggs? As a matter of fact, why in the whole world, are eggs always sold in batches of twelve? It is that way universally in all major cultures. And not just eggs, but it is common with agricultural products generally — at least ones that are sold in small groups instead of by the pound or as a batch, i.e., a peck of potatoes. Does it have anything to do with the egg as a symbol of fertility (actually a source of fertility)? Or of agricultural products generally as representing the earth's fertility? And if it represents fertility, does that have anything to do with the fact that there are twelve constellations in the Zodiac, and the majestic, divine order of the Zodiac governing the earth's fertility? Most would at least tepidly acknowledge that it does. So does it have anything to do with there being twelve tribes of Israel or twelve Apostles? Whoa!! Watch

The Bible and the Origin of Religion

out with that one! There will be an explosive denial among the Bible proponents. We will be adamantly told that this is pure coincidence.

And what about the fact that in every part of the world there is a seven day week? Must it naturally be so? That a year is 365 days — yes, that is understandable, because it is readily observable that the sun's solar cycle takes 365 days. From the earliest times man could map the sky and see the starting and ending points of the night sky on a daily basis and see when we were back where we started - so 365 days was unavoidable. On day 365 the sky would be back at twilight in exactly the same position it had started at. And man has always been able to see that the moon would go through all of its phases roughly twelve times during the course of that year — but not exactly. The moon would complete twelve of its cycles of phases in 354 days. So there was an epact, the time period between when a new lunar cycle would commence and the new year would begin. So a 365 day year and twelve months a year, even though they did not completely synchronize the way we would like, were natural phenomena and so we adopted that which was natural and unavoidable. We discussed the luni-solar year in Chapter 5, in regard to Daniel and the "prophetic year" nonsense. So all of the foregoing makes sense.

But 365 days is not divisible by seven. Neither is 354. So why a seven day week in the *whole world*? Now Christians have a ready answer. "You ignoramus!", they tell me, "just read your Bible - God made the world in seven days!" So this *historical* fact, they claim, is so imprinted on the human mind from time immemorial, that it became a tradition in all cultures that there was a seven day week, and once this tradition became implanted, no culture would ever deviate from it. And so it became foundational to world calendar systems. In all justice, if you believe the Bible is a credible document, then this is one possible answer. Of course the Bible also says that this is the origin of the Sabbath — that God rested on the seventh day. But in Deuteronomy 5:12, which we have seen in chapter 9 as being much older than the Genesis creation account, the children of Israel are told by Moses that the Sabbath exists to commemorate the exodus from Egypt, which seems to put in disarray the entire Bible creation account. So alternatively, what about the fact that to ancient man's perception there were seven planets in the heavens, associated with divine beings and powers? And so, in his Zodiacal astrological system there were (and are) seven *planets* interacting with the twelve constellations? Sheer coincidence?

Let's look then at some other coincidences. Let us look at some coincidences in the stories that religions tell. I will only mention a few, by way of example, at this introductory level. In Genesis 3:15 we have an unusual passage of Scripture which Christians ascribe as the first Messianic prophecy of the Bible, and one which they claim foretells the sacrifice of Christ. Shortly after the story of the temptation of Adam and Eve in the Garden of Eden and the Fall of man, God puts a curse on mankind. The ground is cursed with "thorns and thistles" and man must lead a dire life of hard work to survive; and childbirth is difficult for women, who are to be subject to their husbands. The serpent, who deceived Eve, is also cursed for his treachery and rebellion against God. He is to crawl on his belly. And in a very curious, mystifying passage, God tells the serpent, "I will put enmity between you and the woman, and between your seed and her seed. ***He shall bruise your heel. And you shall bruise his head.***" Bible proponents say this represents Satan crucifying Jesus (the heel bruised by the nails), but in the end Jesus, the son of the woman — a descendant of Eve, triumphs and destroys evil in the world.

Christians also say this prophesies the virgin birth, because *a woman does not have a seed* (even though in fact there is no *seed at all* in a virgin birth, and the delivery of a seed to a woman portends a natural conception process). The term *seed* here, absent some fantastic result-oriented verbal acrobatics, means precisely what we would think that it means — the *seed* of the woman is her descendants, or *son*. The Jewish Bible Society's more natural translation bears this out: "*I will put enmity between you and the woman, and between your **offspring** and hers; **they** shall strike at your head, and you shall strike at their heel*" (Tanach Translation 1999, Jewish Publication Society). This reasonable translation shows the passage for what it really is — a mythical explanation of the fact that most people do not like, and are even afraid of, snakes, and that correspondingly at least some species of snakes will actually bite your heel if you accidentally come across them on the ground. A bruise to the head is more severe than a bruise to the heel. A bruise, or kick, to the head may represent death. What

The Bible and the Origin of Religion

does it mean when we call a person a "snake"? What is the origin of this usage? Why do we not call the same person a chipmunk or a woodchuck? But more importantly to our present inquiry, why does a parallel, regarding the serpent, *"He shall bruise your heel, but you shall bruise (or crush) his head"*, appear, of all places, in Indian Hindu mythology and religion, where Vishnu's heel is bruised by the serpent of evil, but he crushes its head? [3] And more significantly, why is there a tale of a tree of life in a primordial paradise, and of a serpent in conflict with God who is intent on deceiving and corrupting man, and who causes man to fall from his favored pedestal with God and suffer the calamities of our present world, in so many world religions, including Hinduism, Zoroastrianism, and countless others?

The Christians will give us the same, pat answer: God planted it there so when the missionaries came with their Bibles people would recognize it; *or*, alternatively, this story really happened at the dawn of time, and people remembered bits and pieces of it and it became a part of subsequent myth and religion. This is a logical, linear explanation. But is it the only one? Is it the most reasonable one? All of these similarities do indeed portend a common origin — but it may not be the origin which the Bible proponents wish to accept.

When we look at world historical religions, at least at ancient pagan cults, man's earliest religions, it is as though there were a huge box, like a toy box, full of bits and pieces — shreds of myth and strange tales —and the people of the world are like little children who have delved into the box and pulled out random pieces and built our own religions. But the structures we have built are all from the same box, and so they share common features. The serpent biting the heel of the man, but the man crushing his head; a serpent in a garden who speaks and deceives man; man expelled from a position of grandeur and companionship with God — these are all parts of the universal religious panoply, which appear continually in historic world religions. And the serpent, or dragon, takes shape throughout the world as the enemy of God and man, and the great deceiver in the world, whether it be in Zoroastrianism, Hinduism, Greek mythology, China, Egypt, or the Semitic religions, and whether he have the name Typhon, Python, Ahriman, Leviathan, Hydra, or Satan. We shall explore all of this in greater detail below. First, Let us look further into the historical and cultural milieu in which early man developed his religion. When we do, we will see a common tapestry for all world religions.

The World of Early Man and his Religions

To approach the mind of early man, as he developed religions, requires us to attempt to see the world through his eyes, not our own. This is exceedingly difficult. It requires us to cast off momentarily that which we take for granted, including our knowledge of the world around us. Indeed, to replace knowledge with calculated ignorance is, I fear, beyond our mental capacity. It is intellectually unringing the bell. All we can do is to attempt to replace our knowledge of the natural world around us with ignorance, and then to try to *imagine*. Early man's world was filled with fear, desperation, awe and mystery. The latter two categories especially related to observations of the world around him, wherein we possess knowledge, and that corresponding ignorance on his part only intensified the first category of fear. The turn from a hunting and gathering society to an agricultural one could only have intensified the elements of fear and desperation. The increase in the human population, and the growing relative scarcity of the animal population, alone would have aggravated his struggle for existence. In an agricultural setting, he was now especially dependant on the vicissitudes and uncertainty of nature. A drought, a flood, a heavy storm, or even an early frost, could mean starvation and the end of his existence. His reliance upon nature, in an agricultural setting, was now more stark than ever. But he did not understand that nature which governed and enslaved him.

His attitude could only have been like that of what psychologists call the "intentional stance" of infants. The infant sees the world swirling around him in its crib, and can track movements of objects, but the line between an object that moves on its own motion, or that moves volitionally, and an object that is propelled by another force, is not a clear one. The line between inanimate and animate is even less clear. Any movement is interpreted as volitional and deliberate. So early man possessed a similar outlook. Personal volitional forces must govern the natural world. If a wind came, someone propelled it. If it rained, a personal, volitional force was behind it. If it did not rain at

The Bible and the Origin of Religion

all, and your crops were drying up, the creek was drying up, and you were dying of hunger and thirst, then someone was deciding to do this to you. These forces had to be confronted, dealt with, propitiated, and appeased. How could he do this? He soon found that if he tried to talk to these unseen, powerful beings, that they didn't answer. He was merely, as it were, talking to himself. That didn't do any good. So to him, the natural way to accomplish this was a system of sacrifice and worship. So fear, ignorance, mystery, and desperation led to a religion linked to nature. The result was that for thousands of years - at least approximately 30,000 years - man's religion was comprised of nature or fertility religions, of which solar cults, following the solar agricultural cycle, would form the centerpiece and crux.

We must not take the element of mystery referred to above too lightly. Rudolf Otto, in *The Idea of the Holy*, written in 1909,[4] claimed that the origin of religion was in the *numinous* — those things in nature which were mysterious and generated awe, and so were regarded as holy. Early man felt the existence of the otherworldly — an existence beyond and above our own, which he felt a need to worship and attempt to be in companionship with. A spectacularly beautiful sunset, with bright orange clouds and the intense imagery and colors generated around us thereby, could create a feeling of the numinous, and cause man to believe that these represented powers and personalities beyond our world. These things were *holy* and holiness existed within our world. The numinous was precisely a part of the mystery of life referred to above. To Otto it was this sense of holiness that directly led to the origin of religion.

Let us determine more closely how these religions — closely identified with nature or fertility — developed. Once again, let us stretch our power of imagination to imagine ourselves as early man - surrounded by, and dependent upon, an uncertain nature. His study of nature, a part of his involvement in agriculture, led him to a study of nature's routines, order and rhythm. In fact, his world seemed to be controlled on the one hand by order and regularity, which could be depended on for his existence and prosperity; and on the other hand by disorder and unpredictability, leading usually to catastrophe. The greatest apparent regularity was in the night sky. The regularity of the celestial bodies stood out as against the chaos and unpredictability of his world. He found an anchor in the stars. His ignorance, and undoubtedly, as Rudolf Otto would say, his sense of reverence and awe, led him to see the celestial bodies as moving in their course volitionally — the stars in fact were identified with gods. They either *were* personal gods, with characters, wills and desires, or they were at least inhabited by gods. And now here is the crucial link —man saw his fate as obviously tied to that giant, mysterious, awe- inspiring, unknowable expanse called the sky. The sky controlled the fruitfulness of his soil, and gave him life or death. It gave him the warmth of the sun or the cold of winter. The regularity of the sky was best characterized by the patterns and courses of the celestial bodies. That movement was a perfect harbinger of the seasons — of the solar cycle —which brought annual harvests and prosperity, followed by cold, darkness, decay, and death - in other words corruption.

But rather than seeing the sky as a part of a giant, all-embracing natural *system* of which we and the celestial bodies all formed dependant parts, the sky and its celestial bodies were seen as ordering that natural world that we lived under. Rather than seeing the sun, the moon, Jupiter, or the constellation Taurus as existing under, and subject to, a natural system, just as we were, they were seen as divine beings, or controlled by divine beings, who created that order at their own whims, and so could either give or withhold from us sun, rain, and agricultural plenty, at their pleasure. And of course not just an agricultural cycle and its ingredients, although this was the most obvious and needed, but also such things as disease and health. This is the origin of early religion and its forms — in the worship of celestial bodies, the association of divinity with the celestial bodies, and a system of sacrifices and worship to reach and appease the gods. How to "reach" the gods became a source of man's efforts and studies. It was believed that the gods could be reached through sacrifices, such as the sacrifice of first fruits to god — sacrificing to god the first of your harvest as a sign of gratitude — and also through oracles. Oracles could be persons believed to be in contact with a god, and who might be relied upon to speak the god's will, sometimes by even becoming the mouthpiece of god in ecstatic utterance (a phenomenon we still see today in Pentecostal circles); or by interpretation of the will of the gods through inanimate objects, such as an animal's entrails or through particular stones that could grant access to the will of a god.

The role of human intermediaries to the divine order led directly to the emergence of priestcraft as an institution that would influence human society for generations. In his classic work *Primitive Religion*, Paul Radin presented a comprehensive overview of the growth of religion in primitive societies.[5] The results are fascinating, and most instructive for an understanding of the path religion would have taken in all early human cultures. In the most simple hunting and gathering societies we see the predominance of the "neurotic-epileptoid" character as priest or shaman who is prone, either by a neurological disorder or by superior acting skills, to fits or trances which are believed by the societies to represent possession by spiritual forces. Ecstatic utterances are seen as the oracle of God to the community.

Anyone who wants to see traces of this in familiar literature should just read I Samuel chapter 1-19 of the Bible, where ecstatic utterances are commonplace when the "Spirit of God came upon" someone and the Bible simply tells us that the person "prophesied"(I Sam. 10:10-13). At that time there were groups of roaming "prophets" (I Sam.10:10), all of whom presumably were prone to have the Holy Spirit come upon them, leading to ecstatic utterances. In chapter 19, King Saul repeatedly sends messengers to a meeting (a "camp meeting" my Pentecostal friends would insist) of prophets led by the prophet Samuel in Naioth in Ramah to apprehend David. But the messengers, as they arrive at the meeting, are all caught up in the Spirit and they begin "prophesying" themselves. Finally, in frustration, Saul goes himself to the meeting of prophets, where the "Spirit of God" comes upon him and he strips off his clothes and prophesies, then lays naked on the ground all day and all night (I Sam. 19:18-24). Modern Pentecostals claim this is an example of Saul being "slain in the Spirit." I Samuel is from the royal period, possibly even the early royal period, and so demonstrates an earlier stage of Hebrew religion. Although Israel at this stage was already an established agricultural society and a primary culture, we can still see the traces of early religion that Radin described, as indeed we can still see today in our own culture, especially in the Pentecostals and some of their antics.

However, as the societies become agricultural and more advanced, the role of shaman or priest becomes sought after by those seeking prestige, power and wealth, which includes those who do not have the neurotic-epileptoid propensities or capabilities. The society becomes wealthier and the priesthood acquires increasing emoluments of office. So the society, under the influence of the new order of priests, gravitates away from its reliance upon the neurotic-epileptoid. [6] Corresponding with these changes, there is a transformation from early proto-religion, which is based almost entirely on magic - a linking of the ego with the object, and an effort, or supposed capability, of an individual to coerce, or manipulate, objects to achieve his desires. Radin does not even classify this as religion *per se*. But later, the magic, under influence of the priesthood, develops definite, delineated religious contours, with the rites, rituals, and concepts we identify with religion. At the same time, Radin recounts multitudes of examples from primitive cultures around the world which demonstrate the members of the priestly class as everywhere intent upon aggrandizing power and wealth through cunning, conniving manipulation of their societies.[7]

Primitive man thus saw himself surrounded by multitudes of unseen forces and powers. Sometimes these were impersonal forces and spirits, which anthropologists often speak of as *mana*, from a South Seas Island expression. Mana is denoted as a secret, unseen mystical force of great power, which is used to explain much natural phenomenon, such as the weather. It can also be manipulated by individuals. It can reside in a particular person, or in a particular plant or rock. Mana would often be incorporated into a particular object, such as a bracelet, to ward off evil. Obviously, at this point, we are skirting the issue of magic. Animism is closely related to *mana*. Animism is simply the belief in more personalized spirits that inhabit natural objects. Therefore, a particular tree or fire or rock could have an individual spirit.[8]

The dedication to particular natural objects, in turn, is related to the development of *totemism,* a tribal kinship to a particular type of plant or animal, and by the practice of *tabu*, a social restriction upon particular persons or things. Generally, a person, place, or thing is so full of a divine aura that a common person must keep his distance or shun contact. One of the most common subjects of tabu would be any corpse, blood, or even a dying person.[9] Just as Radin, others consider magic and religion to be two separate, but closely related, matters. Sir James Frazer, in *The Golden Bough* (1900), [10] contended that magic represented man's understanding of the impersonal forces which controlled life, whereas religion grew out of a conception of a personal relationship with personal gods, centering on sacrifice and propitiation, and gave man more sense of personal security than the impersonal and uncontrollable elements he saw as magic.

Man was Originally an Atheist

One of the chief claims of Christian apologists has always been that God must be real because man has always been obsessed with the idea of God, and human beings have always believed in the concept of deity. However, we find that the opposite is true. A belief in magic and spirits is not the same thing as a belief in God, or gods. This is not religion as we know it. In fact, what man has always been obsessed with is his own fear and awe of the unknown, and terror at his uncertain fate. These ingredients eventually became translated into religion. But early man, from what we can adduce from the study of primitive peoples in modern times, was actually an *atheist*. He was an atheist according to the true denotation of that term — he had *no* god, so he was an *a*theist. Certainly there is a connotation to the term *atheist* today — of a person who does not believe in the *unseen*, who does not believe in supernatural forces. But this is not the precise denotation of the term. The term simply describes a person who does not worship, or believe in, any god. Paul Radin has shown this to be the most primitive state of man.[11]

It was a process of development that led to man's theism, or a belief in deities. There were many stages in this development, including ghosts, totemism, and ancestor worship. Through these stages, amorphous spirits developed personalities and character. They could become angry, affectionate, or jealous. Their attention could be gained, or their anger propitiated, through sacrifice and offerings. At each stage, the shaman or priest was instrumental as a religious formulator - as someone who explained the supernatural world around and formulated man's beliefs and responses. By explaining the workings of the spirits or gods, the shaman or priest also justified his own status and explained his own failures and his own function. Why was he unable to cure the small child who was sick, and instead the child died? It was because of something that the father did. There was a violation of taboo. So the burden was placed on the applicant rather than the priest. Taboo is obviously related to the concept of sin. This coincided with a god who could be angry or pitiful. The coercion of spirits in magic eventually gave way to propitiation by offering or sacrifice. Incantations became prayers. And spirits became gods.[12]

Christians claim that the concept of Jesus as a substitutionary sacrifice for sin is novel, and that it is novel because it is a revelation from god. Most persons in our day and age also accept it as novel, because they have never heard of it. But primitive man would have been quite familiar with the concept. The idea is not at all unique. It is very common in primitive societies for the shaman to cure an illness by taking the ailment of another person onto himself and then getting rid of it through his spiritual powers. Likewise the idea of blood sacrifice as propitiation of deity is widespread, including the sanctification of an animal about to be sacrificed and the imputation of that sanctity to the faithful. Even the sacrifice of a sanctified human being for sin is widespread. [13]. "Surely he has borne our griefs, and carried our sorrows…"(Is. 53:4). And so the author of Ecclesiastes is very correct when he proclaims there is "Nothing new under the sun."

To the primitive tribesman, there was no distinction between religion and the secular, because religion and spiritual powers were mixed with all of life. Many contend that it was this mixture of magic and religion which led to the concept of the *numinous* — the idea of the holy, which Rudolf Otto attempted to capture and explain — the fear, dread, awe, and reverence that man was confronted with when he considered what he believed was the supernatural or divine. Early man, obviously without our level of knowledge concerning the world around him, lived a life absorbed with the numinous.

Human society thus is transformed from an obsession with a vague *mana*, or a belief in a supernatural world of spirits that can be swayed and influenced by appropriate human action, and related magic, mediated by often half-mad neurotic-epileptoid characters, who see themselves, and/or are seen by their societies, as bearing a special relationship to the supernatural, toward an established normative set of beliefs, practices and rituals to communicate with, worship, and appease the gods, under an established, authoritative priesthood. We

The Bible and the Origin of Religion

can also see the development in the nation of Israel, as we discussed in chapter nine, as Israel made its long transition from its ancient Yahwism to Second Temple Judaism. Just as we saw roving bands of ecstatic prophets in I Samuel, so later in this chapter we will see more glimpses of pre-existing religious forms which, like the lingering stars of a pre-dawn sky, will still be visible during the Hebrew transition. The height of this transformation was the transition to a book religion, and the complete end of prophecy, by the fifth century B.C. We can now see in a clearer light the basis for the railing of Israel's prophets against Israel's increasingly powerful priesthood.

Early Religion as the Religion of the Concrete — Light versus Darkness = Good versus Evil

The world was seen in terms of the good things, identified with the sun — light, heat, fertility, harvest, health, life; and their opposites — darkness, cold, disease, death. This was the fertility/ nature/ solar religion which was universally man's early religion. The winter solstice represented the greatest advance of darkness and all of its negative attributes. But with the winter solstice also came the birth of the new sun for the following cycle, which began its slow advance against the darkness and the cold. The spring equinox represented a victory of the sun. The sun was now equal to the darkness and from that day onward would actually overtake and surpass it. With this victory would come rain, warmth, planting time, and growth of all plant life. The summer solstice marked the ultimate victory and domination of the sun, of warmth, and of light.

The science of the will of the divine led to the development of the Zodiac, which became an essential part of this early religion. The Zodiac was developed at least 4,000 years ago, and arguably 6,000 years ago. [14] Many of the twelve constellations of the Zodiac were identified with animals, and those animals eventually were worshiped themselves. The representations, and later the myths, identified with the Zodiac marked the events of the solar year. For example, between approximately 4,000 and 6,000 years ago the spring equinox, that event that represented the victory of the Sun and its light over the forces of darkness, occurred while the Sun rose in the constellation Taurus — the bull. It is therefore not strange, that all religions which have their origins in the third or fourth Millennium B.C., or 2,000 to 4,000 B.C., have enormous Tauric symbolism.[15] The bull is prominent in worship and in fact is worshipped itself. Hence, the worship of the bull in ancient Egypt, ancient Persia, Japan, and in Hinduism. The origins of Hinduism date to this time period. Remember when the children of Israel, wandering in the wilderness, flirted with returning to their former gods while Moses tarried on Sinai? What symbol did they return to for worship? It was the golden calves. "Behold, Oh Israel, these are your gods, that brought you out of Egypt!" The bull was a holy symbol in Egyptian religion, worshipped as the god Apis (but unfortunately this is not the only bull in the Bible). The religious symbols and practices, once they became embedded in a culture, remained far after the astronomic events that inspired them had ceased.

And what, contrarily, was the most important animal symbol for the nation Israel? On what feast was the exodus centered, and at which would it be remembered for all future generations? And at what stage of the solar cycle did that feast take place? The answers are obvious. At the time of the spring equinox a lamb was slaughtered. Coincidentally, starting about 2,000 B.C., the spring equinox occurred with the Sun rising in the Constellation Aries — the lamb or ram. The expression emerged in the ancient world, "Behold, the lamb of God, who takes away the sins of the world." This phrase did not begin with John the Baptist in the Gospel of John. However, this was a common saying at the time of Jesus, which the Christians conveniently borrowed. The "lamb of God" who takes away the sins of the world, was *not* blessed Jesus, but rather was the constellation Aries, who at the spring equinox reconciled us to God's good will, bringing us light, warmth, and fertility and ending a long, cold, winter.

An understanding of why world religions would change from Tauric symbolism to that of the lamb or ram requires a brief explanation of the phenomenon called the earth's "ecliptic", or "precession of the ecliptic", which is relatively little understood, but which is vitally important to an understanding of the history of the Zodiac. Most of us know that the earth is at every moment hurtling through space at

The Bible and the Origin of Religion

about 66,000 miles per hour on a circular orbit around the sun. This is the earth's revolution. At the same time, it is spinning 1,000 miles per hour, so that it does one complete turn every 24 hours. This is the earth's rotation. This is very evident to us, but only indirectly. If you are sitting at your desk, such as I am right now, and you happen to be near San Diego, and you continue sitting there the next three hours, the space you occupy — the floor, your room, your desk will still be there, and you will be in the same position. But the actual spot in space, in the space of the Universe, which you occupy will in three hours be where Gainesville, Florida is right now, because the earth spins from west to east. You will only notice this because you will see the Sun move from east to west across the sky and if, like me, you happen to be near the Pacific Ocean on the west coast, you will eventually see it set over the ocean. But at the same time as this rotation of the earth, there is also a *precession* of the earth, wherein the earth is also wobbling backwards in the opposite direction. But this backwards wobble is at an angle, because the earth is at a 23 degree cock-eyed angle, and it is very slow - taking over 26,000 years to complete a single rotation. So while the spot that you are in is hurtling away from you from west to east, the earth, like a drunk, is slowing reeling sideways and backwards in the opposite direction, from east to west. The phenomenon is actually quite familiar to us if you have seen a spinning top. Eventually, as the velocity of the top's spin declines, the top begins to wobble, but always in the opposite direction from the spin.

So what this means is that the earth is not always looking at the same part of the sky. It gradually points in another direction. For instance, the North Star is the star Polaris, used as a principle landmark for navigators of all stripes for millennia. Theoretically, if you were standing at the North Pole, it would be directly overhead. However, about 5,000 years ago the North Star was not Polaris, it was Draco. And about 15,000 years ago it was Vega. Likewise, although the Constellations remained the same, their appearance in the sky at different seasons would change because of the earth's precession. So there was a "precession of the equinoxes", as all of the Constellations rotated.

The ecliptic is like the face of a clock. Ideally we have 12 o'clock at the top and 6 o'clock at the bottom, opposite it. We have 9 o'clock to the left and 3 o'clock to the right. So if Taurus is 12 (call that the spring equinox), then Scorpio is at 6 (call it the fall equinox). But if we take the face of the clock in our hands and twist it to the right, then we move to 11 o'clock (the *preceding* position - let's call it Aries) at the top position, but now 5 o'clock (Libra) is at the bottom, and 2 and 8 are now at the left and right side. The precession of the ecliptic functions in the same way. We already have seen how the spring equinox was an especially crucial event, especially for the agricultural, i.e., fertility, cycle. At the time of Jesus, and at the time of the Hebrew exodus, the spring equinox occurred when the Sun rose in the constellation Aries — imaginatively figured as the lamb or ram. And so the then popular exclamation, "Behold the lamb that takes away the sins of the world." But from roughly 2,000 B.C. to about 4,000 B.C., the spring equinox occurred in the constellation Taurus — the bull. Hence, as we have seen, we have a Mosaic religion based upon a Paschal lamb, which by a process of rather natural symbolic extrapolation becomes metamorphasized as a human substitute for the sacrificial lamb — the crucified Jesus. Since roughly the time of Jesus, ironically, we are in Pisces, the fish. Curiously, the symbol of the fish is a symbol of Christianity since very early times. Most Christians believe this is because Jesus' disciples were fisherman and because Jesus said, "I will make you fishers of men." They would also point to the fact that Jesus fed the 5,000 with two fish (curiously there are two fish in the Constellation Pisces). We also have the two incidents of the miraculous drought of fish, in Luke and John. However, considering the fact that the early converts in the Roman Empire were pagans, it is more likely that this was an astrological symbol of a new age.

By this process of looking at the precession of the equinoxes we can also establish the age of the Zodiac. This is because the graphic designations of the Constellations of the Zodiac have meaning — meaning which was placed there by the creators of the Zodiac. For instance, Libra — the scales: What do scales determine? Equality of course. Today this is seen as the Fall equinox. And so it is positioned in the signs of the Zodiac that we know — the period from late September to late October. But then again, we possibly have something very similar in the Constellation Gemini — the twins: why twins? What is the characteristic of twins? Think about it? The answer is that they

The Bible and the Origin of Religion

are identical, right? What is another term for "identical"? Yes, that is correct — equal! And what is equal? Day and night — the equinox, by definition and etymology. At some point in time was this one of the equinoxes — the spring equinox? You can imagine some of the rest — the victory of the sun, represented by long days and plentiful heat — in other words a *strong* sun — the strength of a lion, is Leo. The days retreating backwards and getting shorter, as a crab moves backwards, is cancer, which means the crab.

The oldest extant Zodiac we have is that of Sargon of Accad, from 3800 B.C. Emmeline Plunkett, in one of the most thorough studies of world calendar systems, estimated the creation of the Zodiac to approximately 6,000 B.C. She believed that it was founded when the winter solstice was in Pisces and the spring equinox was in Gemini (*the twins* - equal day and night). Religious practices, once established, gravitated toward the veneration of the spring equinox as the beginning of the year, and eventually became fixated on the bull of Taurus, represented in Egypt as the bull god Apis, as well as in Persia and India; and later on the lamb of Aries.[16]

The Next Phase — Solar Fertility Cults Translated into Ancient Religions

Next, we must examine the content of ancient religions to see how the themes of the solar cycle, and the fertility religions, were played out in ancient myth. When we do, we see a rather monotonous repetition of identical themes, played out throughout the ancient world in widely disparate climes and cultures. They all go something like this: Man is in a primordial paradise, in friendship with god. A nefarious serpent of some type deceives man and he falls from grace. Corruption enters the world. God becomes a man, by impregnating a virgin, and the man is born at the time of the winter solstice, often on the same, identical date - December 25. The man is a god-man, or a "son of God", who does wondrous things and champions the cause of man. He in one form or another often fights and gains victory over the serpent, but often not before he is killed. But alas, he is resurrected at the spring equinox, and he is worshipped as a god, and will one day return to save all of us. Many who read this will immediately feel that I am exaggerating. But let us just look at the record below.

In Greek mythology, Bacchus was born of God, through the conception of his mother, Ceres, who was then a virgin. He was called the "son of God." He did miracles in his lifetime, including miraculously filling three pitchers with wine, paralleling Jesus' miracle at Cana. He was born at the time of the winter solstice. His disciples expected his return after his death. Although we see Bacchus as a mythological figure, the entire point of his story is that he was depicted as a real human being that walked the earth, and Bacchus always had disciples which contended the same. Bacchus was originally worshipped under the symbol of the bull — Taurus — but in later times as the ram, during the period when the earth's ecliptic caused the spring equinox to occur in the constellation Aries — the lamb or ram. Hercules was also born by a god conceiving a virgin. After his birth the wicked king tries to kill him, as also happened in the supposed early life of Cyrus, king of Persia, and with Moses and Jesus. He was also called "son of God", a miraculous benefactor and protector of mankind. The cult of Hermes was very similar.

In Egypt, the identical cult of Bacchus was worshipped under the name of Osiris. Osiris dies and was resurrected three days later at the spring equinox. In Persia, and indeed later throughout the Roman Empire, the same Sun God is worshipped as Mithras, who is born on in a cave on December 25, and dies, descends to hell, and after three days is resurrected at the spring equinox. In the later Roman Empire the birth of Mithras was worshipped as "Natalis Invictus" eight days before the calends of January, or December 25. Mithras, whose cult was at its height in the first century A.D., was called by his many adherents throughout the Roman Empire *"the light that lights every man that comes into the world."* This phrase was plagiarized by the author of the Gospel of John to describe Jesus. [17]

In Phoenicia the cult existed under the name of Adonis. Being Phoenician, the cult of Adonis was the closest geographically to the land of Israel. Adonis was claimed to have been born on December 25, and even more amazingly, he was born in, of all places, Bethlehem (Yes, the same "little town of Bethlehem" we sing Christmas carols about). Adonis died and descended into the underworld of Tartarus, or the Greek equivalent of hell, and was then resurrected. The feast of the resurrection of Adonis was on March 25, *three days* after the spring equinox. The concept of "the third day", or "after three days", a phrase so commonplace in the Bible, and used extensively by Christian commentators as a *type* or prediction of the resurrection, is in point of irrefutable fact a near universal phenomenon in pagan religious cults. And there is always the ubiquitous serpent to enliven the story. In Egypt, Horus fights the serpent Typhon, who persecutes him. He is killed by the serpent but is then reborn. In Greek mythology it is the hero Apollo who is killed by the serpent Python, but then he is born again. His resurrection is celebrated at the full moon at the spring equinox.

All of the above festivals of the spring equinox involved days of mourning followed by a time of rejoicing. The Persians celebrated the feast of Neuruz, commemorating the entry of the sun into the constellation Aries, signifying the renewal of all things. Just before this celebration was the "feast of the cross." We will deal more with the ancient mystical symbolism of the cross below. The Trojans consecrated a lamb as a victim to the Sun at the spring equinox. The Phrygians tied their Sun god to a tree with a lamb at the foot of the tree. The festival of Atys, the Sun god, lasted three days, concluding with the triumph of Atys at the third day after the spring equinox. The Egyptian Feast of Spring actually speaks volumes as to the origin of the Jewish Passover festival. They placed three piles of ten pieces of wood each, each representing ten degrees of the Zodiac within the constellation Aries. Over each a lamb was tied and the piles were set ablaze as a sacrifice. During the festival all living things were marked red, symbolizing that fire from heaven renews life. In all ancient religions their cult god is a metaphor for the Sun, that begins growing longer and stronger, and therefore overcoming darkness, at the winter solstice, when all of our earthly heroes and representatives of the divine are born. But his final triumph, matching that of the Sun, is the spring equinox, when the days actually become equal to, and then longer than, the night. Universally, at least in the west, God is worshipped on *Sun*day. The sun is worshipped through the medium of the earthly demigod hero who personifies the sun. In all religions the Sun God triumphs over death and corruption in the world.[18]

The Persians, Egyptians, Greeks, Chaldeans, the ancient Britons, and the druids all saw in the Constellation Virgo the figure of a virgin holding two ears of corn and suckling a child. In astrology, Virgo was called an "ascendant" on December 25, and so December 25 was celebrated as the Mother of God day. Curiously, because of the precession of the earth's ecliptic, we can only imagine the position of the constellations 6,000 to 8,000 years ago. One of the features no longer readily visible in most of the world is the Constellation Hydra, or the serpent. This huge, coiled expanse of a constellation, obviously not a part of the Zodiac, stretched across the top of the sky. Naturally given the almost universal cosmogony, or accounts of the origin of our world, which ancient cultures held, and the universal representation of a serpent malefactor, this constellation had great significance. This constellation was visible at about 40 degrees latitude before 4,000 B.C., or at the time of the origins of the Zodiac. Although not visible at lower latitudes, such as Egypt or India, it was visible to Central Asian ancestors of many modern civilizations, and known most commonly as the Aryans that invaded the Asian subcontinent and the farther reaches of the Middle East.[19]It has been surmised that in the course of the movement of the Constellations across the horizon there was an annual occasion when contact appeared to be made between Hydra and the other Constellations. In particular, the Hydra "bruised the heel" of the offspring, or seed of the virgin — which could be the "seed" in her hand — the star Spica, seen as an ear of corn, with a sheaf of wheat in the other hand - or the two Gemini twins, but eventually, by summertime, or the height of the sun's power, Hydra faded from view, and hence had his head bruised or "crushed", meaning he was metaphorically vanquished.

Whatever the setting, or the ceremony, these are all solar fables that originally stem from the Zodiac. What is the crucial link between the basis of religion in the fertility/nature/solar cycles, and its reflection in the Zodiac, is the transformation of that cycle into a moral cycle, as well as a natural cycle. The cosmic struggle between light and darkness, portrayed in the heavens, was easily translated and reinterpreted as a cosmic struggle between moral light and moral darkness — between good and evil. Just as the solar hero - a "son of God" - born three days after the winter solstice, who would help humanity, would represent the power of the gods in human form, and would die and be resurrected three days after the spring equinox, so mankind would come to seek a savior from its sins.

Christ and Chrishna

Among the most astounding parallels between the Jesus of the Bible and the divine hero figures of other religions, there is none more remarkable than the comparison of Christ and Chrishna, sometimes spelled Krishna. Now Krishna is the *incarnation* of the god Vishnu, part of the holy triad of Hinduism. I use the word *incarnation* deliberately, knowing there will be intense opposition from Bible proponents, who will claim that traditionally Krishna is portrayed only as an *avatar* of Vishnu. So Vishnu stayed in the heavens and a human figure representing him came to the earth, much like Mithras and Ahura Mazda. The Bible account is distinctive, they will claim, because Christ was "God the Son", a separate *person* or individual within a single God, and that God the Son came wholly into a human being, so that while Jesus was on the earth, God the Son was entirely on the earth also. The argument assumes the validity of volumes of post-Jesus later theology, as we have already seen in chapter eight, and early Nazarean, or Ebionite, Jewish Christians would probably have been quite content with the *avatar* concept of Jesus representing the anointing of a human with the "Spirit of God", with neither the "Spirit" nor the "Son" being separate personalities of God, much less God in their own right. They would see only one, single God, who stayed in heaven the whole time. But despite all of the foregoing, as far as we can determine, the idea was that *God became a man and dwelled among us* — for my money that is an *incarnation*, and no amount of words or convoluted theology can change that. There is not a dime's worth of difference in the world's incarnation accounts, whether they be of Krishna, Mithras, Adonis, Hercules, or Christ.

But let us look at the historical narratives of their lives. Krishna was said to have been born in 1156 B.C., but the date of the written narrative of his life, contained in the Bhagavat Purana, is subject to some dispute. The present state of the narrative existed in its present form at least in the century before Jesus, but there is considerable evidence that the present form of the narrative dates to at least 300 B.C. [20] So the Krishna legend is undoubtedly the older tradition. What are the historical facts of that narrative and how do they parallel the Gospel of Jesus? We have already seen that both represent an incarnation of God, although Christian theology has since the time of Jesus developed a comprehensive orthodox theology both of God (the Trinity) and of the incarnation, which would deny that Jesus could have been an avatar, or anything other than the full embodiment of one of the "persons" of the godhead (the "godhead" constituting and being the sole "God" — no fun, however inescapable, intended). Additionally, both were born of a virgin. Jesus was born in a stable, although the Protoevangelion of James calls it a cave (as was Hercules, Hermes, Dionysus, Adonis, and Mithras before him), and Krishna was born in a dungeon.[21] The parents of both children were on a journey to pay a tax when the birth occurred (at least this is so for Jesus in the Gospel of Luke — In Matthew they are from Bethlehem and no tax plays any part). The birth of both infants was welcomed by a chorus of angels. As soon as Krishna was born he had the power of speech. Although not in the canonical Gospels, this is a part of the non-canonical Infancy Gospel of Jesus, rejected by the orthodox church, but of very early origin, claimed to have been written by the apostle Thomas. [22] Shepherds attended the birth of both new born babes. In the Krishna legend, immediately after the birth, Cansa the king, feared the newborn baby and sought to kill him, but the child is taken away by night to a remote region. The king orders the murder of all of the children in his kingdom, in an attempt to eliminate the baby. An ancient sculpture discovered in a cave in Elephanta, India, commemorates this event, showing a huge drawn sword surrounded by slaughtered infants and weeping mothers.[23] In the Gospel of Matthew we have the wrathful Herod seeking to kill Jesus; his parents are forewarned at night and take him away in haste; and Herod murders the infants in Bethlehem. We should add at this point that numerous other divinely incarnated heroes were born to face wrathful kings that sought to kill them, including the Emperor Cyrus of Persia, Horus, and the Assyrian King Sargon, not to mention Moses. Horus, Sargon, and Moses were put into the river to save them. In the case of Cyrus, the magi told the king that Cyrus would one day be powerful. According to Herodotus, one of the myths of Cyrus, who became a literal "messiah", or savior, of the Jews, is that he met his death through crucifixion at the hands of the queen of the Scythians.[24]

In the Krishna legend, Krishna performs many miracles in his boyhood. He subdues a serpent, that vomits streams of fire from its nose and mouth; and raises the dead to life. Other than the scene at the Temple, when he was twelve, which only attests to superior knowledge, we know nothing of the boyhood of Jesus in the canonical Gospels, but in the non-canonical Infancy Gospel of Jesus he performs Miracles, overcomes serpents, and raises the dead to life. After his escape, Krishna grew up at a town called **Mathurea**. The Gospel of Matthew states that the baby Jesus was taken to Egypt. We are not told for what length of time. The Infancy Gospel however, which Charles Waite argues is at least as old as the canonical Gospels, and not later than the second century A.D., tells us the name of the Egyptian town they stayed in — it was named *Maturea*. This naming of the exact, same place name leaves little down as to a direct connection.[25]

In the Krishna narrative, Krishna's ministry is preceded by that of an older brother, who is also seen as an enemy by King Cansa. In the Gospel, Jesus' ministry is preceded by an older cousin, John the Baptist, who is later imprisoned and killed by a successor King Herod. One of the recorded miracles of Krishna was the healing of a leper, which was the first recorded miracle of Jesus in the synoptic Gospels.

The similarities are so striking that that biblical scholar Charles Waite believed that the apostle Thomas, who was believed by early Christians to have traveled to India and died there, had before his death collected these myths, and either he or his disciples transported them back to Egypt — Egypt being on the natural trade route to India at the time. The Infancy Gospel of Thomas is from Egypt, and was believed by Waite to be the original and complete Gospel narrative, portions of which found their way eventually into the Gospels of Matthew and Luke. Mythologist historian J.M. Robertson, in *Christianity and Mythology,* also believed that the Christian Gospel borrowed from the Krishna legend, or that they came from a common source.[26]

Conviction Overturned

The Cross, the Crown, and the Eucharist

J.M. Robertson, in *Christianity and Mythology*, provided one of the most comprehensive and insightful comparisons of Christian narrative and symbolism with world mythology. He found that "Not only was the cross-symbol, as all scholars now admit, absolutely universal in pre-Christian times, and, as a rule, a recognized symbol of life or immortality, but the actual idea of a mystic or exemplary crucifixion was perfectly familiar in Pagan theology. Obvious myth combined with real and legendary history to crystallize the conception...as we shall see, the cross was itself a myth element peculiarly likely to be bound up with the cult of any Savior God of that period." **[27]**

Robertson cites countless examples to support the sweeping conclusions above. The earliest use we know of the cross in early religion is from Egypt. The symbol of the cross is on the foundations of numerous temples, consistent with the Egyptian obsession with the afterlife. Fourth century church historian Eusebius recounts how a Christian mob sacking the Temple of the god Serapis in Alexandria were amazed to find numerous crosses in the temple. The cross is the sign by which Osiris gives eternal life to the righteous dead. In a striking comparison, how many crosses mark graves in western civilization? Even in many battlefield deaths of old, when even the name of the fallen may be ignored - for lack of time, lack of knowledge of identity, or lack of anything to write with or on - there was time to erect a simple cross to mark the grave. How many of those crosses represent the claim that the deceased was "a Christian", or had any religious convictions; much less that "Jesus saves." The cross at the grave, at the most, usually merely represents that the soul of the deceased has passed from this world, and perhaps that he has passed into an afterlife. The cross merely reflects respect for the dead, and so most people see it. The act may be seen as nominally Christian, but this practice, in its origins, is equally a pagan act fully consistent with the usage of Egyptian religion and represents the soul crossing the trajectory of the ecliptic to its continuing afterlife. Early Hebrew religion stands out for its absence of any theology of the afterlife, absent until the rise of the Pharisees and the Essenes in the Second Temple Period, and so did not utilize the cross.

The Bible and the Origin of Religion

The lamb of the Zodiac was seen as being crucified on a cross, because for a period of seven hundred years it was positioned at the crossing of the arcs of the equinoxes. This would be crucial to astrology- bound early pagan religion and the use of the sacrificial lamb at the spring equinox, in addition to the historically pre-existing bull sacrifice devoted to Taurus. This was the "lamb of God who takes away the sins of the world" that became the cornerstone of the Hebrew religious system, and metaphorically of the Christian atonement by Jesus.

Hermes, the Greek God of boundaries, was considered the embodiment of the Greek *logos*, or "word", conceived of by Plato as the wisdom of God working within human reason. Hermes was indeed the *word made flesh*. Hermes was commonly depicted in the form of the cross, with his head as the top of the cross. We are reminded of the famous statute of "Christ the Redeemer" in Rio de Janeiro. Hermes is also the "Ram-bearer", the archetypal "Good Shepherd." Plato, in his *Timaeus,* depicted the soul of man as two parts joined together as an "x" cross. Although many might see this reference as a stretch, it was in fact early church father and apologist Justin Martyr, of the mid-second century, that cited this as proof that the logos, as Jesus, had been crucified. On a more sanguinary note, in ancient Gaul, Strabo tells us that sacrificed victims were crucified and then eaten as a type of communion.[28]

The cross symbolism is frequently linked to the sacred tree motif, so significant in the Genesis account, and later revivified in Revelation. In the Mithras cult ritual, an unblemished male lamb is sacrificed at the foot of a sacred tree. In pre-colonial Mexico, a sacred tree called "the tree of life" was made into the form of a cross, and then a baked dough figure of a Savior God was crucified on it and was later taken down and eaten. In the cult of Atys, the God-man born of a virgin, the sacred tree, with the image of a youth attached, is cut down and carried to the temple three days before the spring equinox to represent his death. After three days of searching for him and mourning there is a celebration of his resurrection. Curiously, we have seen in many of these religious cults, that the day of remembrance, rather than being the day of the winter solstice - December 22, or the spring equinox — March 22, is actually *three days later*. In the Egyptian cult of Isis and

Osiris an image is also affixed to a tree. In ancient Assyrian religion, God is also seen in the form of a cross; with the upright part a human figure and the transverse part a pair of wings. In Mithraism, this is transformed into a crucified figure holding a wreath, or crown, which we will see below carries its own significance. Then we have the well-known mythological figure of Prometheus, the fire-bringer, or fire-stealer, chained to a rock in such a way that he cannot prevent an eagle from eating his liver, with a mock crown of weeds on his head - a variant of crucifixion. [29]

But in addition to the above mythological background, there were more recent actual historical events to give life and force to the abstraction of the cross. Cyrus, king of Persia, the liberator of the Hebrews, whom the Hebrews saw as a savior, even being dubbed messiah by the prophet Isaiah (Isaiah 45:1-4), according to the historian Herodotus, was crucified by the queen of the Scythians.

And what of the detail of Jesus' crown of thorns? Does this have any antecedents in pagan religions? We find some version of this circumstance commonplace. Prometheus and Herakles, the Egyptian version of Hercules, both were forced to wear a mock crown of weeds and osiers (rough twigs from a willow tree). According to Herodotus, Herakles, the savior son of God, arrived in Egypt to be hailed as a savior. He was crowned and led in a parade procession by the people only in order that he could be sacrificed. As we have seen, Mithras was depicted as both crucified and holding a crown in his hand. Mithraist initiates were given some sort of crown. In the festival of Thargelia, in Athens, common criminal were sacrificed for the sins of the people after they were crowned. The bodies of the criminal were then carried far away to be interred, reminiscent of the carrying away of the body of Jesus from Calvary. It was common for animals to be crowned in animal sacrifice. [30]

But there are even some more striking examples of parallels and antecedents. What of such details as sacrifice of the only son, of the mocking with royal attire, and of the notion of the substitutionary sacrifice of the righteous on behalf of the unrighteous to expiate sin? Celebrated religious mythologist J.G. Frazer, in *The Golden Bough*, cites the ancient Babylonian festival of the Sacaea, in which a prisoner condemned to death is dressed in the king's robes, placed on the throne, and allowed to act as the king for five days, after which he is stripped, scourged, and crucified. This was a combination of two traits that Frazer found as common in the ancient world — the use of a criminal as a scapegoat for sin; and the sacrifice of a divine personage in order to renew life.

An even more astounding example is from the North American Indians, who sacrificed their captives after first putting a crown of feathers on their heads and placing a chief's scepter or baton in their hands — once again, a highly unusual effort to make their sacrificial victim a sort of a "king for a day" before the sacrifice. It may be equated to a moral "fattening of the cow" for slaughter. The phenomenon must be more understandable in terms of human psychology than it is by reference to any religious ideals. In an even more revealing parallel, this time from a cognate Semitic culture, Christian church historian Eusebius cites a Babylonian festival in which the father-god Kronos sacrifices his *only-begotten son* Ieoud *after the son is dressed in royal robes!* [31]

The parallel is obvious to the Gospel account, but it also calls to mind the sacrifice of Isaac by Abraham. And this incident of the binding of Isaac, in Genesis chapter 22, is widely used by Christian apologists as an example of a prophecy (really of typology, or prefigurement by historical parallels) of the death of Jesus. This argument has superficial merit if we are to assume that the Gospels' Jesus account is otherwise credible, reliable and, as the Christians argue, a complete and verified fulfillment of established, verified prophecies. As we have seen in chapter five, that is simply not the case. And the same Genesis account, when not pre-determined to be a *type*, or prefigurement, of the crucifixion of Jesus, is relegated to the status of a prior event which was highly influential in the imaginations and anticipations of ardent, even fanatical, Second Temple Jews in search of a messiah — someone that would be the figure of Isaac, bound to the wood, as Jesus would be; and would at the same time be the ram (what else? The typical equinoctial beast) caught in the thicket.

And what of the actual historicity of the Jesus story? Curiously, both the apostle Paul, in Galatians 3:13, and Peter, in his supposed Pentecost sermon, in Acts chapter 10:39, depict Jesus as "hanged" on a tree. In Galatians 3:13, Paul indicates Jesus as being in violation of the law by being "hanged" on a tree, a clear reference to Deuteronomy 21:23, the only part of the law addressing being hanged on a tree. But Deuteronomy 21:23 clearly states that "he who is hanged is accursed of God." Now this is entirely reconcilable with the idea of being nailed to a cross in a crucifixion, and most Christians see this as merely a variant way of speaking of the same event. However, we have the interesting historical case of Jesus Ben Pandira, whom the Talmud tell us was stoned to death and then "hung on a tree" for the crime of blasphemy "on the eve of Passover", in the reign of Alexander Janneas, who ruled from 106 to 79 B.C. This early Jesus, was also killed for *blasphemy*, or apparently making himself God, exactly what Jesus was accused of (John 10:33).

This earlier Jesus account just so happens to be often conflated with the myth of one Jesus Ben Stada, another Jesus that was a *persona non grata* of the Jewish ruling religious elite, who was also stoned to death and hanged on a tree. According to legend, the mother of one or the other was a woman named Mary Magdala. As we know, in the Gospel accounts, Jesus' mother was named Mary, and Jesus was also associated with Mary Magdalen, a principal disciple, and even the one that first found the open grave and announced the resurrection in the Gospel of John; and there was at least one other Mary. The Jesus accounts may be a compilation of various Jesus myths throughout the years. But the Jesus of these earlier accounts, executed at Passover, as the Gospel Jesus, is not crucified, but "hanged on a tree", apparently after being killed. Are the versions of Acts and Galatians referring to Jesus being hanged an original understanding of Paul and Peter that Jesus was actually hanged, showing an early conflation of various legendary Jesus accounts? One of the most notable facts is that unlike Jesus of Nazareth, the Jesus Ben Pandira execution for blasphemy may have occurred almost at the exact time predicted by the prophet Daniel for the arrival of a messiah. I will not repeat the details of this here, but rather refer to the section in chapter 5 entitled "Prophecy: The Bible Correctly Foretold the Exact Time of Jesus' Ministry and Crucifixion Hundreds of Years Before."[32]

The actual Christian ritual which celebrates the death and resurrection of Jesus is the Holy Communion, or Holy Eucharist, the supposed existence of which at an early date, is hailed by Christian apologists as proving the truth of the resurrection. But this ceremony of the consuming of bread and wine was practiced thousands of years earlier in Hindu rites; was especially prominent in Mithraism, a powerful worldwide religious movement in the first century after Christ; and was practiced for centuries before Jesus in the rites of Dionysus. Justin Martyr strenuously and famously complained that the Mithraists of his day (c. 140 A.D.), according to him, had stolen the Christian Eucharist lock, stock and barrel from the Christians. Like many of his future counterparts, he had a poor conception of history. [33]

Robertson correctly observed that "a theological crucifixion-motive pervaded mythology both in the East and the West." None of the foregoing implies, as Christian apologists are fond of naively characterizing this type of evidence, that early Christian writers and evangelists sat down and copied over popular religious myths into the Gospels and then tried to "sell" them to the general population. What it does suggest, as so accurately and eloquently summarized by Robertson, is that "Ancient mythology is a shoreless sea of dreams, of which we can only say that in their strange way they too must represent the working of constant psychological law, if we could but catch and follow the clues." [34]

Genesis and Ancient Cosmogonies

Let us now examine the issue of ancient cosmogony — how ancient man saw the origin of the world and its condition. We are all most familiar with the Genesis Bible account. However, all of the rudiments of the Bible's view of man's origins are in fact derived from Persian cosmogony identified with the teacher Zoroaster, who lived about a thousand years before Jesus. The outlines of this cosmogony were undoubtedly transmitted to the Hebrews during the time of the Babylonian captivity, initially through Persian influence upon Babylon, and later through Persia's conquest of Babylon. We must remember that the Persian king Cyrus was also eminently popular among the Hebrews, so much so that he was even called a "messiah" in the book of Isaiah.

Conviction Overturned

The Persian cosmogony is included in the *Boundesh*, the Persian equivalent of Genesis. The principle of good versus evil as a cosmic battle is fundamentally and originally Persian - modern day Iran. Here originated the *moral* dimension of the conflict between light and darkness, as well as the idea of angels, of a primordial paradise, of a serpent who brought evil into the world, of the "fall of man", and of a future redeemer who would save the world. [35]The redeemer ultimately was Mithras, the embodiment, or incarnation of Ahura Mazda (Ormuzd), whose religion, as we have seen, was very close to Christianity and in the first few centuries after Jesus closely vied for dominance. Jews and Christians are fond of saying that their "holy land" is holy because all of the above concepts originated there, and that God presumably especially blessed the land of Israel with knowledge of his presence, his character, his power, and his design for the world. But unfortunately for them, the claim rings hollow. All of their fundamental notions were imported from farther east. All of these notions are far older and are from the land of Persia and the teachings of Zoroaster. As usual, the Bible is merely a book of borrowed concepts and ideas.

In this cosmogony, Ormuzd was the god of light, and Ahriman was the god of darkness. God placed man in a primordial paradise called *Eiren*. Except for a difference in pronunciation of the letter "r", which is then transcribed as a "d", this *is* "Eden." We can parallel, as an example in the Spanish language, how the letter "r" is often pronounced such that English speakers think the Spanish speaker is pronouncing a "d" when he is pronouncing an "r." The paradise is a place of perfect harmony and tranquility, but Ahriman makes a great adder, who tempts man and brings upon the earth death and corruption. Now one contrast in the Persian cosmogony is that there is a seasonal character added to this. The adder brings in winter. So in this early cosmogony there is still a trace of the solar cycle. In fact, there are in this cosmogony six portions of the good principle, which are the six months following the spring equinox, and there are six portions evil portions following the fall equinox. The "fall" of man, in this view, happened in "the fall." Now this is crucial, and quite amazing. I always thought, and was taught, that the verb and noun "fall" was merely a homonym of the season *fall*, or autumn. In fact, they are not homonyms at all — they are the same word!

Man awaited a savior at the time of the spring equinox, corresponding to the "victory" of light over darkness — day catches up to night, and from that illustrious moment on, overtakes it, under the sign of the lamb — "the lamb who takes away the sins of the world." Centuries later, God sent that savior, the incarnation of God in the flesh, born of a virgin, who was killed and resurrected at the time of the spring equinox, and who will return one day to judge the living and the dead. His name was Mithras, not Jesus, and his religion was Mithraism. He was worshipped under the sign of the cross, and the sacrament held in his observance was a sacrament of a meal of bread and wine, which should be taken until his return. This was probably the principle worldwide religion, stretching across the Roman Empire, at the time of Jesus, but was also a religion that had almost identical contemporary counterparts in the cults of Hercules and Bacchus of the Greek world, Osiris in Egypt, Adonis in Phoenicia, and Atys in Asia Minor.

We have pointed out the seasonal part of this "fall of man" chronology as distinctive to the Persian cosmogony, however the Persian cosmogony also claims that our world will have a 12,000 year history. In the Boundesh, evil is ushered into the world by the serpent at the seventh sign after that of the lamb (Aries) that represents redemption. This was at the 7,000 year mark, and the world is in the midst of a cycle of decay, corruption, death, and domination by dark forces. The centrality of the number seven is of course carried over to the Bible. As another odd parallel, in Hebrew the number seven is *sheva,* or *shivah* (feminine). In Hinduism, a god of the divine triad is Shiva, who not so strangely is known as the *destroyer.* Also in Hebrew, the word *sheva* is also the same as the word for an oath — to swear something is to *seven* it, rendering it holy. [See Strong's Concordance # 7650-7651]

Similarly, the concept of the life cycle of sin, fall, redemption is fundamental. Many Bible proponents throughout the ages have attempted a similar calendar of world history. Some variant of this view is still held by many Christians. This was especially popularized by the Rabbi Elijah during the first century A.D. in the Talmud. He and many authoritative Hebrew commentators believed that the world had a 6,000 year history to fulfill before its pre-appointed conclusion with a 1,000 year Millennium. Amazingly, although the fall of man in the Bible was not followed, at least according to what we are told, by a winter, we are told that the first thing God did after man's rebellion was to cover him with furs. This curious side note speaks volumes as to the ultimate origin of this fable.

This approach to biblical history has been highly influential among modern Christian Millennialists, who believe that the period from Jesus to the return of Jesus and the Millennium predicted in the book of Revelation, will be 2,000 years. Needless to add that this view was *extremely* popular a few short years ago and, I should say somewhat tongue-in-cheek, less popular today, since it is now 2011. However, others insist that the date should be from the resurrection of Jesus, and so would be about 2032 or 2033. As we have seen a thousand times in the past, the Bible proponents always have ready an explanation, a *spin*, and a recasting.

However, there is also another famous "genesis" account which, although far distant geographically, forms an interesting crossroad between the Persian and Bible account. This is the Tuscan, or Etruscan, account (Tuscany is situated in Northern Italian). In this cosmogony, which predates that of the Bible, God had a 12,000 year labor in the world. In the first 1,000 *years* God *made the heavens and the earth* (Sound familiar? Sort of?) In the second 1,000 years, God made the firmament; in the third 1,000 years he made the sea; and in the fourth millennium he made the sun and moon. In the fifth 1,000 years God made the spirits of birds, reptiles and animals. In the sixth millennium God made man. [36]This is exactly and almost verbatim the Bible Genesis account, with the exception that the Hebrews have made these epics into days — *yom*, with all of the attendant modern debate between the creationists and other religious opponents of creationism over whether or not the Hebrew word *yom* can embrace the concept of "age" (The ire of the creationists over this idea is not diminished by the fact that there exists no other word in ancient Hebrew for "epic" or "age", and that in Genesis chapter two, the exact same word, *yom*, is used to denote "the *day* that God created the heavens and the earth"). But let us not digress into this exciting topic. I am sure we could locate other differences in the accounts (such as that in the Tuscan account, on the seventh day God madea Lasagna and rested). The point is, as we have seen elsewhere, that the cherished Bible creation account of Genesis, unknown to a prophet of the seventh century B.C. such as Isaiah, is not original to the Bible, but like much biblical content is borrowed from outside sources and incorporated into its religion. [37] And in both the Tuscan, Persian, and Hebrew accounts, there are always six periods of time which lead to the world we live in today.

Ninian Smart, in the classic *The Religious Experience of Mankind*, summarized the elements universal to the cosmogonies of early man. How did early man see the emergence of themselves and their relationship to the divine? The following almost universally characterizes these beliefs: 1) That man once lived in a primeval "Golden Age" — a world free of suffering and strife; 2) That man lived in close harmony and communion with God in the Golden Age; 3) That man disobeyed God and God became angry with man; 4) That man has fallen from his close position with God and the world has been plunged into a state of suffering, death, and misery ever since. [38] We might add to this formula a common observation that we have noted from the foregoing narrative: 5) That man has almost universally been involved in the practice of blood sacrifice, usually animal, sometime human, apparently or overtly attempting to propitiate God. Therefore, we have a common cosmogony — origin of the world; a common anthropology — or view of the rise of man and an explanation of his condition; and we might also add, as the Biblicists would say, a common hamartiology — which is the study of the origin of *sin*, which in a larger sense might be seen as a study of the separation of man from the divine, or conversely, the origin of physical and moral evil in the world. Now Christian apologists would explain this by claiming that primitive man was closer in time to these origins and to these supposed actual events and so the oral tradition was preserved. They would claim that modern religions and cults clouded over and eventually obliterated this true original religion, and that only the Bible has preserved the true story and true religion.

Let us now examine the traditional Christian responses to the foregoing series of pagan parallels. The traditional response, not strangely, was to unconditionally admit the above parallels to the

Christian Gospel, but provide an explanation. Tertullian commented on the frequency with which his pagan contemporaries cited the similarity of the Gospel concepts to their own religion and so disparaged the new Christian religion. The explanation by early church fathers Justin Martyr and Tertullian was that the devil planted these myths in people's minds to provide a false alternative to Christianity.[39] The second, closely akin to this, held by later apologists, and by others even today, is that *God*, not the devil, planted these myths in people's minds in order to prepare them for the fundamental concepts of the Bible — that all of the elements of the above myths really did occur, but with Jesus! If that is the argument, then it would appear that God just plain miscalculated, since Tertullian tells that the similarity of pagan myth with Christian doctrine was a common obstacle presented by pagans as a pretext *for not accepting* the Gospel — 'What is new or distinct in all of this from what they already believed?' they would ask. They saw the "good news" as simply repackaged paganism.

Summary of Comparison of Bible with Pagan Mythology

Should we not begin by resorting to the law of circumstantial evidence, in the manner we have modified it for our applications, to determine which explanation is more viable?

"**Before you may rely on circumstantial evidence to find the[truth of the claim], you must be convinced that the only reasonable conclusion supported by the circumstantial evidence is that the [claim is true].**

If you can draw two or more reasonable conclusions from the circumstantial evidence, and one of those reasonable conclusions points to the [truth of the claim and another to its falsity] you must accept the one that points to [falsity]

However, when considering circumstantial evidence, you must accept only reasonable conclusions and reject any that are unreasonable."

What shall we conclude with regard to these striking similarities which have always challenged and perplexed Christians? At the outset, let us look at our options. When two texts are similar, or identical, we may conclude that A borrowed from B, or that B borrowed from A. This was the original allegation of Tertullian and Justin Martyr. If A is the Bible, and B is the compiled pagan mythologies, or the musings of astrology, we obviously cannot make this conclusion. In every single case, the mythologies are centuries, sometimes millennia, older. The position of the Constellations is billions of years older, and the Zodiac — man's interpretation and representation of the Constellations - thousands of years older. Of course, Christian apologists may claim that God made the Constellations exactly as he did in order to engender the very mythologies that man developed, as a prelude to the Bible stories, in order that when human beings heard the Gospel it would not be something strange to them. It was a form of evangelical pre-conditioning for the Gospel. Or, alternatively, it was an original "Gospel" which was distorted. As we mentioned above, if this was God's plan, then he probably should have consulted with an advertising professional in advance. According to Tertullian, these background similarities were used as a pretext for rejecting the Gospel as merely plagiarized paganism.

Another possibility, undoubtedly the only one reasonable and obvious, is that all of these concepts — Christian and pagan alike, are descended from common sources — "the shoreless sea of dreams" which Robertson referred to, and which are ultimately more reflective of human psychological needs than anything else. The incorporation of pagan myth into an original messianic idea of Jewish origin, was a natural result of the religious and cultural milieu of the time, whose influence was certain to enter into the rudiments of the new religion. But can we find confirmation of this anywhere else in the Bible itself?

Pre-Bible Hebrew Religion

Let us return to an inquiry we originally had at the outset to this chapter. What did Hebrew religion consist of before the Mount Sinai sojourn? What were the religious beliefs of the Hebrew people? To define this is a daunting task, with few definite resources at our disposal. Jewish religious history, as we have seen, is a sacred history written centuries later, with heavy editing, especially in the Second Temple period of the fifth century B.C. The Hebrews, as we have seen, sojourned in Egypt for a period of between approximately 150 and 400 years. They grew to have a population which, according to the Bible, consisted of over 600,000 men of fighting age — estimated at two to three million total. Some have questioned the reckoning of numerical figures in the translation and so have estimated the number of Hebrew warriors as only about 60,000 — one "zero" less. There was obviously some set of religious beliefs among such a numerous population. But was there an established religion, including a priesthood? It is rather hard to believe that such a large community of people, living in a separated community, such as slaves would be, would not develop its own priesthood. Such a concept would really be utterly unthinkable, since all communities have developed a religion and a type of priesthood, even to the shamans and medicine men of small, primitive tribes.

With the substantial amount of editing of the Old Testament that we saw in chapter nine, it should seem surprising to us that we would ever find any trace of pre-existing religious practices in the text. After all, according to the Bible, God chose Abraham as his friend to have a direct relationship with him, as patriarch, nation founder, and prophet. And yet later we also saw a priesthood dealing with traditions and texts that were regarded as God-given and holy, so there would naturally be tension between the need to edit, and the reverence for God's word. That leaves us in the position of observing texts which seem discordant and incongruous, and of being forced "to read between the lines" in order to understand. And yet there is abundant material to review.

We should begin with Moses' encounter with his brother Aaron in Exodus chapter 4. Moses, after the burning bush incident is leery to return to Egypt to lead his people. God shifts much of the burden of interaction with the Hebrews to Aaron. God says, "Is not Aaron, the *Levite*, your brother? ...Look he is coming out to meet you"(Ex. 4:14). Now what is interesting is that God refers to Aaron as *the Levite.* Now the Levites were a tribe of Israel, but of course also became a tribe of priests, according to the Bible after the rebellion of Israel in the golden calf incident, and not before. Bible proponents will be quick to point out that God is naturally only referring to the tribal designation of Aaron, because he *was* of the tribe of Levi, and could have just as appropriately stated, "Aaron the Danite", or "Aaron the Gadite."

However, in the first place, at least at this point in Scripture, we have no tribal designations until later in the Bible narrative, such as when they approach the promised land, so this designation as "a Levite" seems to be singularly important in this narrative. And secondly, and more importantly, if Moses and Aaron have the same father and mother, why does God refer to Aaron as a Levite? Wasn't Moses a Levite too? It is as though, let us say, you have a full brother, born of the same French father and French mother as you, and I said to you, "Here comes Maurice, the Frenchman." Why would I call him "The Frenchmen" to you, if presumably you are French also? It would seem that God is referring less to clan lineage, than he is to function. It would appear that Aaron was *functionally* a Levite, and that Moses was not. This would suggest a functioning priesthood *before* the exodus and before the Mount Sinai encounter which, as mentioned above, is exactly what we would expect from a developed culture with a substantial population. We will find greater corroboration of a pre-existing priesthood and religion as we proceed with this study.

What can we know of the substance of any pre-existing Hebrew religion? We all know that the Bible unequivocally condemns astrology. 'Take heed, lest you lift your eyes to heaven, and when you see the sun, the moon, the stars, all the host of heaven, you feel driven to worship them and serve them, which the Lord your God has given to all the peoples under the whole heaven as a heritage..."(Deut. 4:19). Through the prophet Jeremiah, God promises destruction on Jerusalem in the early sixth century B.C., supposedly "because of all the houses on whose roofs they have burned incense to the host of heaven..." (Jer. 19:13).

But historically, we see some incongruities and contraindications. Exodus chapter 39 describes the breastplate designed for the high priest: "...They made the breastplate...And they set in it four rows of stones: a row with a sardius, a topaz, and an emerald was the first row; the second row, a turquoise, a sapphire, and a diamond; the third row, a jacinth, an agate, and an amethyst; the fourth row, a beryl, an onyx, and a jasper...And the stones were according to the names of the sons of Israel: according to their names, engraved like a signet, each one with its own name according to the tribes of Israel" (Ex. 39:9-14). The actual names of some of the stones are a subject of mystery and dispute, despite the obvious need of our Bibles to present a straightforward presentation. It is well known that astrologers designate particular stones to match the Constellations of the Zodiac, whence today we have our supposed "birth stones."

But be that as it may, the above passage of the Bible seems somewhat innocuous — twelve tribes, twelve stones. But the Jewish historian Josephus, writing in the late first century A.D., in the *Antiquities of the Jews*, tells us, "And for the twelve stones, whether we understand by them the months or whether we understand the like number of the signs of the circle which the Greeks call the Zodiac, we shall not be mistaken in their meaning." (*Antiquities*, 3.8.75). The Jewish philosopher Philo, also in the first century A.D., in his *On The Life of Moses*, said "Then the twelve stones on the breast, which are not alike in color, and which are divided into four rows rows of three stones in each, what else can they be but emblems of, except of the circle of the Zodiac?" The correspondence of four rows of three stones each with the four seasons, or four points of the ecliptic — the equinoxes and solstices - is obvious. So the idea of the twelve stones as being representations of the Zodiac is an understanding that is derived from within Judaism. But there is much more evidence yet from within Scripture itself.

The Bible refers to the Zodiac as the "Mazzaroth." It is a Hebrew original word, not borrowed from outside the Hebrew culture, as we would expect if it were a foreign concept. The book of Job is a work which Bible proponents frequently claim is from the patriarchal period, because of the listing of "Job" in the list of those who went with the children of Israel to Egypt, and because its utter lack of reference to the Law of Moses. In Job chapter 38: 31-33, God says to Job: "Can you bind the cluster of the Pleiades, or loose the belt of Orion? Can you bring out *Mazzaroth* in its season? Or can you guide the *Great Bear* with its cubs? Do you know the ordinances of the heavens? Can you set their dominion over the earth?" The author of this passage, from this work that Bible proponents claim to be written by the direct inspiration of God and infallible, obviously believed that Pleiades and Orion contained some inherent, volitional power over the earth and that they maintained a "dominion" over the earth.

The Bible and the Origin of Religion

But the blessing of Jacob upon his twelve sons in Genesis chapter 49 is even more revealing. Reuben, the eldest, and so the first in order, is called as "unstable as water"(v. 4). The reference to water has been argued to be a reference to Aquarius, which would have marked the winter solstice, in which the solar god or hero is almost always born (And which Emmeline Plunkett, remember, believed was the original beginning of the year). Simeon and Levi are called "brothers" even though all the sons are brothers, unless the reference is to twins, in which case they could be related to the sign Gemini (v.5). They took justice into their own hands, referring to the Dinah incident in Genesis 34, and so they seem to grasp the scales of justice, represented by balance, the seventh month, or our Libra. Judah, naturally is called a lion (v.9). Issachar, is called a "strong donkey" (v.14), and so the beast of burden inference has been depicted as a substitute for the bull of Taurus. Zebulon, dwelling "by the haven of the sea" has been likened to Pisces, the fish. Dan, for some unknown reason, is called "a serpent", who bites the horse's heel, so that its rider falls off (v. 16-17). The serpent is always seen as Scorpio. Asher, called "rich", who shall "yield royal dainties" (v. 20), has been compared to Virgo. Napthali, the "hind let loose" is depicted as referring to the ram of Aries. Of Joseph we are told that "his bow remained in strength" (v.24), and so is likened to Sagittarius, the archer. This list has had various, and debatable interpretations, but the references to Reuben, the "firstborn", as Aquarius; to Dan as Scorpio; to Naphtali, as Aries; to Judah, as Leo; and to Joseph as Sagittarius, seem the strongest.

But whatever the etiology of the above prophetic designations, there is a much stronger, although admittedly different, correlation elsewhere in the Bible. We know that each of the signs of the Zodiac came to be identified with various animals. We also know that each of the twelve tribes of Israel had its own standard or emblem, usually an animal. Judah, obviously, had the standard of the lion, and the well known term "lion of Judah" has stood the test of time. The correlation with Leo is obvious. Ephraim had the emblem of the ox, or bull — the relationship to Taurus, the site of the spring equinox between roughly 4,000 and 2,000 B.C., and as such central to religion of that period, is obvious. Dan was the eagle. The symbol of Reuben, the "firstborn", was a man.

Conviction Overturned

The camp of the Hebrews, while on the march during the desert sojourn, is carefully orchestrated and defined in the book of Numbers, chapter two. Each tribe had its assigned location in the encampment. What is highly fascinating is that the four corners of the camp *represented exactly the four corners of the Zodiac* as they existed in the immediately preceding stage of the Zodiac, and as they were still worshipped at that time in Egyptian religion! According the book of Numbers, chapter two, the four corners of the camp were always to be occupied by Judah, the lion, as the summer solstice; Reuben, represented by a man, for reasons we discuss below, takes the place of Scorpio as the fall equinox (although some might surmise the answer may lay in the ubiquitous number of seven we have already discussed, and man's betrayal of God, compared with Reuben's betrayal of his father and his condemnation in Genesis chapter 49, but there is a more appropriate explanation that we shall see); Ephraim, the bull, is the spring equinox; and Dan, the eagle, is the winter solstice. Interestingly, we know from *Calendars and Constellations of the Ancient World* by Emmeline Plunket,[41] that in ancient Babylon and Persia the eagle represented Aquarius, based on the star Aquila, or *the Eagle*, even though Aquila was not in that Constellation, but was instead a nearby bright star, in contrast to the dim stars that comprised the Constellation Aquarius. Now, interestingly, this is almost the *exact, same* order of the Constellations worshipped at Persepolis, Persia, dedicated to Mithras, where the bull (Taurus), the lion (Leo), the scorpion, (Scorpio); and the Eagle (Aquarius) are represented. [42]

However, a variation of this pattern, exactly consistent with the Hebrew encampment, also existed in the ancient Middle East. The chief God of the Medes, Ahura Mazda, is represented as an Archer, or Sagittarius, having its origin before 4,000 B.C., when the spring equinox was in Gemini, and the fall equinox was in Sagittarius. However, this image was conflated with the bull on its standards, representing a later spring equinox. Assyria, with its related chief god, Assur, had the same symbolism of the archer and the bull (or in other words, a man standing over a bull), which became the Assyrian royal standard, as it was also the standard of the Medes. The archer, positioned over the bull, dominated this standard, which was merely an astronomic monogram. The emblem of Sargon II of Assyria also included a water jar for Aquarius (the eagle of Dan), and a lion for Leo (the lion of Judah).[43] So here we have the exact, same configuration of the Hebrew camp, from fellow astrology-bound Semites.

The reason for the commonality is because around 4,000 B.C., an Aryan people, the Manda, ancestors of the Medes, invaded and inhabited the area that became Media, north of Persia, in modern day western Iran. When they conquered ancient Babylonia, that Semitic culture assimilated much of the conqueror's religion, who worshipped a chief god, Asura, who became Ahura of the Persians, and Assur of Assyria. The Aryans also invaded India, among whom the Vedic god Asura emerged. The Aryan Medes, their Persian successors, and their Semitic successors - the Babylonians and Assyrians — worshipped the four cardinal points of the Zodiac as Sagittarius and Taurus, and Aquarius and Leo [44].

Now this configuration requires some concentration, considering that theoretically this is absurd, because Sagittarius is never six months, or six Constellations, away from Taurus, but *it is* from Gemini, which Plunkett believes was the spring equinox in the original Zodiac, about 6,000 B.C. The spring equinox *preceded* to Taurus, but the Aryans and their successors kept on worshipping Sagittarius. As we said, the ecliptic is like the face of a clock. In other words, twelve o'clock must always be opposite six o'clock. If Taurus is the spring equinox at 12 o'clock, then Scorpio must be at 6 o'clock, and Sagittarius must be at 7 o'clock. And yet in ancient Media and Assyria it was seen as 6 o'clock! But they had the 3 o'clock and the 9 o'clock right. This accounts exactly for the symbol of the man (the equivalent of the archer) in the Hebrew encampment. This is the same *error* and the same symbolism of their fellow Semites — the astrologically- oriented cognate peoples, the Babylonians and Assyrians. Apparently God's omniscience does not extend to his knowledge of the Zodiac!

It has also been observed by Christian commentators that there may be a theological representation to be discovered in the proportions represented in the encampment. Numbers chapter two, in addition to providing the order of tribes in camping, also provides the numbers of persons in the tribes. The tribes to the east, behind Judah, equaled a total of 186,000. Those to the North, behind Ephraim, had the smallest number, equaling only 108,000. Those on both wings, east and west, were roughly equal, with 157,000 and 151,000. If you saw this from the sky, you would observe that the long extension to the south, the rather short line at the top, and the equal wings, represented the *cross*. And so it does, assuming the tribes camp one behind the other. The Christians say this is a typological prophecy of the cross of Christ (a historical prefigurement). But is it a prophecy, or *type*, of Christ, or is it the cross of Serapis - the cross of Osiris - the Egyptian cross representing the journey to the afterlife? Of course the Bible never says that the other tribes were to be camped *behind* their sides' standard bearers, but only says they would be "next to" the principle tribes.

All of this is quite fascinating and provides a veiled glimpse of a past that became covered over and obscured by later, more advanced theological concepts and the more structured concepts and theorems of what would become the world of Judaism and Christianity. But let us examine another feature, which was central to early Hebrew religion and later became completely and absolutely lost to it. This is the fascinating world of the Urim and the Thummim.

The Urim and the Thummim

First, let us first go back and review what we have gathered from the origin of religions. The naturalistic, or evolutionary, thesis of historical world religious development holds that man's religious view have evolved over millennia beginning from a simple, primitive view of man and his world and gradually developing into more sophisticated, defined, fixed doctrinal systems which constitute modern religions. Religious thought presumably originated in man's lack of understanding, mixed with awe and fear, of the world around him. He rather naturalistically developed a primitive world view and theology from the world he saw around him. Presumably, this intellectual web of fear-awe-ignorance started with a worship of natural forces and inanimate objects, then inevitably led to a formal priesthood which held dominion over the populace. This in turn led to the development of the role of prophet: certain individuals were seen as enjoying a greater access to divinity than the common man, often as being oracles, the very mouthpiece of divinity.

The Bible and the Origin of Religion

Presumably, this condition could not endure forever within humanity because of two very important things: The first is the fact that any body of doctrine tends to become more defined, structured and legalistic over time, leaving little room for change. Literally, all the great questions have presumably been answered. The defined priesthood was instrumental in this, since any priesthood wishes to define, formalize, ritualize and then control.

Secondly, mankind develops literacy. This facilitates the crystallizing of the past oracles and the tendency to reject any new revelation as unwanted and unfounded. The final form of religion therefore is the existence of a book, or books, which purports to contain all useful and necessary knowledge of God. From this point on, all prophecy is shunned and banned as heretical because it violates the sacred books. However, rebellions against these formalistic, legalistic, priest-bound religious structures will appear. Proponents of this thesis would point to Jesus of Nazareth, and to the Montanists and modern Pentecostals as examples of these periodic rebellions. This, in brief summary, would be the naturalistic, or historical, approach.

The Urim and the Thummim appear suddenly, with almost no explanation, in Exodus chapter 28, are thereafter mentioned very briefly in Scripture, and then suddenly disappear from mention after the immediate post-exilic era. In Exodus chapter 28:30 Moses orders that the Urim and the Thummim be placed in the high priest's breastplate of judgment when he goes into the holy place and "they shall be over Aaron's heart when he goes in before the LORD." The high priest also bears the names of the tribes of Israel over his heart engraved on the breastplate of judgment. "So Aaron shall bear the judgment of the children of Israel over his heart before the LORD continually"(vs.30). The breastplate, remember, also contains the twelve stones representing the twelve tribes, and described elsewhere as the stones of the Zodiac.

But what were the Urim and the Thummim? This is never explained. The names mean "lights" and "perfections". Traditionally it is believed that they were stones. It is fairly clear that they were. We may determine more from their functional use. It appears in Exodus 28:30 that they were used in determining the judgments of God by the high priest standing before God. But in what manner?

We read of them being used in Scripture, but their use is only mentioned directly two, or arguably three, times. One is at the designation of Joshua as successor to Moses in Numbers 27:21, where Joshua is directed to "stand before Eleazar the priest, who shall inquire before the LORD for him by the judgment of the Urim and the Thummim."

The other time is Ezra 2:63 and Nehemiah 7:65, which apparently relate the same manner in which the servant of God is officially seen as acknowledged by God. This is post-exilic. In the return from the Babylonian exile, there were some Levites who could not prove their genealogy and their descent from Levi. They are not allowed to partake of the sacrifices "till a priest could consult with the Urim and Thummim." (Ezra 2:63). These instances seem to confirm that they were used in making a judicial decision.

The use of the Urim and the Thummim has been speculated in I Samuel, chapter 14. The army of Israel, under Saul's son Jonathan, has disobeyed his command to not stop to eat until the Philistine enemy has been defeated. King Saul wants to know if he should go to battle again against the Philistines. The priest says, *"Let us drawn near to God here"* (v.36). *"So Saul asked counsel of God, "Shall I go down after the Philistines? Will you deliver them into the hand of Israel?" But he did not answer him that day."* (v. 37-38). An infuriated Saul threatens revenge against any who have disobeyed him and apparently thereby brought on the disfavor of God, and so *"Saul said to the Lord God of Israel, 'Give a perfect lot."* (v.1). Then Saul said, *"Cast the lots between Jonathan and me."* Jonathan's actions are revealed and admitted. It is believed that this was trial by the Urim and the Thummim, and the lots showed the divine will of God. The use of the lots as representing "drawing near to God" seems to be highly indicative of this conclusion.

Hence, they have been speculated to be some form of divine lots, although we will see that they are far more oracular than merely two stones tossed somehow to give a yes or no answer to questions. They are only mentioned two other times in Scripture, in Leviticus 8:8, merely recounting the placing in the breastplate at the high priest's anointing, and Deuteronomy 33:8, Moses' final blessing on Israel, where he says, "Let your Urim and your Thummim be with your holy one" (apparently referring to the Levites).

Proponents of the naturalistic, or historical approach, to world religion would have a veritable field day with the Urim and the Thummim. They see this as a relic of the most primitive form of religious sentiment - a divine spirit operating through a rock, which is cherished and worshipped. This is not fundamentally different from any other divine rocks, or for that matter tea leaves, tarot cards, crystal balls, or searching the entrails of animals. What this proves is that the whole Mosaic system has been superimposed over pre- existing, naturalistic, pagan religious forms.

Further, they would postulate that this more primitive religion is in the process of transitioning out, to be replaced by a more formalistic, structured, monotheistic religion - even a written one. In time, the Urim and the Thummim are forgotten, as the literally iconoclastic Mosaic religion deprecates any religious idea so primitive as God communicating through a rock, or any religious ritual centering on deference to a rock.

Another observation is that since the Law of Moses nowhere describes, introduces, or even authorizes the use of the Urim and Thummim, but merely acknowledges its presence and use, it is obviously something that pre-exists in Hebrew religion. Such an artifact of religion as divine rocks, or anything else, that tells the will of God in the nature of an oracle, necessarily requires a person authorized and qualified to use it — in other words a priesthood. Now we can understand the designation of Aaron as "the Levite" in Exodus 4:14. Aaron already *was* a Hebrew priest in Egypt, and the Levites represented the traditional priesthood of the Hebrews, who were later displaced by the Aaronite priesthood, and before that perhaps by the Shilohite priesthood.

There are countless other occasions in the early books of the Bible where the use of the Urim and the Thummim is implied under the rubric of "inquiring of God." The books of Judges and I Samuel are regarded as among the oldest writings of the Old Testament, written, some believe, from the time of the Davidic Kingdom and, as we have seen, embracing remnants of incongruous, pre-existing religious forms no where addressed or sanctioned in the Law of Moses. In I Samuel, chapter 23, David and his men are living in the wilderness, engaged in a battle for survival against the armies of King Saul, that are in hot pursuit. After his escape, David had gone for help to the priests, who were at Nob. When Saul discovered this, he murdered the priests of Nob. But Abiathar, later the high priest under King David, escaped and went to the camp of David. David rescued he city of Keilah from the Philistines, but King Saul then sends his army against David at Keilah.

We are told that Abiathar brought "an ephod in his hand." David says to Abiathar, "Bring me the ephod here." The ephod would be the robe over which the priest carries the breastplate, which contains the Urim and the Thummim. Then, when presumably David has the *ephod* in his possession, he prays to God: *"'O Lord God of Israel, your servant has certainly heard that Saul seeks to come to Keilah to destroy the city for my sake. Will the men of Keilah deliver me into his hand? Will Saul come down, as your servant has heard? O Lord God of Israel, I pray, tell your servant.' And the Lord said, 'He will come down.' Then David said, 'Will the men of Keilah deliver me and my men into the hand of Saul?' And the Lord said, 'They will deliver you.'"* (I Sam. 23:10-12). So with such perfect forewarning, David and his men depart the city.

Although the Urim and Thummim is not mentioned directly here, it is clear that "inquiry of God" referred to a direct access to God, in this case directly related to something in the ephod, which could only be the Urim and the Thummim. These are not simple "yes" or "no" answers. He asked a specific question of God, and received a specific answer. Only an object in the nature of an oracle — a direct vehicle to the voice and will of God — could perform this function. From this we can deduce, that in the early works of the Bible, the term *"inquiring of God"* refers to communication with God through the Urim and the Thummim. This is therefore a key to understanding the very specific responses of God to "inquiries of God" in other passages.

Judges chapter 20 is the tale of all of the tribes of Israel going to war against the tribe of Benjamin because of the mistreatment of a Levite visitor in chapter 19. It is considered to be possibly one of the oldest texts, or traditions of the Old Testament. Phinehas, son of Eleazar, the son of Aaron, who is also prominent in the desert wanderings in the book of Numbers, "stood before" the ark in those days — apparently in the role of high priest. If that is the case, then the narrative places the story in the third generation after Aaron and shortly after the advance into the land. So then, it is well before the numerous judgeships narrated in the book of Judges. Only the ark is mentioned. No tabernacle is mentioned at all, and there is definitely no brazen altar because we are told that the people built an altar wherever they took the ark (Judges 21:4). The tribes wanted to decide which tribe should go to battle against Benjamin first. "Then the children of Israel arose and went up to the *house of God* [literally *Beth-El*, or Bethel, which could equally be the place name] to inquire of God. They *said*, 'Which of us shall go up first to battle against the children of Benjamin?' *The Lord said*, 'Judah first'" (Judges 20:18). This could be interpreted as the use of lots. But if that in fact is the communication, in what manner did God communicate so distinctly with Israel? We are not told that Phinehas related the will of God, and no ecstatic prophecy of a seer is mentioned. The only realistic alternative is the Urim and Thummim.

Later, the children of Israel went before the ark and mourned and fasted all day. Then the children of Israel *"inquired of the Lord"* and Phinehas stood before the ark *"saying, 'Shall I yet again go out to battle against my brother Benjamin or shall I cease?' The Lord said, 'Go up, for tomorrow I shall deliver them into your hand'"* (Ju. 20:28). This was clearly not lots. It was presumably a divine communication, administered through the high priest, or person of equivalent stature, who would have possessed the holy stones.

In Judges chapter 18, the tribe of Dan sends a delegation to seek out their inheritance. In the mountains of Ephraim they are surprised to encounter a Levite (which in these early narratives appears to possess all the trappings of full priesthood, and in fact the existence of no other priesthood is even hinted at in these narratives). They ask the Levite, *"Please inquire of God, that we may know whether the journey on which we go will be prosperous."* (Ju.18:5). The Levite assures them the presence of God will be with them. The same Levite also presided over a temple in the mountains of Ephaim full of silver carved and molten images (Ju. 17). The entire incident is totally inconsistent and

Conviction Overturned

incongruous from the dictates and norms of the Law of Moses, and so speaks to an early proto-biblical narrative.

Subsequently, the tradition of the God-possessed oracle continues through the age of the prophets, until the concurrent spread of literacy and the "writing prophets" leads to a reduction of religion to a book. This book-bound, priest-bound religious structure rejects the concept of any new revelation, and consequently, after about 440 B.C., such an idea as any new, direct revelation from God becomes unthinkable. The religion is essentially ossified. Even the ancient rabbis conceded that there were no prophets of God after Malachi[45].

So to summarize, according to the Bible, God spoke to man through two rocks! Then later he spoke through two stone tablets at Mount Sinai. Then he spoke through human beings. And now he speaks through the pages of the Bible, and people argue over what he means! It is a neat historical view, but one which absolutely and entirely corresponds with a naturalistic/historical approach to world religions. In other words, it is entirely what we would expect. The notion of the Urim and Thummim is not significantly different from the concept of a *crystal ball,* something we would nowadays most associate with a gypsy's parlor, and would be a subject of fun among most intelligent people, but which would have been a part of the natural, everyday world of the class of people that devised our Bible. But alas, lest I be too brash or ignorant, or perhaps better said, too facetious in regard to such a holy subject matter, wouldn't we really rather have rocks which give us a definite, specific answer from God? Or else a person, *a la* Lucia Santos, who can communicate directly with divinity? It would seem that this would take all of the guess work out of it.

The naturalistic point of view sees further confirmation of the naturalistic origin of Biblical faith in the extreme ritual avoidance of death and of blood, such as in Leviticus chapter 17, or of bodily discharges, especially menstruation, in chapter 15. They would point to the prevalence of such practices in primitive religion [46]. This ritual *tabu* was something which presumably pre-existed Mosaic religion and was simply assimilated into it. The animal sacrifice practice is viewed similarly. Of course the natural response of the Bible proponents would stress the principles we have already discussed of accommodation, borrowing and condescension. To them the transition away from the

Urim and the Thummim would be a part of God's plan all along — to lead the world to a Bible-based religion. This is despite the fact that we should think that to devolve from the apparently more intimate and direct communication with God we saw in the days of Abraham, Isaac, and Jacob, to hearing from God through rocks administered by priests, would seem like a step backwards, and not forwards.

We would test this hypothesis similarly with the manner we have tested all factual hypotheses and explanations: Is it more reasonable than alternative explanations? Preconditionally, it would appear that our first order of business would be to determine if the Bible is otherwise a credible, reliable document. This is what we have thus far explored. What this chapter has shown us is that what the Bible most claims — to be an *original* and *unique* revelation, which is exclusively the hallmark of a single God of the Universe, who is here, and exclusively *here,* revealing himself, is a groundless claim contrary to facts and logic.

Chapter Eleven

THE EVIDENCE OF CHANGED LIVES

As we mentioned at the beginning, author Josh McDowell cited the third main reason for believing in the Bible to be the evidence of changed lives and the effects of Christianity on history. He is not alone. This is always one of the main arguments of Bible proponents. It is generally classified as "testimony" of changed lives. Indeed, it is the testimonial, "What Jesus did for me" that is the evangelical attention grabber and the tear-jerker. Evidence of changed lives is always appealing and we naturally want to believe what the person is advocating, if only for his sincerity and earnestness. The tales of changing from a life of aimlessness, drugs, crime, alcohol and dissolution to become an admirable, upstanding and stable person is always a story one wants to hear. We are human beings, and we admire the story of victory over odds of another fellow human being of a person rising from the despondency of his plight. And as a jail and prison chaplain and evangelist I knew countless of these stories and the persons that told them first hand. I can testify to changed lives. But let us stand back and look at this as after-the-fact proof that the God of the Bible is real. We shall first see that there is a theological basis within Christianity that not only this *can* be the case, but for the believer this *must* be the case if the Bible is true.

Holy Spirit Influenced Thoughts and Behavior

Christians should and do insist that the believer, or the "saved person", will think differently, and consequently behave differently, because he possesses the Holy Spirit and therefore has the mind of God in addition to his own. There is always admitted the distinct possibility that the saved person will reject the urging of the Holy Spirit and choose to act in a manner different from that the Holy Spirit, God, urges. Then the behavior pattern may not be any different from a person "in the world" that has not received the Holy Spirit. However, it is claimed that having that extra person in your mind telling you what to do — the Holy Spirit — will lead the Christian to think differently and to behave in a manner *generally speaking* different and superior to an "unsaved" or "worldly" person.

Now there will be howls of protest that some Christians are saved, and possess the Holy Spirit, but consistently reject the voice of God and lead a life of sin. So be it! That may easily be admitted, but we should expect that if you look at *all* Christians, and compare them to *all* people in the world, there must be a vast difference in the way they think, and at least the way they think about *ideally* behaving. Their choice-making must be distinctive from "the world."

Now admittedly there are two main Christian views about this division of the human race, derived from a difference over the doctrine of human depravity. All agree that humans have fallen from the grace of God - "all have sinned and fallen short of the glory of God" (Romans 3:23). Whether they believe in a literal Garden of Eden or not, it is agreed that humans have rejected God and so have a "sin nature" — they are cut off from and separated from God and so their nature is dominated by sin — they are depraved — and such is the source of a world of disorder and sin. Just what is the nature or depth of that depravity? Under the Calvinist doctrine of "total depravity" all human beings constitutionally lack even the capacity to do good in the world, or even to think about it. Humans will do good only because they are inhibited from doing evil, or compelled to do good, by circumstances, generally external, such as fear, humiliation, or force, often imposed by reason of Christian influence upon the world. Taken to its logical conclusion (which the holders of this view seldom, if ever do) if you look at a three year old child out in a field alone, your natural instinct and desire is to rape and murder that child. But you look around over your shoulder and you fear that you may be observed, or found out later, so you do not do it. You lack the inherent capacity to feel kindness or a spirit of goodness and kindly goodwill toward the child. Only when you accept Christ, does Christ give you the Holy Spirit, and so you can think good thoughts. And then your life will be radically changed. This is the stark, harsh Calvinist view that many Christians vehemently reject. For one thing, it is hard to believe or stomach, and besides, it makes them look like blasted idiots!

The second school of thought is that of less than "total" depravity. It is modified depravity. A human non-Christian still can be influenced by the Holy Spirit to do good. This is the first role of the Holy Spirit in the world. The extent that a human has good thoughts and actions is the degree that he follows the lead of the Holy Spirit in this life. Ultimately, the Holy Spirit wants to lead all persons to Christ, so that at that point, when he or she hears the Gospel, believes that Jesus died for his sins, and that he is lost and must accept Jesus as his savior to be saved, the Holy Spirit will indwell him, and his journey toward goodness and God-centeredness takes full steam.

There are some Christians seeking to rationalize the obvious existence of persons "outside Christ" who at least *appear* to be basically *good* people — not obviously self-centered, greedy, promiscuous, or materialistic — by cleverly claiming that the devil actually *causes* those persons to be good, or at least allows the Holy Spirit to have access to influencing those people — in order to perversely cause human beings to believe that you can be good without God, or that human goodness is not from God. Did I call this "clever"? So, we see a cynical, conniving devil who actually does good in the world?

In point of fact, under either view, atheists, those that reject even the very notion of God, should be those that naturally have flatly rejected the role of the Holy Spirit in leading them to God, and so therefore ought to be the most removed from God and, since moral notions of any sort are deemed to be from God, then they must be the most ungodly, i.e., "unregenerate" or, to use the vernacular, degenerate and immoral of all persons. Now Christians would not disagree with this hypothesis and actually would loudly claim this conclusion as correct. It could not be otherwise if one accepts the doctrine of the Holy Spirit and its indwelling. They will go further and claim that were it not for the existence of the Holy Spirit - of God - actively working in the world to lead people to the good, humans would be nothing less than demonic, heartless animals without an ounce of human kindness or goodness. God then, to them, is the actual source of all goodness in human beings. Is there a way this hypothesis can be tested? It has been. Let's look at the facts.

A Harvard biologist, Marc Hauser, and a moral philosopher, Peter Singer studied and compared the opinions of religious people with those of atheists in responses to three hypothetical moral dilemmas. [1] The subjects were asked to decide if certain hypothetical courses of action were morally "obligatory", morally "permissible", or "forbidden". In one, a railway train is out of control and about the strike five persons trapped on the railway ahead. The subject is near a switch and knows if he or she throws the switch the train can be diverted onto a siding. But there is a sole person at the siding that will surely be killed. Throw the switch or not? One person will be killed and five saved. In the second, a child is drowning and there is no one to help but you. You can save the child, but your pants will get wet. Do it or not? In the third, five people are going to die immediately in a hospital, all from failure of a different organ. There are no organ donors available. The surgeon then sees that there is a healthy person sitting in the waiting room who has all five organs functioning well. Lose one to save five? Is this any different from the first scenario? The results are really not important for our purposes. What is vitally important for our purposes is that there was *no statistical difference at all* between believers and atheists. What this does surely demonstrate, is that the human moral sense does not derive from God, or from a belief in God. This dispels the notion, believed in by many, and actively taught by not just Christians, but by most religionists, that if it were not for the existence of God, or perhaps as would be stated in a somewhat more cynical fashion, if it were not for the *belief* in the existence of God, there would be no sense of right and wrong and no morality. We will explore later the question of what is the real origin of our morality — of a sense of right and wrong.

In a more in-depth study, Marc Hauser has also written a book, *Moral Minds: How Nature Designed our Universal Sense of Right and Wrong,* [2] in which he posed similar hypothetical situations to a large number of persons — religious and non-religious. They were not conventional scenarios, such as "Under what circumstances would you allow an abortion?", or "Do you believe in abortion?", which are often decided by prior commitments, decisions or instructions. For instance, in the runaway train situation described above, there is an alternative to diverting the train to a siding that will kill one man as a consequence but save the lives of five others that will die. There is a weight that can be thrown from an overcrossing upon the track. But the weight is a very fat man. Another scenario is that the train is divertible to another track, but that track will rejoin the original track and still kill the five people. But there is a very fat man on the diversionary track who will stop the train when it hits him. Pull the switch? What is the difference from throwing the fat man off of the overcrossing then? Is there a difference, between simply using him where he is, and pushing him into danger? All the scenarios involved some thought. One again, the statistics are not important to the study, what was important, and what is important to this book, is that most people reached the same decisions when deciding how to act in response to each scenario, although most could not articulate a reasonable explanation for their decisions. This applied to both the religious and the non-religious equally.

To take this experiment a fascinating step further, Hauser went to Panama and did his experiments among the Kuna Indians, a remote Stone Age group, that live deep in the jungle, and have no formal religion. The facts of the scenario were modified to fit those of a Stone Age people. The *results were the same.* These are the expected results if our moral sense was something genetically intrinsic to our brains, and not implanted by religious instructions, such as the Bible. *All people think alike* when it comes to complex moral decisions. There are not two kinds of people in the world. There is one kind — people with brains. As Hauser concluded, "Driving our moral judgments is a universal moral grammar, a faculty of the mind that evolved over millions of years to include a set of principles for building a range of possible moral systems. As with language, the principles that make up our moral grammar fly beneath the radar of our awareness."

Another major test of the Christian hypothesis should be marriage. There should be a huge difference between saved Christian persons and those of persons in the world —with all their selfishness, sensuality, worldliness, materialism, lack of spirituality, drug and alcohol abuse, etc., etc. The Christian theory of marriage is always stated to be a three-way, triangular marriage, with God as the third person in the marriage, and the top of the triangle. We would expect

The Evidence of Changed Lives

that the work of the Holy Spirit would result in a noticeable incidence of solid lifelong marriages of Christians and a much lower divorce rate than that of "the world"- those that are "outside of Christ." In point of fact, it is a proven and indisputable fact that the highest divorce rate is among those identifying themselves as Baptists and as Evangelical Christians. The lowest divorce rate — you guessed it — atheists, the "heathen" rejecters of God's Holy Spirit.

The divorce rates, taken among a sampling of 3,854 adults in the United States by the Barna Research Group in 1999, were as follows:

- Non-denominational churches 34%
- Jews 30%
- Baptists 29%
- Born-Again Christians 27%
- Mainline Protestants 25%
- Mormons 24%
- Catholics 21%
- Lutherans 21%
- Atheists, Agnostics 21%

The divorce rate, as we can see, was 27% among born-agains and 29% among Baptists, but only 24% among all other adults. [3]

Christians are supposed to be, and are called by Jesus, "the salt of the earth." Gregory S. Paul, in *The Journal of Religion* (2005), also researched seventeen economically developed countries to see if heightened religion and God-consciousness correlated with improvement in the moral character of the population. He found "higher belief rates in and worship of a creator correlate with higher rates of homicide, juvenile and early mortality, STD infection rates, teen pregnancy and abortion in the prosperous democracies." [4] As author Sam Harris points out in his *Letter to a Christian Nation*, of the twenty-five most dangerous cities in America, 76% are in the "red" states that have a high percentage of born-again religious right Christians, and 24% are in *Demon*crat-dominated "blue" states, not controlled by the religious right. Three of the five most dangerous cities in America are in Bible-thumping, preacher-ridden Texas, the evangelical heart of America.[5]

Christians would just love to refute studies such as those outlined above. Unfortunately for them, they have never been able to do so. As psychologist Daniel Dennet has pointed out, "...One thing we can be sure of is that if there is a significant positive relationship between moral behavior and religious affiliation, practice, or belief, it will soon be discovered, since so many religious organizations are eager to confirm their traditional beliefs about this scientifically. (They are quite impressed with the truth-finding power of science when it supports what they already believe). Every month that passes without such a demonstration underlines the suspicion that it just isn't so."[6]

Now if a sense of morality is a programmed part of our brain, is it genetic? If so, is it derived from Darwinian evolution? How can it be? Why would the evolutionary model foster morality within humans? The misinformed objection is usually made that the evolutionary model cannot provide for morality. Why? Because natural selection, the "survival of the fittest", is supposedly a selfish, dog-eat-dog struggle that only produces that which is egoistic and selfish to dominate. Yes, the evolutionary model is selfish and promotes that which is selfish, but not necessarily in a sense of gaining whatever an organism can for itself at the expense of others. In the natural world we see a model of cooperation as often as we see competition, at least within communities, and often with outside communities. Bird communities often have sentinels, who devote sometimes enormous amounts of time cut off from their communities and not enjoying the company of others, or even feasts, in order to perform isolated, lonely security duties. Bees and others have the same. Why do birds and other animals give self- sacrificially of themselves to others, even at the expense of giving away their locations to predators and subjecting themselves to harm? What do they care about others? The concept of dying for one's community is not unique to humans. It is widespread in the animal world. So how could this *altruism* develop in Darwinian evolution?

Richard Dawkins has summarized the results of scientific genetic research. Starting with his classic work *The Selfish Gene*, he has demonstrated how Darwinian genetics can explain the origins of *altruism*, which is by no means the opposite of the concept of selfishness, but rather a byproduct of it. There is the situation of genetic kinship — one is programmed by a gene to support kin because it will lead to the survival of copies of itself. And there is the case of reciprocation — repayment for favors, and the habitual expectation of the return of favors by giving them. These are the principle genetic structures from which altruism in nature flows. There are secondary principles which flow from these, such as reputation. A reputation for kindness and generosity leads to tangible benefits, and yields more than its opposite, such as a reputation for stealing, cheating, and unreliability. [7] We will explore the development of a moral sense more below. Suffice it to say, the following can be proven: 1) Our moral sense does not come from God - it is not implanted in us from God; 2) Our moral sense does not derive from our belief in God; 3) Our moral sense is not derived from the teachings of the Bible or of any religion. Our moral sense is derived from our nature as human beings.

But the Bible proponents will argue — look at the horrific things that humans have done in human history. Very true, but they have been done by Christians and non-Christians alike, and in point of fact, more done in the name of Christ than for any other reason (Christian, let us not get started on what the church has done in history. Don't go there, for your sake! Volumes could be, and have been, written). Presumably this was because they were all humans, and therefore all of the same *kind* — there were not two kinds of humans. And, it should be added, just look at the Bible stories to see if they are any moral guide. Are the stories any better, any less barbarous? God ordered the genocide of the nation of Midian, and the people of Jericho: "Kill every man, woman and child, every ass, sheep, goat, ox and every living, breathing thing" (Joshua 6:21; Numbers 31), and then, in the case of Midian, he punished Israel for keeping the women alive for purposes of debauchery rather than killing them as directed (only the virgin women were to be kept alive for debauchery). Once again, Christian, I wouldn't advise you to go there. There is no balm in Gilead.

But let's look at another key aspect of Christianity to see if is verifiable: the claim of a personal God that we can speak to and that can and will hear us.

The Effectiveness of Prayer

Prayer is a vital part of the Christian religious experience. Any pastor will tell you the importance of prayer. They will also tell you that prayer works — that it is effective; that there is a living, loving, attentive God who — at least if you have believed on his son and are saved by his blood — will hear you and respond. God will not *always* grant your wish, but he delights in his children who are attentive enough to pray, and God *will, sometimes at least,* intervene to change the course of human affairs in answer to your prayer. The Bible itself confirms this. Jesus himself said, *"Therefore I say to you, whatsoever things you ask when you pray, believe you receive them, and you will have them"* (Mark 11:24*); "And whatsoever you ask in my name, that I will do, that the father may be glorified in the son"*(John 14:13); *"Most assuredly I say to you, whatever you ask the father in my name he will give you"* (John 16:23). In Luke, Jesus tells us that like a good father who gives his child what he asks, God will give us and not deny us — *"Ask and you will receive..."*(Luke 11:9-13). We are told that if we had faith "like a mustard seed" [a tiny amount] it would be sufficient to move mountains.

Now pastors and preachers will often not admit that they feel uncomfortable with these verses. Universally, they will admit that God does not grant the prayers of the faithful. The reasons given can for the most part be catalogued:

1. God *always* answers prayer, but the answer is sometimes "No." This is a good answer, but it completely undermines the very premise of the above promises — that God will grant your requests because this is what he wants to do and wills to do. What consolation is it that God heard your prayer but said "no"?

2. A variation of the same argument: You were praying for something contrary to God's will so *of course* you could not get it ("You bad, selfish boy [or girl]! You should know better! God intended that your two year old baby die, as a test to your faith"). Proponents of this view, such as R.A. Torrey, often point to I John 5:14 as a qualification to all of these promises by Jesus: *"Now this is the confidence that we have in*

The Evidence of Changed Lives

him, that if we ask anything according to his will, he hears us. And if we know that he hears us, whatever we ask, we know that we have the petitions that we asked of him." So in other words, all of these grandiose promises have an unspoken caveat: God will only grant our prayers *if he was already planning on doing those things anyway!!* In common parlance this is what we call *false advertising*. I would like to see this on any contract for services — that the company will perform its promises under the contract only under the unstated condition *that it wants to,* and it does not have to perform its promises if it doesn't feel like it. This overwhelming exception renders the promises completely illusory. *They are no promises at all!* This is the kind of ridiculous, circular reasoning we often encounter in the Bible and/or among Bible proponents. Isn't the whole point of Jesus' promises, that God's will *is* to grant our requests? It certainly appears to be so (or am I reading too much into the above, unequivocal promises?) So imagine the above promises of Jesus, with this exception included: *"Therefore I say to you, whatsoever things you ask when you pray, believe you receive them, and* [if the father already has decided to give you them] *you will have them." "And whatsoever you ask in my name,* [if I want to], *that I will do, that the father may be glorified in the son." "Most assuredly I say to you, whatever you ask the father in my name* [if he already wills it] *he will give you"* [unless he doesn't want to, then he will not]. *"Ask and you will receive"* [unless I do not want you to receive it, or have other plans — in that case forget it. You are wasting your time!]. Very consoling isn't it?

3. You have sin in your life, so God doesn't hear you. It is your fault, not God's.

4. You are praying for selfish concerns. It is your fault! This is an unstated, undisclosed exception to the unequivocal promises (you could have fooled me). You must pray altruistically. So it's your fault! You *really* wanted your two year old baby to live and not die of an infectious disease in order that you could *enjoy* his company, not so that his life could honor God! You bastard!

5. You do not have faith. It is your fault. You doubt God. This is a more Pentecostal-oriented argument.

6. A more sophisticated, logical and frankly better argument is the dispensationalist argument. These are "Kingdom" promises to the Jews relating to the time when Christ rules on the earth as King of Israel. So the promises are really to Jews in the Millennium, when they live on the earth with Jesus as king. So these are not promises to the Gentile church at all. Or in another version of dispensationalism, they are promises to the church also, but in the Kingdom Age, when Jesus returns. In either version, the principle is that Jesus was rejected by Israel and crucified, so the promises did not take effect at that time. So in this school of thought, what seem to be clear and present promises are anything but. You need to be a lawyer to understand the whole context of historical biblical dispensationalism (and so one of the founding fathers of this school, C.I. Scofield, was a lawyer).

Regardless of which approach to prayer Christians may take, all Christians will agree, and must agree, with the slogan that "prayer changes things" — it is efficacious. Praying is better than not praying and at a minimum, *"The effective, fervent prayer of a righteous man avails much"* (James 5:16). So, empirically, we should be able to pinpoint a verifiable difference between situations and crises that benefited from prayer of the faithful and those that did not. This has been effectively done.

Dr. Herbert Benson, a cardiologist at the Mind/Body Medical Institute in Massachusetts, is a believer in the efficacy of prayer in medical recovery. He undertook to *prove* the same through a research study funded under a grant from the Templeton Foundation, a foundation of convinced theists which exists to prove the existence of God through science.[8] The foundation's purpose was likewise to *prove,* not to disprove, the efficacy of intercessory prayer, and thereby the existence of a personal, omnipotent God. Dr. Benson's team monitored the recovery of 1,802 patients who received coronary bypass surgery at six different hospitals. The patients were divided into three groups. The first group received prayers but didn't know it was being prayed for. The second group received no prayers and did not know it wasn't being prayed for. The third group received prayers and knew they were being prayed for.

Now the persons praying were genuine evangelical Christians who naturally believed absolutely in the benefits of prayer, wanted to show the efficacy of intercessory prayer, and prayed sincerely for the patients. They were members of three churches, one in Minnesota, one in Missouri, and one in Massachusetts. All prayed earnestly for the patients by their first name and the first letter of the last name. All prayers were directed to be "for a successful surgery with a quick, healthy recovery and no complications."

The results were included in the *American Heart Journal* (H. Benson, "Study of the Therapeutic Effects of Intercessory Prayers"(STEP) in Cardiac Bypass Patients) *AHJ*, 151:4, 2006, 934-42) of April, 2006. Considering those involved in the experiment — with the experiment being originated, contrived, conducted, and financed by those with a vested interest and desire to see the results they wanted — we would normally expect to see the result that the researchers and "prayer warriors" desired. In fact, the results were overwhelmingly disappointing and humiliating to the researchers. The results went in *the exact, opposite direction!* Those that were prayed for and knew that they had been prayed for had substantially more complications than the others. This was the only statistical anomaly from among the groups.

Naturally, the results incensed many Christians. The most likely response and excuse to be given would be the righteous slogan "Thou shalt not tempt the Lord thy God", even though the test was not undertaken by any means to test God's powers, since those undertaking the experiment already believed in God's power and, in fact, the experiment was undertaken to *glorify* the "God of the Universe" and cause others to pray, thereby bringing others to God. What could be more worthy goals? (from the Christian point of view). If the experiment had been successful, it would have been heralded by Christians as demonstrating empirically the power and responsiveness of God. As it is, the experiment demonstrates what the skeptical world already knows, that Christians are unable to demonstrate the existence of their God of the Bible by any means whatsoever. For all apparent purposes, when they pray they are praying to nothing and wasting their time and their breath.

The foregoing merely confirms and corroborates what I and millions of others that have bothered to look have already observed millions of times over — that there are not two kinds of people in the world —distinguished by whether they have accepted Christ or not. I have encountered born-again Christians countless times in the prison setting culpable for the most heartless, selfish bestial crimes — such as child sexual molestation and other sordid crimes. And I have met scores of non-believers with selfless hearts and souls a thousand times greater than any self-righteous "saved" Bible-beater that ever set foot on the earth. God is not glorified by his brood.

The Bible as a Moral Standard

But what about the Christian claim that without the Bible and its moral standard the whole world would go to hell in a basket, and that further, without the Bible the world would be a much more wicked, undesirable place than it is? The foregoing narrative, gauging empirical evidence, should be a satisfactory answer. But to be complete, let's look at the Bible as a moral guide. The Bible is somewhat suspect, to say the least, as a moral standard. When Abraham and two other men are staying at the home of Lot, they are besieged by a mob of men who want to rape Abraham and his companions, but Lot, described as "righteous Lot" by the Bible in II Peter, offers the mob his two virgin daughters instead. Nowadays, we would think of some adjective other than "righteous" to describe such conduct. The Bible thinks there is nothing untoward in Lot's conduct (Gen. 19). Why not just throw your daughters out to be raped? The patriarchs, such as Jacob, have not only multiple wives, but multiple concubines. Jacob cheats his uncle Laban out of livestock and justifies it as a dream he had from God that gave him an advantage. God orders Abraham to sacrifice (murder) his son in order to test his faith (supposedly it's okay because God never intended that it really be done; he was just playing around with Abraham's feelings - which is okay, right? He waited till Abraham's hand with the knife was lifted up to kill Isaac before he stopped him (Gen. 22). Like if I called you and told you your son was in a serious car accident and was dying,

The Evidence of Changed Lives

just as a test to see what you would do, or pointed a loaded, cocked gun at you just to see if you would come to trust me).

God leads the children of Israel on a bloody rampage and murder of all the inhabitants of the city of Jericho, "both man and woman, young and old, ox and sheep and donkey, with the edge of the sword" (Joshua 6:21). He orders the thorough destruction of Midian and is incensed that the Israeli's have kept alive the women and children. He orders all male children killed and only the virgin women to be kept alive "for yourselves." So their mothers were murdered in front of them and they were raped (Nu. 31). It reminds me of Mel Brooks' *Blazing Saddles.* When a band of outlaws is going to attack a town and are ordered to kill everyone in the town, one outlaw asks, "Do we kill all the women too?" The leader of the outlaw says, "Hell no! We rape the hell out of them!" It's very funny unless it is your wife, mother, or daughter. The "Lord God of Israel", at least as portrayed in this time period, is short on mercy. The "God of love" hadn't been invented yet. God's orders for the populations inhabiting the land of Canaan before Israel's arrival are stark: *"...And when the Lord your God delivers them over to you, you shall conquer them, and utterly destroy them."*(Deut. 7:2). *"Also you shall utterly destroy all the peoples whom the Lord your God delivers over to you: your eye shall have no pity on them... "*(Deut. 7:16). *"But of the cities of these peoples which the Lord your God gives you as an inheritance, you shall let nothing that breathes remain alive, but you shall utterly destroy them... "* (Deut.20:16).

Naturally, the Christian argument stresses that these practices were those of humans, not of God — God only *accommodated* natural human bloodlust. But we would think something somewhat loftier — somewhat above the depraved level of humanity — to somehow uplift humanity. We would expect humanity to at least step up in its moral standards. We would hope for something a bit different from the *"God of Love."* In fact, as Thomas Paine, so astutely pointed out in his classic, *The Age of Reason,* Moses was not the only person in history to murder in the name of religion, but historically he was the first one to do so. As such, he is not the spiritual forebear of Jesus, St. Francis, or Mother Theresa. But rather, bearing the distinction of the first person to murder innocent people in the name of religion, I am sure that Thomas Paine, were he here today, would call Moses the spiritual forebear of Osama bin Laden.

But Christians will tell us that there are also the "good things" of the Bible, to be found in the teachings of Jesus in the New Testament. Let's look at the teachings of Jesus to see what kind of a viable, practical moral standard they set. The Sermon on the Mount provides the ethical system of Jesus. *"You have heard it said to you 'an eye for an eye, a tooth for a tooth', but I say to you, that you resist not evil: but whosoever shall smite you on the cheek, turn him the other cheek also"* (Matthew 5:38-39). What kind of a world will it be if we really "resist not evil"? I can tell you: it will be a world where evil takes over very quickly and dominates and controls everything. There will be no reprisals against terrorists, or anyone else. There will be no protection for your home or family. There will be no legal remedy to seek damages for injuries. *"If anyone wants to sue you and take away your tunic; let him have your cloak also. And whoever compels your to go one mile, go with him two. Give to him who asks you, and from him who wants to borrow from you do not turn away."* (Matt. 5:40- 42). Now this is brilliant - give in to oppressors, however wrongful, and help them to oppress you, so that they can later oppress others. Never stand up for your rights or those of others. Never seek justice against oppression.

We are told "not to worry" and in fact to take no concern for the future. *"Therefore I say unto you, do not worry about your life, what you will eat or what you will drink; nor about your body, what you will put on. Is not life more than food, and the body more than clothing?" (*Matt. 6:25-26). Many Christian love these passages and find great comfort in them, but none take them seriously or follow the advice. Should we just stop providing for our families and have no concern for them? Shall we stop saving money, or making sound investments, because then we would be thinking about the future? In the parable of "the rich fool", a man is derided as a fool for building a bigger barn to accommodate a plentiful harvest (Luke 12:13-21). Apparently he should not have provided for his harvest so that it could rot outside, because unbeknownst to him, he was going to die anyway. So just forget about thrift, savings, and making your life and that of the world around you any better. Forget about terrorist alerts and safety precautions too. *"Judge not, that you be not judged"* is just about equally amorphous and pointless. Up to what point should we never judge? With no judgment how can there ever be any standards? Should we not judge murderers, robbers or child molesters? Tolstoy took this maxim to the conclusion that we must completely eliminate our criminal justice system and our penal system.

A man wishes to follow Jesus as a disciple, but he asks for leave to go bury his father first. Jesus callously tells him to *"Let the dead bury their own."* The Christian *spin* was that he really wanted to take care of his father until his death, and this is what he meant by the phrase "bury my father" (Yeah, right). He tells people that *"If anyone does not hate his father and mother, wife and children, brothers and sisters, yes, and even his own life, he cannot be my disciple."* (Luke 14:26) (Do I sense some megalomania here?). Further, he tells us that *"whoever of you does not forsake all that he has cannot be my disciple"* (Luke 14:33). Lest we think this is mere hyperbole, Jesus tells the rich, young ruler that to be perfect he must *"Sell all you have and give to the poor, and you will have treasures in heaven; and come, follow me"* (Luke 18:22).

None of these moral strictures are in any way practical enough to be of any use to human society. That is why, for almost all Christians, these are just "beautiful, wonderful" passages (we cannot decipher what is so beautiful or wonderful about them - it is apparently because they are "otherworldly"), but have no real meaning for them in their lives, because they are impractical. This is no moral guide at all. These are the ranting of a fool, not the basis for a moral code.

If people say they are committed to Jesus, or love Jesus, we should be inclined to ask the question "Who or what is *Jesus* for *them*?" The religionists would wish to believe that it is the biblical Jesus — God incarnate — crucified, buried, and resurrected, who will cleanse you of sin and take you to heaven. But to most that is not the case. To many, Jesus Christ to them means the same thing as it did to many of the worst swindlers and crooks that I have defended — a stained glass figure that would one day take you to heaven so long as he is worshipped with mindless rituals and rote prayers. The families would come sanctimoniously into the courtroom during the trial with prominent crucifixes, or with palm leaves in the shape of crosses during Easter week.

But to others, *Jesus* means something deeper, more pervasive, and more abstract than this. They say they love Jesus, but to them Jesus is not the historical Jesus, but rather *Jesus* signifies the principle of humanity — it consists in the love within their family at Christmas; it is gift-giving and generosity, not just under the Christmas tree at Christmas, but to strangers throughout the year; it is self-sacrifice, as much as the soldier dying to save the lives of his buddies in war, as having heartfelt concern for a destitute person, or visiting people in hospitals and prisons; it is a concern for the welfare of others. There is no theology involved, and for most in this category, which I firmly believe is the vast majority of *Christians,* theology is irrelevant. They would openly scoff at the notion that a person must accept the historical Jesus as their Lord and Savior in order to be *saved* and to get to heaven, or that a Jew, Muslim, or Buddhist will be condemned to hell for eternity unless they convert before they die. This is the Christianity that will never die, and that will remain, and which for the most part, except for the minority of brainwashed cranks and fanatics, has remained.

The Basis of Morality

Isn't the basis of morality really from social empathy — the ability to see ourselves in other creatures, leading eventually to the nearly universal moral axiom, "Do unto others as you would have them do unto you" (or one of the various forms of this rule)? When you witness or contemplate harm to another, you are able to see yourself, or your family, or loved ones, as the victim instead, and therefore to be upset. You wince at a human being with a horrible injury, but injury to an ant or a cockroach doesn't bother you. And how can there be such empathy without first a basis in self-involvement? So the sense of self seems the essence of this concern for others, not at enmity with it.

A classic example of this is man's relationship with his "best friend" — the dog. We are upset at a dog in pain or suffering. We care. Why? They are not human. And yet, we know from experience that although the dog's creative potential, intelligence, and anatomy, are

The Evidence of Changed Lives

quite distinct from our own, that dogs have an emotional capacity that is as acute as our own, and perhaps even more so (at least some dogs have a greater emotional capacity than some people do). This leads to a bonding. The dog's emotional capacity is perhaps higher than any other animal. Many people have much less regard for the well-being of cats (Although some are intensely drawn to cats) because of what is perceived as a reduced emotional capacity — they are seen as more unlike us than dogs. Few would think twice about stepping on an ant, spider, or a cockroach.

So our concern for others — our morality — comes from our nature as human beings. It is not imposed or influenced by religion. On the contrary, original, early religion, just as we have seen in the original Hebrew religion, was essentially amoral. There was plenty of ritual which developed, and plenty of fear, taboo, and totemism, but nothing akin to what we would call a moral code.[9] Keeping your distance from a woman menstruating, is the primitive religionist's view of the height of *morality*. There was a God who was powerful, who had to be appeased, and once appeased he was on your side. It did not depend on how I lived or whom I hurt, so long as I worshipped and appeased God. Then there was a God on my side — right or wrong, he was for me because I was for him. Only later did this God become an essentially moral God, who cared about, and imposed, a sense of right or wrong.

And this depiction of God as a moral judge came about not because a God imposed morality upon us, but because humans had a native moral sense, derived from social empathy, and human beings attributed to God that which was of their own nature (man made God in his own image). It would be strange indeed if humans had a sense of right and wrong but their gods did not. Hence a moral dimension became added to their gods. Indeed, those who interpreted or translated the nature, character and will of God to us (for there soon developed a community of priestcraft in every culture) rather were led to attribute to God at least the moral sense which human culture commonly possessed. But this development of ethics and morality as a dimension of religion was a much later development in the history of religion, although it eventually became a part of all major religions. Religion co-opted morality. It did not provide the world with morality. So humans owe nothing to religion (I must qualify this - at least nothing worthy. I am sure we could think of many things we can attribute to religion, such as the loss of 3,000 lives in the World trade Center for a start.)

America — a "Christian Nation"

On September 11, 2001, the infamous "911", when the news of the World Trade Center bombing was released, very many members of a church in Oceanside, California — in fact my church — spontaneously, and with no urging, suddenly found it very natural to get in their cars and drive to church. There was no church service planned, announced or expected. It was an ordinary weekday morning and afternoon. But so many members showed up at the same time that the church swelled to capacity, almost as though this was indeed a "sanctuary" in which they could be safe and secure. The pastor came out and gave a sermon. He told the crowd that "America was a Christian nation", and that in case they did not realize it until that moment, "We are at war with Islam", and essentially the sooner every red-blooded American realized it, the better off we would all be.

This is a consistent theme of the Christians. Apparently they are not aware of the fact that George Washington, John Adams, and the almost unanimous United States Senate declared that America unequivocally was "not a Christian nation." The circumstance was an undeclared war with the Muslim Barbary pirates in North Africa in 1796-1797. Under President George Washington, and his Vice-President and successor John Adams, America drafted and signed a treaty with the Barbary pirates, of which George Washington heartily approved. It was finally ratified under the presidency of John Adams in 1797 with the votes of the overwhelming majority of the U.S. Senate. The treaty declared quite proudly, lest the Muslims think there was a religious twinge to this conflict, that "America was not a Christian nation." We had no inherent struggle with Islam or any other religion. The Treaty of Tripoli, a very pubic document, proudly provides:

> "As the government of the United States of America is not in any sense founded on the Christian Religion,-as it has in itself no character of enmity against the laws, religion

or tranquility of Musselmen,-and as the said States never have entered into any war or act of hostility against any Mehomitan nation, it is declared by the parties that no pretext arising from religious opinions shall ever produce an interruption of the harmony existing between the two countries."

Many a loyal, patriotic American will say "Amen" to that. The claim is usually made that "the founding fathers" or "America's founders" were all devout Christians who founded our nation on Christian principles. Indeed, there is certainly a question of what they mean by "the founding fathers." Do they mean those that literally first settled in America, those in the Massachusetts Bay Colony in the early seventeenth century, and in the Virginia Yorktown colony? Or are they referring to the founders of the United States of America, identifying those who held sway and influenced the foundations, institutions, and legal principles of our nation between about 1775 and 1789, and in particular during the period of the Constitutional Convention and its ratification in 1787 to 1789? The distinction is meaningful. In fact, the term is used more than not to refer to the latter. And when we look to this group of individuals, we can state categorically that no nation on earth was ever founded by individuals who possessed a greater hostility to revealed religion, and in particular to the Bible. The record is clear.

George Washington, the father of our country, hardly ever went to church, which he seemed to disdain. Although an Episcopalian, he never received the Holy Eucharist, representing the sacrificed body and blood of Christ, at church services, for reasons only known to him, and which we can only surmise. He was never once seen on his knees in prayer. There is not one word in his public or private papers to indicate the slightest adherence to, or belief in, the principles of Christianity, particularly of the miraculous birth, divine mission, or resurrection of Christ, or of atonement and salvation through his death. [10] Our second president, John Adams, although originally a faithful Massachusetts Congregationalist, eventually became a Unitarian, a group that does not believe in the inspiration of Scripture, that Jesus was the incarnation of God, or in the atonement through

Christ. **[11]**. He summarized his appraisal of Christianity as follows: "As I understand the Christian religion, it was, and is, a revelation. But now it has happened that millions of fables, tales, legends, have been blended with both Jewish and Christian revelation that have made it the most bloody religion that ever existed"**[12]**

Thomas Jefferson, one of the five members of the committee that wrote the Declaration of Independence, the author of our Bill of Rights, and the person whose political philosophy most steered the founding of our nation, as one of his first acts as president abolished all national days of fasting and prayer. He openly hoped that "The day will come when the mystical generation of Jesus, by the Supreme Being as his father in the womb of a virgin, will be classed with the fable of the generation of Minerva in the brain of Jupiter." **[13]**. He wrote his own New Testament, which thoroughly deleted all miracles and all claims that Jesus was the incarnation of God on earth, that his blood was shed in atonement for the sins of the world, or that faith in Jesus led to salvation. Sound like Christianity? How about this? He claimed "Christianity is the most perverted system that ever shone on man." And how about this from this "Christian" forefather:

> *"To talk of immaterial existences is to talk of nothings. To say that the human soul, angels, god, are immaterial, is to say they are nothings, or that there is no god, no angels, no soul. I cannot reason otherwise…I am satisfied, and sufficiently occupied with the things that are, without tormenting or troubling myself with things which may indeed be, but of which I have no evidence."***[14].**

James Madison, the "father of the Constitution" and the most influential person at the Constitutional Convention in Philadelphia, labeled the fruits of Christian influence to be "superstition, bigotry and persecution." Benjamin Franklin famously told Americans that "Lighthouses are more useful than churches." **[15]**. Thomas Paine has been described by Dr. James Kennedy, a leader in the religious right's "Christian nation" campaign, as a great Christian. There could be no greater perversion of the truth, although in this book we have seen plenty at the hands of Christians, who seem so unashamedly deft in this dark art. In point of historical fact, it is no secret, that Thomas Paine was one of the most forceful, outspoken and vitriolic enemies of the Bible and Christianity that *ever lived on the face of the earth.* Dr. Kennedy apparently forgot, or didn't know, that Paine was the author of the book *Age of Reason,* one of the most eloquent, intelligent, uncompromising and thoroughgoing repudiations of Dr. Kennedy's Bible ever written by human hands, which is still one of the principle works heralded by America's Freedom from Religion Foundation in its fight against the Bible, and a book which I recommend that every, single person read. This *"great Christian"* wrote :

> *"Of all the systems of religion that ever were invented, there is none more derogatory to the Almighty, more unedifying to man, more repugnant to reason, and more contradictory in itself, than this thing called Christianity. Too absurd for belief, too impossible to convince, and too inconsistent for practice, it renders the heart torpid, or produces only atheists or fanatics. As an engine of power, it serves the purpose of despotism; and as a means of wealth, the avarice of priests; but so far as it respects the good of man in general, it leads to nothing here or hereafter."* **[16].**

Does that sound like your average Sunday school class? These are the founding fathers of this country. No nation owes its existence to a greater class of "infidels" and unbelievers than America. Somewhat later, Abraham Lincoln, as a young man, was greatly enthralled by the above work by Paine, and also by *Meditations on the Ruins* by Count Constantin de Volney, a classic anti-religious study of the development of religion in the world, and one which ascribed all religious belief to superstition, having its original basis in the ancient Zodiac and astrology. As a young man, Lincoln was known to be outspokenly anti-Christian and anti-religious. In later years, in the somewhat socially compromising and stunted role of politician, and as president, he evinced no solid, formal religious sentiments, other than a belief in an Almighty and divine guidance. It was the opinion of William Herndon, a close, early friend of Lincoln, and one of the few persons with whom Lincoln ever spoke of religion, that his view never changed. **[17].** We should not be misled, as the "Christian nation" people often are, by the fact that he certainly expressed a belief in a God, who supported and inspired justice and mercy, as most of the founding fathers did, but it was definitely *not* the God of the Bible and it was not based on atonement through the blood of Christ.

It is remarkable that in none of the voluminous writings of Lincoln, or of any of the others mentioned, is there a single phrase that would suggest an abiding belief that the center of all human history and existence, and what should be the center of each person's life in this world, or more particularly what was the center of *that* person's life, was the sacrifice on the cross of Christ. If a person is a Christian, at least in anything but name, then that principle must be the center of his life, and it would be hard to miss it in the person's public and/ or private letters. But astoundingly, in the myriads of such letters, we find this theme entirely absent from such luminaries as Lincoln and Washington. This omission is impossible to conceive of, without concluding that these great persons did not believe that Jesus' death on the cross provided mankind an atonement for sins, and for the innate sin nature that separated us from God, and that without faith in that cosmic event each person would eventually wind up eternally lost in hell. And without such a belief, like it or not, *they are not Christians!*

Of all of the lies of the Christians over the past 2,000 years, the claim that to be a *real American* you must be a Christian, is by far the most obscene and perverted, and the one which I most relish in refuting.

The Problem of Self-Esteem

Then where do we start to cure the world's problems? And what is the cure for the antisocial personality. Christianity has a ready response. Their answer is that the world's problems come from separation from God and man's self-centeredness. Man must become God-centered and not self-centered. In fact, evangelicals tell us, that we must lose our selves, by having our selves absorbed in God, then we will become better people. It is the origin of all anti-social tendencies, resulting in criminality and delinquency. A popular Christian counseling book, *Counseling God's Way,* by Bob Hoekstra, emphasizes this principle need for people to lose self-esteem as a way to overcome all the problems

The Evidence of Changed Lives

of life, as they become absorbed in God's grace. It harshly criticizes society's secular approach to building self-esteem in individuals as a step to recover from addiction, delinquency, and sundry anti-social tendencies. Self-esteem must be absolutely quenched under the power of the Holy Spirit, the author contends.

As both a criminal defense attorney and jail chaplain I have known and worked with countless criminals and addicts of all varieties. I have seen transitions and transformations. My reaction to the above comments is based on an observation. Based on the discussion of human social empathy above, an obvious question emerges. What about the person who has no self-esteem, self-love, or self-respect? To what extent can he empathize with the plight of another — to see himself in the position of suffering of another — when he doesn't even care about himself? Or to view it another way, the Bible tells us, "Love your neighbor as yourself." Easily said, isn't it? And what if a person hates himself? Does that mean he should hate his neighbor? What if he wants to kill himself? Should he kill his neighbor? In fact, the latter is exactly what happens increasingly every day of the week. Without a minimum quotient of self-esteem, there is no esteem for the lives or well-being of others. There is no compassion, no human sentiments.

I have seen transformations. I have seen transformations when human beings become attached to something other than, and generally greater than, themselves — NOT because they lose themselves, or lose self-esteem, but rather precisely **because they gain it!** They gain it sometimes through Christianity, but also through Buddhism, Islam, communism, Nazism, white supremacy or many other avenues. They are literally transformed into VIP's. It is because they gain something their lives lacked — **value, identity, purpose.** Their life now has value, as a part of their cause, and it is a transforming value. And they have identity in that cause or movement. They are no longer just Sam Smith, now they are now brother Sam Smith, or Comrade Sam Smith. They have a purpose in life. They are somebody.

I have seen this process at work in the case of young gang members, many of whom I have defended, often for attempted murder and drive-by shooting. In the greater L.A. area they are largely from Hispanic families, very frequently from parents who are from Mexico or Central America, who are poor, often illegal, and speak limited, if any, English. They are low wage earners and are from economically depressed areas. One notable thing, contrary to what most would think, is that the children involved are not children who are *bad* kids vis-à-vis their parents, but rather they are the *good* kids. They are very respectful of their parents and are very well-behaved at home. Within the white, middle class general American population, we picture the disobedient, rebellious, disrespectful child in the family who later becomes society's problem. But within these families the situation is frequently reversed. The parents consider them to be great kids, because within the family *they are*. The reason for this phenomenon is not difficult to find.

Children, when they are small, see their parents as superheroes. They are the models of adulthood. But as these children grow up, they see a different reality. They see their parents as people that are marginalized, despised and rejected by the surrounding society. Their parents are at the bottom end of American society — a society that treats them with contempt and wishes they were not even here. The result is resentment. Society's attitude is the attitude toward them. They see themselves as not a part of American society. Along comes the gang, which gives them a new identity, pride and purpose. The gang seems to extol and be a part of the world that they are from. It adopts names that extol parts of Mexico, or of their culture, with names such as *Mara Salvatrucha* and *Tepatitlan*. The gang is at war with the surrounding culture that has rejected their families. They receive an identity in the gang, and even a new name, a moniker. The gang members bind themselves together in an oath of eternal loyalty. What they have is *self-esteem*! It is a self-esteem that comes at a high cost to society.

And yes, the Gospel can do it. There is no greater sense of pride, to the point of smug self-righteousness, than that of Christian humility — the "losing" of oneself in Christ. To be "under his wings", to be "hidden in Christ", to know that God has chosen you to be his disciple, to have an intimate relationship with you, to have him as your father, brother, king, and best friend, as someone that is with you every moment and that you can speak to any time you want and he is there and hears you and listens. And in a world without God that is on its way to damnation, all your sins are forgiven, you are saved, you are a

The Evidence of Changed Lives

disciple of Jesus Christ, and your future is in his glory in heaven. It is wonderful, warming, tender and poignant, and I have seen it melt the stoutest heart. But there is no external, unseen force — no Holy Spirit — it is the human spirit that has to be ignited.

This is what Kierkegaard called the need of the human spirit for commitment in life — the need for passion, for a leap of faith. Kierkegaard made that leap of faith, and found that commitment, in Christianity, which he essentially married himself to as a substitute for marriage and family in his own life — his greatest crisis in life being the failure of his own betrothal, and so he became betrothed to Christ. Kierkegaard, who admitted that Christianity was fundamentally irrational, is probably one of the best proponents and examples of this phenomenon (He also said everything else in life could not be comprehended rationally anyway, so why not just be a Christian). It is precisely in this existentialist perspective that we see the workings of what I call the VIP process — value, identity, purpose — and the role that the Gospel plays in the transformation of lives.

I have worked for years as a prison chaplain and evangelist. Hundreds have "accepted Jesus" based upon my intervention and instigation. As to the question of whether the persons I intervened for have *benefited* from the influence of the Gospel in their lives, in most cases the answer is "yes." There are those that have never been able to concentrate on anything in their lives. They are often those that are nowadays diagnosed with the popular, and faddish, supposed disorder of "ADD." I taught them techniques of how to blot out everything else around them through the power of prayer, which I would tell them is simply talking to God, talking to Jesus. Even if they were being marched in line through the halls by the guards, or in a jail cafeteria, they could in the back of their minds be talking to God and listening for answers. There are those who *never read anything of substance in their lives*, much less a book, but they read the whole Bible! There are those who went from being gang- bangers, addicts, and derelicts to being good husbands, fathers, and citizens. The benefits cannot be denied. Naturally, the same thing can be said for Islam. In prison, especially among Blacks, Islam is the major competitor to the Christian evangelists, usually through the medium of Nation of Islam. The most frequent explanation that I have heard from converts to Islam is that for the first time in their lives they had *order* in their lives.

In this sense Christianity can serve as a "hothouse" — a resting place for those that have just gained for themselves a sense of self-value, self-identity, and purpose, which can stay with them even when they leave the "cause" — when they realize that they do not need the imaginary friend that they talk to; that they had the power within themselves to relate to the world around them, to love life, and to love others and be loved. The most classic book ever written on religion (a bit of literary license — hyperbole to make a point), and the one I cherish the most, is the children's book *Dumbo*. Dumbo, the humble young elephant that was friendless, withdrawn, dejected, untalented, and clumsy, was transformed by a supposedly magical feather, which helped him to fly like a bird. He finally realized that the feather had no power whatsoever — the power was always in his own spirit. It was there all the time. He realized one day that he didn't need a crutch to live. Once again, in a very existential way, the same is true for most Christians. The greatest purpose of life is life — and living it to the fullest — by employing and indulging in those things which are life-enhancing, life-promoting, and life- fulfilling, not worshipping and praying to an imaginary friend, being led by the nose by pastors who feel a need to dominate others, or by reading a confused, silly, inconsistent, and nonsensical book full of lies, deceit, pomposity, and manipulation.

POSTSCRIPT AND CONCLUSION OF THE CASE

In a work such as this one, if the work has been carried out in a diligent and comprehensive manner, a conclusion hardly would seem necessary, and would be nothing but redundant. All that might seem in order is a comparison of the conclusion reached by Simon Greenleaf in his *Testimony of the Evangelists* — one which is distinctly contrary. What is the basis of Greenleaf's conclusion that the Gospel accounts are absolutely trustworthy? We find that Greenleaf reached this conclusion very early in his work, based on the conclusion that "twelve apostles" operating "with a single voice", against overwhelming persecution, hardship and risk, persisted in promoting the Gospel accounts that we know today. Chapters 2 and 3 of this work have addressed these circumstances fully. As Greenleaf summarized his legal review, "***In the absence of circumstances which generate suspicion,*** every witness is ***presumed*** to be credible, until the contrary is shown; the burden of impeaching his credibility lying on his objector."[18] So Greenleaf early on established his own *presumption* of the truth of the Gospel, deciding that there was an absolute "absence of circumstances which generate suspicion." One thing we have certainly shown in this work is abundant, reasonable, and insoluble suspicion generated by the circumstances. In most instances, those very circumstances are irreconcilable with the truth of the Gospel claims. And yet Greenleaf finds a *presumption* of the truth of the claims. In doing so, he has reversed the traditional presumption that we began with. The life of the fellow on the gallows, facing a capital charge, is now *presumed* to be worthy of the gallows, because the charge against him is *presumed* to be true. In the case at hand, the person whose life is on the line, whose life will be *given* to the Gospel and "to Christ" is yours and mine, and that of your spouse, children, parents and friends. The charge of our being inherently "lost" and damned because of an inherited, constitutional, judicially attributed judgment against us, which can only be reversed by giving our lives to the Christian religion, is to be presumed. We are not told by Mr. Greenleaf if the presumption is a rebuttable presumption or an irrebuttable presumption. But it is clear from Mr. Greenleaf's review that in his opinion there is not the slightest thing in the Bible narratives that would give the slightest cause for doubt, and so no reason to question his presumption — "Give us a conviction, and send that life to eternity!" I would submit that it is only with such a pre-conceived, irrebuttable presumption, in other words the iron- clad mindset, that such a conclusion as that of Mr. Greenleaf can be reached. In Greenleaf's opinion there simply could not exist any fabrication or falsehood — deliberate or innocent — within the Gospel narratives because "It would have been irreconcilable with the fact that they were good men." **[19]**

What has been presented herein is a more objective and comprehensive review of the relevant facts and circumstances surrounding the Bible narrative. There are those who would contend that I have stopped short in several respects. There are those who would say that I should proceed with a review of what human beings *should* believe in, or how we should determine right from wrong. I believe what has been said as to the true basis of morality and the origin of religion is a sufficient foundation in this regard. Indeed, I would be deeply dismayed if a reader of this book reacted by becoming a Muslim or a Buddhist, although that is bound to happen, if only because some people are determined to belong to a religion, or are habituated to seeking some form of higher revelation and imaginary companionship. Although socially conditioned and prevalent, I would hope that they will eventually see this as closer to mental illness than it is to personal comfort.

Others would contend that I should address that issue so popular with born-again Christians: their antipathy to evolution. I find that to be far beyond the scope of this work, which would require a completely new work to embrace these issues. In recent years, a number of Christian authors, usually not scientists at all, such as Philip Johnson, in *Defeating Darwinism by Opening Minds,* and *Darwin on Trial,* have written books questioning the validity of evolution. They also have carefully staged debates, usually in front of churches, with supposed scientist front spokesmen for evolution. I believe that these issues have recently been succinctly addressed in the case of *Katzmiller v. Dover*

School Board, 400 F. Supp.2d 707 (2006). The Christians in that case did not have the burden to prove the truth of creationism. They did not have the burden of proving intelligent design — that our Universe and life forms are the result of an intelligent, thinking being. Neither did they have to prove that Creationism, or "intelligent design" was a better scientific theory than evolution. All that they had to prove was the threshold issue that intelligent design was a viable scientific theory — the absolute minimal threshold test. They had a Republican conservative judge of their own choosing, Judge John E. Jones III, whom they believed they could count upon to not be swayed by liberal social currents in American education. The Christians brought in their biggest guns. Their main expert witness was Michael Behe, a biochemist, and author of *Darwin's Black Box*. After a full, fair trial by the judge of their choice, not only did the judge find that intelligent design was *not* a viable scientific theory, Judge John E. Jones III held that it was "breathtakingly inane." I recommend the reading of his opinion, which I think is the perfect legal summary of this entire area and addresses these issues more appropriately than I could ever hope to do here. The "intelligent design" people were given a full, fair trial on the merits, exactly as they demanded and they received the result they so justly deserved.

A good review of this area are the books by Jerry A. Coyne, *Why Evolution is True,* and *Finding Darwin's God,* by Kenneth R. Miller, which is the best refutation I have seen of the various levels of Creationism. It is significant for me that we now know just what dinosaurs ate from the coprolites, or fossilized feces, of dinosaurs. Even the herbivorous dinosaurs never ate any flowering plants, because they did not yet exist in evolutionary development.[20] Flowering plants are from a later stage of evolutionary development. This defies the Creationist contention that all our current species of plants were created at the same time, before the dinosaurs, and would have existed at the time of the dinosaurs.

I have always found the existence of Neanderthal man to be perplexing from the standpoint of the Bible. The Neanderthals, who coexisted for thousands of years with modern man, are often erroneously described as non-human. But "human being" is a generic term — a layman's term if you will. In fact, they were a variant of human being (Christian Creationists contend that they were human beings with rickets from a vitamin deficiency). They had a brain capacity larger than modern humans — *homo sapiens* or *homo sapien sapiens*. The structure of the larynx suggests a capacity for rudimentary speech. Ritual reverence for the dead at burial suggests an appreciation for the rudiments of religion.[21] In 2010 we found that there was much more extensive cross-breeding with homo sapiens than we had previously thought and so a larger amount of Neanderthal DNA exists within modern man. The cross-breeding is final proof that they are essentially a variation of the same species. Even more surprisingly, in late 2010, evidence of a *third form of human being* was discovered in East Asia, whose DNA is prevalent in many South Sea Island peoples. Where do Neanderthals fit into the Bible account? Did they not have souls? Were they in *the image of God*? Why did God create two, even three, forms of human beings on the earth, of which two have gone extinct?

As we can see, there is an enormous abundance of evidence showing a world other than the world portrayed by the Bible, but I leave the elaboration of that world to others.

A Gaza Postscript

There is not a person in the world today who does not know where Gaza is. Gaza, because of its unique location, by all rights should be, and could be, another Dubai. Instead, it is a shattered, devastated wasteland. The only reason it is a devastated wasteland and not Dubai, is religion. The extremism of Hamas is well-known. But what of the fanaticism of those ultra-Orthodox Jews and their American Evangelical supporters with a firm belief that their god told them "I give to you and your descendants after you [Israel] the land in which you are a stranger, all the land of Canaan, as an everlasting possession…" (Genesis 17:7; 48:4). The land "from the river…even to the Western Sea, shall be your territory." (Deuteronomy 11:24) (How curious, that when Palestinians use the preposition "from the river to the sea", and nothing more, a phrase borrowed from Hebrew Scripture, it is considered racist and anti-Semitic, and yet when ultra-Orthodox or nationalist Jews use it, it is not). And Scripture depicts

The Evidence of Changed Lives

God as telling Moses, "From the cities of these peoples which the LORD your God is giving you as an inheritance, do not let anything that breathes remain alive. You shall surely annihilate them ... just as the LORD your God has commanded you." (Deuteronomy 20:16-17). The Bible recounts God saying, "I will deliver the inhabitants of the land into your hand, and ***you shall drive them out before you.***" (Exodus 23:31). Joshua carried out these orders and cleansed the land of non-Hebrews. As to the Amalekites, God directs King Saul to "kill every man, woman, infant, suckling, ox, sheep, camel, and ass", (i.e., "every living, breathing thing") (I Samuel 15:3). King Saul later is punished by the heartless god of the Hebrews (and the American Evangelicals) by losing his throne for keeping some of the livestock rather than killing "everything that breathes." (I Samuel 15:21, 24-26. "You have rejected the word of the Lord and the Lord has rejected you from being king over Israel").

These are not exactly verses that give rise to a spirit of compromise. Yet these verses are lauded by ultra-Orthodox Jews and American Evangelicals alike who claim that the Palestinians (a name they claim has no meaning and a people they claim do not even exist as a people) have rights or claim in the land in which they were born and their ancestors lived for thousands of years. If the only excuse for atrocities by the perpetrators/victims is to point a finger and say; "Look what they did to us!" then the horrors will continue from generation to generation.

Throughout history, thinkers from all range of political persuasions, the most notable being Robespierre and Edmund Burke, have felt that a belief in God and religion were necessary to human society as a deterrent to the worst parts of human nature, by providing confidence in eventual punishment for misdeeds beyond our unsure, frail human institutions. Looking at the Nova music festival massacre and the destruction of Gaza, one would wonder if any such benefit to society is not outweighed by the evil done to society.

FOOTNOTES

Chapter 1—Law and the Search for Truth
1. Simon Greenleaf, *Testimony of the Evangelists: The Gospels Examined by the Rules of Evidence Administered in Courts of Justice* (1995) Grand Rapids, MI: Kregel Classics, 28.
2. Simon Greenleaf, *Testimony of the Evangelists,* 46
3. Josh McDowell, *The New Evidence That Demands a Verdict* (1999), Nashville: Thomas Nelson Publishers, 203.

Chapter 2—The Resurrection, Part One, The Surrounding Circumstances
1. Josephus, *Antiquities of the Jews,* Book 18, chapter 3, section 1, translated by William Whiston, *The New Complete Works of Josephus,* (1999) Grand Rapids, MI: Kregel Publications, 590.
2. Frank Morrison, *Who Moved the Stone,* (1958) Zondervan,146-166.
3. Paul L. Maier, *Pontius Pilate*, Tyndale House (1968) 366.

Chapter 3—The Resurrection, Part Two, The Appearances
1. Bart D. Ehrman, *Lost Christianities,* Oxford University Press (2003), 234-236, 244.
2. Bart D. Ehrman, *Lost Christianities,* 9-11; Bruce M. Metzger and Michael D. Koogan, *Oxford Guide to the Bible,* Oxford Univ. Press ((1993) 629-631.
3. Frank Morrison, *Who Moved the Stone,* (1958) Zondervan, 124-125; 139; 162-166; 170-172; 183-187.
4. Frank Morrison, *Who Moved the Stone,* (1958) Zondervan, 139,147, 162-166; 170-172; 183-187.
5. Frank Morrison, *Who Moved the Stone,* 160-167

6. Josephus, *Antiquities of the Jews,* Book 20, chapter 5, p1, translated by William Whiston, *The New Complete Works of Josephus,* (1999) Grand Rapids, MI: Kregel Publications, 648-649.
7. Simon Greenleaf, *Testimony of the Evangelists,* 28-30.
8. Edward Gibbon, *Decline and Fall of the Roman Empire,* Dell Publishing (1963), chapter 14, 283-298.
9. Bruce M. Metzger and Michael D. Koogan, *Oxford Guide to the Bible,* Oxford Univ. Press ((1993) 34-36, 192-194; Bart D. Ehrman, *Jesus: ApocalypticPprophet of the New Millennium*, Oxford Univ. Press (1999) 105-123.
10. A.N. Sherman-White, *Roman Society and Roman Law in the New Testament,* Oxford: Clarenton Press, 1963, 188-91; William Lane Craig, *The Son Rises: Historical Evidence for the Resurrection of Jesus,* Chicago, Moody Press (1981), 102.
11. R.A. Torrey, *Talks with Men,* Fleming H. Revell Company (1904) 70-87.

Chapter 4—The Nativity

1. Josephus, *The Jewish War,* Book 2, chapter 8, translated by William Whiston, *The New Complete Works of Josephus,* (1999) Grand Rapids, MI: Kregel Publications, 736-740.
2. Suetonius, *Life of Augustus, The Twelve Caesars,* 38, Penguin Books (1957); Colin Wells, *The Roman Empire*, Harvard Univ. Press (1992), 56, 144.

Chapter 5—Fulfillment of Prophecy in the Life of Jesus

1. Bruce M. Metzger and Michael D. Koogan, *Oxford Guide to the Bible,* Oxford Univ. Press ((1993) 34-36, 192-194; Bart D. Ehrman, *Jesus: ApocalypticPprophet of the New Millennium*, Oxford Univ. Press (1999) 105-123.
2. Frank Morrison, *Who Moved the Stone,* (1958) Zondervan, 160-167.
3. John N. Oswalt, *Isaiah 1-39, New International Commentary*

of the Old Testament (Wm. B. Eerdman Publ. Co, 1984) p. 210

4. Herbert Wolf, "A Solution to the Immanuel Prophecy in Isaiah 7:14, *Journal of Biblical Literature*, v. 91, 1972, p. 449-456; John H. Walton, "What's in a Name?" *Journal of the Evangelical Theological Society* 30 (Sept. 1987) 93.

5. Homer Hailey, *A Commentary on Isaiah*, (Baker House 1985) 84

6. R.E. Clements, *Isaiah 1-39, New Century Bible Commentary* (Eerdmans Publ., 1980) 88; Brevard Childs, *Isaiah, Old Testament Library* (Westminster John Knox Press 2004) 64

7. John Walton, "What's in a Name? " *supra*, 295-296

8. Herbert Wolf, "A Solution to the Immanuel Prophecy in Isaiah 7:14, *Journal of Biblical Literature*, v. 91, 1972, p. 449-456; John H. Walton, *supra,* at 293.

9. Homer Hailey, *A Commentary on Isaiah*, (Baker House 1985) 84

10. Herbert Wolf, "A Solution to the Immanuel Prophecy in Isaiah 7:14, supra, 450-454

11. R.E. Clements, *Isaiah 1-39, New Century Bible Commentary* (Eerdmans Publ., 1980) 95

12. Herbert Wolf, *supra* at 454

13. John M. Robertson, *Christianity and Mythology,* London: Watts and Company (1910)

14. Josephus, *The Jewish War,* 2.13.5, translated by William Whiston, *The New Complete Works of Josephus,* (1999) Grand Rapids, MI: Kregel Publications, 747.

15. Sir Robert Anderson, *The Coming Prince,* Kregel Classics, 1957

16. J.J. Collins, *The Apocalyptic Imagination: An Introduction to Jewish Apocalyptic Literature* (1998) Wm. B. Eerdman Publishing, 60-61,74-82; Emmeline Plunket, *Calendars and Constellations of the Ancient World* (1903) by Cosimo Classics, 2005.

Chapter 6—Failed Bible Prophecies

1. John De Marchi, *The Immaculate Heart*, New York:Farrar, Strauss & Young (1952)

2. Samuel Driver, *The Book of Daniel*, Cambridge Univ. Press, 1900

3. Robert Gurney "The Four Kingdoms of Daniel 2 and 7", *Themelios* 2 (1977) 39-45

4. Robin Lane Fox, *The Unauthorized Version*, London: Penguin (1992), 335-336.

Chapter 7—Jesus: Savior and Sodomist

1. Augustine, *Incomplete Work Against Julian*, 4,57, quoted inWilliam Phipps, *The Sexuality of Jesus*, Harper Row (1973) 18

2. William Phipps, *The Sexuality of Jesus*, 44, quoting the *Yehamoth* 6,6, 62b

3. Mark Magnier, "A Small Victory for Pakistan's Transgenders", *Los Angeles Times*, March 10, 2010

4. Ben Witherington, "The Last Man Standing", *Biblical Archeological Review*, (March-April 2006) 24, 76.

5. Morton Smith, *Clement of Alexandria and the Secret Gospel of Mark*, Cambridge: Harvard Univ. Press (1973).

6. Bart D. Ehrman, *Lost Christianities*, Oxford Univ. Press (2003) 78.

7. Bart D. Ehrman, *Lost Christianities*, 81-89.

Chapter 8—Progressive Development of Doctrine: The New Testament

1. Bart D. Ehrman, *Lost Christianities*, Oxford Univ. Press, pp. 91-94, 113-126

2. Bart D. Ehrman, *Lost Christianities*, Oxford Univ. Press, 163-180.

3. Bart D. Ehrman, *Misquoting Jesus*, (2005) Harper Collins, 45-62; 90-98.
4. Bart D. Ehrman, *Misquoting Jesus*, (2005) Harper Collins, 158-160
5. Bart D. Ehrman, *Misquoting Jesus*, (2005) Harper Collins, 144-149
6. Ehrman, *Misquoting Jesus,* 157.
7. Ehrman, *Misquoting Jesus,* 178-186.
8. Ehrman, *Misquoting Jesus,* 211.
9. Porphyry, *Against Celsus* 2, 27, quoted in Ehrman, *Misquoting Jesus,* 199.
10. Ehrman, *Lost Christianities, 48.*

Chapter 9—Progressive Development of Doctrine: The Old Testament

1. Richard Elliott Friedman, *Who Wrote the Bible,* Harper Collins Publishers (1997) 70-88.
2. Jewish Publication Society, Tanach Translation, Notes to Isaiah, ch. 26,53; J.M. Robertson, *Christianity and Mythology,* 104-107; M. Dupuis, *The Origin of all Religious Worship,* 217-224.

Chapter 10—The Bible and the Origin of Religion

1. Richard Elliott Friedman, *Who Wrote the Bible*, Harper One (1997), 67-69, 86-88.
2. Julius Wellhausen, *Prolegomena to the History of Israel, (1876)* Kessinger Pub.
3. Constantin Francois de Volney, *The Ruins Or Meditation on the Revolution of Empires And the Law of Nature,* Echo Library Edition (2007) 107-108
4. Rudolf Otto, *The Idea of the Holy*, 2d Ed., New York: John W. Harvey (1950)

5. Paul Radin, *Primitive Religion,* New York: Dover Publications (1957)
6. Paul Radin, *Primitive Religion,* New York: Dover Publications (1957), 13-39, 56-58.
7. Paul Radin, *Primitive Religion,* Ibid., 40-77.
8. Ninian Smart, *The Religious Experience of Mankind,* Chas. Scribner's Sons (1969) 29-33.
9. Ninian Smart, Ibid., 33-35
10. James Fraser, *The Golden Bough,* MacMillan Publishing Co. (1922)
11. Paul Radin, *supra,* 192-253.
12. Paul Radin, *supra,* 169-253.
13. Paul Radin, *supra,* 156-187.
14. Emmeline Plunkett, *Calendars and Constellations of the Ancient World (1903),* New York: Cosimo Classics (2005), 11-15, 29,42, 145-148.
15. Plunkett, Ibid., 56-80
16. Plunkett, Ibid., 218, 233-235
17. M. Dupuis, *The Origin of All Religious Worship* (1794), New Orleans (1872), Univ. of Michigan Press, Michigan Historical Reprint Series, 232-240; 258-265.
18. Dupuis, Ibid., 254-256.
19. Plunkett, supra., 117-123, 131-132.
20. Charles Waite, *The History of the Christian Religion to the Year Two Hundred,* Chicago: C.V. Waite & Co. (1881), 175176.
21. John M. Robertson, *Christianity and Mythology*, London: Watts & Co. (1910) 180-191
22. Charles Waite, *History of the Christian Religion,* supra., 170-174; J.M. Robertson, *Christianity and Mythology,* supra, 180-191.

23. Waite, Ibid., 175
24. J.M. Robertson, *Christianity and Mythology,* supra, 180-182.
25. Waite, supra, 171
26. Robertson, *Christianity and Mythology,* supra, 189; Waite, *History of the Christian Religion,* 174.
27. Robertson, Ibid., 364, 369.
28. Ibid., 374-377.
29. Ibid., 369-377.
30. Ibid,, 365-367.
31. Ibid., 367..
32. Ibid., 284, 298, 363-364.
33. Ibid., 358-362; Charles Waite, *History of the Christian Religion,* supra., 391.
34. Robertson, Ibid. 370, 378.
35. M. Dupuis, *Origin of All Religious Worship*, (1794), New Orleans (1872), Univ. of Michigan Press, Michigan Historical Reprint Series, 217-224.
36. Ibid., 223-232
37. Ibid., 225-232
38. Ninian Smart, *The Religious Experience of Mankind,* Chas. Scribner's Sons (1969) 53-54.
39. Waite, *History of the Christian Religion,* supra., 389.
40. Ibid., 356.
41. Emmeline Plunkett, *Calendars and Constellations of the Ancient World (1903)*, New York: Cosimo Classics (2005), 64-70.
42. Ibid.
43. Ibid., 77-79
44. Ibid., 81-87
45. Alfred Edersheim, *Life and Times of Jesus the Messiah,*

Hendrickson Publishers (1993) 18-19.

46. Ninian Smart, *The Religious Experience of Mankind,* Chas. Scribner's Sons (1969) 34-35.

Chapter 11—Evidence of Changed Lives

1. M. Hauser and P. Singer ,"Morality without Religion" *Free Inquiry* 26:1 2006, 18-19.

2. Marc Hauser, *Moral Minds: How Nature Designed our Universal Sense of Right and Wrong,* (2006) Ecco Books.

3. Darrel W. Ray, *The God Virus,* (2009) IPC Press, p. 194.

4. Quoted in Richard Dawkins, *The God Delusion,* (2006) Houghton Mifflin, pp. 262-263.

5. Sam Harris, *Letter to a Christian Nation,* (2006) Knopf Publ., 44-45.

6. Daniel C. Dennet, *Breaking the Spell,* (2006) Penguin Books, 280.

7. Richard Dawkins, *The God Delusion,* (2006) Houghton Mifflin, pp. 245-254.

8. H. Benson, "Study of the Therapeutic Effects of Intercessory Prayer (STEP) in Cardiac Bypass Patients" *American Heart Journal* 151:4, (2006) 934-42. Quoted in Dawkins, *The God Delusion,* Houghton Mifflin, (2006) 85-88.

9. Ninian Smart, *The Religious Experience of Mankind,*(1969) New York" Charles Scribner's Sons, 27-40

10. Franklin Steiner, "What was Washington's Belief?". in the *Religious Beliefs of Our Presidents from Washington to FDR* (1936) Prometheus Books

11. Peter Marshall and David Manuel, *From Sea to Shining Sea* (2000) Fleming H. Revell, 184-186.

12. Richard Dawkins, *The God Delusion,* 65

13. Marshall, *From Sea to Shining Sea,* 106-108, 111

14. Thomas Jefferson, Letters to John Adams, Aug. 15, 1820;

Lester J. Cappon, ed., *The Adams-Jefferson Letters,* Vol. 2, Univ. of North Carolina Press, 1959.

15. James Madison, *A Memorial and Remonstrance,* addressed to the General Assembly of the Commonwealth of Virginia, 1785; Benjamin Franklin, *Poor Richard's Almanac;* Franklin Steiner, *The Religious Beliefs of Our Presidents From Washington to FDR,* Prometheus Books, 1936.

16. Thomas Paine, *The Age of Reason,* G.P. Putnam Sons, New York: Knickerbocker Press (1794), 189-190.

17. William Herndon, "Abraham Lincoln's Religious Views", William Herndon, from Franklin Steiner, *Religious Views of Our Presidents from Washington to FDR*, Prometheus Books (1936)

18. Greenleaf, *Testimony of the Evangelists*, 29

19. Ibid., 33

20. Kenneth R. Miller, *Finding Darwin's God,* (1999) Harper Perennial, 62

21. Fazale Rana and Hugh Ross, *Who Was Adam?,* NavPress (2005) 179-198.

BIBLIOGRAPHY

Ancient Christian Gospels: *Their History and Development*, Trinity Press International).

Anderson, Sir Robert. *The Coming Prince.* Kregel Classics, 1957.

Benson, H. "Study of the Therapeutic Effects of Intercessory Prayer (STEP) in Cardiac Bypass Patients." *American Heart Journal* 151:4 2006.

Childs, Brevard. *Isaiah, Old Testament Library.* Westminster John Knox Press, 2004.

Clements, R.E. *Isaiah 1-39, New Century Bible Commentary.* Eerdmans Publ. 1980.

Collins, J.J. *The Apocalyptic Imagination: An Introduction to Jewish Apocalyptic Literature.* Wm. B. Eerdman Publishing, 1998.

Craig, William Lane. *The Son Rises: Historical Evidence for the Resurrection of Jesus.* Chicago: Moody Press, 1981.

Dart and Riegert, *The Gospel of Thomas*: The Lost Sayings of Jesus, (Seastone Press, 2000).

Dawkins, Richard. *The God Delusion.* Houghton Mifflin, 2006: 245-254.

De Marchi, John. *The Immaculate Heart.* New York: Farrar, Strauss & Young, 1952.

Dennet, Daniel C. *Breaking the Spell.* Penguin Books, 2006. Driver, Samuel. *The Book of Daniel.* Cambridge Univ. Press, 1900.

Dupuis, M. *The Origin of All Religious Worship.* (1794), New Orleans, 1794; Univ. of Michigan Press, Michigan Historical Reprint Series, 1872: 232-240; 258-265.

Edersheim, Alfred. *Life and Times of Jesus the Messiah.* Hendrickson Publishers, 1993.

Ehrman, Bart D. *Jesus: Apocalyptic Prophet of the New Millennium,* Oxford Univ. Press, 1999.

Ehrman, Bart D. *Lost Christianities.* London: Oxford University Press, 2003.

Ehrman, Bart D. *Misquoting Jesus*. Harper Collins, 2005.

Fox, Robin Lane. *The Unauthorized Version*. London: Penguin, 1992.

Fraser, James. *The Golden Bough*. MacMillan Publishing Co., 1922.

Friedman, Richard Elliott. *Who Wrote the Bible*. Harper One, 1997.

Gibbon, Edward. *Decline and Fall of the Roman Empire*. Dell Publishing, 1963.

Greenleaf, Simon. *Testimony of the Evangelists: The Gospels Examined by the Rules of Evidence Administered in Courts of Justice*. Grand Rapids, MI: Kregel Classics, 1995.

Hailey, Homer. *A Commentary on Isaiah*. Baker House, 1985.

Harris, Sam. *Letter to a Christian Nation*. Knopf Publ., 2006: 44-45.

Hauser, Mark. *Moral Minds: How Nature Designed our Universal Sense of Right and Wrong*. Ecco Books, 2006.

Hauser, M., and P. Singer. "Morality without Religion." *Free Inquiry* 26:1 2006: 18-19.

Herndon, William. "Abraham Lincoln's Religious Views." William Herndon, from Franklin Steiner. *Religious Views of Our Presidents from Washington to FDR* Prometheus Books, 1936.

John Dominick Crossan, *The Historical Jesus*, Harper Collins, 1991

Josephus, Flavius. *Antiquities of the Jews*. Book 18, chapter 3, section 1; translated by William Whiston. *The New Complete Works of Josephus*. Grand Rapids, MI: Kregel Publications, 1999.

Maier, Paul L. *Pontius Pilate*. Tyndale House, 1968.

McDowell, Josh. *The New Evidence That Demands a Verdict*. Nashville: Thomas Nelson Publishers, 1999.

Magnier, Mark. "A Small Victory for Pakistan's Transgenders." *Los Angeles Times* March 10, 2010.

Marshall, Peter and David Manuel. *From Sea to Shining Sea*. Fleming H. Revell, 2000.

Metzger, Bruce M. and Michael D. Koogan. *Oxford Guide to the Bible*. Oxford Univ. Press, 1993.

Miller, Kenneth R. *Finding Darwin's God.* Harper Perennial, 1999: 62

Morrison, Frank. *Who Moved the Stone.* Zondervan, 1958.

Oswalt, John N. *Isaiah 1-39, New International Commentary of the Old Testament.* Wm. B. Eerdman Publ. Co., 1984. M. Robertson. *Christianity and Mythology.* London: Watts and Company, 1910.

Otto, Rudolf. *The Idea of the Holy.* 2d Ed., New York: John W. Harvey, 1950.

Paine, Thomas. *The Age of Reason.* G.P. Putnam Sons, New York: Knickerbocker Press, 1794.

Phipps, William. *The Sexuality of Jesus.* Harper Row, 1973.

Plunkett, Emmeline. *Calendars and Constellations of the Ancient World* (1903) by Cosimo Classics, 2005.

Radin, Paul. *Primitive Religion.* New York: Dover Publications, 1957.

Rana, Fazale and Hugh Ross. *Who Was Adam?* NavPress, 2005 Ray, Darrel W. *The God Virus.* IPC Press, 2009.

Smart, Ninian. *The Religious Experience of Mankind.* Chas. Scribner's Sons, 1969.

Smith, Morton. *Clement of Alexandria and the Secret Gospel of Mark.* Cambridge: Harvard Univ. Press, 1973.

Steiner, Franklin. "What was Washington's Belief?" *Religious Beliefs of Our Presidents from Washington to FDR* Prometheus Books, 1963.

Volney, Constantin Francois de. *The Ruins Or Meditation on the Revolution of Empires And the Law of Nature.* Echo Library Edition, 2007.

Waite, Charles. *The History of the Christian Religion to the Year Two Hundred.* Chicago: C.V. Waite & Co., 1881.

John H. Walton. "What's in a Name?" *Journal of the Evangelical Theological Society* Sept. 1987: 30.

Walton, John D. "The Four Kingdoms of Daniel 2 and 7." *Themelios* 1977: 2

Wellhausen, Julius. *Prolegomena to the History of Israel.* Kessinger Pub., 1876.

Witherington, Ben III. "Last Man Standing?" *Biblical Archeological Review* 2006.

Wolf, Herbert, "A Solution to the Immanuel Prophecy in Isaiah 7:14." *Journal of Biblical Literature* v. 91, 1972.

www.ingramcontent.com/pod-product-compliance
Lightning Source LLC
LaVergne TN
LVHW021757060526
838201LV00058B/3135